CU00798252

Brazil
Cruising Guide

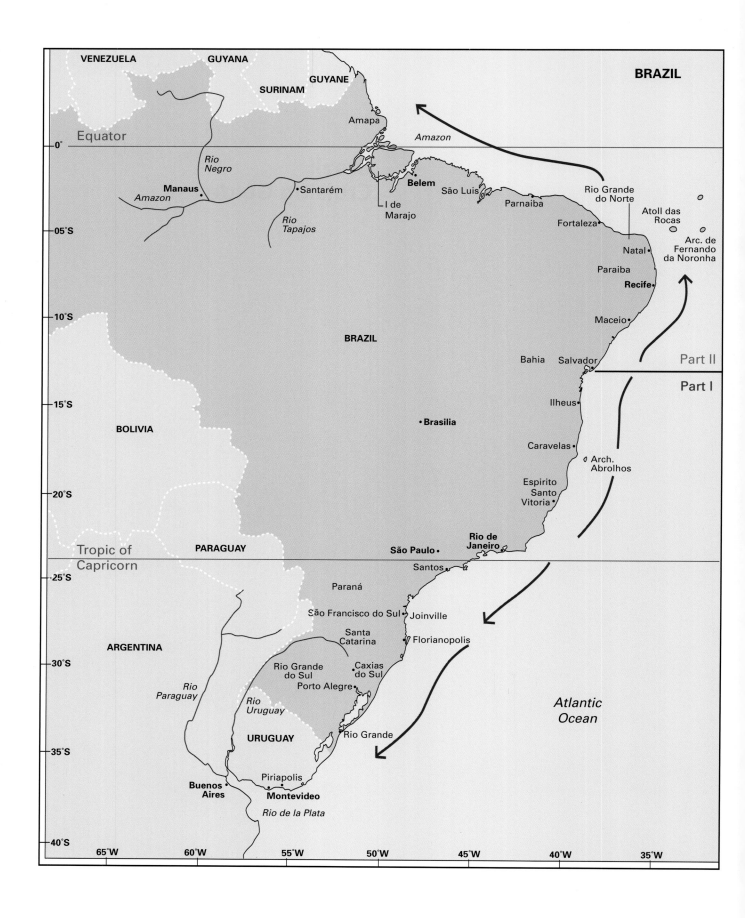

Brazil
Cruising Guide

MICHEL BALETTE

Imray Laurie Norie & Wilson

Published by
Imray Laurie Norie & Wilson Ltd
Wych House, St Ives, Cambridgeshire, PE27 45BT England
☎ +44(0)1480 462114 *Fax* +44(0)1480 496109
Email ilnw@imray.com www.imray.com

All rights reserved. No part of this publication may be reproduced,
transmitted or used in any form by any means - graphic, electronic or
mechanical, including photocopying, recording, taping or information
storage and retrieval systems or otherwise - without the prior
permission of the Publishers.

© Michel Balette 2010

Michel Balette has asserted his right under the Copyright, Designs and
Patents Act 1988 to be identified as the author of this work.

© Translation Imray, Laurie, Norie and Wilson Ltd 2010

Translated from the French by First Edition Ltd, 6 Wellington Court,
Cambridge, CB1 1HZ www.firstedit.co.uk

First English edition 2010

A catalogue record for this book is available from the British Library.

ISBN 978 184623 201 5

Original Published in France as *Le Brésil*
2008
Editions Vagnon, 30, avenue des Ecoles Militaires, 13100 Aix en Provence
www.vagnon.fr info@ codes-vagnon.fr
Author: Michel Balette
Photo credits: Florence Balette-Desplat (unless otherwise specified in the
caption). All rights reserved
Drawing credits: Florence Balette-Desplat. All rights reserved
Chart credits: Diretoria de Hidrografia e Navigação (DHN) Marinha do
Brasil
Michel Balette Permit no. 51000/2006.001/00
With digitizing assistance from MaxSea ® International

CAUTION
While every care has been taken to ensure accuracy, neither the
Publishers nor the Author will hold themselves responsible for errors,
omissions or alterations in this publication. They will at all times be
grateful to receive information which tends to the improvement of
the work.

AUTHOR'S CAUTION
The charts in this work are not to be used for navigation. Whilst they
have been used with permission of the Centro de Hidrografica da
Marina do Brasil, many have been reduced unevenly to suit the format
of the pages. They are no substitute for the official charts. Whilst the
author and publisher have taken all due care in the compilation of this
work, it should be regarded only as an aid to navigation and should
consequently be used with due caution.

To improve future editions, you are invited to let the author know your
opinions and observations. Please post, fax or email them to:

Imray Laurie Norie & Wilson Ltd
Wych House, The Broadway, St Ives
Cambridgeshire PE27 5BT England
☎ +(0)1480 462114
Fax +(0)1480 496109
Email ilnw@imray.com
www.imray.com
Or *Email* MichelBalette@hotmail.com

Printed in Singapore by Star Standard Industries (Pte) Ltd

Contents

Preface

We crossed the Atlantic in our boat *Izarra*, arriving in Brazil with the intention of spending just a few months in the country as many have done in the past. That initial stay has led on to one of several years. We sail from island to island, from anchorage to anchorage and from one port to the next, each place strangely different but friendly, we have discovered new and different scenery, and constantly meet new and delightful people.

The Brazilian coastline extends for over 4,000 miles, and much time is needed to explore its coasts and rivers.

The marine charts published by the Centro de Hidrografia cover the coastal zone very well, but there can be certain risks when navigating the watercourses; there are some areas for which the hydrographical information does not always exist, and at entrances to rivers there may be shifting sandbanks, the position of which can vary as a result of seasonal changes and meteorological conditions.

The coast of this vast country is divided into three very different regions, both in terms of geography and of population and climate.

The north and northeast

- From Belém and its major river port to the mouths of the Rio Amazonas, a river so huge that its milky coffee-coloured waters are discharged far out to sea.
- The state of Bahia, strongly influenced by African culture, many of whose traditions have been preserved and are still practised to the present day; Salvador, a city where the colonial past is evident everywhere, in its architecture, its traditions and the Bahian way of life. The majority of the population here is black or half-caste, smiling, welcoming and obliging, and little concerned about the material side of everyday life.

From the northeast to the southeast

- 1,300 miles of coast, down to the major port of Santos, with endless beaches, inlets and paradise islands.
- The state of Rio de Janeiro, which, though one of Brazil's smallest, is hugely important in terms of tourist activity. Legendary Rio with its fabulous scenery, the huge bay of Guanabara, dominated by the Sugarloaf and the statue of Christ of Corcovado. It has well earned the name of cidade maravillosa, built as it is on the most beautiful bay in the world!
- The bay of Ilha Grande and its 250 islands set in crystal-clear waters.
- The state of São Paulo. It is here that the greater part of Brazil's industrial strength is concentrated. Here, in São Paulo, Latin America's megalopolis, and in Santos with its huge port complex, we sense the pace of manufacturing and economic activity.

As a contrast to this, the region also boasts the beautiful Ilhabela.

The south

- From Paranaguá to Santa Catarina: this is Bavaria, transported to another, exotic realm!
- Rio Grande do Sul, a vast, sandy coast and the route leading on to Uruguay, Argentina and, for the adventurous, the sea channels of Patagonia and the high latitudes of the far south.

Acknowledgements

I should like to express my thanks to the Brazilian navy for their helpful support and advice, in particular the **Diretoria de Administração da Marinha** and the **Diretoria de Hidrografia e Navegação** who granted me permission to copy the Brazilian marine charts.
Almirante Paulo Cesar Dias de Lima.
Capitão de Mar-e-Guerra Persio Soares Souto.
Capitão de Mar-e-Guerra Carlos Alberto Pêgas Ferreira.
Capitão de Mar-e-Guerra Norberto. Superintendente de Segurança da Navegação.
Capitão de Fragata Alexandre Borges Briones.
Capitão de Fragata Sergio A. Pereira Joau E Silva, of the Distrito Naval de Salvador (2003).
Centro Náutico da Bahia
Iate Clube de Bahia
Iate Clube Armaçao de Buzios
Alain Joullié, Commodore of the *Iate Clube*
Clube de Regata Guanabara de Rio
João Enrique, President of the Iate Clube de Santos
Berardino Franganiello, Commodore of the ICS.

Yacht Club do Rio Grande do Sul
Carlos Augusto Vieira da Fonceca (Guto)
MaxSea International, at Bidart
Brice Pryszo, president of MaxSea International.
Les Éditions Loisirs Nautiques
Gildas de Gouvello, president of the nautical magazine *Loisirs Nautiques*
And my Brazilian friends
Marcelino of the Iate Clube de Aratu.
Geraldo of the village of Maraú.
Neblina at Itacaré.
Amir Klink, Luiz and Thalita of *marina do Engenho in Paraty*.
Commodore Newton Righi Vieira and Rocha, of the Club Naval Charitas.

Introduction

This yachting guide to the coast of Brazil is divided into two parts:

Part I southwards, from Salvador de Bahia to
  Rio Grande do Sul.
Part II northwards from Salvador de Bahia to Belém.

General Information

Notes on the crossing

We sailed from France by the classic route via Spain and Cape Finisterre, by way of the Bay of Biscay.

The coast of Galicia with its Rias Altas and Rias Bajas provides a highly characteristic change of scene, well worth a few stop-overs.

Portugal offers a foretaste of Brazil with the welcome of its inhabitants and the opportunity to attune to the language. Phrase books come into their own as you practise a few useful Portuguese expressions for everyday use in Brazil.

To the southwest of Portugal, Cabo São Vincente can deliver some surprises, with very thick fog even in mid-summer.

You then reach the coast of the Algarve, a beautiful region. The weather becomes warmer, and charges in the marinas rise markedly along with the temperature.

The next leg brings you back into Spain, to sun-drenched Andalucia, the Gulf of Cadiz and the tiny village of La Rabida, with its monastery, the place where Christopher Columbus prepared for his expedition to the New World.

A fair breeze in the Gibraltar area will then take you across your first stretch of ocean to the island of Porto Santo and the mild climate of lovely Madeira.

From there, it is just a short hop to the Canaries, with ports of call at Las Palmas, Puerto de Mogan and Santa Cruz de Tenerife, to name but a few. Here you can put the final touches to the boat to prepare it for the ocean crossing itself.

At these various ports of call, you will encounter a good many fellow sailors, most of whom will be heading for the Antilles; but there will also be some setting out for Brazil.

As you pass Pico de Teide, you bid farewell to Europe. It will respond with a few savage gusts, and a strong northeasterly wind will speed you towards the coast of Africa or the Cape Verde islands.

I chose to visit the Cape Verdes, followed by a port of call in Senegal, setting out from Dakar for my crossing of the Atlantic.

This stop-over in Africa enabled me to fill up with water and fresh food supplies more easily than I might have done in the Cape Verdes, where there are fewer options for provisioning.

The northeast trade wind transports you swiftly or slowly, as it wills, to the intertropical zone, notorious for the instability of its weather conditions. Neptune, god of the seas, will baptise you as you cross the equator by depositing on you torrents of rain and spray, to the loud accompaniment of thunder and followed by flat calm.

Brazil is well worth it all!

Approaching the coast of Brazil you will be tempted to make Récife your first port of call, as this is the nearest port after crossing the equator.

Resist the temptation and keep to the old maritime traditions. Famous navigators have sailed this way before you; five centuries ago, Portuguese ships commanded by Pedro Alvarez Cabral discovered this new country. Another who made this voyage was Amerigo Vespucci, and the gods sent winds to drive him to Bahia where he entered Brazil by way of Baía de Todos os Santos … which of course was the right thing to do!

The boat

What kind of boat to take is an ever-open question, whether it be a monohull or catamaran, fixed keel or twin-keel. Whatever your answer, if you have a boat, prepare it for the ocean crossing and set out. Come and discover Brazil.

In preparing this cruising guide I sailed a Passoa 47, with integral aluminium centreboard, built by Garcia Aluminium. The experience of sailing in *Izarra* has been a good one, as she has proved extremely comfortable, reliable and safe. Although there is no such thing as the perfect boat, I appreciated the very real advantages of this one: the robustness of its construction and rigging and the well-ventilated interior, thanks to its generous side hatches.

The variable draught of 1.1m to 2.5m is useful for safe sailing in Brazil; as in many places in the tropics, sailing with keel up or half raised makes it possible to weave through the sandbanks and reefs which are found scattered along the coast.

Many fellow sailors whose boats have a deeper draught had to miss out on visiting interesting places, or had doubts about sailing up river. They endured the stress and tension of sailing over rocky shoals (a feeling I too shared), and sometimes they made huge detours before they could meet up with us at an anchorage.

Another advantage of a lifting keel is that there are not many marinas in Brazil, and those with facilities for lifting out boats are few in number and have long waiting lists.

I was able to bring the boat ashore regularly to inspect the bottom of the hull and clean shell and algal growth from below the waterline. In the warm waters of Brazil, this growth can be particularly obstinate.

Sails and engine

Our boat has a cutter rig with genoa and staysail.

We had little in the way of light sails, and a gennaker, asymmetric spinnaker or other lightweight headsail can be useful when sailing off the wind and in the fairly light winds sometimes found along the Brazilian coast.

Nevertheless, it is always reassuring to have a powerful engine available in certain conditions, and also on the rivers, where the current can often be strong.

A good outboard motor on a semi-rigid dinghy is also useful in order to explore difficult-to-reach areas or those that are at some distance from the yacht at anchor.

Comfort on board

The Brazilian sun is strong. Hoods, biminis and other kinds of awning are one area where you should not spare expense. These will provide protection from the sun, and also from the rain, which can sometimes be torrential, depending on the season.

Another practical consideration in this climate is the frequent need to freshen up, which makes it useful to have a stern shower, for example. This is particularly pleasant after a swim, because of the high salinity of the sea water in these regions.

Our water reserves on board consist of 1,000 litres in reservoir tanks built into the hull and coated with good quality paint.

This water is used both for practical purposes and (once filtered, of course) for drinking, as an addition to our bottles of mineral water.

Energy supply on board

A wind generator or solar panels would be a useful backup for the batteries. However, in Brazil the wind can remain light for several days, and cloudy skies can considerably reduce the output of solar panels.

A generating set is certainly an excellent solution if you have space on board, although these are expensive and you will then need to carry a good stock of diesel.

On the Passoa 47 we have a 650 litre tank, giving us a good degree of practical independence, as refuelling facilities are not always close at hand.

Anchors and cables

The main anchoring equipment I use consists of a 25kg CQR anchor and 80m of 12mm chain, marked every 10m with paint of a different colour. This chain is extended with 100m of 22mm nylon rope.

This anchor has proved very efficient on a bed of sand or mud, which are usual in most anchorages, and holds even in gusts of 40 knots and more.

As a general rule in a depth of three to 5m and in good weather conditions, I play safe and anchor using 25 to 30m of chain, bearing in mind the possibility of a gust while I am away from the boat.

As my secondary anchor and cable I have a FOB anchor and stern mooring line consisting of 10m of 10mm chain and 16mm rope.

This is particularly useful if I bring the boat ashore on a beach or sandbank, or want to set two anchors, as I would, for example, in narrow rivers.

Electronic equipment on board

The GPS will be an indispensable item on your instrument panel, as well as a good depth sounder that can indicate shallow depths accurately.

Our electronic log is reliable enough, although the impeller sometimes becomes blocked by suspended fine weed in the currents.

The radar has proved very efficient, especially at nightfall, because of the many fishing boats encountered all along the coast, especially around the capes.

In the south of Brazil in particular, visibility can be much reduced by blankets of fog, especially at the end of the night and lasting through until mid-morning.

Marine charts

The Centro de Hidrografia da Marinha do Brasil publishes paper charts that give thorough coverage of the coast.

At ports of call, a great many charts will be found on the pontoons, and some of these are very ancient or are photocopies: beware; these charts may not necessarily be up to date with the latest corrections! (*See the list of charts on page 267*).

The Brazilian charts are inexpensive at around R$35, so it is much better to use original ones.

For some parts of the coast and some rivers of Brazil, no hydrographic data exist. It is necessary to approach these areas with care.

If you have an on-board computer, there are electronic charts coupled to GPS, which are very practical to use. However, some systems do not have enough charts giving small-scale details.

The system I used for navigation was MaxSea International. This navigation software is compatible with Mapmedia electronic charts and some others.

Mapmedia has produced digital versions of over 12,000 charts worldwide, through international partnership with hydrographic and topographic departments. These charts are a faithful and continuous reproduction of the paper charts, from which they were scanned; they reproduce the precision and reliability of the paper originals.

Nevertheless, in parallel with the electronic navigation aid, it is important to check and note the navigation information on the marine charts published by the Centro de Hidrografia e Navegação of the Brazilian navy.

History

Brazil is the largest country in South America, with a population today of around 180 million.

In the past, these lands were inhabited by a number of Amerindian tribes spread across the north of the country, the Tupi and Guarani, mainly near the coast, and the Tamoios who made their way to the south.

Still today, many small colonies of indigenous peoples are found all across Brazil, although the main groups are settled in the Amazon region. Most of these indigenous tribes have maintained their traditions and way of life.

It was the Spanish navigator Vicente Yañez Pinzon who first discovered this land in January 1500, but on account of the treaty of Tordesillas (1494), Spain did not lay claim to it.

Portuguese colonisation

On 22 April 1500, the Portuguese navigator Pedro Alvarez Cabral, commanding an expeditionary fleet of 13 ships and following the route of the northeast trade winds, reached the coast of this new continent.

He landed on the eastern coast at what is today Porto Seguro and formally named the land Terra da Vera Cruz.

During 1501, Amerigo Vespucci, also sailing on behalf of Portugal, explored a large part of the coast and discovered Baía de Todos os Santos, at Salvador. In January 1502, Gaspar de Lemos anchored in the bay of Rio de Janeiro.

It was in this region that the first explorers discovered a tree, the dark wood of which was used by the Amerindians to make a red dye. They called this tree the *pau brasil*; on their return to Portugal, Terra da Vera Cruz acquired the name BRAZIL.

The French had already explored these lands some time earlier and had tried to establish themselves in Rio bay, but some bloody conflicts ensued and they were repelled by the Portuguese. Within 30 years the Portuguese began a programme of colonisation, and divided the country into 15 captaincies.

In 1530, Tomé de Souza was named first governor of Brazil. The central seat of government was located at Salvador da Bahia, which became the country's first capital.

The countries of this new continent are particularly suited to the growing of sugar cane, cotton and tobacco, and ideal for the founding of new communities. In order to protect it against foreign incursions, the Portuguese undertook the construction of many fortresses on strategic points of the coast.

The city of Rio de Janeiro was founded in 1567.

The country suffered a number of attacks between 1580 and 1640 by the English, then by the Dutch, who succeeded in establishing themselves at Salvador de Bahia. After many years of fighting, the Dutch were eventually repelled by the Portuguese and gave up all claim to the territories of Brazil.

From 1640 onwards, Brazil became a Portuguese viceroyalty, and a period of stability began which proved favourable to the development of the country.

Brazil prospered rapidly, mainly as a result of the large sugar cane and coffee plantations in the northeast.

During the 1750s, the discovery of the hevea tree, the sap of which is used to produce rubber, led to the development of the Amazon region and the creation of the river ports of Belém and Manaus.

The discovery of gold in the region of Minas Gerais produced a huge influx of settlers and gold-seekers from Europe. Some years later, diamonds were discovered and considerably accelerated the economic growth of the country. Gold was brought across the mountains to the city of Paraty (*caminho do ouro*) to be loaded onto ships bound for Portugal.

Later, with the development of new and safer routes, this wealth was transported by way of Rio de Janeiro, which quickly became a very prosperous city.

The central seat of government was transferred there in 1763. Rio became the new capital, to the detriment of Salvador.

Creation of the Brazilian Empire

In 1807, France under Napoleon was at war and his Grande Armée invaded Spain and Portugal.

The Portuguese Prince Regent João VI was forced to flee, and took refuge at Rio de Janeiro. On his return to Portugal in 1821, João VI named his son Dom Pedro viceroy of Brazil, placing the government of the country in his hands.

However, this was opposed by the Upper Chamber of the Cortes, who wanted to retain Brazil as a colony, and demanded the return of the viceroy to Portugal.

Dom Pedro refused; in 1822 he proclaimed the independence of Brazil, and had himself proclaimed Emperor under the name of Pedro I. His autocratic manner in government produced much discontent among the people, and he was obliged to abdicate in favour of his heir, Pedro II. It was during his reign, in 1888, that slavery was abolished.

Creation of the First Republic

The abolition of slavery led to a rupture between the royal family and the powerful landowners (*fazendeiros*), and in 1889 Pedro II was overthrown by a military coup d'état.

A constitution was adopted and Brazil became a federal republic, with General Manuel Deodoro da Fonseca as its first President. He was to govern as a dictator, quickly becoming unpopular.

A revolt by the army forced him to hand over power to his vice president, Floriano Peixoto, who proved equally unable to maintain order in the country.

A new president, Prudente Jose de Moraes, was elected, and calm was gradually restored to Brazil.

There followed alternating periods of peace and social conflict. The former governor of São Paulo, Samuel Campos Salles, came to power, and his arrival once more brought fresh economic expansion.

The country's coffers were replenished, thanks to large foreign loans, and this enabled industry and commerce to develop, especially that of São Paulo and the south of the country.

However, a fall in the price of coffee and lower prices for rubber produced a serious imbalance in the Brazilian economy, and led to fresh unrest in the second decade of the twentieth century, with severe political and social agitation.

With the start of the first world war in 1914, Brazil at first remained neutral, but German attacks on the Brazilian fleet led the country to declare itself on the side of the Allies in 1917.

The post-war period was marked by more social unrest, and President Arthur da Silva Bernardes, who was elected in 1922, was obliged to declare martial law.

His successor, Washington Luis Perreira de Souza, was also unable to master the economic crisis, and further social unrest erupted, under the pressure of communism, once more paralysing the country.

Estado Novo (the New State)

The presidential election of March 1930 gave victory to Julio Prestes, but he remained in office for only a very short while; a few months later, Getulio Vargas seized power in a coup d'état, with the support of the Army and a large majority of the political class. He was an excellent politician and an able manipulator. He governed in an autocratic manner.

In the very first year following his coming to power, he undertook significant social reforms, such as a guaranteed minimum salary, the creation of a social security system for workers, and compulsory public school attendance.

All these reforms helped draw the support of the popular classes to his side. The centralisation of power enabled him to impose decrees, he reorganised the army, created a political police force and imposed strict control of the press.

In 1939, on the eve of the second world war, he aligned himself on the side of the United States and committed the Brazilian navy to take part in the conflict.

In 1945, a military coup d'état ousted Vargas from power, but he was re-elected in 1951 with the support of the parties of the Left. In fulfilment of election promises, he undertook agrarian reform, but came into conflict with the powerful landowners. The opposition became particularly hostile to him, and he gradually lost the support of the army. He committed suicide in 1954.

Juscelino Kubitschek, whose supporters included both those of Getulio Vargas and also the communists, was elected to the Presidency of the Republic in 1956.

His dynamic policies of economic development, together with a loan of 150 million dollars, enabled Brazil to achieve strong industrial growth. The new capital, Brasilia, was created, and major transport projects carried out; industry and car manufacture developed, and hydroelectric stations built.

The period that followed was more chaotic: Jânio da Silva Quadros, former governor of São Paulo, replaced Kubitschek in January 1961, but had to leave office a few months later.

He was succeeded by his vice-president, João Goulart, ex-minister of Labour under Vargas. Goulart, however, was overthrown by a military coup in 1964, and General Humberto Castelo Branco, chief of staff of the Army, replaced him at the head of the country.

The country remained in the hands of the military for 20 years, from 1964 until 1985, and it was they who provided its presidents.

During this period the country had the advantage of political stability and good economic growth.

Major projects were carried out to exploit natural resources, but to the detriment of necessary social reforms. Discontent gradually set in among the working class, a strong trade union movement took shape, bringing social unrest in a series of disturbances.

This situation was met with a new decree to give plenary powers to the President: the press was censored and the opposition parties of the Left were banned, the only authorised opposition party being the Brazilian Democratic Movement (MDB).

The flag of Brazil

In 1968, fresh social unrest and a student revolt were repressed by force and followed by a wave of arrests.

The country then sank into chaos, with extreme inflation and a high level of unemployment.

The fresh elections of 1985 saw the replacement of military power by a civilian president, Tancredo Neves. However, on the eve of entering office he fell ill and died. He was replaced by Fernando Collor, who was dismissed in December 1992 following a major corruption scandal.

The country remained in a period of crisis, with growing inflation and an enormous foreign debt.

Collor's replacement continued the struggle against inflation with a plan to reduce the foreign debt. A new currency, the Real, was introduced in July 1994.

In December 1994, the former Finance minister, Henrique Cardoso, was elected President of the Republic. This new president managed to restore economic growth with a stabilised currency and resumption of foreign investment.

He was re-elected in 1998. However, society's problems remained unsolved with increasing corruption at all levels and violence a part of everyday life. An increasing gap was opening up between the affluent and the less advantaged sections of the populace.

The Left comes to power

The downturn of these last few years encouraged the birth of a new political party, the Workers' Party (PT), drawing together the parties of the Left, the socialists and leftist radicals.

Luiz Ignacio Lula da Silva, known as 'Lula', a former metal worker and trade union militant, assumed the leadership of this Party. His electoral campaign was based on urgent social measures: the battle to defeat corruption, assistance to the poorer classes, combating hunger, and the more equal distribution of wealth.

On his election in 2002, Lula became the first President of the Republic of Brazil to come from the Left. He assumed leadership of a country in a precarious financial situation, with a currency (the Real) that had been devalued by 30% in 2002, and massive foreign debt.

When Lula next presented himself to the country in new elections in 2006, the country's balance sheet was a good deal better than when he came into office, the currency was recovering and foreign investment was being resumed.

The transfer of votes from parties of the Left and a large vote from the northeast of the country meant that he was re-elected on 29 October 2006 with a comfortable majority over his rival, Geraldo Alckmin, governor of the State of São Paulo.

Geography

With a total surface area of over eight million square kilometres, Brazil is the fifth largest country in the world.

The territory can be subdivided into the following large areas:

- The north, through which flows the Rio Amazonas. This massive river is 6,200km in length (half of which is in Peru). Most of the region is Amazonian rainforest. On the border between Brazil and Venezuela is a mountain massif, the highest summit of which is Pico de Neblina (3,014m).

- The northeast. The African influence is most marked in this region. Along the coast are large, rich agricultural lands, while the hinterland (*Sertão*) tends to be desert, and largely depopulated.

- The centre-west, an extension of the Amazonian territory. This is an area of broad, open spaces, sparsely populated, and mainly used for cattle-rearing.

- The southeast, the richest and most inhabited region, where 40% of the country's population is concentrated. This is where the largest cities are to be found, such as São Paulo, with half the country's industrial potential, and Rio de Janeiro, in the state that attracts most of Brazil's tourism.

- The south, with a subtropical climate and noticeably less warm in winter. This is the land of the gauchos, and the European influence is very strong here.

- The coastal zone, running the length of the country from north to south, has over 7,000km of coastline and is extremely diverse, with extensive beaches, rocky, indented coasts and countless island.

Jaca (or jackfruit), fruit of the jaca tree
(*Artocarpus heterophyllus*)

The torch ginger or porcelain rose (*Etlingera elatior*)

The *mata atlântica*, the coastal tropical forest

Delicate Angels' Trumpets (*Datura*)

Heliconia (*Heliconia rostrata*)

Nature and the environment

Flora

The hot, humid climate of much of the country gives Brazil a luxuriant and very varied vegetation.

Across these vast lands extend immense tropical forests with a wealth of flora beyond compare.

The flowers are an overwhelming celebration of colour, shape and perfume only rivalled by the delicious multitude of fruits. All kinds of fruit can be found in Brazil, both those familiar in our temperate regions (apples, oranges, bananas…) and the immense variety of tropical fruits (mango, papaya, jaca, acerola, pitangua, maracuja, umbu…).

The flora of Brazil falls into several groups, belonging to the different ecosystems:

- The Amazon basin in the north of the country. This region has the largest tropical forest in the world, the luxuriant and very dense vegetation of which contains over one and a half million identified species. However, this ecological treasure is threatened with intensive deforestation.

- The Sertão, the inhospitable semi-arid region of the northeast.

- The Cerrado, which covers the centre of Brazil, consisting of immense expanses of savanna and forests.

- The Pantanal, an immense marshy area of 150,000km², on the borders with Bolivia and Paraguay. It is flooded from December to March, bringing about a renewal of the flowers, savanna and prairies just as soon as the water level falls. This is one of the wildest areas of Brazil, little capable of exploitation for agriculture, but an ecological paradise for the fauna which inhabits it.

- The *mata atlântica* is a dense tropical forest covering the hilly coastal regions and extending down to the sea, and is most striking in the states of Bahia, Espírito Santo, Rio de Janeiro, Paraná and Santa Catarina. At least 90% of this forest has been destroyed over the

The stately Bird of Paradise flower (*Strelitzia*)

The inquisitive lemur

years to make way for plantations of coffee, sugar cane and similar crops. Today it is protected, but it remains under threat from rampant urbanisation.

Fauna

Brazil has a remarkable diversity of fauna: mammals, birds, marine and freshwater fish, insects and reptiles. The Amazon region and the huge expanses of the Pantanal alone form a vast sanctuary.

There is no need to list here all the countless animal species to be found in Brazil, since this has already been done by the experts, but below are some of those likely to be encountered on this cruise or excursions to the interior:

Mammals

Brazil boasts many species of mammals: its forests are inhabited by peccaries and the delightful armadillo, tapirs, ring-tailed coatis, and that large rodent, the capivara. It is less common to encounter jaguar and puma, since of all the cat family these are among the most cautious of being seen and the most difficult to get near. The jacaré, a member of the alligator family, is also widespread in the vast marshes of the Pantanal.

Monkeys, lemurs and other macaques also inhabit the Brazilian countryside, and it is no longer uncommon to encounter them, even around much-frequented areas.

Birds, reptiles, turtles and tortoises

Great numbers of flamingoes, herons, egrets and red ibis (*guará*) are usually to be seen in the flood-prone areas of Pará and the Amazon region. In the tropical forest, there are many species of parrot, and various kinds of toucan and macaw (rarer) can still be seen.

As for reptiles, while you may not often encounter a 10-metre-long anaconda at a bend in the path, there will more probably be water snakes (Salvador, Itaparica) and coral snakes (*cobra coral*), which are pretty to look at but very poisonous.

Turtles and tortoises (*tartarugas, cágados*) are also much in evidence, and you are bound to encounter some when diving (Ilha Grande).

Fish

Marine fauna are also very well represented, both marine fish and a great variety of river and freshwater fish.

The number of recorded kinds of freshwater fish runs into thousands, especially in the Amazon region and the Pantanal. Piranhas, much feared for their razor-sharp teeth, frequent all the rios of the Amazon basin. If you have the opportunity, when visiting one on the many tributaries of the Amazon, you should ask a fisherman to catch you a Tucunaré, or – even better – you might visit him at his house and eat one; this fish is delicious.

The coast of Brazil is also rich in marine fish. Personally, my approach to fishing is always to leave some of each species in the sea to reproduce and take only the minimum I actually need; sometimes I even resort to a tin of sardines... Nevertheless, along these coasts you would have no difficulty in catching a tuna or dolphin fish: I have done it.

The coast of Espirito Santo is well known for marlin fishing. For this, of course, it is necessary to have the right equipment and skills.

In the rivers of Bahia and the Paraíba delta, quantities of shrimp (*camarões*) are caught, as well as sea crabs (*siri*) among the mangroves. Another kind that is much appreciated in Brazil is the land crab (*guaiamu*).

One creature you should not try to catch is the right whale (*baleia franca*): you will certainly encounter many of these in the waters off the *Abrolhos*. Not only because of their size (you would have trouble getting 10 tons of whale on board); these mammals are also a protected species.

Do, on the other hand, aim to harpoon a few delicious forkfuls of *badejo* or *vermelho* in a restaurant. Well recommended.

Warning

The laws that govern the keeping of protected wild animals are very strict in Brazil. It is absolutely forbidden to smuggle animals (such as tortoises or parrots, or other species) out of the country, on pain of very severe fines or even imprisonment.

Population

Brazilian society numbers some 180 million inhabitants, and is made up of a great variety of races as well as people of mixed race.

Around 60% of the population is white, essentially consisting of Portuguese, Italian, German, Polish and French, who are settled throughout the country, but mainly in the south. Most of the rest of the population is mixed race; the *mulatos* (mixed-race black and white) are to be found throughout Brazil, while the *caboclos* (mixed-race white and Amerindian) predominate in the Amazon region and the northeast. There is also a significant Asiatic community in Brazil.

Marked inequalities are seen in society and lifestyles; around the edges of extensive stretches of land under cultivation by rich landowners is found an entire disadvantaged population of rural labourers, the *Sem terra*, living in tumbledown roadside shacks.

In more densely populated areas, it is common to see people living in luxurious homes next to a disadvantaged population housed in very basic fashion in *favelas* around the major Brazilian cities such as São Paulo, Rio de Janeiro, or Salvador.

Despite these visible inequalities there is no sign of jealousy or racism apparent among this population.

Language

The official language of Brazil is Portuguese. It differs in some ways from the Portuguese spoken in Europe, in particular by a pleasing singsong accent.

When reading the language, understanding is helped to some extent by the fact that a number of words are similar in French or Spanish. To understand spoken Brazilian Portuguese demands long practice, especially as the accent is very different from the north to the south of the country (*see the Glossary at the end of this book*).

Religion

Brazil has the largest concentration of Roman Catholics in the world.

There are also many sects and other religions of African inspiration.

With the arrival of the Portuguese on Brazilian soil, and of numerous slaves to work on the plantations, the colonists forbad the practice of the African rites.

In order to avoid the sanctions they would incur, the slaves gave their African deities a Catholic guise, and did homage to their gods (*Orixàs*) through veneration of the saints of the Catholic religion. It is as a result of this practice that a number of Afro-Brazilian cults now exist, a legacy of Yoruba religion, such as Umbanda, Macumba and Candomblé.

The sects and powerful religious organisations such as Igreja Universal and Assembleia de Deus, and many others, are widespread throughout Brazil.

National holidays and festivals

1st January	New Year's Day (*Confraternização Universal*)
21 April	Tiradentes, national hero of Brazil
1st May	Labour Day
7 September	Brazilian Independence Day

12 October	Our Lady of Aparecida, patron saint of Brazil
2 November	Day of the dead (*Finados*)
15 November	Proclamation of the Republic
25 December	Christmas Day (*Natal*)

Health

In general there are few health problems in Brazil, apart from the obvious need to observe a few basic rules of hygiene, especially as regards food and water.

It is advisable to drink mineral water or filtered water, and fruit and vegetables should be carefully washed before eating.

In anchorages or among mangroves, shortly before nightfall, mosquitoes are especially numerous and inclined to bite.

Methods of protection include the use of a repellent and, ideally, sleeping under a good mosquito net impregnated with insecticide.

Dengue, a disease transmitted by a particular species of mosquito (*Aedes aegypti*), is present throughout Brazil, and rare cases have been reported among visiting yachtsmen.

In the state of Bahia, there is a parasite (*Larva migrans*) that is deposited on beaches by dogs. It can become lodged under the skin, especially that of the feet; as it moves around it leaves a red trail.

This can be treated easily by applying an ointment: the advice is to consult a doctor who is a skin specialist.

The risks of exposure to the sun should not be underestimated; the sun in Brazil is strong, and can cause serious sunburn, sunstroke, heatstroke or dehydration.

Safety

It would be a mistake to become obsessed with safety problems and the risk of violence in Brazil.

The larger Brazilian cities such as São Paulo (over 15 million inhabitants), Rio de Janeiro (five million inhabitants) and Salvador (three million inhabitants) have many working-class districts that are extremely disadvantaged, and the risk of physical attack in the street is inevitably greater there than in a rural village or small fishing port.

Nevertheless, by observing the sort of commonsense rules that every traveller knows and by taking sensible care, outings and walking around the city should present no problem, as long as certain quarters are avoided and you keep well away from the *favelas*.

As a general rule, you should avoid drawing attention to yourself by loud appearance or behaviour, or making any display of wealth such as the wearing of watches, chains, jewellery or other valuable objects.

The best way to remain inconspicuous is to dress and behave like the Brazilians.

When you withdraw money from a cash dispenser, be alert to people around you when you leave the bank: thieves may follow you for a long time, waiting for a suitable moment to pick your pockets or mug you in some deserted spot (*assalto*). If this does happen, it is useless and above all dangerous to offer even the least resistance.

Other behaviour that is not advisable in Brazil (or indeed in a good many other countries) is to walk around with a fat wallet bulging from your inside pocket, or leaving your possessions on the beach.

There is in principle no problem during the day in well-frequented places, and the police are all around in the main busy areas of the city and tourist sites.

In the evening, when shopkeepers roll down the shutters and passers-by head home, greater vigilance is needed. Above all, deserted or ill-lit streets should be avoided.

In Salvador, the Comercio district near the port has a rather bad reputation, so when returning to the marina at a late hour, it may be wiser to travel by taxi.

In Rio, after dark in the Copacabana quarter of the city, when the streets empty and all is abandoned to the denizens of the night, a starlight stroll can bring trouble.

In isolated anchorages in deep bays or *rios*, there are not usually any problems, although vigilance is still needed; there have occasionally been attacks in the past and this could happen again.

As a general rule you should not let the occupants of a local small boat attach alongside, or allow its occupants to come aboard under whatever pretext.

It is of course necessary to keep an eye on dinghies and outboard motors. (Rio Bay).

Never forget that, in Brazil, a boat is seen as a sure sign of wealth and will tend to provoke a covetous reaction. A foreign boat is all the more tempting, as it will contain expensive navigation equipment, personal effects, photographic equipment and the like.

Cuisine and drinks

Brazilian cuisine

There are three main meals during the day in Brazil, much as in Europe:

- Breakfast (*café da manhã*)
- Lunch (*almoço*)
- Dinner (*jantar*)

As a rule Brazilians rise early, and breakfast is eaten from 0630.

Breakfast is substantial, consisting of fruit juice, coffee, fruit, sausage, ham, cheese, yoghurt, etc.

The midday and evening meals are eaten at approximately the same times as in Europe, although many Brazilians tend to have just one main meal a day on account of their hours of work. People who eat dinner late nibble a few snack items (*petiscos*) in the evening.

Traditional Brazilian cuisine is generally rather rich, often fried or served in a sauce. Snack bars (*lanchonetes*) have great displays of fritters and doughnuts (*pasteis, folhados, empadas*) of all kinds.

The basic ingredients of a typical meal are tomatoes with onions and salads as a starter, then a main dish of meat, chicken or fish with an accompaniment of rice, black beans (*arroz com feijão*) and manioc flour (*farofa*).

Brazilians seldom end the meal with a dessert, but coffee (*cafezinho*) is ever-present. It is served in a tiny cup and is consumed at all hours of the day.

Restaurants of all kinds are found throughout Brazil.

One type that is commonly found is the *comida a kilo*, a self-service system offering a varied range of dishes. Customers help themselves to whatever they want and pay for their food by weight. It is a practical and inexpensive system, and widespread across the whole country.

Another restaurant system frequently met with in the cities is *rodizio*, where for a very reasonable set price you can eat what you wish from a selection of fish, meats, Japanese or Italian specialities, etc.

Brazilian specialities you will encounter:

Feijoada, the national dish: a stew made of a variety of different meats with beans, manioc flour, and peppers, served with rice.

In the north of the country, the cuisine of the Amazon region has many dishes based on vegetables and fish.

In the northeast, the main style of cooking is Bahian cuisine with its strong African influence. It is characterised by the use of palm oil (*dendê*) and flavoursome spices. The usual specialities include seafood, *moquecas de peixe*, *camarãoes*, *vatapa*, and meats such as *carne do sol* (dried meat); snacks include *acarajés*, a kind of fritter cooked in *dendê*, which can be eaten on every street corner in Bahia.

In the centre and the southeast, look out for *virado de feijão*, in Minas Gerais *carne de vaca* and *porco*, in Rio and São Paulo *feijoada* (traditionally served on Wednesdays and Fridays), and *churrasco*, an assortment of delicious barbecued meats.

Italian cuisine also features, with pizzas and pasta dishes of various kinds.

In the south, cattle-rearing country, there is nothing to equal *comida gaucha*, delicious *churrascos* cooked over a wood fire, found from Paraná down to Rio Grande do Sul.

Drinks

Wine can be drunk with all meals in Brazil (there are vineyards in the south and southeast). However, Brazilians' favourite drink is beer (*cerveja*). A good deal of beer is consumed, served very cold. The commonest brands include: Antarctica®; Bohemia®; Brahma®; Skol®.

There are many kinds of delicious freshly-pressed fruit juices (*sucos*), as many as there are kinds of fruit in Brazil: *laranja*, *abacaxi*, *manga*, *maracuja*, *goïaba*, *acerola*, *umbu*, etc.

Caldo de cana is sugar cane juice, which is made by crushing a sugar cane in a fearsome machine, with noisy gears, found in the streets and squares of Bahia.

Guarana: This is the Brazilian equivalent of Coca Cola®. A popular soft drink in Brazil, it is made from an Amazonian plant that has all kinds of unexpected virtues!

Then, of course, there is the famous *caipirinha*, the Brazilian drink par excellence, which is served on every possible occasion: festivals of all kinds, family reunions, as a drink shared among friends or even to drink alone; it can be enjoyed at almost any hour of day or night.

The rules for making this drink are precisely laid down, and it is made only with Brazilian *cachaça*.

Cachaça is the exclusive designation of origin of Brazilian *aguardente de cana* (a spirit made from the juice of sugar cane), and its alcohol content can be as high as 38 to 48°.

The law of 2 October 2003, decree No. 4851, lays down the technical details of *caipirinha*, which has three basic ingredients: lime, caster sugar, and *cachaça*.

Traditional recipe for *caipirinha*

Take one ripe lime (only lime is used), as full of juice as possible (the skin will be smooth and supple, stretched and a slightly lighter green).Wash it, then cut it in half, in half again, and so on until you have eight pieces.

Place it in a special wooden container for making *caipirinha*, and add two teaspoons of refined caster sugar.

Crush the mixture with a wooden pestle. Avoid crushing the lime peel too much, as this gives the drink a bitter taint.

When the juice and sugar are well mixed, pour them into a large glass and fill it with crushed ice. Gently add about 50ml of *cachaça*.

Drink the delicious brew through two straws. This way, you are able to drink the *caipirinha* from the bottom of the glass.

It is better to use artisan-produced *cachaça* from a *fazenda*, since it has a much better flavour than the industrially produced kind.

There are some variations on *caipirinha*:
Caipirissima, made with rum, *caipirosca* with vodka, *caipirisaquê* with sake. Mother Maria Paolina's recipe is another I have sampled:
- 2 ginger leaves, placed in the bottom of a glass and crushed with a fork,
- 2 tablespoons lemon,
- Fine cane sugar,
- 2 tablespoons iced water,
- Crushed ice,
- 1 generous slug *cachaça*.

On finishing the drink, nibble the ginger leaves and be gently transported to paradise.

Cachaça

Cachaça itself can be drunk on its own, in a small glass, either iced or at room temperature and at any hour.

I recall a Brazilian fisherman on the Rio Paraguaçu who generously offered me a glass of *cachaça* at seven o'clock in the morning; I drank it in small instalments. I found it very warming, especially in its effects on my throat. His cheerful manner and rolling gait told me that this was not his first swig of the day.

Batida

This drink, based on pressed fruit juice (*suco*) and *cachaça*, is another expression of Brazilian hospitality. It usually consists of two parts fruit juice to one part cachaça; sugar and ice cubes are added. This is made with any of a great number of *sucos*: *abacaxi*, *coco*, *morango*, *limão*, *uva*, *caju*, *graviola*, *umbu*, *pitanga*, to name but a few. It can even be made with tomato, coffee, chocolate – the list is endless.

These delicious drinks are accompanied by a variety of tapas-style snacks (*petiscos*) and appetisers (*tira gosto*) of different kinds.

Entering Brazil by Boat

The coastal zones

International waters lie beyond a limit of 200M from the coast; for Brazil as for all countries open to the ocean, three zones are defined:

The exclusive economic zone, which extends for 200M from the coast, gives the country rights over the conservation and management of natural resources, and exploration on or under the sea bed.

The contiguous zone, from 12 to 24M, permits the control of infractions of regulations, including immigration and sanitary laws.

The territorial sea extends 12M from the coast. Authorisation needs to be obtained to enter or stop in this zone, and the presence in these waters must not be prejudicial to the good order of the country.

The skipper and crew of a boat entering Brazil must complete the entry formalities at the various administrative departments concerned, and these formalities can only be carried out at certain official ports of entry where there is an office of the Capitania dos Portos, department of Immigration (*Policia Féderal*) and Customs.

The skipper, as well as the members of the crew, must also visit the Department of Health.

The official ports of entry

Here is a list of the official ports of entry into Brazil, in the various states of the country:

North coast

Manaus	(Amazonas)
Belém	(Pará)
Macapá	(Amapá)
São Luis	(Maranhão)

Northeast coast

Fortaleza	(Ceará)
Natal	(Rio Grande do Norte)
Recife	(Pernambuco)
Maceió	(Alagoas)
Salvador	(Bahia)
Ilheus	(Bahia)

Southeast coast

Vitória	(Espírito Santo)
Rio	(Rio de Janeiro)
Angra dos Reis	(Rio de Janeiro)
Sepetiba	(Rio de Janeiro)
São Sebastião	(São Paulo)
Santos	(São Paulo)

South coast

Paranaguá	(Paraná)
São Francisco do Sul	(Santa Catarina)
Florianópolis	(Santa Catarina)
Imbituba et Itajaí,	(Santa Catarina)
Rio Grande	(Rio Grande do Sul)

Entry formalities (Entrada do barco)

When arriving by sea, it is not necessary to present a visa to enter Brazil. The initial administrative formalities required on landing at an official port of entry should be performed in the following order:

- *Polícia féderal* (Immigration)
- *Alfândega dos Portos, Receta Féderal* (Customs)
- *Ministério da Saude* (Health department)
- *Capitania dos Portos.*

Polícia Féderal (Immigration)

The skipper must go in person with his or her passport and the boat's papers, and a declaration of entry for the boat (*passe de entrada*) will be issued.

The crew and passengers must also attend the office of the Polícia Féderal with their passports.

Alfândega dos Portos, Receta Féderal (Customs)

Fill in the various printed forms, and a special declaration stating the value of the boat. Customs will calculate a tax proportional to the value of the boat (*Termo de Responsabilidade*). This tax is stated for information only, but does not have to be paid.

Ministério da Saude (Health Department)

Fill in the health questionnaire and present vaccination certificates, and the health authority will give you a *certificado de livre prática*.

Capitania dos Portos

Fill in the entry document, the *Declaração de entrada*.

If you wish to visit certain islands, such as Fernando de Noronha, the Abrolhos Archipelago, Ilha da Trindade, or others, you should ask at the *Capitania* who exercise control over these islands.

All these formalities are free of charge.

As a general rule, smart dress is required at all Brazilian administrative offices, i.e. shirt and trousers (not shorts).

Length of stay

Brazilian law allows visitors to the country a total length of stay in Brazil of 180 days (two times 90 days), excepting derogations.

An initial authorisation of 90 days is granted on entry.

Important In order to obtain a extension of stay it is essential to make the request well in advance of the expiry of the 90 days, at the appropriate office of the *Polícia Féderal*, in return for a small fee. This extension of stay is normally granted.

Derogations

There are two other types of permission that allow a longer stay in Brazil:

- A 2-year cultural visa, for study
- A permanent visa for a retired person

To qualify for the second of these visas, the applicant must be over 50 years of age, deposit a dossier of the appropriate certificates, present a certificate of retirement, a non-criminal record (certificate of good conduct; CRB disclosure), and provide proof of adequate income; the applicant must also be in a position to make a monthly credit transfer into the Banco do Brasil.

Entry into the country must then be made within 90 days of the date of obtaining this visa.

This request must be made in the country of origin, at the Embassy of Brazil.

Note: Visa provisions are subject to change, so should be checked as necessary.

In Britain, the address to contact for further information is:

Embassy of Brazil, 32 Green St, London, W1K 7AT
☎ 020 73999000, *Fax* 020 73999100
Email info@brazil.org.uk

New law allowing a 2-year length of stay for the boat

On the proposal of senator César Borges, of Salvador de Bahia, an amendment of the existing regulations (decrees No. 37 of 1966 and No. 4543 of 26/12/2002) was presented in 2005. This relates to the length of stay in the country.

The decree in question is No. 5887, which was passed and published in the official Journal (*Diário Oficial da União*) on 8 September 2006. Article 313 § 5 and § 6 states:

In the matter of a small sport and leisure vessel belonging to a foreign tourist, this will be able to benefit beyond the the regular six months' stay in Brazil allowed to the boat's owner, from a prorogation amounting to two years in total of the length of the stay in the territory.

If the owner is temporarily out of the country the harbour authorities can authorise duty-free mooring or gardiennage in a public area provide you have prior confirmation from the *Capitania dos Portos*.

You should enquire locally at the offices of the *polícia féderal* and customs.

This decree is still fairly recent, so there may be some officials who are not yet aware of it; also, you should not hesitate to ask to speak to a superior authority if your request is disputed.

Exit formalities (Saída do barco)

There are two different categories, and the distinction needs to be made, as they are treated differently: leaving the state and leaving the country.

Leaving the state

Return to the various offices, apart from the Health department, and you will be issued with an exit document (*passe de saída*), **without putting an exit stamp in your passport**.

The formalities must be repeated, in the same order (police, customs, *Capitania dos Portos*), at the port of entry of each state. Even if some of the police and customs offices dispense with these formalities, it is still better to request them.

Leaving the country

When you leave the country, you must revisit all the same offices. It is absolutely essential to make sure that the *Polícia Féderal* put an **exit stamp in your passport** (otherwise you will be considered to be continuing your stay in the country, and if you extend your stay beyond the authorised limit this is punishable by a fine).

Diplomatic and consular missions

Consulate of Great Britain

General Switchboard
+55 (11) 3094-2700
In Brasilia
British Embassy, Setor de Embaixadas Sul, Quadra 801, Lote 8, CEP 70408 900, Brasilia, DF, Brazil
☎ +55 61 3329 2300
In Rio de Janeiro
British Consulate General, Praia do Flamengo 284/2 andar, 22210-030, Rio de Janeiro RJ
☎ +55 21 2555 9600
Email bcg.rj@fco.gov.uk
In São Paulo
British Consulate General, Rua Ferreira de Araujo, 741, 05428-002, Sao Paulo-SP
☎ +55 11 3094 2700
Email saopaulo@gra-bretanha.org.br

Consulate of Argentina

In Rio de Janeiro
Praia Botafogo 228, Sobreloja 201 Edificio Argentina, 22250-040, Rio de Janeiro, Brazil
☎ +55 21 2553 1646, *Fax* +55 21 2552 4191
Email fcrioj@mrecic.gov.ar

Consulate of Belgium

Rua Lauro Muller, 116/602, Torre do Rio Sul, Botafogo, 22290-160, Rio de Janeiro/RJ
☎ +55 21 2543 8558, *Fax* +55 21 2543 8398
Email RiodeJaneiro@diplobel.fed.be

Consulate of France

In Rio de Janeiro
Avenida Presidente Antonio Carlos 58, 20020-010, Rio de Janeiro, Brazil,
☎ +55 21 3974 6699
In Sao Paulo
Avenida Paulista 1842, Torre Norte, 14 Andar, 01310-923 Sao Paulo, SP, Brazil
☎ +55 11 3371 5400, *Fax* +55 11 3371 5401

Consulate General of Germany

In Rio de Janeiro

Rua Presidente Carlos de Campos, 417 Laranjeiras, 22231-080 Rio de Janeiro, RJ, Brazil
☎ +55 21 2554 0004, *Fax* +55 21 2553 0184

Consulate General of Italy

In Rio de Janeiro

Avenida Presidente Antonio Carlos 40, 40 CEP 20020-010, Rio de Janeiro (RJ)
☎ +55 21 3534 1315, *Fax* +55 21 2262 6348
Email segreteria.riodejaneiro@esteri.it

Embassy of the Netherlands

In Brasília

SES Quadra 801 Lote 5, 70405 900 Brasília, DF
☎ +55 61 3961 3200, *Fax* +55 61 3961 3234
Email bra@minbuza.nl

Consulate of Portugal

In Brasília

SES Avenida das Nações, Lote 2, CEP 70402 900, Brasília DF 70402-900, Brazil
☎ +00 55 61 303 296 00/1, *Fax* +00 55 61 303 296 42
Email embaixadadeportugal@embaixadadeportugal.org.br

Consulate General of Switzerland

In Rio

Rua Cândido Mendes 157, 11 andar, 20241 220, Rio de Janeiro, Brazil
☎ +55 21 2221 1867, *Fax* +55 21 2252 3991
Email rio.vertretung@eda.admin.ch

In Recife

Av. Presidente Kennedy 694 A, Peixinhos, 53230 630 Olinda/PE, Brasil
☎/*Fax* +55 81 34 93 70 50
Email recife@honorarvertretung.ch

Consulate of the United States of America

In Brasília

SES Av. das Nações, Quadra 801, Lote 03, 70403 900, Brasilia, DF
☎ +55 61 3312 7000
Fax +55 61 3312 7676

Navigation aids and information

Marine charts

The charts used for navigation in the coastal areas of Brazil are those published by the Centro de Hidrografia e Navegação (CHN) of the Brazilian navy (*see the list of charts in the Appendix, page 267*).

These charts were produced using the Mercator projection.

Because of the scale of these charts, some of the navigation marks have been deliberately omitted, and detailed charts should therefore be consulted for greater precision.

Where to obtain CHN charts

Marine charts are on sale:
- At the Centro de Hidrografia da Marinha, rua Barão de Jaceguay, s/n. Ponta de Armação, Niteroi, 24 048 900, Rio de Janeiro
- In the offices of the Capitanias dos portos.
- In the marinas and from some chandlery and marine equipment stores, such as:
  O Veleiro, rua Teófilo Otoni, 48. Centro, Rio de Janeiro.

Satellite positioning

CHN charts are now produced by the satellite navigation system, using the World Geodetic System 1984 (WGS84). The positions given in this book are based on this system.

Course indications

The course indications given in the text, plans and sketches are always course over ground, expressed in degrees (°).

Distances

The distances are given in nautical miles (M).

Heights

Heights are given in metres (m), above mean sea level.

Depths

On Brazilian marine charts, the low water line is shown in dark blue, and one or two lighter blue colours may be used to represent the depth contours at 10m and 20m.

Note The depths are measured in metres (m) and corrected for the level of mean low water springs, unlike the charts of some other countries, where the depth is measured with reference to the level of the lowest spring low water.

Navigation marks

Lateral marks are in accordance with the maritime buoyage system of the IALA /AISM(*), region B.

(*)IALA: International Association of Marine aids to navigation and Lighthouse Authorities.
(*)AISM: Association internationale de signalisation maritime.

An historic marine chart of Baía de Todos os Santos

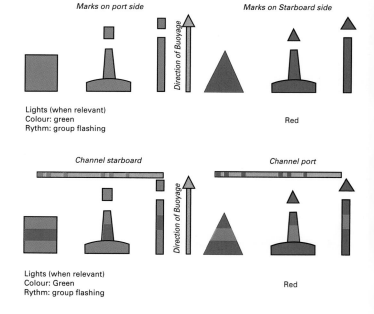

Marks on port side

Marks on Starboard side

Direction of Buoyage

Lights (when relevant)
Colour: green
Rythm: group flashing

Red

Channel starboard

Channel port

Direction of Buoyage

Lights (when relevant)
Colour: Green
Rythm: group flashing

Red

BUOYAGE SYSTEM LATERAL MARKS, REGION B

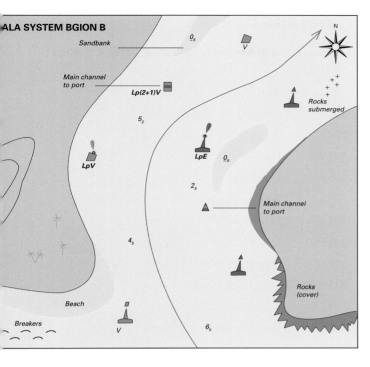

ALA SYSTEM BGION B

Sandbank

Main channel to port

Lp(2+1)V

Rocks submerged

LpV

LpE

Main channel to port

Beach

Rocks (cover)

Breakers

○ : radio mast

⊕ : waypoint

: breaking waves

▲ : starboard buoy

▮ : port hand buoy

⬗ : buoy

: light

: lighthouse

A	*amarela*	yellow
B	*branco*	white
N	*preto*	black
E	*encarnada*	red*
V	*verde*	green
Lp	*lampejo*	flash
Lp.B	*lampejo branco*	flashing white
Lp(..)	*grupo de lampejos*	group flashing
F		fixed
FA		fixed yellow
FB		fixed white
FE		fixed red
FV		fixed green
Alt		alternating
Alt. BEV		alternating white, red, green
Iso		isophase
oc		occulting
oc(.)		group occulting
L dir		direction light
BL		luminous buoy
FAR		lighthouse
FTE		light beacon
Aero		aero light
Aero RC		aeronautical radiobeacon
R		continuous quick
R(3)B		group quick(3)white
MR		continuous very quick
Fre		frequency
Mo(.)		morse code

Some symbols and abbreviations used in the sketch charts and Brazilian charts

: depths in METRES

: rocks with less than 2 metres depth over them

: rock just below or on the surface

: a shoal or reef with the least depth shown

: wreck partially above water

: rock ballasting on a mole or breakwater

: above-water rocks

: cliff

⚓ : anchorage

: prohibited anchorage

: church

: chimney

: castle or fort

✈ : airport

: ruins

: harbourmaster or port police

: fish farm

: yacht club

: water

: fuel

: mangroves

: palms

: bushes

* Note There are two Brazilian words for the colour red: either *encarnada* or *vermelha*.

On marine charts, the word used for red is *encarnada* (E) so as to avoid confusion of the letter 'V' for *vermelha* with that for the colour green, *verde* (V).

When approaching from seaward, a buoy or light will therefore be indicated as Lp.V (green) to port or Lp.E (red) to starboard.

Hydrographic terms used on Brazilian marine charts

Depths

0_5 +0.5m

4_2 -4.2m

Abbreviations

B	baía	bay
C	cabo	cable
La	laguna, lagoa	lagoon
Ens, Ang	enseada, angra	cove
Estr	estreito	strait
Can	canal	channel
Ent, Barra	entrada, barra	mouth, bar
Est	estuário	estuary
I	ilha	island
Fund	fundeadouro	anchorage
Bc	banco	bank
A.F	alto fundo	shallow water
Cor	coroa	coral
Rfe	parcel, recifes	reefs
P	pedra	rock
R	rocha	rock
A	areia	sand
C	cascalhos	gravel
L	lama	mud

Topographic terms used on Brazilian marine charts

m	metro	metre
Pta	ponta	point
Pto	ponto	point
Estal	estaleiro	ship yard
Mt	rampa	slipway
Mo	morro	hill
Cast	castelo	castle
+, e, IG	igreja	church

Tides and currents

Terms relating to tide levels on Brazilian marine charts

CD	Chart Datum
LAT	Lowest Astronomical Tide
HAT	Highest Astronomical Tide
MLW	Mean Low Water
MHW	Mean High Water
MSL	Mean Sea Level
MLWS	Mean Low Water Springs
MHWS	Mean High Water Springs
MLWN	Mean Low Water Neaps
MHWN	Mean High Water Neaps
MLLW	Mean Lower Low Water
MHHW	Mean Higher High Water
MHLW	Mean High Low Water
MLHW	Mean Lower High Water
Sp	Spring tide
Np	Neap tide

List of main lighthouses

From Cabo Orange to Salvador

	Portuguese	English
Cabo Orange	Lp(2)B.15s49m18M	Fl(2)15s49m18M
Cabo Maguari	Lp.B.5s41m16M	Fl.5s41m16M
Ponta de Tijoca	Lp(2)B.10s34m18M	Fl(2)10s34m18M

Rio Pará et Belém
Ponta Algodoal	Lp(2)B.10s.33m.16M	Fl(2)10s33m16M
Salinópolis	LpB.6s60m46M	Fl.6s60m46M
Soure	Lp(2)B.10s34m16M	Fl(2)10s34m16M
Ponta Taipu	Lp(3)B.15s38m16M	Fl(3)15s38m16M
Ponta Maria Teresa	Lp.B.6s41m15M	Fl.6s41m15M
Ponta Chapéu Virado	Iso.V.2s10m13M	Iso.G.2s10m13M

São Luis
Farol de Santana	LpLAlt.BBE.51s56m 31/25M	AlLFl.WWR.51s 56m31/25M

Luis Correia
Ponta de Itaqui	LpB.5s28m15M	Fl.5s28m15M
Ponta de Itapagé	LP(2)B.15s45m20M	Fl(2)15s45m20M
Ponta Baracuru	LpB.10s79m27M	Fl.10s79m27M
Ponta Pecém	LpAlt.BBE.30s74m 26/21M	AlLFl.WWR.30s 74m26/21M

Fortaleza
Farol de Fortaleza	LP(2)B.10s84m43M	Fl(2)10s84m43M
Ilha Rata	LpB.15s62m16M (SG)	Fl.15s62m16M (SG)
Ponta do Mel	LpL.B.30s105m41M	LFl.30s105m41M
Cabo Calcanhar	LpB.10s73m38M	Fl.10s73m38M
Cabo de Sao Roque	Lp(3)B.10s49m21M	Fl(3)10s49m21M

Fernando de Noronha Natal
	LpE.6m7m7M	Fl.R.6m7m7M
Ponta Mãe Luisa	Lp(5)B.25s86m39M	Fl(5)25s86m39M
Ponta Tabatingua	Lp(5)B.60s95m24M	Fl(5)60s95m24M
Cabo Bacoparí	Lp(2)B.10s29m15M	Fl(2)10s29m15M
Ponta da Trincheira	LpB.6s11m12M	Fl.6s11m12M

Cabedelo
Pedra Seca	Lp(3)B.10s15m16M	Fl(3)10s15m16M
Cabo Branco	LpB.10s45m27M	Fl.10s45m27M
Ponta das Pedras	Lp(3)B.15s55m18M	Fl(3)15s55m18M

Recife
Ponta de Olinda	Lp(2)B.35s89m46M	F(2)35s89m46M
Digue	LpE.6s11m11M	Fl.G.6s11m11M
Farol de Recife	LpAlt.BE.12s19m 17/13M	AlFl.WR.12s19m 17/13M

Suape
Cabo S. Agostino	LpB.10s90m22M	Fl.10s90m22M
Ponta Verde	LpB.10s12m13M	LFl.10s12m13M

Maceió
	LpAlt.BE.20s67m 43/36M	AlFl.WR.20s67m 43/36M
São Francisco do Norte	LpB.6s10m14M	Fl.6s10m14M
Farol do Peba	LpL.B.15s42m17M	LFl.15s42m17M

Aracaju
Faro de Sergipe	Oc(6)B.60s40m39M	Oc(6)60s40m39M

From Salvador to Rio de Janeiro

Itapoã	Lp B.6s23m15M	Fl.R.6s23m15M
Santo Antõnio	AltIsoBBE.30s38m 38/34M	AlIso.WWR.30s 38m38/34M

Morro de São Paulo	Lp(2)B.15s88m23M	Fl(2)15s88m23M
Ponta Mutá	LpV.3s10m11M	Fl.G.3s10m11M

Camamu
Morro de Taipus	Lp(3)B.15s75m23M	Fl(3)15s75m23M

Itacaré
Farol das Contas	LpB.10s9m10M	Fl.10s9m10M

Ilheus
Ilheus Grande	Lp(3)B.10s19m8M	Fl(3)10s19m8M
Digue do Malhado	Lp.V3s13m5M	Fl.G.3s13m5M
Farol de Ilheus	LpB.10s34m23M	Fl.10s34m23M
Belmonte	LpB.6s35m21M	Fl.6s35m21M
Porto Seguro	Lp.Alt.BBE.30s56m 26/21M	AlFl.WWR.30s 56m26/21M
Digue Porto Seguro	LpV.6s6m8M	Fl.G.6s6m8M
Corumbá	LpB.10s14m12M	Fl.10s14m12M
Cumuruxatiba	Lp(3)B.10s5m7M	Fl(3)10s5m7M
Barreiras do Prado	Lp(2)B.12s41m16M	Fl(2)12s41m16M
Alcobaça	LpB.15s27m15M	Fl.15s27m15M

Caravelas
Ponta da Baleia	LpB.5s18m14M	Fl.5s18m14M
Abrolhos	LpB.6s59m51M	Fl.6s59m51M
Ponta do Catoeiro	LpB.10s19m14M	Fl.10s19m14M
Coroa vermelha	Lp(3)B.15s15m13M	Fl(3)15s15m13M
Nova Viçosa	LpLB.15s63m23M	LFl.15s63m23M
Rio Doce	LpB.6s45m18M	Fl.6s45m18M
Barra do Riacho	Lp(2)B.10s29m14M	Fl(2)10s29m14M

Vitória
Ponta Santa Lucia	Lp(4)B.12s28m34M	Fl(4)12s28m34M
Ilha dos Pacotes	LpB.6s6m8M	Fl.6s6m8M
Ilha Escalvada	R(2)B.6s26m15M	Q(2)6s26m15M
Punta do Ubu	LpB.5s26m14M	Fl.5s26m14M
Ponta do Retiro	Lp(3)B.15s39m23M	Fl(3)15s39m23M
Guaxindiba	Lp(2)B.10s22m15M	Fl(2)10s22m15M
Atafona	Lp (2) B.15s29m16M	Fl(2)15s29m16M
Açu Cabo São Tomé	LpB.3s12m12M	Fl.3s12m12M
São Tomé	LpL.B.67·5s48m40M	LFl(2)67·5s48m 40M
Macaé	LpL.lt.B.20s155m28m/ 22M	AlLFl.WR.20s 155m28m/22M
Buzios – Ilha Branca	LpB.5s37m8M	Fl.5s37m8M

Cabo Frio
	FE.LpB10s139m49M	Fl.10s139m49M
Ponta Negra	Lp(2)B.10s70m21M	Fl(2)10s70m21M
Ilhas Maricás	LpLB.15s79M16M	LFl.15s79m16M
I. Rasa	LpAlt.BBE15s100m 51/45M	AlLFl.WWR.15s 100m51/45M

Rio de Janeiro
Rio de Janeiro	AeroLpAlt.BV.74m22M	Aero.AlLFl.WG. 74m22M
Morro do Pico	R.B.250m30M	Q.250m30M
Ponta de Santa Cruz	IsoE.2s25m14M	Iso.R.2s25m14M
Ilha de Laje	IsoV.2s16m11M	Iso.G.2s16m11M
Marina Glória	LpE.3s6m5M	Iso.G.3s6m5M

From Rio de Janeiro to Rio Grande do Sul
Ilha de Palmas	LpBE.6s31m10/7M	Fl.WR.6s31m 10/7M
Ilhas Tijucas	LpBE.10s86m11/7M	Fl.WR.10s86m 11/7M

Ilha Rasa da Guaratibá	LpB.6s41m18M	Fl.6s41m18M
Ilha Grande		
Ponta de Castelhano	Oc(3)B.10s120m27M	Oc(3)10s120m27M
Ponta dos Meros	Lp(2)B.15s44m15M	Fl(2)15s44m15M
Ponta de Juatinga	LpB.10s174m17M	Fl.10s174m17M
Paraty		
Ubatuba – Ponta Grossa	Lp(3)B.10s64m16M	Fl(3)10s64m16M
São Sebastião		
Ponta Caraguatuba	Lp(2)B.12s74m12M	Fl(2)12s74m12M
Ponta das Canas	LpB.6s12m9M	Fl.6s12m9M
Ilha da Vitória	LpB.6s100m16M	Fl.6s100m16M
Ponta Grossa (Ilhabela)	Lp(3)B.15s59m16M	LFl.15s59m16M
Ponta do Boi	LpL.10s69m22M	LFl.10s69m22M
Ilha de Alcatrazes	Lp.B.6s23m15M	Fl.6s23m15M
Santas – Bertioga		
Pedra do Corvo	LpB.6s28m7M	Fl.6s28m7M
Ilha de Moela	Oc.AltBBE.6s109m 40/39M	AlOcWWWR.6s 109m40/39M
Ilha das Palmas	LpE.3s17m5M	Fl.R.3s17m5M
Laje da Conceição	Lp(2)BE12s33m16/17M	Fl(2)WR.12s33m 16/17M
Ilha Queimada Grande	LpB.10s82m23M	Fl.10s82m23M
I Bom Abrigo	LpAltBBE.30s146m 28/23M	
Paranaguá		
Ponta das Conchas	LpB.10s66m25M	Fl.10s66m25M
Ponta da Galheta	LpL.6s42m8M	Fl.6s42m8M
Guaratuba		
Farol de Caiobá	LpB.5s26m15M	Fl.5s26m15M
São Francisco do Sul		
Ilha da Paz	LpB.20s83m26M	LFl.20s83m26M
Ponta do Verrido	LpB.6s49m18M	LFl.6s49m18M
Itajaí		
Ponta das Cabeçudas	Lp.Alt30s57m28/23M	AlFl.WWR.30s 57m28/23M
Ilha da Galé	LpB.10s77m8M	Fl.10s77m8M
Calhau de São Pedro	LpB.3s18m8M	Fl.3s18m8M
Ilha do Arvoredo	Oc(4)B.60s89m24M	Oc(2+4)60s89m 24M
Santa Catarina		
Ponta da Galheta	LpB.10s149m16M	Fl.10s149m16M
Pta dos Naufragados	Lp(2)B.15s42m18M	Fl(2)15s42m18M
Ilha de Coral	LpB.3s80m14M	Fl.3s80m14M
Ponta Imbituba	Lp(3)B.15s68m21M	Fl(3)15s68m21M
Ilha das Araras	LpR(2)B.6s53m11M	Q(2)6s53m11M
Ilha dos Lobos	LpB.5s49m11M	Fl.5s49m11M
Cabo S. Marta Grande	Oc(3)BE.30s73m 46/39M	Oc(3)WR.30s73m 46/39M
Rio Grande do Sul		
Farol da Barra	Oc(6)B.21s31m30M	Oc(6)21s31m30M
Digue (W)	LpE.10s11m11M	LFl.G.10s11m 11M
Albardão	Lp(4)B.25s49m42M	Fl(4)25s49m42M
Arroio Chuí	Lp(2)B.35s42m46M	Fl(2)35s42m46M

Salvamar system of sea search and rescue

The Salvamar sea search and rescue service comes under the responsibility of the Command of Naval Operations (CON), which in turn is under the direction of the ministry of the Navy of Brazil.

The alert system is made up of coast radio stations belonging to the Brazilian ministry of Posts and Telecommunications (embratel).

The area covered is from the coast to the 10° meridian.

This area is made up of five regions. For each region, coordination of the activities of search and rescue (SAR), is placed under the responsibility of the *Comando de Distrito Naval*.

Centro de Coordinação de Salvamento Maritimo Districal (RCC), SALVAMAR BRASIL – MRCC BRASIL
☏ (21) 3870 6056, *Fax* (21) 3870 6038
Email mrccbrazil@com.mar.mil.br

Coordination centres for rescue at sea

There are five rescue coordination centres covering the coast of Brazil; these are, from north to south:

Comando de 4° Distrito Naval
Salvamar Norte, Belém
☏ (91) 3216 4030

Comando de 3° Distrito Naval
Salvamar Nordeste, Natal
☏ (84) 3221 1947

Comando de 2° Distrito Naval
Salvamar Leste, Salvador
☏ (71) 3320 3711, (71) 3320 3730

Comando de 1° Distrito Naval
Salvamar Sudeste, Rio de Janeiro
☏ (21) 3870 6119, (21) 2253 6572

Comando de 5° Distrito Naval
Salvamar Sul, Rio Grande do Sul
☏ (532) 3233 6139.

The RENEC national network of coast radio stations

The 40 coastal stations of the *Rede National de Estaçãos Costeiras* (RENEC) are located along the whole of the Brazilian coast.

These coast radio stations:

- obtain information and transmit it to the RCC;
- process and retransmit warnings to sailors;
- process and retransmit weather reports;
- process and retransmit time signals;
- receive signals, distress and safety calls.

List of coast radio stations

Frequency
VHF: Channel 16.
HF: 500 MHz.
2 MHz, 4 MHz, 8 MHz, 12 MHz, 16 MHz, 22 MHz, 156 MHz, 174 MHz by radiotelephone.

Capitanias dos portos

The *capitanias dos Portos* make means of search and rescue in the emergency area available to the RCC. In each *Distrito Naval*, there is a ship ready to intervene, and if necessary the RCC will call in air-sea assistance.

Station name	Call sign	Type	Geographic Coordinates	
Belém radio	PPL	radiotelephone radiofax & radioteleprinter	01°24'·32S	048°26'·23W
Breves radio	PRI	radiotelephone	01°40'·45S	050°29'·25W
Macapá radio	PTL	radiotelephone	00°01'·33S	051°08'·05W
Santarém radio	PPT	radiotelephone	02°26'·36S	054°41'·41W
Almerím radio	PTT	radiotelephone	01°29'·43S	052°36'·06W
Manaus radio	PPM	radiotelephone	00°06'·57S	059°54'·32W
Tabatingá	PPU	radiotelephone	04°15'·08S	069°56'·46W
Itacoatibá	PTM	radiotelephone	03°08'·44S	058°35'·47W
Parintins	PRM	radiotelephone	02°36'·43S	056°44'·00W
São Luis	PPB	radiotelephone	02°09'·31S	044°17'·22W
Tefe radio	PPE	radiotelephone	03°21'·10S	064°43'·53W
Fortaleza radio	PPN	radiotelephone	03°45'·34S	038°26'·40W
Aracatí radio	PTF	radiotelephone	04°35'·16S	037°41'·34W
Mossoro radio	PRQ	radiotelephone	05°04'·52S	037°27'·28W
Natal radio	PPN	radiotelephone	05°45'·18S	035°13'·59W
Olinda radio	PPO	radiotelephone radiofax & radioteleprinter	08°03'·35S	034°55'·26W
Maceió radio	PRO	radiotelephone	09°39'·56S	035°44'·11W
Cabedelo radio	PTN	radiotelephone	07°07'·31S	034°53'·02W
Fernando de Noronha radio	PTO	radiotelephone	03°50'·49S	032°24'·05W
Palheiros radio	PRM	radiotelephone	05°30'·42S	037°07'·19W
Aracaju radio	PTA	radiotelephone	10°54'·40S	037°03'·01W
Salvador radio	PPA	radiotelephone	13°00'·21S	038°30'·24W
Ilheus radio	PPI	radiotelephone	14°51'·52S	039°01'·29W
Teixera de Freitas radio	PTI	radiotelephone	17°24'·02S	039°45'·03W
Vitória radio	PPV	radiotelephone	20°25'·32S	040°19'·50W
São Mateus radio	PRV	radiotelephone	18°33'·10S	039°54'·00W
Campos radio	PTV	radiotelephone	21°47'·35S	041°26'·27W
Casimiro de Abreuradio	PRR	radiotelephone	22°26'·04S	042°03'·49W
Rio radio	PPR	radiotelephone radiofax & radioteleprinter	22°57'·53S	043°40'·23W
Angra dos Reis radio	PTR	radiotelephone	23°02'·21S	044°13'·09W
São Sebastião	PTS	radiotelephone	23°44'·00S	045°25'·00W
Santos radio	PPS	radiotelephone	23°59'·18S	046°18'·17W
Paranaguá radio	PPG	radiotelephone	25°31'·01S	048°30'·21W
Caiobá radio	PTG	radiotelephone	25°51'·00S	048°32'·00W
Itajaí radio	PPC	radiotelephone	26°51'·17S	048°38'·20W
Florianópolis radio	PTC	radiotelephone	27°35'·18S	048°31'·59W
Porto Alegre radio	PPP	radiotelephone	30°04'·46S	051°10'·57W
Ozorio radio	PTP	radiotelephone	29°52'·50S	050°17'·15W
Morro Reuter radio	PRP	radiotelephone	29°32'·09S	051°05'·24W
Junção radio	PPJ	radiotelephone	32°11'·01S	052°10'·10W

In addition, the control system for maritime traffic (Siscontram) makes it possible to call on the services of ships under the Brazilian flag, foreign going ships and those engaged in home trade and small coasting trade, as well as foreign merchant ships over 1,000 tonnes. Ships in the emergency area must give their locations to the RENEC fixed radio stations, which transmit the information to the *Comando Naval do Controle do Trafego Marítimo* (Concontramar).

The navy hospitals of each district also provide help in emergencies.

List of Capitanias dos Portos

Northeastern area

Capitania dos Portos da Amazona Oriental, Belém
☎ (91) 242 6551, 3242 7188
Capitania dos Portos do Estado do Rio Grande do Norte. Natal
☎ (84) 221 2631, 3201 9630
Capitania dos Portos de Estado da Paraiba. João Pessoa
☎ (83) 221 0945, 3241 2805
Capitania dos portos do Estado de Pernambuco. Recife
☎ (81) 224 17 12, 3424 7111
Capitania dos Portos do Estado de Alagoas. Maceió – Jaraguá
☎ (82) 223 54 00, 221 6797

Eastern and Southern areas

Capitania dos Portos do Estado da Bahia. Salvador
☎ (71) 3320 3779, 3320 3777
Capitania dos Portos de Ilheus
☎ (73) 231 2912, 3634 2912
Capitania dos Portos do Estado do Espírito Santo. Vitória
☎ (27) 3334 6400, 2124 6500
Capitania do Porto de Cabo Frio
☎ (22) 2643 2774
Capitania dos Portos de Rio de Janeiro
☎ (21) 3870 6119, 3870 5320
Capitania dos Portos de Santos
☎ (13) 3221 3453, 3221 3454
Capitania dos Portos do Paraná
☎ (41) 3420 1100, 3422 3033
Capitania dos Portos de Santa Catarina
☎ (48) 222 5634, 258 5500
Capitania dos Portos do Rio Grande do Sul
☎ (53) 3233 6188.

Climate and weather

The coast of Brazil has a length of about 7,500km, stretching from the Amazon to the frontier with Uruguay. Consequently the weather conditions experienced in these various regions in the same period of the year are very different.

Despite this variety, the climate can be seen as falling into two main categories:

- A tropical climate north of the Tropic of Capricorn, with an average maximum temperature above 26°C and an average minimum temperature not above 18°C
- In the south, a subtropical climate: more temperate, with a mean maximum temperature above 22°C and mean minimum temperature below 13°C

Rains are not excessive; although copious at times, they tend to be of fairly short duration.

In view of the importance of climate in determining sailing conditions, the following regions can be distinguished, working down the coast from north to south.

The north

There is a rainy season during the first five months of the year and a dryer season in the second half of the year. However, in the Amazon region, an important feature is heavy rain that can produce significant flooding.

The prevailing winds are from the northeast in the dry season and southeast during the rainy season.

With regard to navigation, rivers can carry down trees and masses of uprooted vegetation, called *amazonas*. These form floating islands, which can be a danger to small boats.

The intertropical convergence zone

This lies between 0° and 10° North in winter and spring and does not much affect the north of Brazil, which is subject to the southeasterly trade winds of the southern hemisphere.

In summer and autumn, this zone is displaced to the south, between 5° South and 5° North. The winds are from the northeast and rains are intense.

The east

Here too there is a dry season and a rainy season, with maximum precipitation in July. The prevailing winds are mainly southeasterly, Force 4 to 5.

The Bahia region

The geographical situation of this region, between the equator and the tropic of Capricorn, means that it enjoys a pleasant climate in all seasons.

There is little variation in the average annual temperature, which remains in the range between 26 and 32°C. Some maximum temperatures may be as high as 35°C in summer.

Nevertheless, a pattern can be observed giving a summer period or dry season from November to March, with oppressive heat tempered by a tropical breeze and brief showers of rain. Winds belong to the tradewind pattern, usually blowing from the northeast, Force 3 to 4.

The winter period or rainy season sets in during the months from May to August, with precipitation becoming more frequent and copious. Depressions coming from the south bring strong south and southwest winds that can reach 30 knots with a choppy sea and moderate to heavy swell.

The Rio de Janeiro region

Here too the climate is hot and humid in summer with brief showers; the temperature can rise as high as 35°C, with considerable humidity.

The rest of the year in the winter period, the weather is generally dryer and fresher than in the northeast, with daytime temperatures between 20 and 25°C, night-time temperatures down to about 18°C. Rain can sometimes last several days.

The prevailing winds are northeast trade winds, Force 3 to 4, setting in around the middle of the day in the form of

The Pampeiro

Cold fronts that form over Argentina affect the coasts of Brazil, giving rise to a southwesterly wind, the *Pampeiro*.

Before the front arrives, there is a noticeable rise in atmospheric pressure, together with an abrupt fall in temperature.

On the arrival of the cold front, there is a fresh southwest wind, which gradually strengthens to around 40 knots or more in strong gusts, and also rain and violent storms in the case of a particularly active depression.

The violence of this weather phenomenon depends on the characteristics of the warm air, on how long the adverse weather lasts, and on the characteristics of the cold air.

- If the air is dry with a southwest wind, the bad weather may be only very temporary.
- If the air is unstable and humid, the bad weather may last two to three days.

The Carpinteiro

This very strong southeast wind blows on the south coast of Brazil, often following on after a cold front. Its strength can reach the order of 40 knots or more, and it presents a danger in that it tends to blow vessels irresistibly in to the shore. It is therefore advisable to be prepared for it by keeping sufficiently out to sea.

a coastal breeze. During the night, a land breeze takes over, blowing from the northwest sector and a little less strong. The sea is usually smooth with a moderate swell from the northeast and a one-knot current running southwest.

In the summer, a few rare northerly gusts of up to 30–35 knots may be experienced. These are in most cases short-lived.

In the winter period, incoming cold air masses from Argentina create cold fronts, producing the inverse of the normal weather pattern, with prevailing winds from the southeast to southwest, Force 4 to 5 or even Force 6, accompanied by heavy rain. The sea becomes rough, the current is halted or reversed and runs northeast, its speed varying according to the strength of the wind and the state of the sea.

Another weather feature to note in the Rio region is the presence of fog banks near the coasts and within bays at the end of the night and at daybreak, lasting until well into the morning. These fog banks cause a significant reduction in visibility.

The south

This region has a more temperate climate, with fog being frequent in the autumn and winter. The wind pattern is variable, north and northeast from September to January, and with winds from the southern sector in autumn and winter, usually accompanied by cold fronts.

Weather forecasts

By VHF

Weather forecasts and severe weather warnings are given on demand by the *Capitania dos Portos*, in response to a call on Channel 16.

Station Estação	Mode Modo	Fréquency Frequencia Khz	Schedule Horário
RENEC*	VHF Ch 16 HF Ch 28	156.8 4.125	on request (a pedido)
PWZ-33**	RD (J2D) radiodados Radiodata	4.266 (a pedido) 6.448	0230–0330
	RI radiotele-impressão	8.580 12.709 16.974	0600–0730 1845–1930

They are given in Brazilian Portuguese by the main RENEC radio stations; possibly in English depending on the operator, and broadcast on VHF on Channel 16.

Transmission of marine weather forecasts and severe weather warnings
Transmissao de Meteoromarinha e Avisos de Mau Tempo

* **RENEC** National Network of Coastal stations
Rede Nacional de Estações Costeiras (**EMBRATEL**)
** **PWZ-33** Navy Radio Station in Rio de Janeiro
Estação Rádio da Marinha no Rio de Janeiro (**ERMRJ**)

By HF

Frequency: 12 709 kHz   Schedule: 0645 hours UTC
Frequency: 16 974 kHz   Schedule: 1845 hours UTC

By Internet

www.cptec.inpe.br
www.dhn.mar.mil.br/infmeteo.htm
www.inmet.gov.br
www.buoy.weather.com

The sites I consult myself are: cpte.inpe.br or dhn.mar.mil.br, which generally give good 5-day forecasts.

The weather forecasting coverage of the Brazilian coast is divided into two ocean areas, north and south, and 10 coastal areas, A to H, working from south to north. These areas are (*see map*):

- **N** north ocean area
- **S** south ocean area
- **A** Arroio Chuí to Cabo de Santa Marta
- **B** Cabo de Santa Marta to Cabo Frio (sea area)
- **C** Cabo de Santa Marta to Cabo Frio (coastal area)
- **D** Cabo Frio to Caravelas
- **E** Caravelas to Salvador
- **F** Salvador to Natal
- **G** Natal to São Luis
- **H** São Luis to Cabo Orange

Notices to mariners (avisos aos navegantes)
This information is transmitted by radio and internet. The notices concern hydrographical and topographical information, nautical marks and signals, meteorological information and other general information relating to navigation.

A bulletin is published regularly every fortnight by the *Centro de Hydrografia e Navegação* and is available free at the *Capitanias dos Portos*.

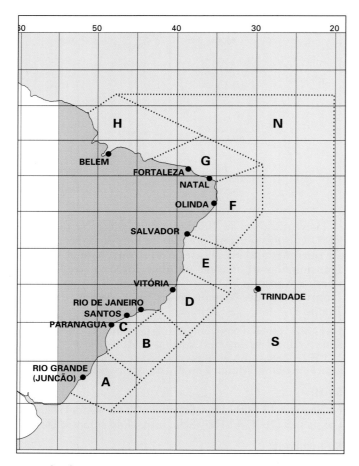

By Telephone

Metéo marine de Rio de Janeiro ℡ (21) 2189 3010, 2630 8861.

Grading of the marinas and anchorages

A grade of one to four stars has been given for the marinas and anchorages. This was based on the following features and criteria:

Quality of mooring
*   Mediocre
**   Satisfactory
***   Good
****   Excellent

The assessment looked at the comfort of a marina or anchorage, taking account of such things as the composition of the bed to provide holding ground for anchors, swell, current, undertow, the safety of the anchorage with regard to the wind, other possible dangers, etc.

Facilities and services
*   Few facilities
**   Some availability
***   Satisfactory services
****   Excellent

The facilities available in the location: administrative formalities, banks, communications, Post Office, telephone, internet access, fuel, washing and toilet facilities, restaurants and bars, etc.

Services for boat maintenance: port installations, mechanical resources, electricity, sail loft; options for dry storage ashore, maintenance services in general, etc.

Water
Supply to the pontoons of a marina, public water supply of reasonable quality or filtered water; water supplied free of charge or payment required.

In the case of a basic anchorage: drinking fountain or public water tap; other means of supply.

Electricity
Power to the pontoons: 110 volts or 220 volts; other options.

Fuel
Filling station at the location or nearby.
Oil, filtration.

Supplies
*   Few facilities for obtaining supplies
**   Some facilities for obtaining supplies
***   Good for obtaining provisions
****   Excellent

Facilities for purchasing basic supplies, or for complete provisioning for a cruise or crossing; supermarket, grocery store, public market, fishermen, etc.

Mooring fees
*   Inexpensive
**   Modestly priced
***   Expensive
****   Very expensive

Harbour charges; possible supplementary charges or all inclusive; free days, partial or total freedom from charges, reductions; possibility of payment by cheque or cash; whether or not bank cards accepted.

Note:
The mooring fees given for the marinas are a guide for information only. They may vary considerably depending on the length of stay in the marina, low or high season (*temporada baixa* or *alta*). During festival times, at New Year, during carnival or other events the prices in some marinas can double.

It is always possible to discuss the price or ask for a reduction (*desconto*); also, where possible, there need be no hesitation about making play of the competition.

Location and surroundings
*   Mediocre
**   Average
***   Good
****   Very good

Location
Closeness to the centre of town or place of interest, marina outside the town or isolated anchorage. Means of transport: on foot; by bus, taxi, passenger boats and ferries.

Surroundings
Peacefulness of an anchorage or quietness of a marina, noise, boats passing, nuisances. Safety, risk of aggression, port security.

Places of tourist interest
Sights and centres of tourist interest. Places to visit in the immediate locality or excursions into the surrounding area.

I. Southwards from Salvador de Bahia to Rio Grande do Sul

STATE OF BAHIA

The state of Bahia is the part of Brazil where the country's African culture and heritage are to be found in its religion and music, in the typical cuisine of the region and in its dance and popular festivals. Its capital, Salvador da Bahia, has preserved the best of its colonial past in its historic buildings, its churches and its traditions.

The city's historic centre, Pelourinho, has a striking air of the exotic. Nightly the air pulsates with the fascinating rhythm of its music.

A *saveiro* on the Rio Paraguaçu

Salvador da Bahia

Tourism and culture

Baía de Todos os Santos was discovered by the navigator Amerigo Vespucci in 1501, following his crossing of the Atlantic in 67 days. Salvador was to become Brazil's first capital.

For sailing vessels crossing the Atlantic Ocean today, the port of Salvador is the preferred place to make landfall on first entering Brazil.

As a port of call it offers exceptional tourist and cultural interest. The opportunities for discovering the interior of the country are also many and varied.

The visitor is instantly struck by the fascinating character of the city and the warmth and welcome of its people. This is Africa transported to the South American continent together with all its ancestral traditions, culture, colours, music and mysticism, brought here in times past by African slaves.

This is a complete change from the accustomed scene, with a magical atmosphere and intensity of emotion.

Lower city, upper city and beaches
(cidade baixa, cidade alta, praias)

Salvador, a city with a population of around 2.5 million inhabitants, is essentially made up of three parts:
• the lower city, *cidade baixa*,
• the upper city, *cidade alta*,
• the seaside area with its beaches.

The lower city: this is where you disembark, and your first steps on land will naturally lead you to the district of Comércio, the port installations and official departments, the police, customs and *Capitania dos Portos*.

This district is also where to find the central Post Office, banks, stores selling nautical and fishing supplies, as well as the Mercado modelo, an imposing building of the colonial era housing a great number of local handicraft shops.

Further afield, beyond the commercial port, is the huge São Joaquim market, where you can find just about everything, a profusion of regional produce, plants, spices, stall upon stall displaying all the many fruits that Brazil produces, and all kinds of other things –

Salvador. Elevador Lacerda, which leads to the city's historic district of Pelourinho

hardware, handicrafts, sculptures, pottery, basketware, medicinal plants with miraculous properties... all gaily intermingled and the whole suffused with an atmosphere of frenetic energy.

An imposing elevator called the *elevador Lacerda* will whisk you 60m upward in a matter of seconds to reach the upper city.

The upper city, called Pelourinho, is the historic centre, the old city. It is a harmonious assembly of restored, old colonial residences with beautiful, pastel-coloured façades. Among these are some majestic historic buildings such as the Palácio Rio Branco, residence of the first Governor of Bahia, Tomé de Souza.

There are also several museums here, including the Museu da Cidade and the Casa de Jorge Amado, a famous Brazilian novelist and figurehead of Bahia.

This district comes especially alive on Tuesday and Friday evenings, when Bahian music groups set up podiums in various squares (*largos*) to give performances. Some of these groups are particularly famous, such as Olodum or Timbalada.

This is also the place where most of Salvador's craft and artisan activity is to be found, as well as many shops displaying paintings, sculptures, pottery and ceramics, clothing, musical and percussion instruments, jewellery, necklaces and bracelets and much more.

Salvador. São Joaquim market

Salvador. The church of Nossa Sra. Do Rosário dos Pretos, built by slaves at the end of their working day

The seaside area and beaches: Surfing, diving and undersea fishing are all carried on here, and there is a series of spacious beaches extending northwards: Barra, Ondina, Rio Vermelho, Costa Azul, Boca do Rio, Corsario, Praia dos Coqueiros, on through to the magnificent Itapoã beach!

The beaches are the meeting place for the local Bahians who come to swim, to eat the regional specialities in the multitude of cabanas with their terraces crammed with tables and the umbrellas extending right down to the sea.

Salvador and its 365 churches

This is the city of 365 churches – a church for every day of the year – built on Baía de Todos os Santos (All Saints' Bay). A visit to some of the more famous of these churches is not to be missed: for example, the Igreja Conceição da Praia in the lower city, the Catedral Basílica da Sé and the Igreja São Francisco in the upper city. In the lower part of the Pelourinho district is the Igreja Nossa Senhora do Rosário dos Pretos, whose pretty pastel blue façade can be seen on all the postcards. This church was built in the 18 century, the work of slaves at the end of their day's labours.

Around 10km to the north of Salvador is the Igreja Nosso Senhor de Bomfim, which stands out on a hilltop. This is one of the most famous in Bahia. Each year a vast procession several kilometres long makes its way here from its starting point near the fishing port.

Faith is strong among the Bahians. They may practise more than one religion, honouring the saints of the Catholic religion, São Salvador, Santo Antônio, São Paulo, São Francisco, and Nosso Senhor do Bomfim or Nossa Senhora da Conceição, and also venerating the *Orixás*, deities such as Ogum, the god of war, Oxala, god of the universe and protector of peace, and Lemanja, goddess of the sea, in many religious ceremonies, processions and *candomblés*.

Candomblé

Candomblé is an Afrobrazilian rite, and this religious ceremony is frequently practised in the region of Bahia.

The ceremony is performed at a *terreiro*, a sacred location or village casa where the people assemble to honour a deity (*Orixá*) with prayers, chanting, dancing and sacrifices.

The presiding mistress of the ceremony (usually an older woman), assisted by initiates, invokes Exú, the messenger to the *Orixás*. Exú's role is to establish communication between those present and the gods, and is represented clothed in black and red and bearing a trident. She enjoys great respect and is possessed of considerable powers, and capable of both good and bad actions to influence the deity being invoked.

Salvador, the *candomblé* deity, Orixá

Salvador, the upper city, Museu da Cidade (City Museum) and Casa de Jorge Amado museum

A group of musicians, playing percussion instruments, and chanting singers enliven the ceremony with their rhythms and psalmodies.

The Bahians, dressed in traditional costumes and headdresses, dance to the rhythm of the music, swaying in their voluminous white robes, the dancers arrayed in the beautiful finery of the *Orixá*.

As an offering of food during the ceremony a traditional dish such as *feijoada* is served, first to *Exú* and then to those present. Exú loves *feijoada*, but also has a taste for *aguardente* (a spirit made from sugar cane). The people eat and drink, often in considerable quantities, in a sticky and smoky atmosphere where the strong smell of tobacco mingles with that of incense.

The *Orixá* is honoured with prayers and offerings. Meanwhile the atmosphere of the assembly is heavy with tension and the people are enveloped in a strange mysticism. The music takes on a more and more obsessive rhythm and the women intone rhythmic chants alternating with lamentations. Some of the dancers reel, then fall into a trance, literally possessed by the spirit of the *Orixá* that has entered them.

Exú is satisfied, the assembled people receive their assurance, and the celebration may continue late into the night.

If you wish to attend a *candomblé* ceremony, you should try to find an authentic one rather than one organised by some local agency for groups of curious tourists. You should succeed in finding one by asking around, listening out, or getting into conversation with older folk among the Bahians.

Capoeira

Another traditional event of African origin among the street spectacles to be encountered in Salvador is *capoeira*.

This is a martial art that the slaves used to practice under the guise of a dance, and is a formidable method of hand-to-hand combat developed for use in the revolts organised in the plantations without the knowledge of their masters.

Coffee in Brazil, street style

The musical rhythm is provided by a small group of percussion players and a remarkable stringed instrument called the *berimbau*, a sort of musical bow with a resonating gourd.

The entire performance is accompanied by a monotone chant in a syncopated rhythm.

Two individuals engage in hand-to-hand combat in a graceful ballet. Each makes a feint at attacking his adversary, dodges the blows, pirouettes with amazing agility and the two men confront each other in a twirling tangle of legs and arms without ever actually touching, in perfect harmony.

This spectacle can be seen in several parts of the city in Salvador, during the day in the Mercado modelo, and in the evening in Pelourinho, on the main square and in certain of the city's restaurants and hotels, where good professional groups put on high quality performances.

Carnival

It is not possible to do justice to Salvador without mentioning its carnival:
- four days of popular festivity,
- almost the entire population of over two million people on their feet to celebrate,
- 150 *trios eléctricos*, gigantic vehicles equipped with deafening sound systems and surmounted by a large platform on which a group of Bahian musicians fires up the crowd. Behind them comes the banda, followed by the whole troupe of singers and dancers in gaily coloured *camisas*, all dressed in matching style and hue.

All the streets from the historic city centre and on through the districts of Campo Grande and Barra as far as Ondina are taken up with the parade; traffic is banned; priority is entirely given to the processions and the *trios eléctricos*!

Street carnival in Salvador de Bahía

Enormous podiums are erected in the main districts of the city, and here performances are given by some of Brazil's greatest singing stars, to huge applause from the crowd.

The maze of alleys of Bairro do Pelourinho, where the *trios eléctricos* cannot go, sees a street carnival for the most eager revellers: groups of musicians and percussionists, a delirious crowd singing and dancing, extravagant costumes, shouts and laughter everywhere. The people are bent on enjoyment; they drink, they eat from smoke-wreathed barbecues, and the whole place resembles some gigantic ant-heap swarming with brightly-coloured creatures.

An amazing atmosphere!

Nautical events and regattas

Salvador has become the centre for nautical events in Brazil and, with support from the Terminal Náutico da Bahia, a great number of events and regattas are organised throughout the year.

The festival of Bom Jesus dos Navegantes
1st January. There is a procession at sea in which all the local vessels and other pleasure boats escort the statue of Jesus along a route from the *Capitania dos Portos* to the beach of Boa Viagem.

Rallye les Iles du Soleil
In December-January, around thirty cruising yachts call in at the Terminal Náutico de Salvador before sailing up to the Amazon and French Guiana.

João das Botas, the *saveiros'* regatta
Saveiros are the traditional sailing boats of Bahia. Constructed out of wood, they have a mast without shrouds, made of a tall, slender tree trunk and a large sail with an area of over 100m², which is the vessel's sole means of propulsion.

These boats provide a constant link between Salvador and the various islands of Baía de Todos os Santos, they sail up the Rio Paraguaçu and transport anything and everything that can be loaded on board: materials and

Capoeira at Bairro do Pelourinho

Salvador. *Saveiros* sailing in the João das Botas regatta

building equipment, earthenware pottery items and various craft objects, crates and packages of all kinds, provisions, cows and calves, pigs and poultry...

The festival of Yemanja

On 2nd February a great procession of boats takes place in which *Yemanja*, goddess of the sea, is promenaded through the Baía de Todos os Santos to Rio Vermelho. The accompanying boats are profusely decorated in blue and white and the music of the percussion groups on board pounds out its rhythm. Visiting yachts are of course invited to join the festival.

Bahiazul Regatta

An all-category regatta from Salvador to Itaparica. Organised by the Government of Bahia.

Around Alone

Arrival and departure point for competitors when the South American leg of the race calls here. The boats are moored at the Terminal Náutico.

Les Voiles du carnaval de Bahia

During the carnival, in February.

Canaries-Salvador

Arrival of the regatta.

Salvador-Maragogipe Regatta

In August. Around 100 sailing boats take part, with great festivities in the village of Maragogipe.

Salvador-Recife-Fernando de Noronha rally

In September. The great nautical festival of Pernambuco. Over 100 sailing boats take part.

Transat 6.5m

Every two years, in October (2007). Arrival of the single-handed race.

La Rochelle-Salvador

Every two years, in November (2007).

Transat Jacques Vabre
Le Havre-Salvador

Single-handed race for monohull and multihull sailing boats.

Salvador. Base of the Brazilian navy, and Capitania dos Portos

Practical information

Administrative formalities when entering the country at Salvador

See page 11, section 'Entering Brazil by Boat' for the various formalities.

Polícia Féderal (Immigration)

The port office of the maritime Polícia Féderal is to be found on the quayside of the Commercial Port, building No. 2, on the first floor. ➁ 3243 3952.

The entrance is 100m from the Terminal Náutico, in avenida da França, on the left.

Alfândega do Porto de Salvador (Customs)

This is also situated at the Commercial Port, in the same building as the Polícia Féderal, but on the ground floor. ➁ 3236 3028.

Ministério da saude (Health department)

At the Commercial Port, building No. 8, going through the main port entrance. ➁ 3241 0276.

Capitania dos Portos

Beside the Terminal Náutico marina, just beyond the fishing port, in the Brazilian navy building.

All these formalities are free. ➁ 3220 3812.

Extension of stay

If the duration of stay in Brazil is to extend beyond 90 days, an extension of stay must be obtained from the Polícia Féderal. This needs to be requested in good time. In the past, this was done by applying at their main office at avenida Oscar Pontes 339, but applications are now handled at their office at Deputado Luís Eduardo Magalhães International Airport. It would be wise to check the arrangements.

British Consulate General
Praia do Flamengo 284/2 andar, 22210-030, Rio de Janeiro RJ
➁ +55 21 2555 9600, *Fax* +55 21 2555 9671 (Consular)
Email bcg.rj@fco.gov.uk

Useful addresses and telephone numbers

Tourist office

Bahiatursa: Jardim Armação, Centro de Convenções de Bahia
➁ (55 71) 3370 8400, *Fax* (55 71) 3371 0110.
Offices:
- at the Mercado modelo, from 0800 to 1830
- at the Rodoviária bus station
- at Luis E. Magalhães international airport
  Emtursa: (55 71) 3380 4200

Travel agencies

There are many travel agencies in Salvador. These include:
- Pinheiro: rua Portugal, edificio Augusto Borges – Comércio (250m from the Terminal Náutico)
  ➁ (71) 3242 4599
- Farol Turismo. rua Belo Horizonte, 70 – Barra avenida
  ➁ (71) 3267 4433 (There will almost certainly be an English speaker available)

Public transport within the city

Salvador has an extensive city network of buses, and these provide the best means of transport to its various districts. There is a bus stop just opposite the marina, and another at the foot of the *elevador Lacerda*.

Underground railway: the map can be obtained from the tourist office.

Excursions

Bus station, all destinations.
Rodoviária – Av. Tancredo Neves
➁ (71) 3358 0765.
(Rodoviária or Iguatemi bus).

Airline companies

- TAM: ➁ (71) 3123 1000
- VARIG: rua Carlos Gomes, 103 ➁ (71) 3788 7000;
  and Shopping Barra, 2nd floor.
- TAP-Air Portugal: ➁ (71) 3204 1105.
  Avenida Tancredo Neves, 1632/1206.
This is one of the quickest flights, to Lisbon with connections from there.

Others fly via Rio de Janeiro and São Paulo (Air France, TAM, etc.).
- GOL: ➁ (71) 3789 2121
- VASP: rua Miguel Calmon, 27, Comércio
  ➁ (71) 3789 1010
  (internal routes only)

Tourist protection

Delegacía de proteção ao tourista (Deltour)
➁ (71) 3322 1188

Consumer protection

Procon: rua Carlos Gomes, 746 ➁ (71) 3321 4288

Banks

The Brazilian currency is the real (R$), divided into 100 centavos.

In January 2010, there were nearly four réais to the sterling, and three réais to the euro (€).

Most of the major banks are centred in the Comércio district (Banco do Brasil, Citibank, Bradesco, etc.) and it is easy to withdraw money from cash dispensers by card using Visa, Mastercard, or American Express.

It is also possible to withdraw money safely from the cash dispenser at the Banco do Brasil in the commercial centre of Barra (2nd floor).

Travellers' cheques or currency can be exchanged in banks, but the commission charged by the banks is often considerable, so it may be better to try some of the bureaux de change, for example in Pelourinho, where there are several.

Post and telecommunications

Central Post Office (*correio*), 200m from the Terminal Náutico, Praça da Inglaterra, all services. Opening hours from 0900 to 1700.

Telephone and fax

Telephone area code for Salvador: ☏ 71.

Brazilian Phone Numbers now have eight digits. An initial 3 or 2 has been added recently

Note: The area code of the city is preceded by a '0' when dialling from inside Brazil but outside the city concerned. There is no initial '0' when dialling from abroad or from inside the city. So, for example, telephone numbers in Salvador begin with the code '71' when calling from Salvador, but the city code is '071' when calling from elsewhere in Brazil.

At the central Post Office, using a phone card. DDD phone cards are for calls within the country and DDI cards for international ones.

There are three call boxes for local and international telephone calls inside the precincts of the marina. These operate using cards that can be obtained from the desk at the central Post Office.

Internet access

- Internautas.com, Passage av. da França/ av. Estados Unidos, loja 04 (opposite bus stop).

There are also many cybercafés in Bairro do Pelourinho and Praça da Se.

Supplies

Several large supermarkets in the city, in the Bompreço chain of stores. The most accessible from Salvador's marinas are the Bompreço supermarkets in Barra or Iguatemi.

Water

The water of the Salvador mains supply is unsuitable for drinking straight from the tap. Brazilians drink either filtered tap water or bottled mineral water.

Carbon filters that can adjust to fit over water taps are sold in places such as large supermarkets or hardware shops (*feragem*).

Ice

Sold in bags of 10 or 20kg at the shipping terminal or at Bahia Marina.

If the ice has been made from filtered water, the words *gelo de agua filtrada* appear on the bag.

Refilling of gas bottles

These can be deposited at the Terminal Náutico to be collected and sent to the firm Brasilgas for refilling. They are returned a few days later.

Health emergencies

- Pronto socorro ☏ 192
- Hospital Aliança ☏ (71) 3350 5600
  Private establishment covering all specialities including a paediatric department. There will almost certainly be an English speaker available.
- Hospital Portugues ☏ (71) 3203 5400
  Reliable; all departments.
- Instituto cardio-pulmonar ☏ (71) 3203 2200
- Fundação Bahiana de Cardiologia (FBC)
  ☏ (71) 3336 0300
- Hospital Sarah Kubitschek (orthopaedic hospital)
  ☏ (71) 372 3333

Pharmacies (*droguerias*): in Brazil these are numerous and well stocked. There seems to be no problem over equivalent drugs.

Boat maintenance services

Some overhaul of the boat and equipment, maybe even a few repairs, may of course be necessary following an ocean crossing. Here is a list (not exhaustive) of firms offering such services:

Boat lifting facilities

- Bahia Marina: ☏ (71) 3322 7244. Travel lift, 40-ton capacity. This is the only place on Baía de Todos os Santos with a travel lift; service is faultless.
- dos Saveiros Marina: ☏ (71) 3312 1737
  Boat hauled up slipway (limit 15t)
- Aratu late Clube: ☏ (71) 3216 7284
  Boat hauled up slipway (limit 13t)
- Base Naval de Aratu: ☏ (71) 3307 3400, 3521 3154
  Facilities for lifting out larger vessels

Hull cleaning

Green Servicios Náuticos (Carlinhos): ☏ (71) 3124 7551.
Services satisfactory

Painting, antifouling

Several brands of antifouling for polyester boats are available in Salvador.

This is not always the case for aluminium hulls, so it may be advisable to carry some stocks of this on board, bearing in mind the length of time for which it can be kept at temperatures below 30°C.

- TISA Nordeste. Agent International, av. Jequitaia, 2 079, Agua de Meninos Salvador ① (71) 3243 3933
- Jotum, at Ribeira ① (71) 3316 7923

Mechanical services

- Volvo – SOS Náutica ① (71) 3312 5932
  Mobile (71) 9138 7119
- Yanmar-Ventec: ① (71) 3313 7598
- Polidiesel – injection ① (71) 3312 5421
- Yamaha – Dumar ① (71) 3242 5697

Electricity

- Djalma Sà ① (71) 3359 4644
- Tecmar serviços tecniços ① (71) 3377 7271
  Mobile 9974 7994
- Tecnick ① (71) 3356 9409, *Mobile* (71) 9975 4381

Electronic equipment

- Igor F. Stelli ① (71) 3322 2293, *Mobile* (71) 9967 0774

Refrigeration

Silvano ① (71) 3398 4609, *Mobile* (71) 9606 7421.
- ELI (air conditioning, refrigeration): ① (71) 3218 5234

Sails, awnings

- Vinx Veleria ① (71) 3356 5299,
  Mobile Edouardo (71) 9143 8557
  Work is of satisfactory quality
- Maxwell Vela ① (71) 3207 1445. Close supervision needed to ensure careful work
- Delta Sails ① 3353 8511 (Marcelo), *Mobile* 9963 2611

Always specify precisely the quality of cloth and thread (UV-resistant) required.

Chandleries

- Regatta, at Bahia Marina ① (71) 3321 3799
- Dumar (opposite the Capitania) ① (71) 3243 8688

Stainless steel welding, fitting out

Juthay: av. Contorno ① (71) 3322 8797
The workshop is 50m from the entrance to Bahia Marina, and overhangs the avenue; it is reached via a staircase which leads up directly from the road.

For all welding jobs, construction of bimini frames and poles or stern gantries, etc.

Stainless steel (Inox)

- Regatta, at Bahia Marina
- OGOSIL. Gomes Silva Ltda (specialist wholesaler): rua Barao de Cotegipe, 126 Calçada Salvador ① (71) 3312 1352

As a general rule, the Calçada district is the place to look for everything to do with mechanics, filtration, hoses, electricity, batteries, etc.

Take the Ribeira bus; it is about 4km to Calçada.

Fuel

There is a floating pontoon with pumps, diesel and petrol anchored at the exit of the Terminal Náutico marina, behind Fort São Marcelo.

At this pontoon it is also possible to take on supplies of packs of mineral water and all kinds of other drinks (beer, cola, guarana, etc.).

Two service stations on either side of the *Capitania dos Portos* also sell motor oil and most current types of filter.

There is a service station on the pontoon at Bahia Marina where payment can be made by Visa card.

Photocopies

CopyArt, Largo 2 de Junho, between the districts of Pelourinho and Campo Grande, provides all kinds of photocopies, including large format.

Nautical charts

Charts can be purchased at:
- the Capitania dos Portos; offices open from 1230 to 1600.
- Regatta, at Bahia Marina.

Import of spare parts

In theory, boats in transit do not pay customs duty on the import of spare parts. In practice, Customs put a 60 to 100% tax on all imported equipment. Information can be obtained from the marina office.

- DHL. MKS. Transportes especiais: rua Princesa Isabel, 573, Salvador Barra ① (71) 3264 2655

The transport service provided by this company is prompt and the import taxes are paid on reception.

Baía de Todos os Santos

There are many reasons behind the popularity of Salvador as the place to make landfall on first arrival in Brazil: its geographical situation, the ease of entry to the port and its reception facilities. From the practical point of view, too, it is an excellent port of call, and a good departure point for boats intending to sail down to the south of Brazil, Uruguay, Argentina, or the channels of Patagonia. It is also a good choice for those aiming to visit the northeast coast of Brazil and the Amazon, and on towards French Guiana, the Caribbean or Panama.

Navigation

Brazilian chart DHN No. 1110.

Tide and currents

The tides in the bay of Baía de Todos os Santos are semi-diurnal, with an average height of 1.3m above chart datum and a maximum tidal amplitude maximum of around 2.6m.

The flood current and ebb current are particularly strong at the entrance to the bay, especially to the north and west of the Banco de Santo Antônio shoals.

The flood current lasts five hours and runs N-NE.

The ebb current lasts seven hours and runs S-SE.

In both cases, the speed of the current averages 1.5 knots, but can reach three knots or more in spring tides.

After heavy rain, the current can exceed these values.

Attention must be paid to the currents when navigating in the channels and rivers, as they can be strong in some areas such as the Itaparica channel, the sea channel leading to the Almirante Alves Câmara terminal and also the Rio Paraguaçu.

When entering Baía de Todos os Santos it is therefore preferable to make landfall at the end of a rising tide.

Approach

Approach by day The buildings of the city will be seen on the horizon from a considerable distance when coming from the north.

The coastline is low, with some hills. Around 10 miles to the north of Salvador, the dunes of white sand of the Abaete lagoon can be seen from the open sea.

Conspicuous landmarks
The white tower with horizontal red bands of the Itapuã lighthouse, 10M to the northeast.

More to the west, the Santo Antônio lighthouse, a cylindrical tower with black and white horizontal bands. This is situated at the southern extremity of Salvador and marks the entrance to Baía de Todos os Santos.

Approach by night The exceptional setting of the bay means that it is far better to enter Baía de Todos os Santos by day; nevertheless, sometimes it is necessary to make landfall by night.

Hazards

To the south of the Santo Antônio lighthouse and at the entrance to the bay, care should be taken when approaching the shoals of the Banco de Santo Antônio, indicated by a north cardinal mark and a south cardinal mark.

When the winds are from the southern sector, the waves break on these shoals. It is vital to pass round the shoals to the south (south cardinal mark).

⊕ 1 • 13°59,95'S 038°31,90'W Iate Clube de Bahia

If the sea conditions are good and the tide full, there is nevertheless the possibility of passing close to the coast, between the north cardinal mark and the coast. When taking this route, however, the current may be considerable.

Locate the Itapuã lighthouse LpB.6s24m15M with a luminous range of 15M and more to the south the Santo Antônio lighthouse Alt.IsoBBE.30s38M, at the entrance to Baía de Todos os Santos.

The lights of the city of Salvador can be seen from some distance from out at sea. For the approach to the coast, the course is the same as that for the approach by day, passing to the south of the Banco de Santo Antônio.

Salvador approaches. Itapuã lighthouse

BAIA DE TODOS SANTOS

São Roque

Rio Paraguaçu

Canal de Itaparica

Itaparica

BAÍA DE TOD

Pia

Lp

I. DE ITAPARICA

Fte. Barra do Pote

L. B. 6

Lp(2)B. 6M

15₅

Pta

9

ALT. ISO

16₅

8₅

Oc. B. 3₅ 7m 6M

TR. (NOT.)

Pta. da Cruz

14

18

I. Carapeba

Pta. Aratuba

9₂

17

18₅

19₅

Jaguaribe

Rio Jaguaribe

Pta. Cacha-Prego

10₇

16₅

20

Rio da Dona

Pta. Garcia

8₇

18₅

7₈

17₅

5

30

13₉

12₃

25

10₂

18

11₉

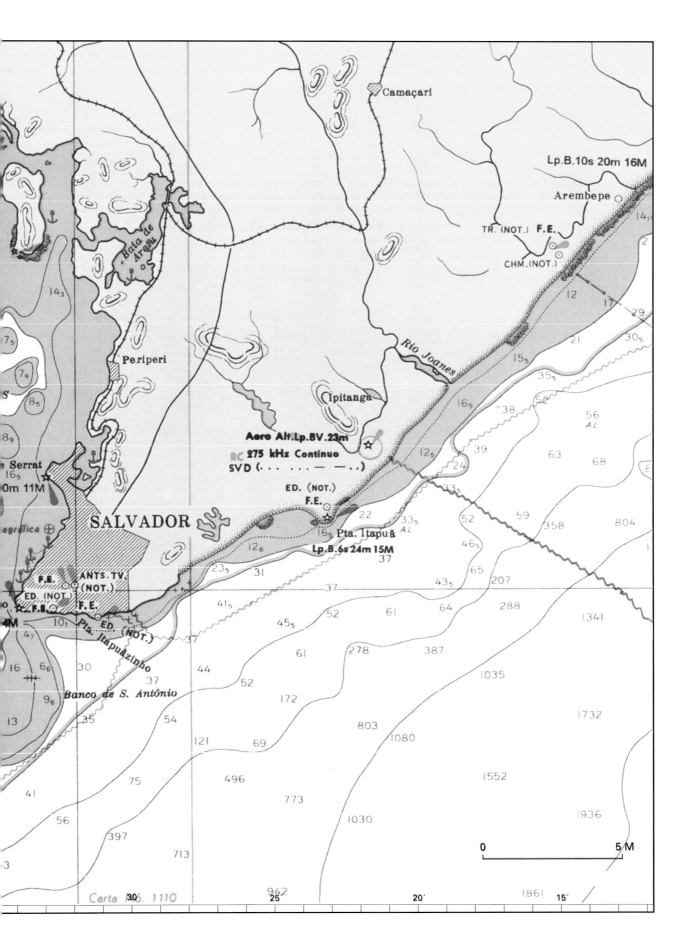

Camaçari

Lp.B.10s 20m 16M

Arembepe

TR. (NOT.) **F.E.**

CHM.(NOT.)

Baía de Arena

14₃

Periperi

Rio Joanes

15₅

16₅

Ipitanga

Aero Alt.Lp.BV.23m

RC 275 kHz Continuo

SVD (· · ·   · · ·   —   — ·)

ED. (NOT.)
F.E.

Serrat
16₅
0m 11M

SALVADOR

12₆

16₅ Pta. Itapuã

Lp.B.6s 24m 15M
37

egrafica

F.E.   ANTS. TV.
(NOT.)

ED. (NOT)
F.E.   F.E.

10₇ Pta. Itapuãzinho
ED. (NOT.)

4₇

16   6₆   30   37

9₆   37

Banco de S. Antônio   35

13

41

56

397

713

0   5 M

BRAZIL CRUISING GUIDE **35**

Baía de Todos os Santos marinas

Baía de Todos os Santos is made up of around thirty islands scattered over an immense stretch of water. Only one part of the bay is navigable for yachts, as there are some areas in the northern part where the depth of water is not very great.

At the entrance to the bay and past the Santo Antônio lighthouse, the conical red beacon that marks the channel entrance should be left to starboard.

You next encounter, in order:

- at 1M the anchorage of Porto da Barra and the anchorage of the Iate Clube da Bahia
- 2.5M further north, Bahia Marina
- at about 3M, the Terminal Náutico da Bahia (CENAB) marina
- 8M further north, there are two small marinas in Baía da Itapagipe; these are Angra dos Veleiros, Marina

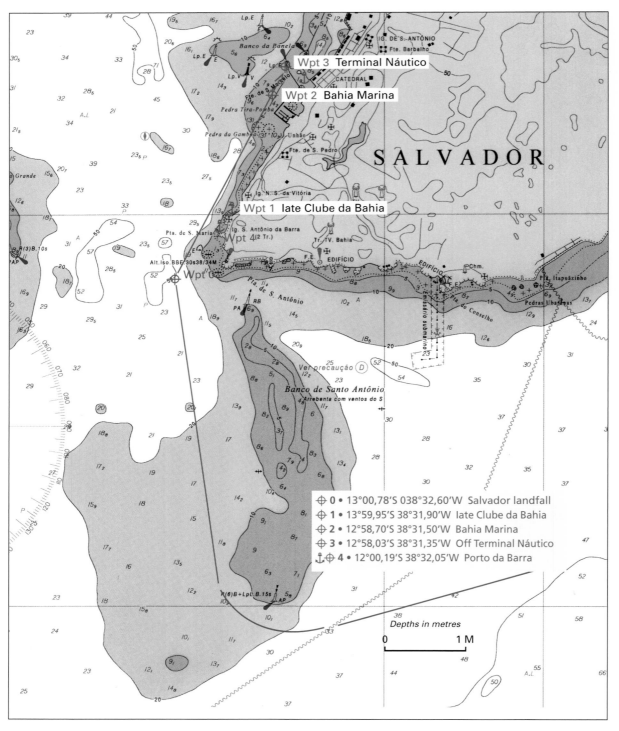

⊕ 0 • 13°00,78'S 038°32,60'W Salvador landfall
⊕ 1 • 13°59,95'S 38°31,90'W Iate Clube da Bahia
⊕ 2 • 12°58,70'S 38°31,50'W Bahia Marina
⊕ 3 • 12°58,03'S 38°31,35'W Off Terminal Náutico
⚓⊕ 4 • 12°00,19'S 38°32,05'W Porto da Barra

Depths in metres

0 — 1 M

LANDFALL AT SALVADOR

Saveiro Clube and Marina Pier Salvador. These marinas are not equipped for visiting boats and have limited facilities

- at around 18M from the entrance to Baía de Todos os Santos, there is also a well protected stretch of water at Baía do Aratu, containing the marina of the Iate Clube do Aratu, as well as another anchorage, Aratu Marina
- lastly, the island of Itaparica, on the western side of the bay, has a very pleasant marina, with certainly one of the most attractive sites in the whole of Baía de Todos os Santos.

The Terminal Náutico da Bahia and Bahia Marina are certainly the most accessible, and clearly to be preferred from the point of view of comfort and services following an ocean crossing.

IATE CLUBE DA BAHIA

Iate Clube da Bahia is a private Salvador boat club with around 3,000 members (*socios*). Of these, about 400 actually own boats, most of which are motor boats (*lanchas*) and are kept in nearby marinas.

It is affiliated with several other Brazilian and foreign clubs, some of which do not necessarily have any marine focus; the Paris Country Club, for example.

It is happy to welcome boats that are passing through and to make the facilities of the club available to them.

A stop here enables visiting sailors to spend a few days in a pleasant location. Many boats come for the day to enjoy the surroundings and the comfort of the club's facilities.

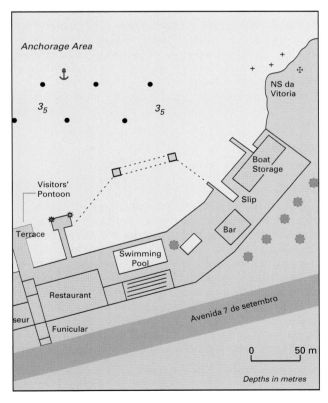

IATE DE CLUB DA BAHIA

Salvador. Entrance to Baía de Todos os Santos. Santo Antônio da Barra lighthouse abeam

Navigation

Brazilian chart DHN No. 1110.

⊕**1** • 13°59,95'S 038°31,90'W Iate Clube da Bahia

Approach

From the entry into Baía de Todos os Santos ⊕0, about 1M to the north of the Santo Antônio lighthouse, a small church can be seen to starboard, situated high up and overlooking the beach of Porto da Barra.

Just after this, the Iate Clube comes into view in a small cove, easily recognised by the presence of a number of boats at anchor, and behind them, the prominent installations of the club.

Quality of moorings

There is no marina at the Iate Clube. There are buoys moored to dead weights on the sea bed opposite the arrival pontoon, and it is possible to anchor at one of these. A boatman provides a link between the anchorage and the pontoon, day and night.

The anchorage is sheltered from winds coming from the north round to the southeast, but very exposed to winds from the southwest and northwest, which make the water here very choppy.

Anchorage of the Iate Clube da Bahia, as seen when arriving from the south

View of the Iate Clube da Bahia

Facilities and services

The club has toilet facilities, showers, a bar, restaurants, swimming pools, etc.

There are few services in the immediate area and for boat repairs you will need to head for the other Salvador marinas.

There is a slipway where small boats (low tonnage only) can be brought ashore on a trailer and kept under cover.

Water Water tap at the arrival pontoon.

Electricity There is an electric point on the arrival pontoon. Temporary use of this may be possible as long as the connection is for a short time only.

Supplies

There is little available in the immediate locality, although there is a supermarket (Bompreço) quite nearby, and also the Barra shopping mall (Shopping Barra).

Mooring fees The Iate Clube is open to all boats arriving by sea and their crews, and allows visitors to anchor here for a courtesy stay of three days. Beyond that period a charge is made, in the range of R$30 per day for a 45ft boat.

Location and surroundings The club is situated at the entrance to Baía de Todos os Santos, in the district of Barra, close to the Santo Antônio lighthouse and beaches.

Tourism

Barra is a modern, tourist district with a pleasant seafront and a good number of well-frequented bars and restaurants.

An interesting visit can be made to the lighthouse, which is close by, and its maritime museum, which traces the history of Baía de Todos os Santos since the period of its discovery in 1501.

⚓ THE IATE CLUBE

Although the anchorage of the Iate Clube is not always comfortable (it can be a bit 'rolly'), the reception here and the comfort and range of facilities are excellent, providing:

- a complex on three levels, with lift, offering luxurious reception rooms and a restaurant,
- shops,
- a 50-metre swimming pool with bar and restaurants on a large terrace projecting out over the sea (good restaurant; reasonable prices).
- facilities for children: they are not forgotten, as there is a large swimming pool with water slide and a play area.

In all, the club is a friendly and popular place for members to meet up with family and friends, especially at weekends, when it is particularly lively. It is a very agreeable stop-over after a few days' sailing.

Even those not using the anchorage of the Iate Clube, can make use of its facilities if they make a request in advance to the management and provide proof that they have a boat in one of the Salvador marinas.

Iate Clube da Bahia, Av. 7 de Setembro, SALVADOR, Ba, CEP 40 130 001
☎ 55 (71) 2405 9111
Email icb@icb.com.br

BAHIA MARINA

Opened in 1999 to coincide with the commemoration of the 450th anniversary of the founding of the city of Salvador, today Bahia Marina is the most modern pleasure port of Baía de Todos os Santos. It is situated at the entrance to the bay. With a surface area of 178,000m², the marina is not yet fully occupied and still has considerable accommodation capacity.

Its clientèle consists mainly of Salvador pleasure craft, whose owners make sailing trips at the weekend or go sea fishing in motor boats.

Visiting boats will find good quality mooring in this modern marina, with a range of facilities and services available.

Navigation

Brazilian chart DHN No. 1110.

Approach

Approach by day From ⊕0, Salvador landfall, take a 25° course towards the harbour wall of Salvador's commercial port. About 2.5M from the Santo Antônio lighthouse, a harbour wall made up of boulders will be seen to starboard. At the end of this, a cylindrical beacon tower with horizontal black and white bands indicates the entrance to the marina.

VHF Channel 16, alternative frequency on Channel 12.

On arriving in the marina, wait for a port employee to arrive in an inflatable dinghy and guide you to a mooring.

Approach by night From ⊕0, take a 25° course towards the red beacon Lp.E, which marks the end of the protective harbour wall of the commercial port of Salvador.

Salvador. Entrance to Bahia Marina

Conspicuous landmark At a distance of around two nautical miles, the *elevador Lacerda* can be seen to starboard. The tower of the elevator is 60 metres tall, and its entire height is well illuminated, providing an easily distinguished landmark by day or night.

The *elevador Lacerda* is 0.5M north of Bahia Marina. Steer a course towards it, and the entrance to the marina will be seen to starboard, marked by a fixed red light that is easily visible on the harbour wall of boulders.

⊕ 2 • 12°58,70'S 38°31,50'W Bahia Marina

The marina has 300 spaces available, with berthing by means of mooring lines, bow or stern to the pontoon. On

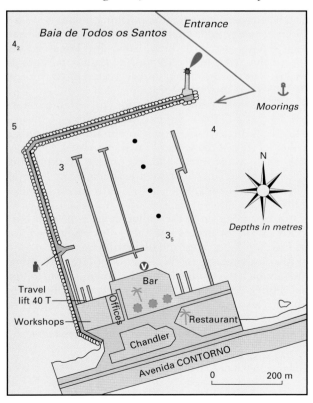

BAHIA MARINA

disembarking you should report with the boat's papers to the reception office.

There is no problem in obtaining a berth as the marina has several pontoons, many of which are still unoccupied.

Quality of moorings***

The port installations of Bahia Marina are modern, sited in and area that is completely calm and well sheltered from winds and currents. Nevertheless, gusts from NW, rare as they are, can cause the water to become choppy inside the marina.

There is also a slight undertow, noticeably more so during the period of spring tides.

Facilities and services ****

The marina has bars, restaurants, chandleries, a variety of other shops, etc. and booking office for cars. The toilet facilities are good in terms of quality, although provision is rather limited for a marina of this size (just two toilets). They can be accessed by day or night.

Water The water taps are locked, and users need to ask at the marina for them to be opened.

An adaptor is needed for the connection (19 diameter male hose connector).

Electricity The berths are equipped with electricity sockets (110 and 220 volts, 60 Hz), in sufficient number.

Fuel Service station on a small pontoon in the marina, with pumps for petrol and diesel.

All general maintenance services are available in the technical area: marine motor mechanics, electricity and electronics, soldering, polyester repairs, hull cleaning team, general maintenance, etc. It is also possible to call in companies from outside the marina.

Salvador, general view of Bahia Marina

Salvador, Bahia Marina, the only 40 tonne travel-lift in Bahia

Boat lifting facilities

The marina has a travel lift with a 40-tonne capacity for lifting boats, together with the necessary props and blocks, and has a very professional team of staff.

This is the only place in Salvador with modern equipment to lift out yachts in excess of 10 tonnes.

Hull cleaning

In the warm waters of Brazil, hulls soon become thickly and firmly encrusted with algae and shells. It may be more efficient to scrape the bottom before hauling the boat out of the water; this makes it easier to detach the shells.

Carlinhos charges a reasonable price for his team's hull-cleaning services, either in or out of the water.
Green Náutica — Serviços náuticos, Carlinhos
☎ (71) 9124 7551.

Supplies***

There are several supermarkets in the city; the nearest is Bompreço Barra, which carries a good stock, and the shopping mall, Shopping Barra.

*Mooring fees**** As a guide, fees are from R$3 per foot and per day.

Connection to the water supply incurs a supplementary charge. The charge is pro rata, based on consumption, and costs R$5 per m³.

Card payment is accepted.

Location and surroundings***

The marina is in a pleasant setting, with a vast complex surrounded by green spaces.

The technical installations are well managed and the companies working on site appear reliable.

The one source of nuisance may be the motor boats, since there are many of these in the marina, and the noise

and exhaust fumes can be annoying when eager mariners in charge of maintaining them rev the engines loudly, especially as they prepare for weekend outings.

The marina is situated near the Comércio district, close to the administrative departments and banks, and 10 minutes on foot from the bus stops and *elevador Lacerda*, which provides access to the upper city and historic centre of Pelourinho.

However, there can be some problems of personal safety in this area, which is near to a disadvantaged district. This should especially be borne in mind when returning from an outing at night, when it is advisable to take a taxi back to the marina. After dark, it is wise to avoid going through this area on foot. It is also wise to avoid using the *Lacerda elevator* after early evening.

Port security

An assistance team is available on the pontoons between the hours of 0700 and 2200.

The marina is completely enclosed and there is a security service with 24h video surveillance.
Bahia Marina, Av. Contorno, 1010, Comercio, SALVADOR, Bahia, CEP 40015-230
☎ (71) 3320 8888
www.bahiamarina.com.br

TERMINAL NÁUTICO DA BAHIA

Previously 'Centro Náutico da Bahia'. Still known by various names, such as CENAB, it belongs to the Bahia state department for sport, SUDESB.

The origins of the Terminal Náutico da Bahia go back to 1994, when the state government created a special commission to promote the development of nautical sports and events.

Two years later, in December 1996, the marina was built between the commercial and fishing ports.

The marina would enable major ocean races and passing yachts to call here, and its construction reinforced the position of Salvador de Bahia and Baía de Todos os Santos on the nautical scene, giving them enormous significance as a location.

In 2007, following a change of Bahia state government, the Centro Náutico was renamed Terminal Náutico da Bahia, whilst largely maintaining the policy regarding its role in the world of watersports.

With such a favoured and hospitable background, what better place for yachtsmen arriving from Europe, the Cape Verde Islands, Senegal or South Africa to make landfall?

Its strategic position in the sailing environment of Baía de Todos os Santos makes it a natural meeting place for yachts heading for a range of destinations.

Another advantage is the location of the Terminal Náutico, which is in the centre of town, close to the official bodies dealing with the entry formalities for Brazil and also to the historic and tourist centre of Salvador.
Terminal Náutico da Bahia – SUDESB, Avenida da França s/n – Comércio, SALVADOR- Bahia – CEP: 40.010 010
☎ (71) 3242 4082, 8167 7175, *Fax* (71) 3326 3433
VHF Channel 16 (manned between 0700 and 1900).

General view of Terminal Náutico da Bahia and of the Capitania dos Portos

The marina, with the Lacerda elevator in the background. Above, the Governor's palace

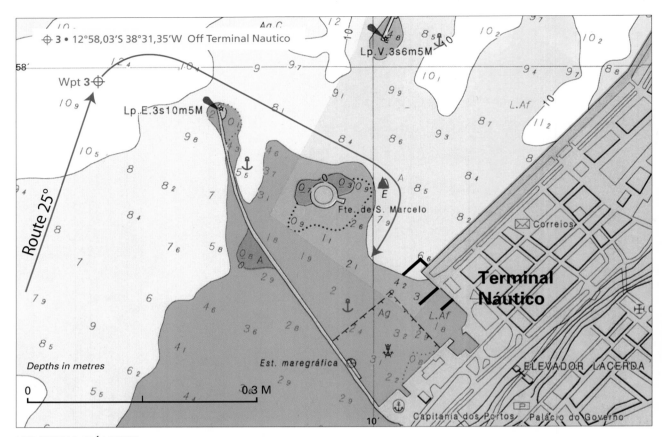

TERMINAL NÁUTICO

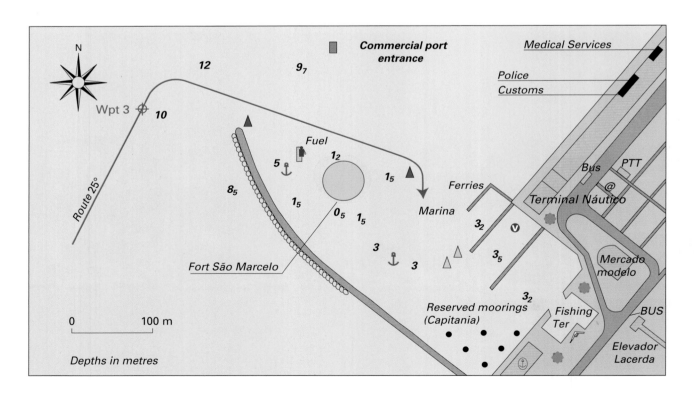

Navigation

Brazilian chart DHN No. 1110.

Approach

Approach by day From ⊕0, Salvador landfall, take a 25° course towards the commercial port of Salvador, situated about three miles from the Santo Antônio lighthouse.

Leaving Bahia Marina to starboard, head towards the small red tower, which is clearly visible at the end of the harbour wall of the commercial port.

Conspicuous landmarks On the approach, the tall white tower of the *elevador Lacerda* will be seen to starboard, and beyond it the long harbour wall protecting the commercial port of Salvador. In the background is the imposing silhouette of the fort, Forte São Marcelo, only the upper part of the fort being visible above the jetty.

Once you have passed the harbour wall, head towards Forte São Marcelo, leave the fort to starboard. Pass round the conical red buoy to enter a vast stretch of water. In the foreground, to starboard behind the fort, is an anchorage area used by local boats and some yachts at anchor.

To port, there is first of all a pontoon reserved for passenger boats providing pleasure trips and a shuttle service to Itaparica and other islands.

Just behind this pontoon can be seen the pale blue painted façade of the elegant building that houses the administrative services of the Terminal Náutico da Bahia. Here there are two pontoons with the capacity to accommodate 60 to 80 yachts, monohulls and catamarans.

In the background the installations of the Brazilian navy can be seen. The mooring buoys here are reserved for the launches of the *Capitania dos Portos* and boats belonging to the pilot station.

Beyond, in the depths of the harbour, between the Terminal Náutico and the naval base, is the small fishing port. This contains small craft and pirogues belonging to local fishermen.

Approach by night From the entrance to Baía de Todos os Santos, ⊕0, leave Santo Antônio lighthouse, Alt.Iso.30s38/34M, to starboard. Take a 25° course, towards the commercial port.

At a distance of about three miles, leaving to port the light of the green buoy Lp.V marking the channel, a red light Lp.E, will be seen opposite, on the beacon at the end of the protecting harbour wall of the port.

When entering at night you will see the marina to be full of moored boats of all sizes. Very great care is therefore needed to avoid the large local tourist boats (*escunas*), which have bowsprits that project well beyond their bow, sometimes by as much as 10 metres.

These bowsprits are almost impossible to see at night, so pose a real risk of collision. It may therefore be preferable to wait for daylight before entering Terminal Náutico, and instead to anchor near the harbour wall, in an area between the end of the harbour wall and Forte São Marcelo, on a bed of sand and mud that provides good holding ground, in 3–4m of water.

⊕ 3 • 12°58,03'S 38°31,35'W Off Terminal Nautico

Quality of moorings ***

Mooring

Mooring is by means of a mooring line, to a buoy, and either bow or stern to the pontoon, under the direction of Amilton. Strict as he is with the staff of the marina, he is pleasant and friendly in his dealings with passing yachtsmen.

On disembarking you should go to the office, where you will be given information on the entry formalities, the various services attached to the marina, tourist events and the like.

The staff are efficient, both administratively and in terms of surveillance and security. The motto 'service, efficiency and friendliness' could be said to sum up the team.

This is a safe mooring, but troubled by an undertow (especially around the time of spring tides), and by the frequent passage of pilot launches serving the commercial port.

It is therefore wise to check your moorings and even double them.

Facilities and Services ***

All facilities; toilet facilities are satisfactory but limited, and can be inadequate when the port is busy.

Some overhaul of the boat and equipment, maybe even a few repairs, may of course be necessary following an ocean crossing. A list (not exhaustive) of firms offering such services is given in the section on boat maintenance services on page 31. Some of these are attached to the marina. Repairs can be obtained more quickly by asking the Terminal Náutico office to contact the company direct. Do not to be in too much of a hurry; you are in Bahia!

Terminal Náutico's location in the Comércio district places you close to all the administrative departments for formalities, banks and communications.

Water The pontoons are adequately equipped with water outlets.

Nevertheless it is advisable to keep your own reserves of water well topped up: not only does the marina often suffer the problem of damaged water pipes; technical deficiencies can also affect the city's supply.

The service station, on a barge at the exit to the marina, and ships waiting at anchor

Electricity There is adequate provision of electricity outlets, with 110 volt and 220 volt sockets (60 Hz).

Fuel This is provided on a floating pontoon at the exit to the marina, behind Forte São Marcelo.

Supplies ***

There are several supermarkets in town. The most convenient of these is Bompreço in the district of Barra.

For fruit and vegetables, there are many stalls selling these in the Comércio district, although the São Joaquim market definitely offers the best choice.

Mooring fees **

Mooring fees are satisfactory, representing a good balance of quality and price.

As a guide, the cost for a 45-foot boat is R$30 per day.

Location and surroundings ***

Terminal Náutico is ideally situated in the Comércio district, just a stone's throw from the official departments dealing with the entry formalities required on arrival in Brazil, and close to the *elevador Lacerda*, which leads directly to the city's historic and tourist centre.

Almost everything can be found either in the immediate area or nearby.

Bus stops for the city services to all destinations are to be found opposite the entrance to the marina or at the foot of the *elevador Lacerda*.

Although this district is very busy during the day, since it is the business quarter, it becomes deserted at night, so that there can be security problems on returning to the port. It is advisable to take a taxi when returning to your boat late at night.

At the marina itself, there is a 24h security service.

There is a snack bar with terrace on the upper floor of the building, but unfortunately it is only open during watersports events, rather than permanently, which would have added to the social amenities of the marina.

Salvador. Entrance to the Terminal Náutico. In the centre, Forte São Marcelo. Pass around the fort, leaving it to starboard

Salvador, anchorage of Porto de Barra

Porto da Barra

There is a pleasant anchorage for a day trip near the Iate Clube da Bahia, 2.5 miles from Bahia Marina and the Terminal Náutico marina.

It is situated at the entrance to Baía de Todos os Santos, in a cove that is well protected from large ocean waves and facing a small beach.

Navigation

Brazilian chart DHN No. 1110.

As you sail along the coast towards the exit from Baía de Todos os Santos, the anchorage is 2.5 miles from the Terminal Náutico and just beyond the Iate Clube da Bahia. Leave the Iate Clube to port, and you can anchor opposite the little beach of Porto da Barra.

⊕ 4 • 12°00,19'S 38°32,05'W Porto da Barra

Anchorage

Quality of moorings

Boats can anchor in 4–5m on a bed of sand and rocks.

This anchorage is well sheltered from winds from the northeast, but can be rather 'rolly' and exposed to tidal currents.

It is not advisable to use it when the wind is from the southern or western sector.

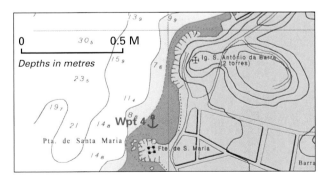

PORTO DA BARRA

Location and surroundings

The anchorage is in a pleasant setting, between two historic buildings, the church of Santo Antônio da Barra and Forte de Santa Maria.

It is possible to come ashore by dinghy on the right-hand part of the beach, behind the jetty.

This little beach is very popular and on days when it is crowded it can be difficult at high tide to find any space on the narrow strip of sand.

Baía de Itapagipe (Ribeira)

Locally this bay is commonly known as Ribeira. Although passing yachts seldom visit it, the bay provides a possible stop in the Ribeira district, near the port of Salvador.

Itapagipe is almost completely surrounded by sea, and a delightful place to stroll around. The western part has a long stretch of sand.

In the northern part there is an anchorage area, and two small marinas further inside the bay.

Navigation

Brazilian chart DHN No. 1110.

Ribeira. Entrance to the bay and anchorage area

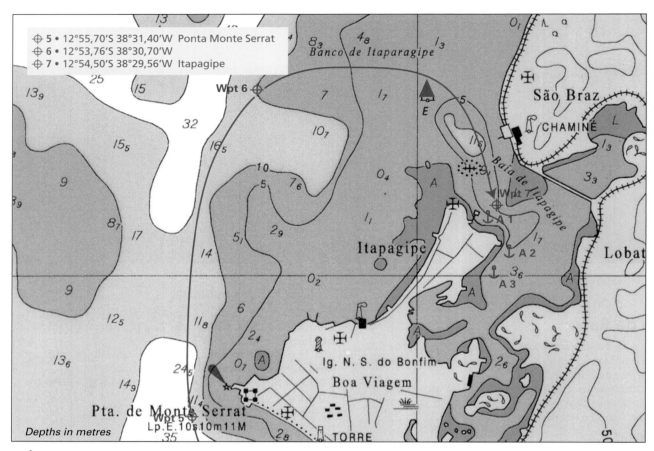

BAÍA DE ITAPAGIPE

Approach

Baía da Itapagipe is situated about eight miles north of the entrance to Baía da Todos os Santos and five miles from the marina at Terminal Náutico, but access is not easy since there is an extensive sand bank across much of the entrance, with depths of water between one and 1.5m at low tide.

Access to the bay is therefore restricted to boats with a shallow draught, and for most yachts it is essential to wait until the end of the rising tide in order to enter this stretch of water.

From the Salvador marinas, head towards the Ponta de Monte Serrat, a small red and white banded tower shaped like a flattened cone, until you reach

⊕ 5 • 12°55,70'S 38°31,40'W Ponta Monte Serrat

After this you bear to starboard on a 20° course for two miles to enable you to make the approach to the Itapagipe sandbank,

⊕ 6 • 12°53,76'S 038°30,70'W

Then, to starboard, you will see a red conical buoy. Head for this, taking care because the sea bed rises rapidly over a distance of about half a mile.

Once you have passed this buoy, steer a course of 160° to enter Baía de Itapagipe, where you once again find depths of 8–10 metres.

⊕ 7 • 12°54,50'S 38°29,56'W Itapagipe

As you enter the bay you will see to starboard a concrete pier jutting out and an extensive anchorage area ⚓A1.

A little further into this stretch of water is a small marina called Angra dos Veleiros, and the Saveiro Clube marina.

The district within Baía de Itapagipe is called Ribeira. This is a quiet district of typical local character, quite close to Salvador. It has a long promenade along the edge of the bay.

At the entrance to the bay is a popular beach, and along its length runs a row of small *cabanas* that give a touch of local colour to the scene.

The entire outer part of the bay extending southwards is made up of a long sandy beach.

ANGRA DOS VELEIROS MARINA

This is a small private marina, with a single 80-berth pontoon. Its size means that it can only accommodate small vessels (maximum 10m).

The berths are reserved in the first instance for members, and there are very few moorings available for passing yachts; anchorage ⚓A2.

Quality of moorings **

The mooring area is calm on the whole, but northwesterly gusts (which are rare) can make the mooring uncomfortable.

It is also possible to anchor nearby in four to five metres of water on a bed of mud, providing good holding ground.

Ribeira. The beach at the point of Itapagipe

Facilities and Services **
There are few facilities on site, but the services of outside companies can be used.

There is a gantry with straps which enables low-tonnage boats to be suspended out of the water at low tide.

The marina has toilet and shower facilities and a terrace with a small restaurant bar.

Water Adequate availability of water taps on the pontoon.

Electricity 110 volt and 220 volt electricity sockets.

Supplies ***
There are some *mercadinhos* here; there is also a frequent bus service, so that it is easy to reach the supermarkets in Salvador.

Mooring fees **
The inclusive price for a boat is about R$25.

Location and surroundings **
The surroundings are not the best and the water may not be particularly clean, one possible cause being the chemical factory on the shore opposite.

SAVEIRO CLUBE MARINA
Quality of moorings **
The general features of this marina are similar to the previous one.

It is mainly frequented by *escunas*, the traditional sailing boats of Baía de Todos os Santos, but also used by all categories of yachts.

It has a single pontoon, 150m long; anchorage A3.

Facilities and Services ***
A slipway enables boats of up to about 15 tonnes to be hauled out, onto an area that is usually somewhat congested.

Bar and restaurant on site.

On the exterior of the same building is a store for chandlery and fishing equipment.

Water The pontoon is equipped water taps.

Electricity 110 volt and 220 volt electricity sockets on the pontoon.

Ribeira. Angra dos veleiros marina

Ribeira. The single pontoon of Saveiro Clube marina

Mooring fees *
A berth at the pontoon costs about R$25 per day.

Location and surroundings **
As for the previous marina Angra dos Veleiros.

Both these marinas have closed access from the side adjoining the road, and a 24h security service.

MARINA PIER SALVADOR
This is the newest of the marinas near Salvador in Baia de Itapagipe. It is located at the head of the bay on the starboard side after Angra dos Veleiros and Saveiro Clube marinas and is next to the latter.

⊕ • 12°54,82'S 038°29,46'W Marina Pier Salvador

Marina Pier Salvador, Av. Porto dos Tainheros 1704, Salvador BA - 40421-580
VHF Channel 16
☏ +55 71 3316 1406
Internet by Wi-Fi
Email piersalvador@piersalvador.com.br

Rates
R$0.60–1 per foot per day, R$18 per foot per month.

Baía do Aratu

Baía do Aratu, situated about 10M to the north of Salvador, has a number of possible anchorages to offer, in perfectly calm waters.

The surroundings, on the other hand, are not particularly exotic, and to reach it the route takes you past an industrial area, with a backdrop of port installations, disused quarries and grain silos.

Despite this, it is one of the most protected sites in Baía de Todos os Santos, where a boat can be left safely in the marina of the Iate Clube during an absence of several days or even months, to allow for an excursion to the interior of the country or a stay outside its borders.

Navigation

Brazilian chart DHN No. 1110 and No. 1104.

Approach

Approach by day Leaving the Terminal Náutico de Salvador, take a 350° course as far as Ponta de Monte Serrat, then 6° towards the red channel mark No. 1. This takes you into a marked navigation channel leading to the entrance to Canal Cotegipe which gives access to Baía do Aratu.

Conspicuous landmarks

To starboard, the long pier of the Terminal da Usiba will be seen, which is for the loading of ore tankers. Further to the north is a tall mast with antennas and large gas storage tanks.

This is Ponta da Areia, which lies at the entrance to Canal Cotegipe. It is marked by a small red beacon topped with a red light.

Ponta do Marinho lies opposite, on the northern side of the canal entrance, and the basins adapted to receive large vessels of up to 65,000 tonnes, at Porto Aratu, can be seen. Once past channel mark No. 7, bear to starboard towards the entrance to Canal Cotegipe:

⊕ 8 • 12°47,20'S 038°30,00'W Cotegipe

Access to Baía do Aratu

Enter Canal Cotegipe, which is S-shaped and fully marked.

Follow this channel as far as another red buoy No. 7 opposite Ponta do Criminoso. Here you enter Baía do Aratu, and a 170° course leads directly to the Iate Clube, which is situated in the depths of the bay, at the foot of a prominently visible group of buildings.

Aratu. Pass round buoy No. 7. The Iate Clube is in the depths of the bay, in the background

Approach by night Follow the marked channel (*see approach by day*) as far as ⊕8, abeam of Ponta da Areia, which has a red light Lp.E.5s5m5M.

Then take the marked channel of Canal Cotegipe to beacon No. 7 which is topped by a red light Lp.E.3s. This indicates the entrance to Baía do Aratu.

At the southern end of the bay the lights of a group of buildings on a hill can be seen. The Iate Clube is at the foot of this hill, and can be reached by a direct 170° course.

There are two marinas in Baía do Aratu:
• Aratu Iate Clube
• Aratu Marina

ARATU IATE CLUBE

This is a private club which is happy to receive visiting yachts. It has pontoons available for mooring as well as a mooring area, with mooring buoys installed by the club.

⊕ 9 • 12°48,75'S 38°27,67'W Aratu Iate Clube, A1

In port

Most of the boats in the marina are yachts.

The Iate Clube has a number of mooring buoys available; also two large pontoons with a number of berths available for visitors.

Quality of moorings ★★★

Although the water is somewhat muddy, as a place to leave a boat this marina is thoroughly safe, well sheltered from the winds and totally free of undertow of tidal currents.

Facilities and services ★★★

Bathroom facilities are respectable and spacious and the club offers every comfort: a swimming pool, television room, bar and good restaurant with a large terrace built out on piles.

The marina has capable maintenance staff and the site is well supervised day and night by a specialist surveillance company. This includes making rounds of the mooring area, ⚓A1, at night.

There is a slipway enabling boats up to 12 tonnes to be hauled out on a trailer. A number of maintenance services are available on site, joinery, electrical, mechanical and painting.

Water The pontoons are equipped with water taps, and there is drinking water, with a fountain with filtered water in the technical area near the sheds.

Electricity There are outlets on the pontoons (110 volts only). It is therefore advisable to have a suitable voltage transformer.

Fuel There is a diesel pump on the arrival pontoon.

Supplies ★★

The village of Ilha São João is situated near the marina, but there are few facilities for provisioning in the immediate locality. However, around ten kilometres away there is a supermarket in the village of Paripe which carries quite good stocks.

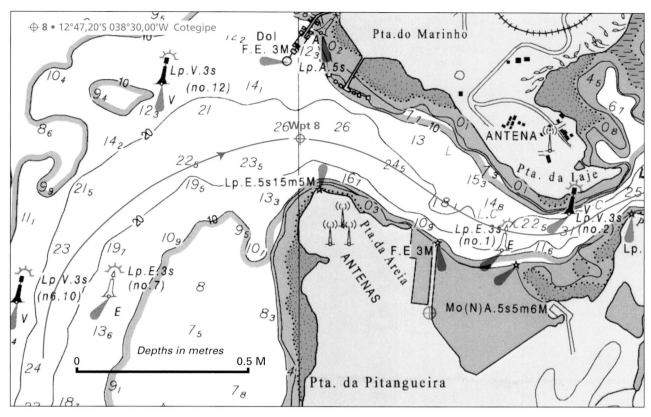

CANAL DE COTEGIPE

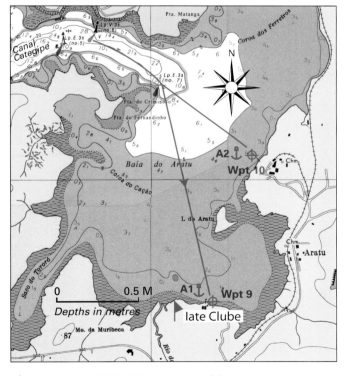

⊕ **9** • 12°48,75'S 38°27,67'W Aratu late Clube
⊕ **10** • 12°47,80'S 38°27,41'W Marina Aratu

BAÍA DO ARATU

Aratu, the late Clube marina in the depths of the bay

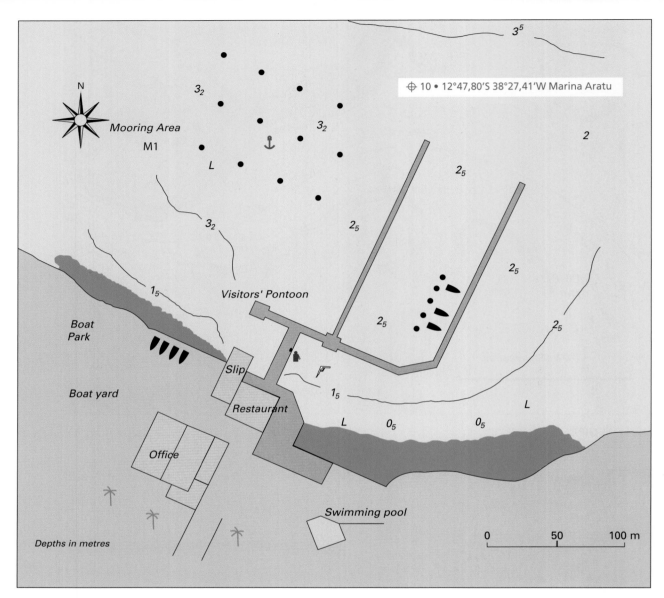

ARATU IATE CLUBE

For other purchases, Terminal França buses in the direction of Salvador and the commercial centre of Iguatemi are frequent. The bus stop is about 500 metres from the marina.

Mooring fees * These are about R$20 per day for a mooring, and R$30 per day at the pontoon. The charge for a boat out of the water, on the hull-cleaning area of the boatyard and not enrolled with the club, is R$80 per day.

For a stay of longer duration it is possible to pay by credit transfer to the Banco do Brasil, Branch 12 378.

Location and surroundings **

The Iate Clube is in a completely isolated location, but several buses leave the village regularly in the direction of Salvador. The internal organisation of the club is good and there is a 24h surveillance and security service.

There is little of tourist interest in the village, but the club is friendly and organises frequent week end regattas, social evenings and various activities, and visiting boats are of course invited.

Aratu Iate Clube, Rodovia Paripe Cia – Ilha de São João, SIMOES FILHO – Bahia
☏ 71 3216 74 44, *Fax* 71 3216 72 84
Email aratuclube@uol.com.br

ARATU MARINA

This lies a short distance north of Aratu Iate Clube (about 1M).

The port installations are easily recognisable with a disused cement works as background, by an old wharf with transporter and the abandoned hulks of disused vessels.

⊕ 10 • 12°47,80'S 38°27,41'W Marina Aratu
Anchorage ⚓A2

The anchorage at Aratu Marina

Quality of moorings ***

There are some mooring buoys and two pontoons, used by local sailors to berth their boats.

Boats anchor on a bed of mud that provides good holding ground, in 3m of water.

Facilities and services ***

A number of services are available on site, including mechanical repairs, polyester, and painting. There is a slipway for lifting out large boats for maintenance and repair or storage in the technical area.

Small restaurant on site.

Water Taps on the pontoons.

Electricity 110-volt electricity outlets on the pontoons.

Supplies *

There are no provisioning facilities at all on site.

Location and surroundings *

The marina is well away from all facilities, so car or taxi transport is more or less indispensable. The surroundings have only slight appeal in view of the abandoned factory.

There is a great deal to be done here to modernise the installations afloat; on the other hand, the naval yard holds a degree of interest.

Marina Aratu
① (71) 3594 7369/73
Email maratu@svn.com.br

Ilha da Maré anchorage

Ilha da Maré

The contrast could not be more striking between the port installations and storage tanks of the huge industrial area of Porto Aratu and the pretty hamlet of Ilha da Maré, nestling amidst greenery.

As you leave Baía do Aratu, this anchorage is one not to be missed!

Navigation

Brazilian chart DHN No. 1110.

Approach

Approaching from Salvador

Follow the Baía do Aratu route as far as red beacon No. 7 of the main channel.

Then steer a 345° course towards the Ilha da Maré landing stage, used by tourist excursion boats.

Anchor 200m further to the north, opposite the *Nilson* restaurant.

Approaching from Baía do Aratu

Ilha da Maré is opposite the entrance to the Canal Cotegipe.

From ⊕8, head for the Maré landing stage and moor a little further north:

⊕ 11 • 12°46,78'S 038°30,86'W Ilha da Maré

Anchorage

Quality of moorings **

Anchor in three to four metres of water, on a bed of sand which gives good holding ground.

This is a calm stretch of water, but account must always be taken of a strong tidal current in this part of the bay.

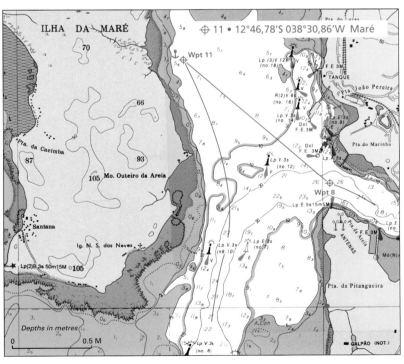
ILHA DA MARÉ

Facilities and services *
No availability on the island.

Supplies *
Little in the way of provisioning facilities.

Location and surroundings ***
Ilha da Maré is near Baía de Aratu, so it is possible to call in here either before entering the bay or afterwards.

Tourism
During a stop-over here, a visit can be made to the southern part of the island on foot.

The route takes you along a coast bordered with beautiful vegetation, to the village of Santana.

There are two lovely beaches, Praia Grande and Praia das Neves.

The speciality of the *Nilson* restaurant is *camarãoes a vapor*.

Ilha Itaparica

General information
Measuring 30x20km, Ilha Itaparica is the largest island in the Baía de Todos os Santos. It lies just some 10 miles from Salvador, and is without doubt one of the most pleasant and frequently visited in the bay.

It is also a favoured destination for holidaymakers and for the inhabitants of Salvador, so although it may be quiet during the week, it becomes very busy from Friday evening onward.

The island makes an excellent port of call for yachtsmen, and a point of departure when setting out to visit the other islands of Baía de Todos os Santos and the Rio Paraguaçu.

On the northern end of the island is Itaparica marina, and at the southern end the anchorage of Cacha Pregos.

There are plenty of possible places to anchor along the west coast in the Canal de Itaparica. One of the most popular is the one at the Tororó waterfall. The southeast coast is less accessible in any kind of sailing boat because the approach is obstructed by a barrier of reefs.

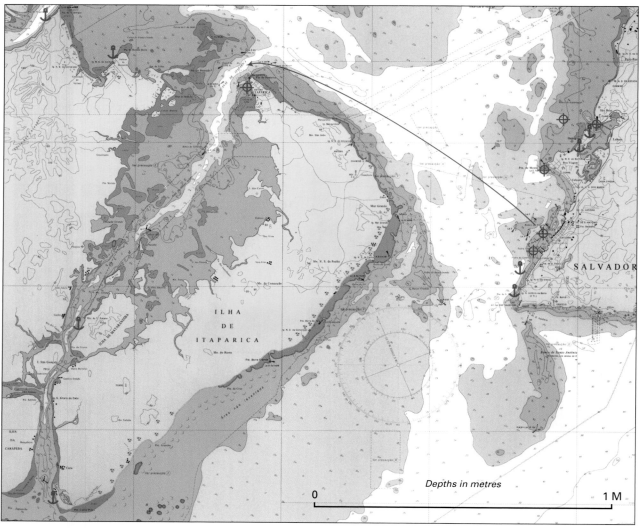

Depths in metres

0   1 M

ILHA ITAPARICA

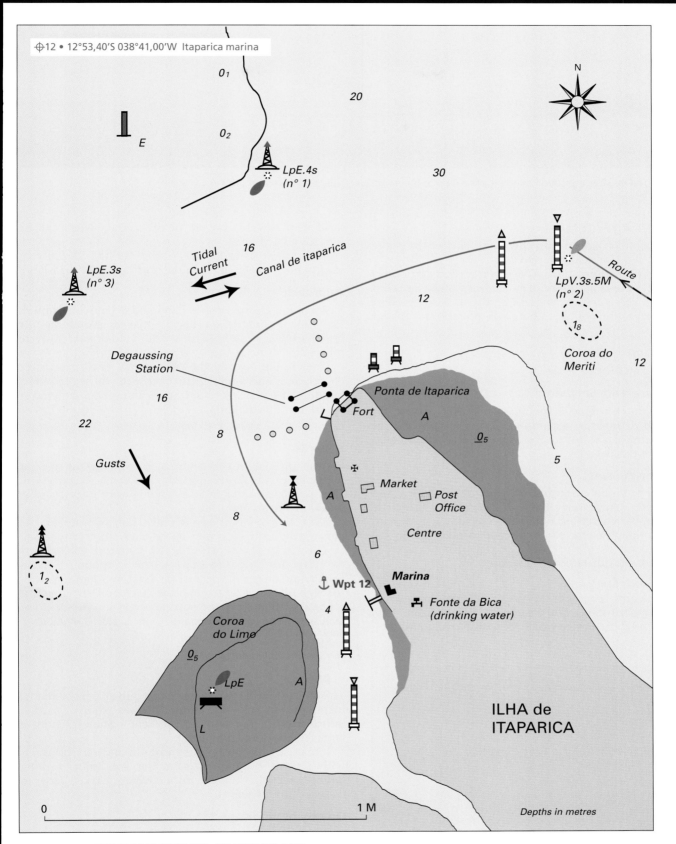

ITAPARICA. THE NORTHERN TIP OF THE ISLAND

Itaparica. The degaussing station on the northern tip of the island. Boats need to pass round this

ITAPARICA MARINA

This small marina in the northwestern part of the island is run by the Terminal Nāutico.

It is fairly quiet during the week, but on Friday evenings there is an influx of boats from other Salvador marinas. There are not enough berths to accommodate everyone at the pontoon, but it is possible to anchor nearby.

Navigation

Brazilian chart DHN No. 1110.

Departure from Salvador

Leaving the Terminal Náutico, steer a 300° course for about 10M towards beacon No. 2, Lp.V.3s leaving the shoal Coroa do Mériti to port. The shoal is about half a mile from this beacon.

Tides and currents

The speed of the currents can reach 2.5–3 knots, and even more than this at the entrance to the Canal de Itaparica. When setting out from Salvador it is best to take advantage of the flood current to take you to the island.

Consult the tide table for Salvador.

Conspicuous landmarks

Two beacons mounted on piles, tall red and white banded poles, stand out clearly on the horizon. Pass around the more easterly one (beacon No. 2), and then head west towards the tip of the island, which can be seen about 1M away.

The other conspicuous feature is the degaussing station for military ships on the north point of the island.

Approach

Pass around the tip of the island and degaussing station, leaving to port the special marks indicating its boundaries (yellow beacons and cylindrical concrete pillars).

Then sail along past the village with its clearly visible church and, half a mile further on, you will see to port a building of several storeys. Itaparica marina is situated at the foot of this building.

⊕12 • 12°53,40′S 038°41,00′W Itaparica marina

Hazards

On the approach to the marina, it is important to treat with caution the Coroa do Limo sandbank to starboard. This is a large sandbank, extending widthways, and is uncovered from mid-tide.

Also, at low tide there is only 1.2m of water in the passage that provides entry to the interior of the marina.

This entrance is represented by a conical yellow buoy to starboard and the end of the pontoon to port. Depending on the draught of the boat, it is better to wait for high tide in order to enter the marina. Alternatively it is possible to moor to the outside of the pontoon.

Marina Itaparica, Av. 25 de outubro. Fonte da Bica, ITAPARICA – Bahia – 44460-000
☎/Fax (71) 3631 1645
www.marinaitaparica.com.br

In port

This pretty marina was constructed quite recently, and its installations are well thought out: shops, tourist information, a bar and an excellent restaurant with a large terrace raised on piles.

Itaparica village is fairly spread out and very pleasant, with several restaurants near the sea front, serving Bahian specialities, and with a covered market between its two central squares.

Quality of moorings ***

The water is calm and in general well protected, although gusts from southwest or northwest can be a problem. These in particular can stir up the water of the marina, and the moorings along the outside of the pontoon can become very uncomfortable. In this case it is better to anchor, using a good length of chain.

Itaparica, beacon No. 2, which should be left to port

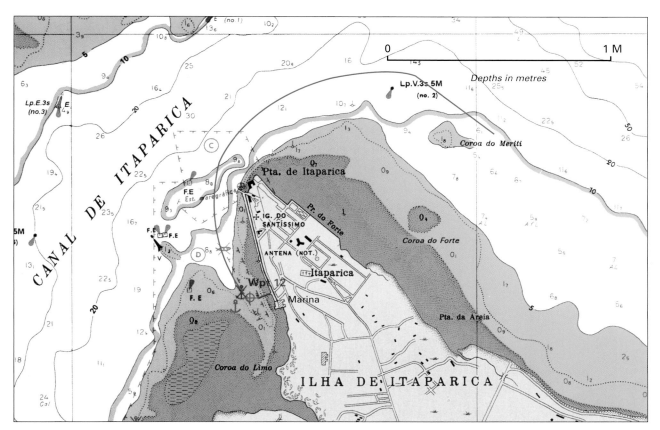

ITAPARICA NORTH

The marina. The sandbank can be seen in the background

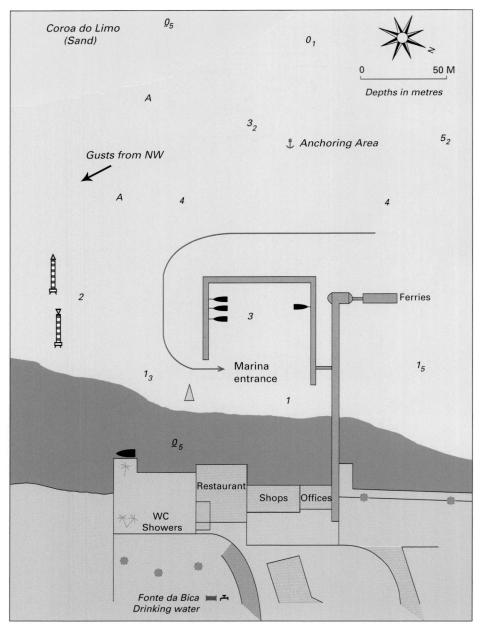

ITAPARICA MARINA

The drinking water fountain Fonte da Bica, next to the marina

Facilities and services *

There are some facilities at Itaparica and at the next village, Mar Grande, which is about 10km away.

In Mar Grande, there can be some problems withdrawing money by card from the automatic cash dispensers, so it is advisable to draw out money in Salvador before coming to the island.

Similarly for maintenance work on the boat there is a greater choice of contractors in Salvador.

Water Just next to the marina is the Fonte da Bica, a mineral water fountain, which provides water of excellent quality. The locals come here from the village to get supplies, armed with cans and plastic bottles.

The water on the pontoons also comes from this source, so it is worth taking advantage of it and filling up the boat's water tanks and reserves for everyday consumption; you might even indulge in the luxury of washing the boat in mineral water.

Electricity The pontoons are adequately equipped with 110-volt and 220-volt outlets.

Hull cleaning Hull cleaning can be done by bringing the boat ashore alongside the quay to the right of the restaurant, or for centreboard boats and catamarans, coming ashore opposite the marina, on the sandbank that is uncovered at low tide.

Anchorage Visiting boats can also anchor in the area opposite the marina, in three to four metres of water, on a bed of sand. They can fill up with water at the pontoons and use the marina's bathroom and sanitary facilities for a small fee.

Supplies ***

There is a small market in the centre of the village, and some *mercadinhos*. On the way out of the village is a bigger supermarket called *Atlántica*.

About 10km away in the village of Bom Despacho is a large, well-stocked Bompreço supermarket.

Mooring fees * Fees are the same as at the Terminal Náutico, from R$30 per day for a 45-foot boat.

Location and surroundings ****

The marina lies in a particularly pleasant setting, with an extensive sandbank opposite, which is a wonderful place to collect seashells when it is uncovered at low tide.

A 24h surveillance and security service is maintained.

Hull cleaning on the sandbank opposite the marina

Tourism

Every Friday evening, the village is filled with the rhythm of music as a public dance (the *Seresta*) is held in the central square, to the lively accompaniment of a small group of local musicians.

Near the marina are several nice little restaurants such as *Cosas e Tal* or *Rosas da Margarida*, as well as a good restaurant on the terrace of the marina, which serves excellent Bahian specialities.

There are two parts to the island: Itaparica in the north and Vera Cruz in the south.

There is a regular link between the island and Salvador, provided by shuttle service boats and a ferry.

The shuttle service boats (*lanchas*) leave every 30 minutes from the Terminal Maritimo and take half an hour to the village of Mar Grande (Vera Cruz).

The ferry, which also takes cars, leaves the São Joaquim ferry terminal and takes one hour to reach the village of Bom Despacho.

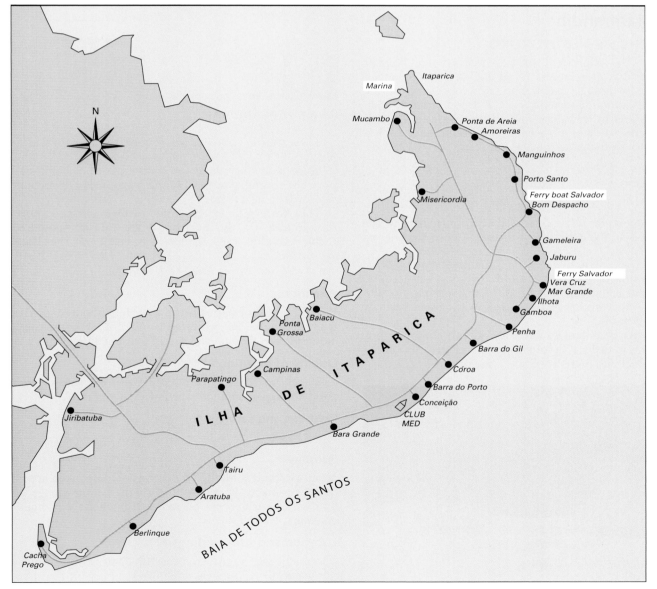

ITAPARICA – PLAN OF THE ROADS ON THE ISLAND

The beaches along the east coast and down to the southern tip of the island, among them Ponta de Areia, Amoreira, Barra Grande, Barra do Gil and Aratuba, are some of the loveliest of Baía de Todos os Santos. It is also on this coast, incidentally, that Club Méditerranée has chosen to site its village.

Transport, trips and tours of the island

The entire island is served by collective taxis (*kombis*) which stop anywhere in response to a hand signal.

The friendly French proprietor of a *pousada*, Philippe, will also organise trips around the island and local surroundings and help you discover various typical sites of the region, such as:

- The Senhor do Bomfim fazenda, an extremely old *cachaça* distillery, a small village where most of the region's pottery is made, diving trips, and several other interesting sites.

Philippe, Pousada Zimbo Tropical, Aratuba, ITAPARICA
℡ (71) 3638 1148

Ilha Matarandiba

⚓ CACHOEIRA DE ITORORÓ

Towards the southwest of Itaparica island, Ilha de Matarandiba offers access to an anchorage surrounded by greenery and so calm that even the sound of the waterfall cannot disturb its peace. During the summer, in fact, there is little if any water in the waterfall, which only begins to deserve its name once there have been a few good showers or during the rains of the winter season.

Navigation

Brazilian chart DHN No. 1110.

On leaving Itaparica marina, resume a course of 300° for half a mile in the direction of the green buoy that lies to the northeast.

This enables you to enter the Canal de Itaparica. Steer a course first of 204° for about 4.5M and then of 235°, which will bring you first of all to the red buoy of the Tubarão bank and then to the following green buoy at about 3.5 miles.

However, it is best to keep to a depth contour of at least 10m, in order to avoid a shoal marked 1.5m on the chart, which lies halfway between the two buoys.

The light-coloured rocks of the waterfall

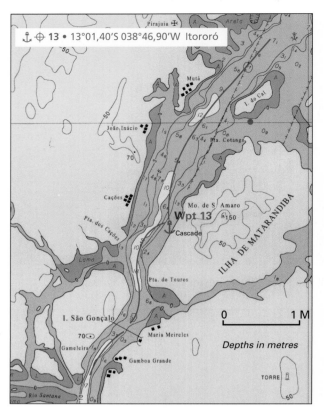

ILHA MATARANDIBA

Then steer a 220° course, leaving the Ilha do Cal to port.

Once past this island, at a distance of 1.5 miles to port, the shoreline advances, and a group of tall coconut trees will be seen there.

The waterfall is ½ mile further on, to port, recognisable by the horizontal line of light-coloured rocks standing out against the green of the thick vegetation.

⊕ 13 • 13°01,40'S 038°46,90'W Itororó waterfall

Anchorage

Boats can anchor opposite the waterfall, about 80 metres from the shore. The waterfall is in a hollow in the rocks alongside the channel and is easily reached by dinghy.

Quality of moorings ****

The anchorage is very calm, in 2.5 metres of water with good holding ground on a bed of sand and mud.

Facilities and services *

None at all.

Supplies *

None available, although a dinghy could be taken across to the opposite shore, to the small fishing village of Cações, where it is possible to buy fish when the *pirogues* come in.

Location and surroundings ***

The anchorage is utterly peaceful. During the summer the waterfall is one in name only for most of the time, with no water in it, though maybe just enough for a refreshing shower.

Access to the south of the island is through a bridge with limited headroom

Note

Access to the south of Ilha Itaparica: bridge
1.5M south of the waterfall, the river is spanned by a
bridge with a height of approximately 19 metres*
(height at low tide, tide coefficient 47) beneath the
roadway at its highest point.

Sailing boats requiring a headroom close to this figure
must exercise great caution when considering whether
to use this route to reach the south of Itaparica island
and the anchorage of Cacha Prego.

The electricity cables before the bridge are considerably
higher.

CACHA PREGO

To the south of Ilha Itaparica, the beautiful beaches of
the tip of the island look directly out to the ocean,
protected by a barrier of rocks.

The village of Cacha Prego is very appealing, with its
small harbour where the tourist excursion boats are
moored, and constantly busy sea front.

Navigation

Brazilian chart DHN No. 1110.

Access to Cacha Prego is possible by way of the northern
part of the Canal de Itaparica. However, it is important
to bear in mind the caution above, concerning the bridge
(*see note at the end of the section on Cachoeira de
Itororó*).

If the headroom required by the boat will not allow it
to pass under the bridge, the alternative is to go right
round the island and approach via the southern section
of the Canal de Itaparica.

Another possibility is to come direct from Salvador:
steer a course of 230° for about 20M, taking care to
leave the cardinal buoy that guards the shoal of Baixo
Grande, at the exit to Baía de Todos os Santos, to
starboard.

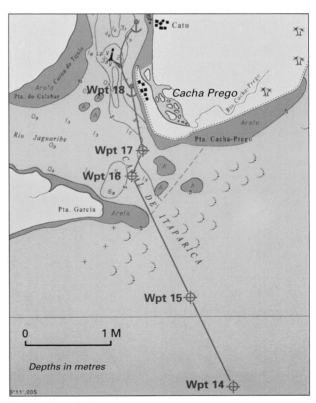

ITAPARICA SOUTH

⊕14 • 13°10'.80S 038°46'.55W Prego landfall

⊕15 • 13°09'.70S 038°47'.07W

⊕16 • 13°08'.20S 038°47'.80W

⊕17 • 13°07'.90S 038°47'.68W

⊕18 • 13°07'.15S 038°47'.80W Cacha Prego

This route remains at a distance of about 2.5 miles from the coast, and so avoids the barrier of reefs that extends all along the southeast coast of Ilha de Itaparica. It then joins up with ⊕14, which lies opposite the southern entrance to the Canal de Itaparica. (Beware: there are no hydrographic data for the reef-strewn edge of the coast).

⊕14 • 13°10,80'S 038°46,55'W Prego landfall

Good weather and a calm sea are needed in order to enter the canal. It is best to wait for a rising half-tide.

Navigating with the sun at your back, it is possible to make out the brown patches of stirred-up sand over the shoals that partially obstruct the passage.

Steer a course of 330°, and an interrupted line of breaking waves will be seen ahead, in the distance.

There is no need to be worried by these waves; continue at reduced speed in the direction of ⊕15.

⊕15 • 13°09,70'S 038°47,07'W

This waypoint brings you into a good position opposite the entrance to the canal. You are then able to sail in depths of 6–8m, between two sets of reefs, visible at the surface. Continue on this course for 1.8M, through a narrow passage between Ponta Garcia (the extension of a small island of sand with some vegetation) to port and Ponta Cacha Prego (which is also extended by a large, covered sandbank, reaching halfway across the entrance to the canal) to starboard.

⊕16 • 13°08,20'S 038°47,80'W

Now head for ⊕17.

⊕17 • 13°07,90'S 038°47,68'W

Then make your way along the coast in the direction of the village and the landing stage, which will be seen to starboard, less than a mile away.

There is an anchorage with several small local boats, but the sea is often rough here and it is better to continue on beyond the landing stage to find a more comfortable anchorage.

Suggestion

⊕18 • 13°07,15'S 038°47,80'W Cacha Prego

⚓ CACHA PREGO ANCHORAGE

Quality of moorings ★★★

Boats can anchor on a bed of sand giving good holding ground, in 4–5m of water.

This stretch of water is calm, but can be slightly rough in a falling tide when the wind is against the current.

Facilities and services ★

There are few repair facilities in the immediate locality, but there is a small boatyard in the village of Catu, run by a Frenchman called Robert; enquiries can be made there.

Transport on the island is available by *kombi*. These depart regularly from the small village square by the canal.

Supplies ★★

This is no problem in the village, where the usual basic supplies are available.

For complete reprovisioning, you will need to go to the north of the island, where there is a large supermarket in the village of Bom Despacho.

Location and surroundings ★★★

The activities carried out in the village are fishing and tourist-related. Many excursion boats are moored in the river in the north of the village.

There is a pleasant sea front with several small restaurant bars along the canal. The area is always very busy at summer weekends.

The long beaches of Cacha Prego point continue around the entire southeast coast of the island, which has a string of beaches protected by a barrier of reefs, and where the water is deliciously warm.

⚓ CATU ANCHORAGE

Strong winds from the northeast to south bring the swell into the canal and make the anchorage at Cacha Prego uncomfortable, especially when the tide is falling.

This may make it preferable to anchor further north in the canal, near the boatyard or opposite the small village of Catu, about one mile away.

The anchorage beyond the landing stage

Note

According to some of the local fishermen, the sandbanks at the southern entrance to the Canal de Itaparica can shift considerably from season to season and as a result of the currents and weather conditions. The entrance to Cacha Prego calls for good local knowledge. If using this route, sailors are urged to pay constant attention to the depth sounder. In case of doubt, seek the guidance of a local sailor.

Ilha do Frade

Frade is one of the largest islands of Baía de Todos os Santos, and daily attracts many day trippers and holidaymakers, as well as Bahians at the weekend.

The eastern part of the island has beautiful beaches, while the interior is covered with dense tropical forest; its luxuriant vegetation is ecologically protected.

There are two possible anchorages, one in the north of the island, well sheltered from all winds, and the other in the south. However, this one is more a day anchorage, as it is only sheltered from winds coming from the northeast.

⚓ FRADE SOUTHERN ANCHORAGE

The south of Frade island can be reached directly from Itaparica and boats can anchor to the left of the landing stage where the tourist excursion boats come in to moor.

Navigation

Brazilian chart DHN No. 1110 and No. 1107.

Approach

From Itaparica marina, return to the north tip of the island. Opposite can be seen Ilha do Frade. A course of 33° for about 5M will bring you to Ponta do Farol, at the southern end of the island.

ILHA DO FRADE

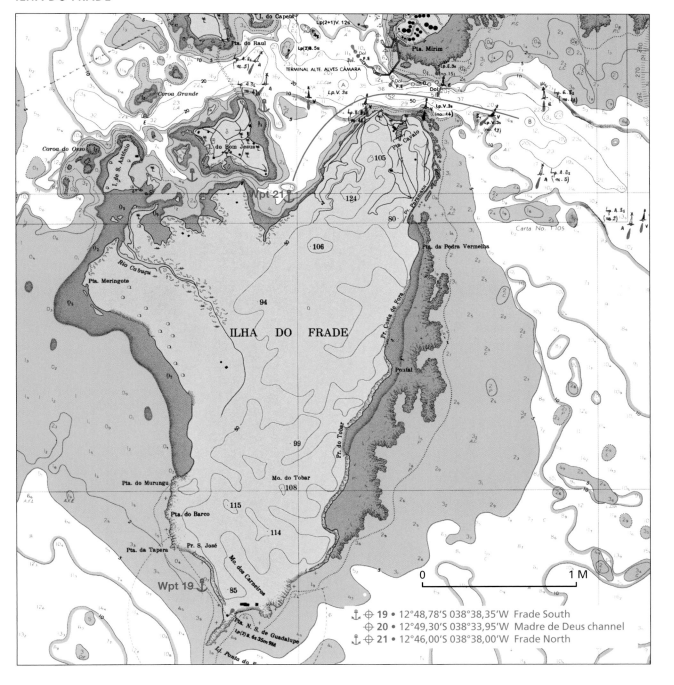

⚓ ⊕ **19** • 12°48,78'S 038°38,35'W Frade South
⊕ **20** • 12°49,30'S 038°33,95'W Madre de Deus channel
⚓ ⊕ **21** • 12°46,00'S 038°38,00'W Frade North

Escunas moored at the landing stage of Frade

Hazards

A rocky shoal extends out for some distance at Ponta do Farol, so it is important to take a wide enough course to avoid this shoal if rounding the island to the south.

Anchorage

Boats can anchor behind the landing stage, which is reserved for tourist excursion boats; these come alongside at the end of the landing stage.

⊕ 19 • 12°48,78'S 038°38,35'W Frade South

Quality of moorings ***

Boats anchor on a bed of sand and rocks that provides good holding ground, in four to five metres of water.

However, in some places there is smooth rock, which makes the grip of the anchor much less certain.

The anchorage is well sheltered from the flood current and from northeast winds.

Overnight it is better to find another anchorage, because the water can become rough when the wind is from the southwest to northwest, and the anchorage then becomes uncomfortable.

Location and surroundings ***

This is a practical anchorage near Itaparica island, useful for a day trip or an outing for a pleasant walk or swim or to visit one of the restaurants in the south of the island.

⚓ FRADE NORTHERN ANCHORAGE

Navigation

Brazilian chart DHN No. 1110 and No. 1104.

Approach

Leaving from Terminal Náutico, steer a 343° course in the direction of buoy No. 1 of the access channel for the Alves Câmara oil terminal, at the south of Madre de Deus island. This channel is marked with buoys along its entire length:

⊕ 20 • 12°49,30'S 038°33,95'W Madre de Deus channel

Take care to leave the south cardinal buoy to starboard; this marks a series of shoals.

Note In the Madre de Deus channel there is always a strong tidal stream, and it is preferable to take advantage of this.

Follow this channel as far as green buoy No. 16; then, once you are past this buoy, the small church of Our Lady of Loreto will be seen to port on the northern tip of Frade island.

Anchorage

There is plenty of choice of anchorages along the northwest coast, with a depth of 3–5m throughout.

⊕ 21 • 12°46,00'S 038°38,00'W Frade North

Quality of moorings ****

The water is very calm and the anchorage area well sheltered.

Boats anchor on a bed of sand and mud that provides good holding ground, in a depth of 4m.

There is absolutely no current at this anchorage.

Location and surroundings **

This is a quiet anchorage in which to spend the night, despite the nearness of the brightly-lit oil installations.

Ilha Bom Jesus dos Passos

To the northwest of Ilha do Frade, the charming Ilha do Bom Jesus offers the visitor a typical small village with square and church.

The south of the island has a completely calm mooring, barely ruffled by the wakes of a few small craft returning from a day's fishing; the backdrop is exceptionally beautiful, with spellbinding sunsets.

Navigation

Brazilian Charts DHN No. 1110 and No. 1105.

A strong ebb current that should not be ignored

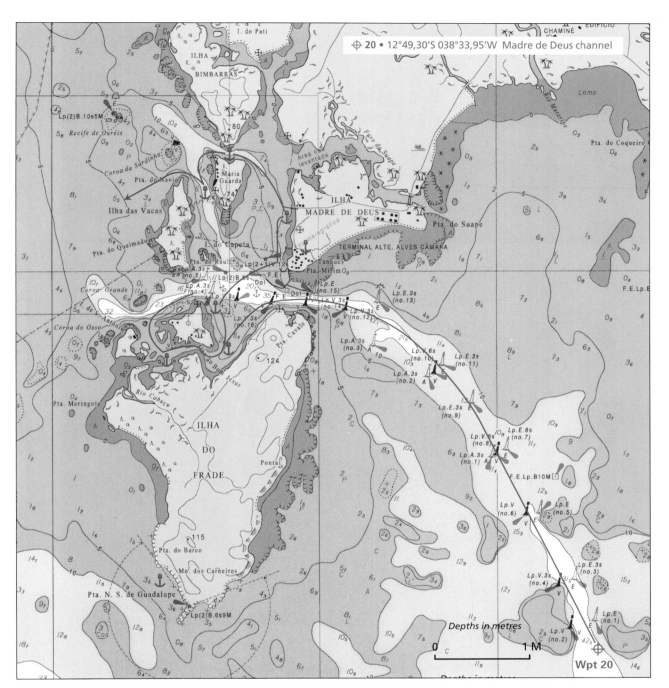

Depths in metres

0   1 M

Wpt 20

ANCHORAGES NORTH OF ILHA DO FRADE

The small church of Nossa Senhora de Loreto on the northern tip of Ilha Bom Jesus dos Passos

⚓ BOM JESUS NORTH

Approach

Follow the route leading to the northern part of Ilha do Frade as far as green channel buoy No. 16, leading to the Amiral Alves Câmara oil terminal. Then steer a course of 275° towards the church on Bom Jesus, which is clearly visible from just over a mile away, and head towards the island's jetty where the passenger boats are linking the island to the mainland moor.

Anchorage

It is possible to anchor near the jetty.

⊕ 22 • 12°45,32'S 038°38,33'W   Bom Jesus north

Bom Jesus anchorage

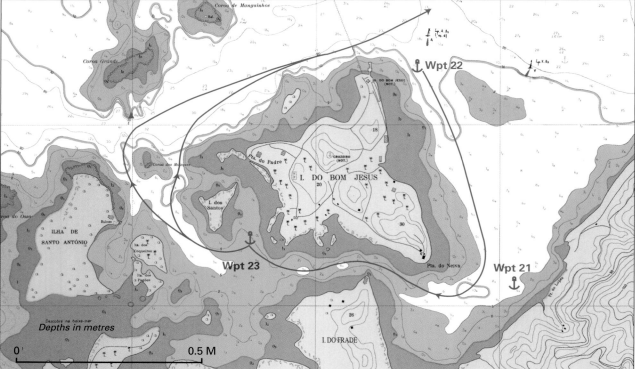

Depths in metres

Wpt 22

Wpt 23

Wpt 21

0   0.5 M

ILHA BOM JESUS DOS PASSOS

The jetty and church on the north of the island

Quality of moorings **

Holding is good in 4–5m of water on sand and mud.

Location and surroundings **

The oil terminal in the background mars the surroundings, but the mooring is convenient for going ashore in a tender.

⚓ BOM JESUS SOUTH

Approach

From the Bom Jesus jetty, go around the east side of the island, staying a good distance from the shore in depths of 5–6m.

A narrow passage can then be seen to the west, behind Ponta do Neiva, leading through an S-shaped channel to an anchorage on the south of the island.

This anchorage can also be reached directly from ⊕21 (*see Ilha do Frade north anchorage*).

Precautions

The passage between the two islands is particularly narrow and the water is shallow in the middle section (1.5 to 2m at mean low water).

Yachts with a deeper draught should wait for half-tide and go carefully in this passage, where cautious progress on the depth sounder is strongly recommended.

Anchorage

⊕ 23 • 12°45,87'S 038°38,70'W Bom Jesus south

Quality of moorings ★★★★

Holding is good in 3–4m of water on sand and mud.

The mooring is completely calm and very well sheltered.

There is no current.

Location and surroundings ★★★★

The mooring is close to a fishing community and a small boatyard that repairs and caulks traditional craft using traditional techniques (such as caulking with coconut fibre).

The site is particularly peaceful against an attractive backdrop of greenery, but the water is muddy and cloudy, even at high tide.

Departure from Bom Jesus south anchorage

Leaving the south anchorage, go around the west side of the island, through the passage between Ilha do Bom Jesus and Ilha de Santo Antônio.

In the middle of the channel, watch out for a shoal, Coroa dos Moleques, which is covered from half-tide and only marked with a wooden pole topped by an X.

If passing to the right of the shoal, navigate cautiously through this narrow passage, or alternatively take the passage to the left of the shoal where the water is deeper.

A little further north, a red buoy marks the Coroa Grande shoal. Either head west towards Itaparica and the Rio Paraguaçu, or northeast towards the islands of Madre de Deus and Maria Guarda.

A completely calm mooring

Ilha de Santo Antônio, to the east of Bom Jesus

The marking of Coroa dos Moleques, a shoal covered from half-tide onwards

Ilha Madre de Deus

To the north of Ilha do Frade, Ilha Madre de Deus has a contrasting landscape; on the south of the island, the long white sandy beach of Suape is overlooked by an oil terminal, with huge port facilities and enormous tankers at their berths.

Navigation

Brazilian Charts DHN No. 1110 and No. 1105.

Approach

Follow the marked access channel to Ilha Madre de Deus to the Alves Câmara terminal, the petroleum facilities of which can be seen on the south of the island.

⊕ 24 • 12°45,00'S 038°37,57'W Terminal A. Câmara

From the terminal, steer a course north for approximately 0.7 miles, between the green beacons and the mooring posts, along Ilha Madre de Deus' anchor after the jetty.

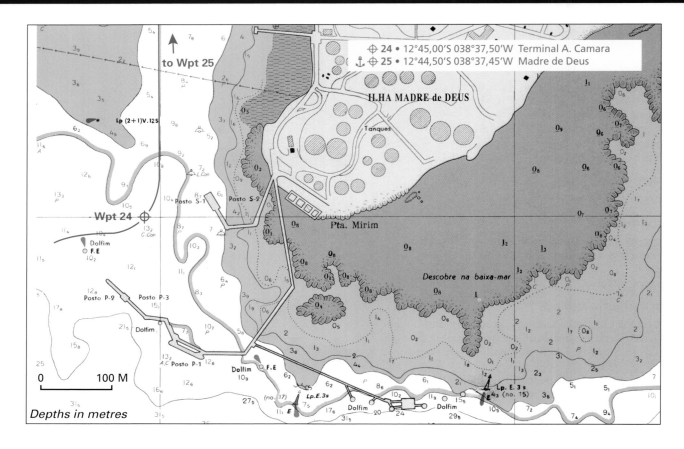

```
24 • 12°45,00'S 038°37,50'W  Terminal A. Camara
25 • 12°44,50'S 038°37,45'W  Madre de Deus
```

ILHA MADRE de DEUS

Tanques

Posto S-1   Posto S-2

Wpt 24

Dolfim
F.E

Posto P-2   Posto P-3

Dolfim

Posto P-1

Dolfim   F.E

to Wpt 25

Pta. Mirim

Descobre na baixa-mar

0   100 M

Depths in metres

⚓ ANCHORAGE

✛ 25 • 12°44,50'S 038°37,45'W Madre de Deus

Quality of moorings ***

Anchorage in 3–4m of water; the mooring is calm with reasonable holding on mud.

Location and surroundings *

The jetty can be used for going ashore in a tender.

The surroundings are not of great interest near the enormous fuel storage tanks, but Suape beach on the south of the island is beautiful.

Ilha Maria Guarda

Right next to Madre de Deus, Ilha Maria Guarda is accessible via a channel of a good depth that goes round the north of the island.

Sailing at the start of the incoming tide makes the passage more clearly visible as the shore and sandbanks are largely uncovered at low tide.

Navigation

Brazilian Charts DHN No. 1110 and No. 1105.

From ✛25, Madre de Deus anchorage, steer a course towards

✛ 26 • 12°43,90'S 038°37,60'W

✛ 27 • 12°43,68'S 038°37,78'W

which will allow access from the north to the passage that can be seen between Ilha Bimbarras and Ilha Maria Guarda.

The Madre de Deus anchorage

The passage to the north of Ilha Maria Guarda

⚓ NORTH ANCHORAGE

It is possible to anchor on the north side of Maria Guarda, between a small floating pontoon and Ponta Gravatá.

⊕ **28** • 12°43,66'S 038°38,03'W Maria Guarda north

West anchorage

Then go around the island, staying well off the northwestern section in order to avoid the low-tide elevations of Coroa Gravatá and Coroa Maria Arcanjo. Head for the jetty and choose an anchorage near the village,

⊕ **29** • 12°44,03'S 038°38,23'W Maria Guarda west

When tying tenders up to the concrete slab of the jetty, watch out for the protruding bolts, which are only visible at low tide.

Quality of moorings ***

Anchor holding is good in three to four metres of water on sand and mud.

The mooring is generally calm and the currents are weaker in this part of the bay.

Facilities - services

Very limited.

Supplies *

Very little on the island, with just a mini-market.

Location and surroundings ***

This is a peaceful little island with a pleasant walk through the small village with its coloured houses, built along the shore. Complete peace and quiet in an attractive setting, but the water is muddy, especially at low tide.

Ilha Bimbarras can be reached easily in a tender from the north anchorage and Ilha das Vacas can be reached from the west anchorage.

Stay well off the northwestern tip and Coroa Maria Arcanjo

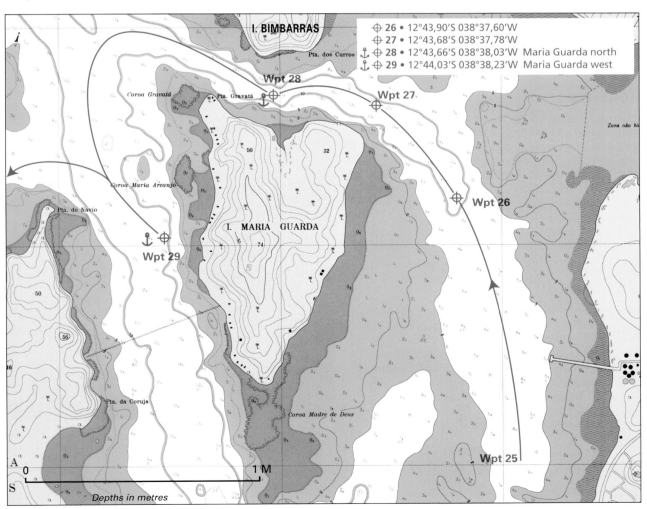

⊕ **26** • 12°43,90'S 038°37,60'W	
⊕ **27** • 12°43,68'S 038°37,78'W	
⚓ ⊕ **28** • 12°43,66'S 038°38,03'W Maria Guarda north	
⚓ ⊕ **29** • 12°44,03'S 038°38,23'W Maria Guarda west	

ILHA IMARIA GUARDA

The Ilha Bimbarras anchorage

Ilha Bimbarras

Ilha Bimbarras is located to the north of Ilha Maria Guarda and easily accessible in a tender from the north anchorage on Maria Guarda, ⊕28.

There are only 250m between the two islands.

Bimbarras is a private island under an ecological protection scheme. It is covered by a beautiful forest with a wide variety of trees providing homes for numerous types of birds, including some rare species.

Go ashore on the small beach of Ponta dos Curros, near a private jetty belonging to a house, where permission to land can be sought.

Ilha das Vacas

Located to the west of Ilha Maria Guarda, Ilha das Vacas is largely wooded with rocky shores that offer a few white sandy beaches at low tide.

There are few places to anchor on the east and south sides of Ilha das Vacas, but it is easy to reach the island in a tender from ⊕29 Maria Guarda west anchorage.

There are only 300m between the two islands.

Leaving the anchorage on Ilha Maria Guarda, go round Ponta do Navío to the north of Ilha das Vacas, staying well off.

To go towards Itaparica or the Rio Paraguaçu, head southwest, going along Ilha do Frade at a good distance offshore.

Ilha das Vacas. The northern tip with its small beach

Salinas de Margarida

Although in the past the salt marshes (*salinas*) and farming were the main activities in Salinas de Margarida, these have now diversified into fishing, tourism and crafts.

The village is pleasant but there is most activity in the seafront square, fringed with bars and restaurants. At the weekend, trip boats from Salvador bring large numbers of tourists and visitors to the island.

Navigation

Brazilian Charts DHN No. 1110 and No. 1107.

From Itaparica marina, head towards red buoy No. 1, to the north of the tip of the island, then steer a course of 355° to the green buoy that marks the Coroa das Pedras shoal.

A course of 253° leads after four miles to a second green buoy marking the Coroa de Fondo Grande bank. Approximately half a mile after the buoy, turn towards the church of Nossa Senhora do Carmo, which can be seen to port.

Anchorage

Head towards the beach, where a concrete jetty protrudes around 100m.

It is possible to moor on the jetty when there are no trip boats, but the wind and tidal current can make mooring alongside uncomfortable, and it might be preferable to anchor off nearby for the night:

⊕ 30 • 12°52,00'S 038°45,90'W Salinas de Margarida

Quality of moorings ***

Holding is good in three to four metres of water on sand and mud.

The mooring is calm but the winds from the north and the ebb current make mooring alongside uncomfortable and it is preferable to anchor off nearby for the night.

Facilities – Services *

Very little on shore.

Supplies **

Supplies can be found in the village.

A number of fishermen on the island sell fish, crabs and shellfish.

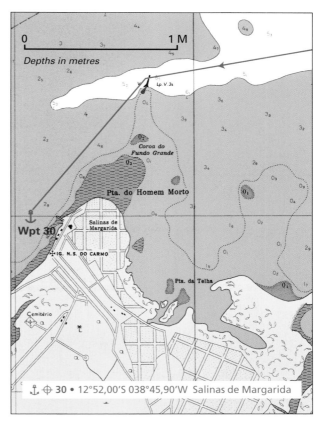

SALINAS DE MARGARIDA

Note Make sure you leave Ponta do Homem Morto well to port. This sandbank rises rapidly and is uncovered at low tide.

Location and surroundings ***

Located near the Rio Paraguaçu, there are some very pleasant walks from here to Ponta de Guadalupe at the mouth of the river.

Tourism

The villages of Salinas de Margarida and Conceição de Salinas are close by.

The church of Nossa Senhora do Carmo, a conspicuous landmark, and the jetty

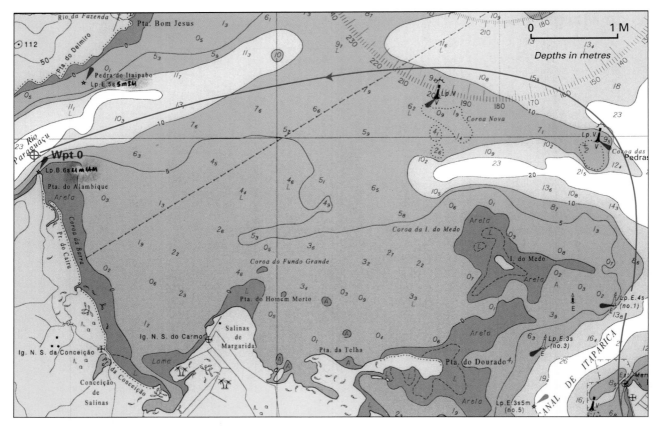

RIO PARAGUAÇU APPROACH

A little further away, towards the Rio Paraguaçu, are the beautiful beaches of Conceição and Cairú, which stretch to the mouth of the river.

At low tide, this huge expanse of sand is largely uncovered and forms an immense sandy plateau providing rich pickings of shellfish.

Ilha do Medo

This island is located between Itaparica and Salinas de Margarida, close to the former.

Several legends hang over this island, some morbid, others terrifying, hence its name – the island of fear.

In centuries past, it is said to have been used at one time as a leper colony and at another for Candomblé and black magic rituals to frighten white people.

The Jesuits in turn are said to have introduced wild cats to keep the natives away.

It is a fact that over the years, the island has always been uninhabited.

It is now an ecological reserve in Baía de Todos os Santos and, in principle, landing is prohibited.

It is mainly covered with forest and surrounded by a large sandbank that prevents it being approached by yacht.

However, the shoal surrounding it makes an interesting dive site in shallow waters.

There is a wide variety of fish around, particularly rays and also dolphins, who seem to appreciate the calm of this site.

Rio Paraguaçu

Leave Baía de Todos os Santos and head up the Rio Paraguaçu to discover a different Brazil, unspoilt by tourism and far from the hustle and bustle of the large towns.

This is a region of small fishing and farming villages that has kept its authentic character and where people live life at a slower pace. The river snakes inland through a varied landscape that is a mixture of tropical vegetation, ochre coloured rocks and mangrove-covered shores.

Navigation

Brazilian Charts DHN No. 1110, No. 1107 and No. 1108.

Navigation is largely in depths of 15 to 30 metres, staying in the middle of the river, and does not pose any particular problems. However, caution is the order of the day as in the mooring areas, the depth decreases rapidly and there are numerous sandbanks in the northern section of the river.

It is preferable to take advantage of the tidal currents, which run at approximately 2–3 knots.

From Salvador or the island of Itaparica, head for the green buoy marking Coroa das Pedras, located to the north of the tip of Itaparica. A course of 283° leads to the green buoy at Coroa Nova; then come round onto 260° to head towards the entrance to the Rio Paraguaçu.

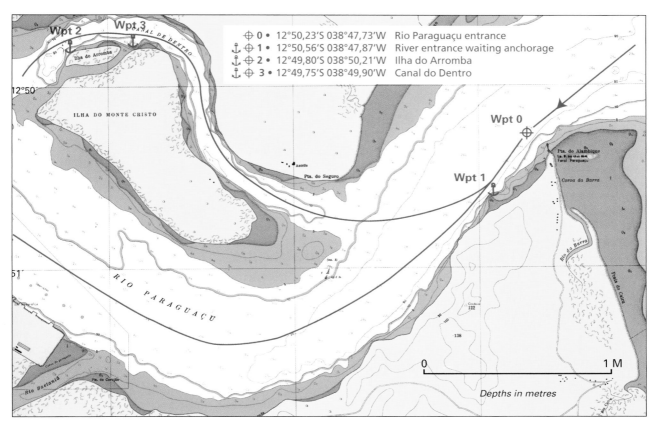

RIO PARAGUAÇU (1)

⊕ **0** • 12°50,23'S 038°47,73'W	Rio Paraguaçu entrance
⚓ ⊕ **1** • 12°50,56'S 038°47,87'W	River entrance waiting anchorage
⚓ ⊕ **2** • 12°49,80'S 038°50,21'W	Ilha do Arromba
⚓ ⊕ **3** • 12°49,75'S 038°49,90'W	Canal do Dentro

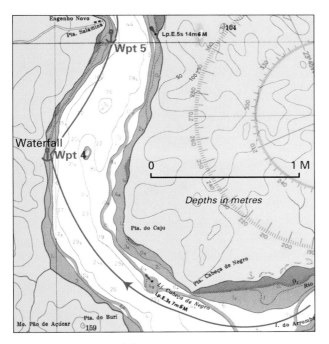

RIO PARAGUAÇU (2)

⚓ ⊕ **4** • 12°48,80'S 038°52,05'W Waterfall
⚓ ⊕ **5** • 12°47,95'S 038°51,68'W Forte Salamina

⊕0. The tower on Ponta do Alambique at the entrance to the river

⚓ A SELECTION OF ANCHORAGES ON THE RIO PARAGUAÇU

The anchorages on the Rio Paraguaçu are many and varied depending on individual tastes, but they all have one thing in common: the calm, the tranquillity, the silence, the strange feeling that time has stopped…

When waiting for the flood current, it is possible to anchor at the entrance to the river in 4m on sand, behind Ponta do Alambique, opposite a small beach.

⊕ **0** • 12°50,23'S 038°47,73'W Rio Paraguaçu entrance

There is another waiting anchorage half a mile further on, to port, near the jetty of an attractive private residence, which is brightly lit at night.

This is the same type of anchorage as the previous one with, however, several rocks near the bank, which should be left at a distance.

Four miles from the mouth of the river there is an anchorage near Ilha do Arromba in 4m on sand.

⊕ 2 • 12°49,80'S 038°50,21'W Ilha do Arromba

Half a mile further on in the Canal de Dentro, there is a good anchorage in 4m of water on sand, where the night can be spent in pleasant surroundings.

⊕ 3 • 12°49,75'S 038°49,90'W Canal do Dentro

Heading 10 to 12 miles up to the north of the river on the port side, opposite an old *pousada* (hostel), now a private residence, there is an interesting anchorage from where a waterfall can be visited. Ask the owner or caretaker for permission to cross their land.

After 30 minutes' walk in thick forest you will come to a deliciously cool waterfall, perfect for a refreshing dip.

⊕ 4 • 12°48,80'S 038°52,05'W Waterfall

Further north, Ponta Salamina can be seen to port, and at its tip the fort that defended access to Maragogipe in the 16th century.

Half a mile after the point, the ruins of an old *engenho* (sugar mill) are just managing to resist being engulfed by vegetation.

⊕ 5 • 12°47,95'S 038°51,68'W Forte Salamina

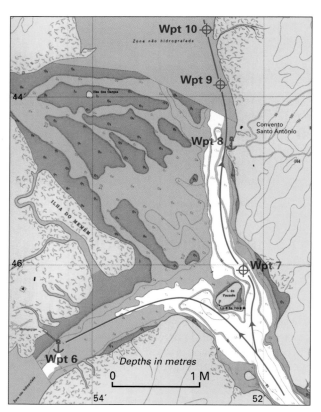

RIO PARAGUAÇU (3)

⚓ ⊕ 6 • 12°47,05'S 038°54,37'W Maragogipe
⚓ ⊕ 7 • 12°46,05'S 038°52,28'W Ilha do Francés
⚓ ⊕ 8 • 12°44,58'S 038°52,47'W São Francisco

The fort on Ponta Salamina

Maragogipe

This small town, with a population of 20,000, is an unmissable stop on the Rio Paraguaçu.

The town is located in the Recôncavo, a region to the north of Baía de Todos os Santos that was previously extremely prosperous due to its agricultural, sugar cane and tobacco production, as well as its livestock; it remains an important centre for trade in agricultural products.

Arrive on a Friday evening, as there is a large traditional market on Saturday morning that transforms the town into a hive of activity.

Navigation

2.5 miles to the north of Ponta Salamina, Ilha do Francés splits the river in two.

To reach Maragogipe, about two miles away, turn to port to the south of Ilha do Francés, and then head towards a long jetty opposite which boats can anchor.

⚓ ⊕ 6 • 12°47,05'S 038°54,37'W Maragogipe

Quality of moorings ***

Holding is good in 3–4m of water on mud.

To go ashore, it is preferable to leave the tender at the end of the jetty rather than tying up near the village as, at low tide, it is very difficult to refloat; the bank uncovers significantly, leaving a knee-deep layer of mud.

Similarly, it is more advisable to put out two lines, a stern anchor and a bow line to the jetty, as when the tide turns there is a risk that the current will drag the tender and it will become wedged under the concrete slab of the jetty, or get damaged on the pillars, which are heavily encrusted with sharp shells.

The jetty at Maragogipe

Maragogipe. Saturday is market day

Facilities – Services ***

Some repair facilities on shore.

Bus service for visiting the neighbouring villages of São Felix and Cachoeira.

Supplies ***

No problem in town, where there are several mini-markets.

Location and surroundings ***

The anchorage is close to the town, and is heavily frequented by passing boats.

Tourism

The Salvador-Maragogipe regatta takes place in August every year, with no fewer than 200 participants, all categories.

There are huge celebrations at the finish line!

Maragogipe is a very lively town, particularly on Saturday, which is market day, when the farmers of the Recôncavo region come down from their holdings on horseback to sell their crops and livestock, horses, zebu, bulls, and so on.

There is also a market selling fresh and dried meat, multi-coloured displays of fruit from all over Brazil at very low prices, and a phenomenal variety of types of grain and flour. This colourful scene of Bahian rural life is out of this world!

Baía de Iguape

Few people visit this bay and its traditional villages. However, there is a peaceful atmosphere and serene tranquillity against a backdrop of mangroves and tropical vegetation, and the locals are very friendly.

Navigation

Baía de Iguape is a large, calm stretch of water, but caution is required as it is also a vast sandbank area, only part of which is uncovered at low tide.

The northern and western parts of the bay are uncharted, so care must be taken when navigating in this area.

SÃO FRANCISCO DO IGUAPE

This small village is mainly inhabited by fishermen and farm workers from the surrounding holdings.

Its sandy streets converge on the shady central square.

A very fine church and the monastery of Santo Antônio, which is undergoing restoration, stand on the banks of the Rio Paraguaçu.

Approach

Brazilian Chart DHN No. 1107.

From Maragogipe, steer a course towards Ilha do Francés, leaving the entire Baía de Iguape sandbank area to port; most of the sandbanks are covered by very little water.

⊕ 7 • 12°46,05'S 038°52,28'W Ilha do Francés

Then head directly north upriver for about one mile, towards the small village of São Francisco and the church of Santo Antônio.

⊕ 8 • 12°44,58'S 038°52,47'W São Francisco

Anchorage

Quality of moorings ***

Boats can anchor opposite the church and Convento de Santo Antônio (a former monastery), in 5m on sand and mud, near an old concrete jetty.

It is a peaceful anchorage with good holding.

However, account must be taken of an ebb current of up to three knots, more in spring tides, and the anchor should be checked when the tide turns.

On the school run in the village square

The anchorage opposite the Convento de Santo Antônio

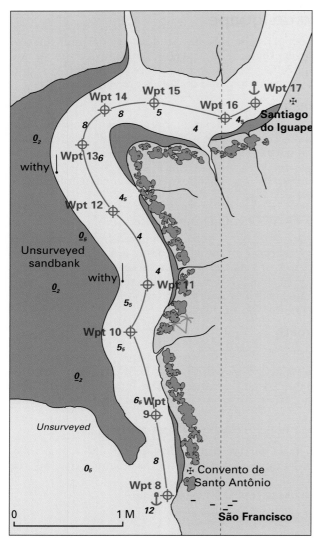

ROUTE TO SANTIAGO DO IGUAPE

⊕ **9** • 12°43,86′S 038°52,56′W
⊕ **10** • 12°43,20′S 038°52,73′W
⊕ **11** • 12°42,67′S 038°52,69′W
⊕ **12** • 12°42,01′S 038°52,92′W
⊕ **13** • 12°41,38′S 038°53,23′W
⊕ **14** • 12°41,07′S 038°53,05′W
⊕ **15** • 12°41,04′S 038°52,58′W
⊕ **16** • 12°41,17′S 038°52,20′W

Supplies **

Limited to basics, in the mini-market near the square. Fish and shrimps are available directly from the fishermen.

Location and surroundings ***

To go ashore in a tender, land on the small sandy beach near the jetty.

A small sandy road leads to the square in the village of São Francisco. The church and monastery are undergoing restoration, but with a little luck they can be visited.

SANTIAGO DO IGUAPE

Heading upriver, to the north of the previous anchorage, chart DHN No. 1107 shows an uncharted area. It is however possible to continue further upriver to the small village of Santiago do Iguape, approximately five miles away.

Navigation

Leave the anchorage at São Francisco at the start of the rising tide, so that the riverbed and partly uncovered sandbanks are more clearly visible.

Anchor opposite the beautiful church in Santiago which, given its great age, could also do with some serious restoration.

⊕ **17** • 12°41,03′S 038°51,68′W Santiago de Iguape

Sandbanks on the river

Anchorage opposite the village of Santiago

The children hunt for blue crabs (*Gaiamu*)

Santiago do Iguape village square

Quality of moorings ***

Completely calm anchorage with good holding in three to four metres of water on mud.

Account must be taken of the current, which can be up to 2.5 knots on the falling tide.

Supplies **

Very little in the village.

There is a lot of shrimp fishing in the river and these can be bought directly from local fishermen.

Location and surroundings ***

Exceptional surroundings in a peaceful village where the calm pace of life is from a completely different age.

CACHOEIRA

To the north of Baía do Iguape, the Rio Paraguaçu continues to São Felix and Cachoeira, through a maze of sandbanks and sometimes rocks.

The significant silting of the bay makes access to the northern part of the river difficult.

Saveiros

Saveiros, traditional Bahian craft, are frequently encountered in Baía de Todos os Santos and on the surrounding rivers.

They are large, pot-bellied wooden sailing boats around fifteen to twenty metres long, with a carefully selected mast made from a straight, slender tree trunk, curved at the top.

A large mainsail and a small jib provide propulsion. There is no engine, of course!

Saveiros are generally crewed by two men, one handling the sails and the other at the helm. On arrival in Salvador, near the marina at the Terminal Náutico, they lower the mainsail and, using the boat's momentum, manoeuvre with amazing dexterity to come alongside near the fishing port on the quay set aside for them.

Previously, *saveiros* were the only link between the villages in the Bahia region.

Although times have changed, there are still a great many saveiros in the Baía de Todos os Santos and, as in the past, they provide links between Salvador and the most remote villages on the Rio Paraguaçu.

They generally carry anything they can take on board en route. They can often be seen, loaded to the gunwales with cases of equipment, crates of beer, miscellaneous consumer goods, building materials, sand, bricks, cement, timber, as well as livestock and poultry … in short, anything and everything!

Using the winds and favourable currents, they jauntily ply the Rio Paraguaçu, the helmsman stretched out on the stern, steering with his foot.

Try racing them – there's no guarantee you'll win!

But whatever you do, don't follow them. Their shallow draught (about 60cm) means that they can go over pretty much any of the shoals, whatever the state of the tide, and even without charts they know every route and short-cut in Baía de Todos os Santos and the rivers.

If they go aground, no problem! The men just stretch out on deck and wait calmly for the next high tide.

Of course, their delivery times aren't guaranteed, but hey, we're in Bahia!

A *saveiro* on the Rio Paraguaçu

However, it is possible to go as far as Cachoeira with a shallow draught boat.

A local boatman, if he is reliable, can also give advice or act as a guide through the shoals and obstacles that litter the river.

Tourism

Cachoeira and São Felix can also be reached by bus from Maragogipe, on a road that winds through a landscape of hills, some of which have been largely cleared for crops.

The town, which is famous for its exceptional colonial architecture, was declared a Brazilian Historical Heritage site in 1971.

It is currently attempting, in the face of many problems and limited financial resources, to restore its architectural heritage, the last vestige of its past.

There are churches, museums, historical monuments and a large number of residences from bygone days, some of which have been abandoned and are now little more than beautiful frontages.

São Felix

On the right bank of the Rio Paraguaçu, the small village of São Felix is accessible on foot from Cachoeira over an old railway bridge. A lane for cars has been built out of wooden sleepers on the railway itself.

When a train comes, road traffic stops on either side of the bridge and the road becomes a railway once more to let the train past. Interesting!

The region is also known for producing excellent tobacco with an exceptional aroma; the cigar factories, which can be visited, are in São Felix.

Arquipélago de Tinharé

To the south of Salvador da Bahia, the coast is sandy, fringed with long beaches and adorned with abundant vegetation.

This is known as the Costa do Dendê and it owes its name to the exuberant landscape of palm trees, the fruit of which hangs in heavy bunches and is used to produce *dendê* oil (palm oil). This flavoursome brown oil is one of the basic ingredients vital in the preparation of Bahian culinary specialities such as *vatapa*, *moqueca* and many others.

However, the Costa do Dendê also offers visitors 100km of largely deserted beaches. The hinterland has a very varied landscape and its historical buildings recall the prosperous days previously enjoyed by the region.

The Tinharé archipelago on the Costa do Dendê is made up of three main islands:

- Ilha de Tinharé
- Ilha de Cairú
- Ilha de Boipeba

There are two ways of reaching the islands:

- from Valença, in a *lancha* (motor boat), through a maze of rivers and canals in the middle of thick vegetation of mangroves, tropical forest and coconut palms,
- by sea from Salvador, in which case the first port of call is Morro de São Paulo.

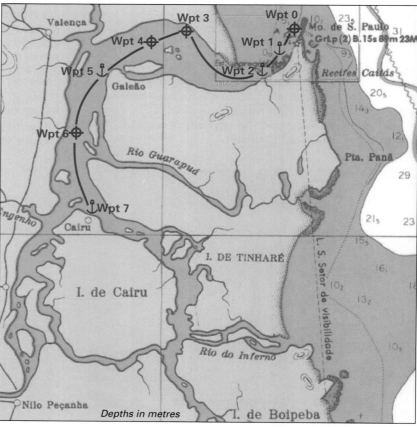

ARQUIPELAGO DO TINHARÉ

Ilha de Tinharé

⚓ MORRO DE SÃO PAULO

Morro de São Paulo is located on Ilha de Tinharé, approximately 30 miles from Salvador.

Accessible only by boat, this attractive Bahian resort village stretches along its five beautiful beaches against a backdrop of greenery.

Enjoy the charming surroundings during the week because come Friday, it is inundated with holidaymakers, tourists and the bright young things of Salvador.

They arrive by sea in *lanchas* and fast catamarans, and on the numerous passenger boats that ply the river from the town of Valença.

There are no cars in Morro de São Paulo and everybody gets around by foot in the small sandy streets that snake between the *pousadas*, bars, restaurants and numerous fashion boutiques.

Navigation

Brazilian Charts DHN No. 1100 and No. 1100A.

Leaving from Salvador, once out of Baía de Todos os Santos, steer a course of 225°, leaving the island of Itaparica a good distance away.

This is to avoid the barrier of reefs all along the coast, where the sea breaks on the rocks just above the surface of the water.

Approach

There is no difficulty in reaching Morro de São Paulo, or in entering the broad river, which is seven to 10 metres deep. However, in spring tides, a 2.5–3 knot ebb current against a northeasterly wind can make the channel choppy.

Approach from the northeast. The lighthouse and fort

Conspicuous landmarks

The tall white tower of the Morro de São Paulo lighthouse stands out clearly on the top of the hill overlooking the village, Lp(2)B.15s89m23M.

⊕ 0 • 13°22,10'S 038°54,90'W Morro de São Paulo landfall

Right at the entrance the ruins of the old fort can be seen to port, followed by a long jetty where the trip boats moor; this is the main arrival and access point to the village for tourists coming to the island.

It is possible to anchor nearby, but this anchorage is crowded, noisy and constantly disturbed by the comings and goings of the passenger boats.

It is preferable to carry on about half a mile up the river, where there is an anchorage at the Iate Clube.

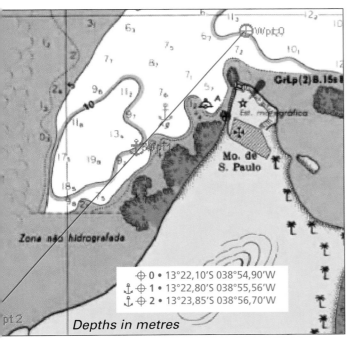

⊕ 0 • 13°22,10'S 038°54,90'W
⚓ ⊕ 1 • 13°22,80'S 038°55,56'W
⚓ ⊕ 2 • 13°23,85'S 038°56,70'W

Depths in metres

MORRO DE SÃO PAULO

Forte da Ponta, at the entrance to Morro de São Paulo

⚓ MORRO DE SÃO PAULO IATE CLUBE ANCHORAGE

Heading upriver, a few sailing boats can be seen to port on mooring buoys, opposite a wooden jetty. Anchor nearby.

⊕ 1 • 13°22,80'S 038°55,56' W near Iate Clube

A few years earlier, I had stopped over at the Iate Clube, which was a dreary-looking place with its ramshackle pontoon and unwelcoming facilities.

Then, a Frenchman called Daniel, helped by his partner Juliana, renovated the Iate Clube and transformed it into an attractive place with a well-decorated interior, a crêperie and a welcoming bar/restaurant, all in an extremely pleasant setting. Skippers and crews could avail themselves of Daniel's local knowledge and he gave out advice, addresses, an internet weather forecast and information on local sailing conditions.

Unfortunately, the Iate Clube closed down in 2006; we hope that someone can breathe new life into it soon.

Although it is a great shame that the Iate Clube has closed, the site is still one of the good anchorages at Morro de São Paulo.

Quality of moorings ***

Anchor close to the old Iate Clube with good holding in three to 4m on sand.

The anchorage is on the route of the trip boats but it is possible to anchor closer to bank in two metres of water, looking out for a few rocks close to shore. Fishing boats often anchor here overnight, waiting for the tide, and it is a good idea to leave some swinging space for when the tide turns.

In a strong northerly or northeasterly wind, the offshore swell comes into the river and on the ebb, the mooring can be choppy and uncomfortable.

In this case, it might be preferable to anchor after the first bend in the river, behind Ponta do Curral, or further upstream in front of the village of Bom Jardim.

Morro de São Paulo. The Iate Clube jetty

Facilities – Services **

Trips out of Morro are made in *lanchas*, the passenger boats that almost constantly ply the river, and leave from the jetty. There is a regular link to Gamboa and Valença every hour from 0700, and there is always a fast boat (*lancha rápida*) available for journeys.

Water Emergency supplies in the mini-markets in Morro.

Fuel None in Morro, but three miles upriver is a floating pontoon with a diesel pump at the Bom Jardim jetty.

Communications Post, telephone and internet in the main street.

Supplies ***

Basic foodstuffs in the mini-markets in Morro de São Paulo.

For more comprehensive supplies, the neighbouring village of Gamboa do Morro has two supermarkets.

Location and surroundings ***

The Iate Clube anchorage is approximately 1km from the centre of the village, which is reached by walking along the beach.

However, at high tide, part of the path is impassable but you will have to get a *lancha* to drop you off at your boat. If returning later in the evening, there is a small path through the forest that leads to the beach, near the old Iate Clube.

The anchorage is in an exceptionally beautiful setting, with the only nuisance being the passenger boats, which pass nearby, and sometimes very close to the boat.

Tourism

- The beaches of course! Completely protected by a barrier of reefs that form natural pools of clear, still water.

- The Forte da Ponta, built by the Portuguese in 1728, which is unfortunately falling to ruin through lack of maintenance.

- The path along the shore between Morro and Gamboa is a particularly pleasant walk, alternating between beaches, rocky stretches and tropical forest, where the branches of the trees hang into the sea.

- A little before the village of Gamboa, a huge rock fall has resulted in a flow of pink clay that runs along the wall; the clay is renowned for its therapeutic properties and people come to roll around and cover themselves in the mud, before jumping in the sea.

- Also unmissable is the walk up the winding path through the forest to the top of the *morro* (hill) and the lighthouse (1855) that overlooks the village, and from where you can admire the fantastic view of the beaches that stretch out around it.

After dark, Morro de São Paulo has a vibrant nightlife.

There are a great many bars and restaurants lining its sandy streets; the discos are more concentrated towards the second beach.

Morro de São Paulo. Beautiful beaches with natural pools

The Barraca do Zé beach bar

⚓ GAMBOA DO MORRO

The anchorage at Gamboa is located approximately one mile after the Iate Clube, opposite the village.

⊕ 2 • 13°23,85'S 038°56,70'W

It is a passenger and trip boat stop on a long jetty.

Quality of moorings ***

It is possible to anchor before the jetty but you will have to put up with the constant comings and goings of the passenger boats, which don't slow down as they pass through the middle of the anchored boats. There is less disruption after the jetty, and the water is calmer on this curve of the river. However, like the Iate Clube anchorage, some swell can make its way in and leave the anchorage choppy on the ebb current.

Despite this, it is a very safe place and holding is good in three to four metres of water on sand.

Facilities – Services ***

The village of Gamboa is like Morro de São Paulo with no cars and sandy streets, but without the touristy side, and prices are accordingly lower.

A little before the village of Gamboa there are cliffs of clay renowned for its therapeutic properties

There are some boat maintenance services.

Before the jetty, there is a small beach where shallow draught boats, dinghies, catamarans and motor boats can easily be pulled out between tides for a quick service or repair or to clean the hull.

Supplies ***

There are two well-stocked supermarkets in the village; gas cylinders are also available.

Location and surroundings***

The village is pleasant with several seafront restaurants, and it's easy to reach the neighbouring village of Morro de São Paulo, which is a short walk away.

⚓ BOM JARDIM

Located to the north of Gamboa, Bom Jardim is reached by going up the Canal de Taperoá in 8–10m of water.

However, be sure to stay well clear of Ponta de Bicudo, which has a large sandbank and several rocks off its tip.

⊕ 3 • 13°22,07'S 038°58,40'W Bom Jardin

Quality of moorings ***

Anchor after the jetty, where there is good holding in three to four metres of water on sand.

The anchorage is well protected from the wind, particularly from the north and northeast when it is blowing steadily.

Facilities – Services ***

The proximity of the town of Valença makes it easier to find boat maintenance services; there is a bus service that runs from 0800.

Another advantage of this stop is the opportunity to fill up with fuel at the floating pontoon shortly before the jetty.

Location and surroundings ***

Nearby, Ponta do Curral is an interesting site with its beach and the large sandbank that stretches out to the point.

Valença

Further up the Canal de Taperoá, the small town of Valença (population 12,000) is unfortunately largely inaccessible to sailing boats due to their draught. It would be possible to get close, anchor off and then continue in the tender, but the anchorage would be uncomfortable due to the constant passenger boat traffic on the Rio Una.

The best way to reach Valença is to take one of the many *lanchas* that depart from Morro and Gamboa.

Departures are hourly from 0700, by two different means: the fast *lanchas*, which take around half an hour and travel at over 30 knots, and the traditional *lanchas*, which take an hour and a half but are popular and much more pleasant.

Valença is one of the liveliest towns in the region and has a great deal of commercial activity with a vast market along the Rio Una.

It has a marked seafaring tradition and the port offers almost every boat service imaginable.

It is also an important centre for the construction of traditional Bahian *pirogas* (dugout canoes) and *escunas* (sailing boats).

The town is a noisy, bustling hive of activity with something out of the ordinary happening on every street corner.

The 17th century church of Nossa Senhora do Amparo dominates the landscape from its position on the hill outside the town.

Cairú

To the southwest of Ilha de Tinharé is Ilha de Cairú, with the small village of Cairú.

It is said to be the first village built in 1501 after the discovery of Brazil by the Portuguese.

Ilha de Cairú can be reached by sailing boat by going up the Canal de Taperoá, which extends into the Rio Cairú.

Navigation

Leaving Gamboa do Morro, head up the Canal de Taperoá towards Bom Jardim, staying in the middle of the channel.

Then head towards:

⊕ 4 • 13°22,33'S 039°00,10'W North of Ilha dos Manguinhos

After Bom Jardim, cross to the left-hand section of the channel in depths of 6m, to avoid a sandbank that stretches 1.5–2 miles along the right-hand half of the channel.

Then steer towards Ponta Galeão, where the church on the hill stands out as a conspicuous landmark,

⊕ 5 • 13°23,76'S 039°02,20'W Galeão

Galeão is a small fishing village and makes a pleasant stop.

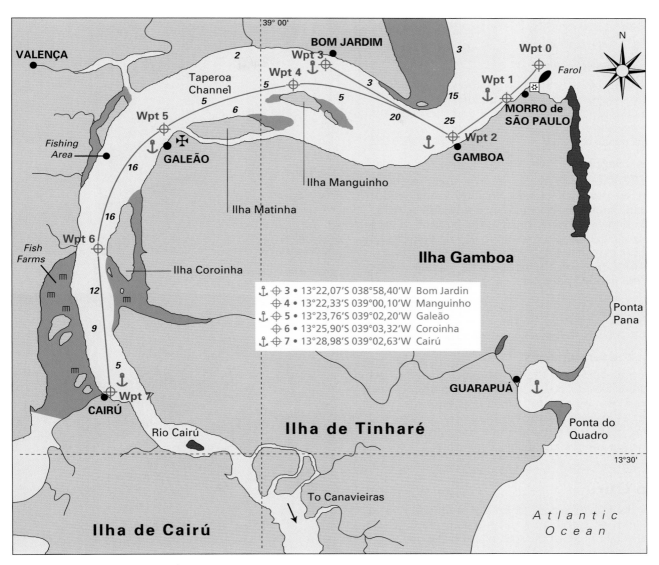

ARQUIPELAGO DE TINHARÉ

The church dominates the entire landscape, and from the top of the hill there is a magnificent view from Morro de São Paulo right round to Valença.

Anchor upstream of the jetty, where holding is good in four metres of water on sand and mud.

For over one mile after the village of Galeão, watch out for the numerous fishing nets stretched right across the river (float visible on the surface).

Then continue in the middle of the channel in up to 16m of water until abeam the tip of Ilha Coroinha.

⊕ 6 • 13°25,90'S 039°03,32'W Coroinha

Once past the island, with the mouth of the Rio Tanengo to port, the small village of Cairú can be seen in the distance and is reached through waters that gradually become shallower to depths of three metres.

The channel is very wide at this point, but the entire right-hand half is shallow and littered with fish traps. It is therefore wise to stay on the left-hand side, where the water is deepest.

The completely calm anchorage at Cairú

Anchorage

⊕ **7** • 13°28,98'S 039°02,63'W Cairú

Quality of moorings ***

Anchor shortly after the floating pontoon, where holding is good in 3–4m of water on sand and mud.

The anchorage is completely calm and sheltered from all wind directions.

There is no current.

Facilities – Services

Few services in the village. If you have technical problems on the boat, talk to Vivaldo, a boat builder with a ready smile who may or may not be able to help.

He also knows the river well and the position of every sandbank and submerged rock up to Ilha de Boipeba and the southern exit channel.

His workshop is on the bank of the channel, 500m south of the floating pontoon.

Supplies

Some supplies available in the village, which has a bakery and a fairly well-stocked supermarket.

Location and surroundings

This is a neat village, at the top of which there are two churches side by side, Nossa Senhora do Rosario, built in 1610, and the Convento São Francisco, the third monastery to be built in Brazil in 1654.

A young guide will tell you about the construction of the monastery and the life of its occupants.

Rio do Cairú

The Rio do Cairú snakes along the south of Ilha de Tinharé and its entrance is accessible from Cairú to shallow draught boats at the start of the rising tide.

The river passes the small fishing villages of Canavieiras and Carvalho, and then empties into the sea approximately fifteen miles further south. This itinerary requires in-depth knowledge of the river and riverbed, which is littered with rocks.

Barra do Carvalho at the river exit is a passage between two large shoals of sand and reefs, and caution is required when approaching this area. Account must be taken of the tide, the wind and the weather conditions at sea, as these can be very different from those on the river, which is completely sheltered.

It can be a great help to have the assistance of a local boatman for this passage, as long as he is reliable; bear in mind that local fishermen, who generally use dugout canoes, do not always have much concept of the draught of a sailing boat.

Caution is therefore recommended when taking this itinerary.

Boat builder Vivaldo

Bending planking for *escunas*

Ilha de Boipeba

To the south of Ilha de Tinharé is Ilha de Boipeba, with the village of Velha Boipeba on the northeastern tip of the island.

The eastern part of the island is fringed with around twenty kilometres of deserted beaches, protected by rocks and coral reefs that form natural pools at low tide.

The beaches of Moreré and Coreira are without doubt among the most beautiful beaches on the Costa do Dendê.

Passenger boats regularly call at Cairú and go on to Canavieiras and Ilha de Boipeba.

A convenient way to reach the island is to take the *lancha* that leaves Valença at 1200 every day and comes up the Canal de Tinharé, stopping in at Cairú, where you can join the boat at around 1230.

The village is very lively in the summer season and has several *pousadas*, as well as numerous beach-side bars and restaurants serving excellent fish dishes.

⚓ ENSEADA DE GARAPUÁ

Enseada de Guarapuá is located approximately eight miles to the south of Morro de São Paulo.

The cove shelters a small fishing village and is encircled by a beautiful beach lined with coconut palms. In calm seas, there is no particular problem on entry and the channel is easily identifiable from offshore.

Navigation

Brazilian Chart DHN No. 1100.

On leaving Morro de São Paulo, stay well clear of the lighthouse point, navigating 1.5–2 miles to the east, in order to avoid the Caitás reefs, on which the sea breaks violently, then steer a course of 170°.

The shoals make the sea rough near the coast and taking a route in 15–20m of water makes the passage more comfortable until you are abeam Ponta Paná.

⊕ **8** • 13°27,00'S 038°51,70'W Ponta Paná

Then steer a course towards ⊕**9**, which is located opposite the entrance to the cove.

⊕ **9** • 13°28,94'S 038°53,00'W Guarapuá entrance

The small village of Guarapuá can be seen in the background; head for the channel, which is clearly visible between two rows of reefs on which the sea breaks.

The channel is wide and in the cove it is calm with no current or undertow. A few fishing boats can be seen to starboard on mooring buoys; anchor near these.

⊕ **10** • 13°28,42'S 038°54,48'W Guarapuá anchorage

Quality of moorings ***

The mooring is generally well protected and undisturbed by the swell, but it is open to easterly and southeasterly winds.

Holding is good in 2–4m of water on sand.

Facilities – Services

None in Guarapuá.

Supplies *

Essentially fish and fruit.

Location and surroundings ***

Excellent location in a pleasant setting, with a long, practically deserted beach on the edge of a forest of coconut palms.

The village is very small and there are a few restaurants beside the beach serving good fish, shrimp and shellfish dishes.

A good catch at Guarapuá

Guarapuá, entrance to the bay

The village of Guarapuá

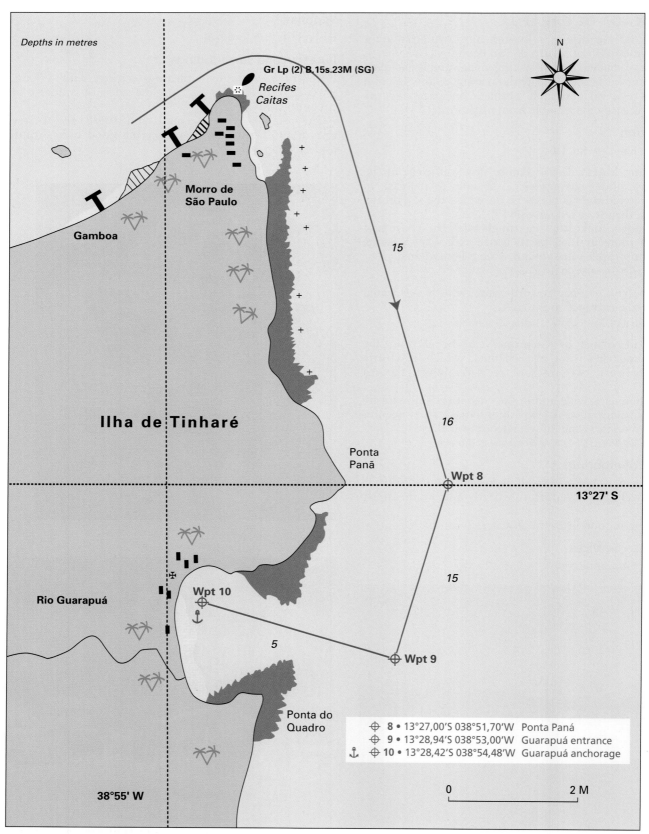

Depths in metres

Gr Lp (2) B.15s.23M (SG)

Recifes
Caitas

N

Morro de
São Paulo

Gamboa

15

Ilha de Tinharé

16

Ponta
Panã

Wpt 8

13°27' S

15

Rio Guarapuá

Wpt 10

5

Wpt 9

Ponta do
Quadro

8 • 13°27,00'S 038°51,70'W	Ponta Paná
9 • 13°28,94'S 038°53,00'W	Guarapuá entrance
10 • 13°28,42'S 038°54,48'W	Guarapuá anchorage

38°55' W

0   2 M

ENSEADA DE GUARAPUÀ

Baía de Camamu

The exploration of Baía de Camamu and the start of the construction of the town go back as far as the 16th century, very soon after the discovery of Brazil.

The town of Camamu quickly became one of the most prosperous in the region, thanks to the bounty of its particularly fertile soil, which produced large quantities of basic commodities such as manioc flour, sugar cane and wood for building houses, boats and dugout canoes.

Today, part of the region has kept its traditions intact, as the town is far from the urban centres and part of the archipelago has no road links; agriculture, fishing and other traditional activities still take place.

For sailors, it is a calm, completely protected bay, with varied anchorages and unusual destinations against a backdrop of coconut palms and mangroves.

Tourism hasn't really reached Camamu yet and the people of the islands are certainly among the most welcoming in the Bahia region.

Here, they are concerned with naturalness, simplicity, hospitality and the pleasure of giving, and giving everything – drink, food, friendship and more.

Navigation

Brazilian Charts DHN No. 1100 and No. 1131.

The entrance to Baía de Camamu is located approximately 35 miles south of Morro de São Paulo, on a low stretch of coast without any marked geographical features.

On leaving Morro de São Paulo, stay well clear of the point, navigating 1.5–2 miles to the east, in order to avoid the shoals and the Caitás reefs, on which the sea breaks violently.

Then steer a course to:

⊕ 0 • 13°49,15′S 038°51,00′W Camamu landfall

This route, in depths of 30 to 40 metres, makes the passage a little more comfortable, as the shallower waters near the coast make the sea choppy.

Approach

Conspicuous landmarks

The lighthouse of Taipus, a tall tower with red and white horizontal stripes, can be seen from a long way offshore Lp(3)B.15s76m23M.

The white tower on Ponta Muta at the entrance to Baía de Camamu

Entrance to Baía de Camamu. Steer a course to Ponta da Pedreira, on the north of Ilha Grande de Camamu

Coming from the north, the reefs of Sororocuçu, with the sea breaking on them, and the tower on Ilha de Quiepe are clearly visible from offshore and are left well to starboard.

To port at the entrance to the bay, Ponta Mutá has a small white tower topped with a green light Lp.V.3s11m11M.

From the south, come along the coast a good distance off and steer towards ⊕2, near Ponta Mutá.

Tide and currents

The tide is semi-diurnal with a mean level of 1.1m above the chart datum.

The current is generally 2–3 knots, but can reach five knots on the ebb in spring tides. Under these conditions and with a northeasterly wind (prevailing wind), the entrance to the bay can form a particularly choppy bar.

The ebb current can be felt around one hour after high tide; it is particularly strong in the second hour and then decreases until low tide. The flood current starts around one hour after low tide and becomes strong in the second hour.

The best time to cross the bar is at the start of the rising tide, in order to take advantage of the flood current and have a clearer view of the reefs just on the surface.

⊕ 1 • 13°50,74′S 038°53,95′W Entrance to bay

Steer a course of 242° to:

⊕ 2 • 13°52,00′S 038°56,39′W Near Ponta Muta

This waypoint allows you to monitor your route and note any drift due to the current, which carries you towards Ponta Mutá.

Then continue towards:

⊕ 3 • 13°53,40′S 038°59,00′W Campinho approach

In practical terms, from ⊕1, go through the entrance of Baía de Camamu on a direct heading of 242° on Ponta da Pedreira, which is clearly visible from offshore to the north of Ilha Grande de Camamu.

Precautions

To port on entering the bay, the reefs of Pedra Cioba and Banco das Taipavas, on which the sea breaks, can be seen at low tide but are covered from half-tide onwards.

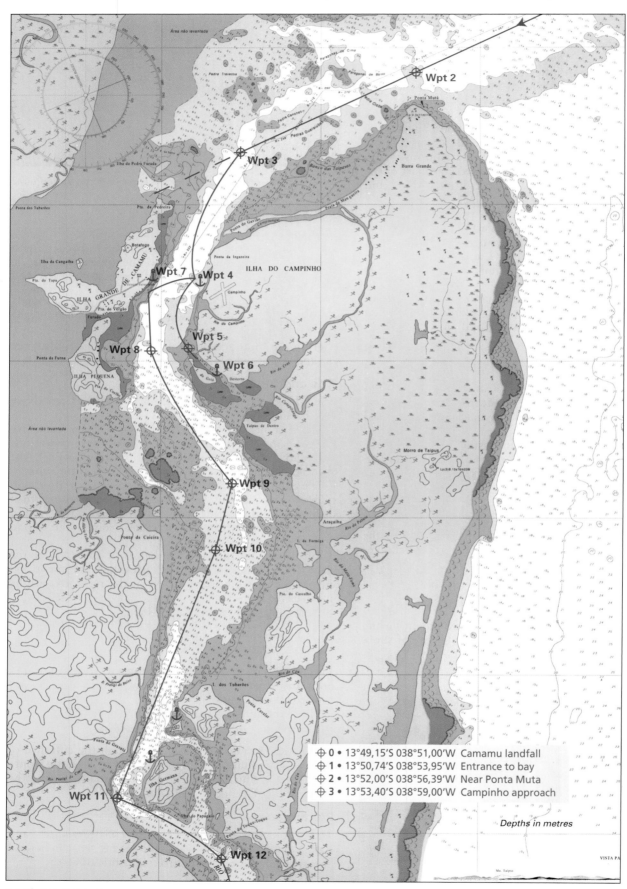

⊕ 0 • 13°49,15'S 038°51,00'W Camamu landfall
⊕ 1 • 13°50,74'S 038°53,95'W Entrance to bay
⊕ 2 • 13°52,00'S 038°56,39'W Near Ponta Muta
⊕ 3 • 13°53,40'S 038°59,00'W Campinho approach

Depths in metres

BAIÁ DE CAMAMU

⚓ BARRA GRANDE

This is a small seaside resort located to port at the entrance to Baía de Camamu, and the only place really affected by tourism. The village is no less pleasant for this, and its sandy lanes are lined with attractive houses and a number of nicely decorated *pousadas*, and everything visitors might need to fully enjoy the wonderful landscapes of the peninsula is available.

Quality of moorings *

This is the first anchorage on entering Baía de Camamu, but it is far from the best.

The mooring is exposed to northerly and northeasterly on-shore winds, and the ocean swell comes in to the anchorage, making it rough and very uncomfortable.

A more sensible solution is to avoid this anchorage and go to Barra Grande in a tender or passenger boat from the anchorage of Campinho (*see Campinho, Location and surroundings*).

Facilities – Services **

Transport to the other islands and to Camamu.

Camamu passenger boats:
- The normal *lanchas* run from 0540 every morning from the Barra Grande jetty.
- The fast lanchas run on request by calling *Camamu Adventura* on Channel 16 and then switching to Channel 6 or 10.

Telephones and Internet service in the village.
No boat maintenance services.

Supplies **

There are several mini-markets and bakeries in the village, as well as a variety of small shops and boutiques.

Location and surroundings

Tourism

Barra Grande is located on Ponta Mutá and has two beaches, a large one inside the bay and another on the ocean side that is particularly worth visiting.

This is the Costa do Dendê, made up of mile after mile of wide beaches fringed with coconut palms. The beaches are protected by a coral reef which, at low tide, forms a series of natural pools of warm, clear water such as Praia de Taipus da Fora.

Further south there are two large lakes on the seashore, Lagoa Azul near Taipus lighthouse and Lagoa do Cassange; both are just 100m from the ocean.

There are no metalled roads here and these beaches, together with the entire region, can only be visited in off-road vehicles, pick-ups, motorbikes and other 4x4s, on sandy tracks that are often pot-holed and in very poor condition. If you have a bad back, avoid it!

All along the route there are traditional restaurants, bars, *pousadas*, etc.

For information about transport and tourist routes, consult the travel agencies or tourist office in the village.

The jetty at Barra Grande

Ilha do Campinho

Ilha do Campinho is the first island in Baía de Camamu, and is also one of the most pleasant and unusual.

It is located at the entrance to the bay and is a good starting point for visiting the other islands. It is on the route of the *lanchas* that run regularly between Barra Grande and Camamu.

There are two mooring options:
- the Campinho anchorage,
- the Sapinho anchorage.

Approach

From ⊕3 a course of 199° leads to Ponta da Ingazeira 1.5 miles away, and an old jetty, the concrete piles of which are easy to see and are the unattractive vestiges of an abandoned port project.

After Ponta da Ingazeira there is an anchorage to port.
⊕ 4 • 13°55,00'S 38°59,41'W Campinho anchorage

⚓ CAMPINHO

Quality of moorings ***

The water is completely calm and holding is good in 4–5m on sand and mud.

Northerly and northeasterly winds can generate an unpleasant chop, especially on the falling tide. Nearer the shore, this nuisance is slightly alleviated by the presence of a counter-current, as long as the draught of the boat is such that you can get in close enough.

Note

The old charts took into account a project to build a port at Campinho and showed an entrance channel marked with beacons; all of the beacons have been removed and the project abandoned.
There are no opportunities to moor alongside in Baía de Camamu, but there are several anchorages.

The Campinho anchorage

Facilities – Services **

There are few facilities and no services.

Passenger boats pass regularly and connect Barra Grande and Camamu, where there are several services such as a bank and communications (*see Camamu*).

Times: Normal *lancha*: leaves Campinho at 0540 in the morning, returning at 1130. Journey time to Camamu: One hour 30 minutes.

Fast *lancha*: call *Camamu Adventura* on VHF Channel 16; they will give you times and will collect you from your boat. Journey time: 30 minutes.

Water On the pontoon of Pousada Apoio Náutica (R$25 for 500 litres) or from the locals in an emergency.

Gas A small depot sells 13kg cylinders in the village.

Supplies **

There is very little in Campinho, with just a small mini-market selling a few basics and bread, but there is a wide variety of fruit all over the island which, most of the time, the locals will kindly give you for nothing.

Location and surroundings ***

The anchorage is near Barra Grande, the smart tourist resort just three miles away, which you can reach by *lancha* or tender in calm weather (however, watch out for the current and two large sandbanks on which the waves can break). You can also go by foot along a small path through the forest (crossing the river in a dugout canoe).

Opposite the anchorage, less than one mile to the west, Ilha Grande de Camamu can also be reached by tender.

The friendly atmosphere on Ilha de Campinho, particularly with the locals near the anchorage, is enough in itself to create the special feeling you get here.

You might meet a couple of Brazilian yachtsmen, Breno and Lao, who decided to live on the island and have built their house opposite their moored boat.

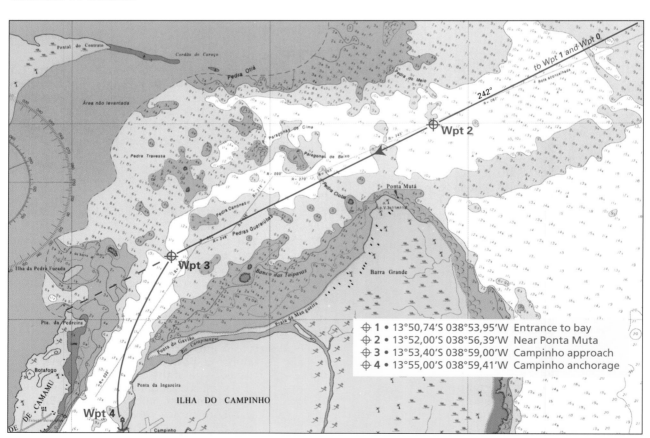

⊕ 1 • 13°50,74'S 038°53,95'W Entrance to bay
⊕ 2 • 13°52,00'S 038°56,39'W Near Ponta Muta
⊕ 3 • 13°53,40'S 038°59,00'W Campinho approach
⊕ 4 • 13°55,00'S 038°59,41'W Campinho anchorage

CAMPINHO

Welcome to Campinho (strange, it's alcoholic fruit juice...)

Pousada Lotus, Campinho

Then there are Aurora and Onilia, two sisters who were born on the island over 75 years ago and have never left. Onilia knew the famous French author Antoine de Saint-Exupéry, creator of the *Little Prince*, who stayed near her house by an old landing strip; she talks of him emotionally, wiping away a tear with the back of her hand, and still feels great nostalgia (*saudade*) for the period. Nearby, Sonhia will welcome you to her *pousada*, the Lotus; the walls of her restaurant are lined with miniature sails that she embroiders with the name of your boat in her spare time. Make sure you sign her log!

Campinho, the jetty at Pousada Apoio Náutica

Further along, Apoio Náutica Vida Marinha, which can be recognised by its large pontoon jutting out, is a beautifully-kept *pousada* run by Juvencio and his lovely daughter Julie.

They extend a warm welcome in pleasant surroundings, with excellent food, a huge breakfast and several other services (showers, telephone, internet connection and water for your tanks). Passenger boats to Camamu stop at the pontoon.

Pousada Apoio Náutica
☼ (73) 3655 5158
Email juvenciomendes@car.ba.gov.br

⚓ SAPINHO

This anchorage is on the south of Ilha do Campinho; the location is charming, the mooring is very calm and, for lovers of Bahian specialities, there are two good restaurants on either side of the anchorage.

Access is through a narrow channel between Ilha do Campinho and Ilha do Goió.

However, watch out for two sandbanks that obstruct the entrance to the channel; despite the apparent width of the channel at high tide, the passage is relatively narrow.

From the anchorage at ⊕4, go along Ilha do Campinho, staying well clear in around five metres of water.

After less than one mile, the small Rio do Sapinho can be seen to port, straddled by a wooden bridge, and opposite, the northern tip of Ilha do Goió. The water depth decreases rapidly at the northern entrance to the river and at the very tip of Ilha do Goió, where again the sandbank protrudes a long way into the passage.

⊕ **5** • 13°55,85'S 038°59,62'W

⊕5 is in between the two sandbanks, approximately on the centre line of the southeast oriented channel.

Sail on the left-hand side of the channel in depths of three to four metres, along Ilha do Campinho.

A little distance away to port, the small jetty at Sapinho can be seen; go past it and anchor a little further on to starboard...

⊕ **6** • 13°56,03'S 038°59,46'W Sapinho anchorage

Baía de Camamu: the mouth of the Rio Saphinho

Sapinho, the bridge over the river

Anchor in the right-hand section of the channel, where holding is good in 4m of water on sand.

Quality of moorings ****

The mooring is excellent and well-sheltered; only easterly to southerly winds can cause a slight chop.

Little current in the channel.

In strong northerly or northeasterly winds, it is far preferable to the Campinho anchorage.

Facilities – Services *

There is very little in Sapinho, but a passenger boat for Camamu stops at the pontoon of the *pousada Sapinho* at 0600.

Supplies *

Nothing; possibly water in an emergency from the locals.

The island is also populated by a large number of crabs (*gaiamu*), which are a beautiful blue colour.

The *gaiamu* is a land crab that moves with surprising speed. Watch out for their sharp claws! They are delicious grilled over a wood fire.

Location and surroundings ****

The small hamlet of Sapinho, which has remained true to tradition, can be reached from the anchorage. There is a pleasant walk between the small houses built along a sandy track that winds through greenery to the small bridge over the river.

Ilha do Goió, which is just opposite, can also be reached from this anchorage.

Ilha do Goió

Approximately one mile to the south of the Campinho anchorage, opposite the hamlet of Sapinho, is the small Ilha de Goió, a narrow stretch of sand fringed with several lovely beaches.

There are few buildings on the island, with just a restaurant located on the northern tip. At the southeastern end of the island there is a beautiful white sandy beach shaded by coconut palms.

Anchorage

This is the same anchorage as the Sapinho anchorage, ⊕ 6, described in the previous entry.

Land crab (*gaiamu*)

The Goió – Sapinho anchorage

Ilha do Goió. The northern tip of the island

Ilha Grande de Camamu

Ilha Grande de Camamu is located opposite Ponta da Ingazeira, less then one mile from Ilha do Campinho.

A protruding jetty can be seen on arrival at the island, and it is possible to anchor slightly to the south of it.

⊕ 7 • 13°55,00'S 038°39,02'W Ilha Grande

Near the jetty is a plant that processes barite, a very dense rock used in petroleum exploration, and not far from there, the village stretches along the shore; it has a small landing stage where the passenger boats serving the island stop. There are a few pleasant inlets on the northeastern coast and a good walk to Ponta da Pedreira, surrounded by rocks.

Ilha Grande, the passenger boat jetty

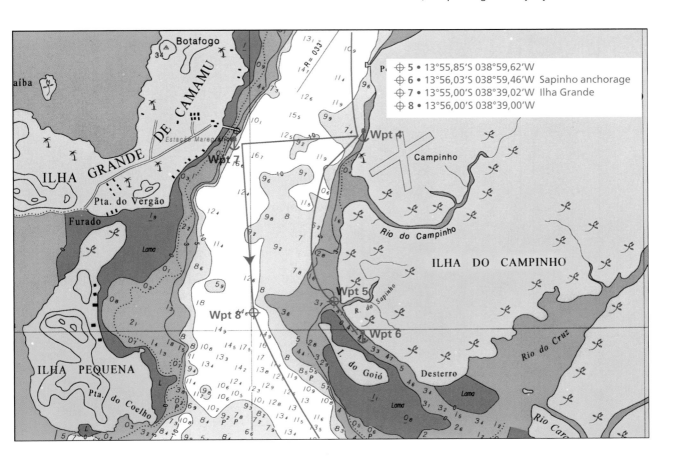

⊕ 5 • 13°55,85'S 038°59,62'W
⊕ 6 • 13°56,03'S 038°59,46'W Sapinho anchorage
⊕ 7 • 13°55,00'S 038°39,02'W Ilha Grande
⊕ 8 • 13°56,00'S 038°39,00'W

Ilha de Pedra Furada, which means 'pierced stone'

Ilha de Pedra Furada

This island, located to the north of Ilha Grande de Camamu, is one of the smallest in Baía de Camamu, but it is full of charm, which is a good thing for its lucky owners.

It is defended by a barrier of particularly dangerous rocks, which are covered as soon as the tide starts to rise. There is also a strong current in the narrow passage between Ponta da Pedreira and the island.

The best way to visit the island is by tender at half-tide, from the Campinho anchorage.

Watch out for the submerged rocks on the southeastern side and proceed cautiously to land on the island.

Visitors can cross the island for a contribution of R$1, which goes to an environmental protection agency for the conservation of the island.

It is an interesting site with a peculiar chaos of rocks; some form little caverns and others arches, creating a bizarre landscape.

Camamu, view of the town

Camamu

The town of Camamu is located approximately 12 miles to the southwest of the entrance to the bay of the same name, and is reached by going round Ilha Pequena to the south of Ponta do Coelho.

Beyond Ilha Pequena the waters are uncharted, and the town is reached through a maze of channels fringed with thick mangroves.

The channel at the entrance to the town is relatively wide, but the bottom is littered with rocks and sandbanks. Only a narrow passage is practicable for shallow draught boats. It is preferable to seek help from a local boatman to reach Camamu.

The jetty on the right is only for the use of passenger boats and fast *lanchas*, which jostle around the single floating pontoon.

It is possible to anchor on the left-hand side of the river, just before the São Jorge boatyard.

However, the simplest way to visit Camamu is to take a passenger boat, leaving from Barra Grande, Campinho or Sapinho at 0500.

If you call on the VHF the previous evening, the boat will collect you from and take you back to your yacht.

Facilities – Services **

There are excellent road links from Camamu, and there are buses to Salvador, Ilhéus, Porto Seguro and other destinations.

All of the administrative services are available in town, including the police, the public health department, Banco do Brasil, the Post Office, internet access, etc.

For boat maintenance services, it is best to contact the São Jorge boatyard on the opposite bank to the town centre.

There is also a small machine shop on the channel, and an auto electrician at the top of town.

There are a number of boutiques along the channel, as well as a chandlery and fishing tackle shop.

Supplies ***

Supplies can be obtained easily. There is a market in the town centre, together with several very well-stocked large supermarkets. One of the village children will carry your shopping bags from the supermarket to the jetty for a small tip.

Location and surroundings

Tourism

The town is lively during the week, but the main event is the Saturday morning market.

The entire population of all of the villages in the region converges on the town to buy, sell, exchange and barter.

They come from all over, on foot, on horseback, by donkey, by boat, and flock to the enormous market square. There's no need to ask the way, just let the crowd take you there!

There is a flour market where the locals will guide you through their huge range of products, letting you examine, touch, smell and taste flour, semolina, manioc, *farofa* and more, most of which are, according to the signs, blessed by God himself.

The doorway of the building that houses the meat market is decorated with two enormous cattle heads, oozing blood and looking at you curiously.

There are no flies on the displays of meat and the cleanliness is exemplary; God is also omnipresent here for blessings.

Outside is the fruit and vegetable market, a colourful, perfumed feast for the eyes. Everything is attractively laid out, in rows, pyramids, towers, arranged in woven baskets or on coloured fabric – you'll want to take everything with you, including the vendor's smile!

On the other side of the road are spices and *dendê* oil, shrimps, fish and dried meat – all the ingredients for making Bahian specialities. A little further on are the clothes, with brightly-coloured shirts and t-shirts, shorts, hats, shoes, etc.

If you want to discover a piece of old Brazil, make sure you visit the Saturday morning market in Camamu!

The market; Bahian style tripe

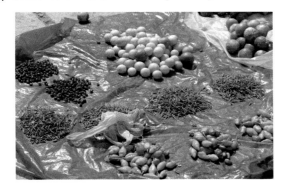

A colourful display

Dried meat on sale at the market

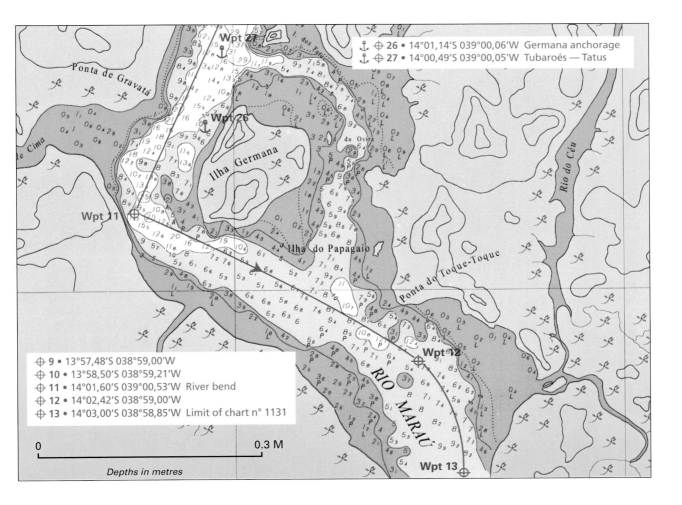

⚓ ⊕ **26** • 14°01,14'S 039°00,06'W Germana anchorage
⚓ ⊕ **27** • 14°00,49'S 039°00,05'W Tubaroés — Tatus

⊕ **9** • 13°57,48'S 038°59,00'W
⊕ **10** • 13°58,50'S 038°59,21'W
⊕ **11** • 14°01,60'S 039°00,53'W River bend
⊕ **12** • 14°02,42'S 038°59,00'W
⊕ **13** • 14°03,00'S 038°58,85'W Limit of chart n° 1131

0   0.3 M

Depths in metres

⚓ MARAÚ

15 miles from the Campinho anchorage, at the south of Baía de Camamu, is the very traditional village of Maraú. Although modest in size, with a population of 1,100, the village is the administrative centre of the region.

It is located on a narrow strip of land between the river and the ocean and the people travel along roads or tracks that are often in very poor condition.

The village has retained its charm, with a large church tower dominating the landscape.

One curiosity is a giant fresco painted on a wall around fifteen metres high facing the river, showing some of the Brazilian fauna.

The inhabitants of the village live as they always have, peacefully, far from the bustle of modern life and tourism, and nothing seems able to disrupt this daily routine.

The main activity is fishing from dugout canoes using traditional methods, in an inextricable maze of tiny channels deep in the mangroves.

The anchorage at Maraú

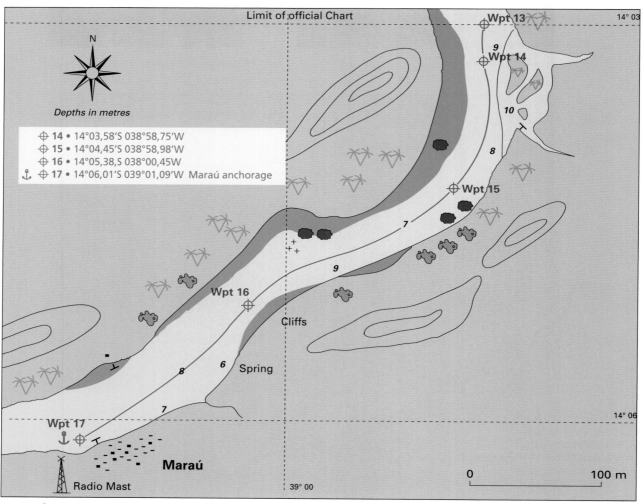

MARAÚ

Navigation

Brazilian Chart DHN No. 1131.

See plan page 93.

(Chart No. 1131 ends at latitude 14°03,00'S and the region is uncharted beyond this point).

Set off from the anchorage at Ilha do Campinho or Ilha Grande de Camamu at the start of the rising tide and head south to ⊕8.

⊕ **8** • 13°56,00'S 038°39,00'W

Then steer a course of 148° towards:

⊕ **9** • 13°57,48'S 038°59,00'W

and then towards:

⊕ **10** • 13°58,50'S 038°59,21'W

Ilha dos Tubarões, Ilha dos Tatus and Ilha Germana can be seen to port.

These islands have two attractive anchorages, but it is better to take advantage of the flood current to go directly to Maraú and stop at the islands on the way back.

Steering a course of 203°, a passage can be seen in the distance narrowing between Ponta de Gravata and Ilha Germana:

⊕ **11** • 14°01,60'S 039°00,53'W   River bend

Continue on a course of 122° towards:

⊕ **12** • 14°02,42'S 038°59,00'W

Chart DHN No. 1131 ends at:

⊕ **13** • 14°03,00'S 038°58,85'W   Limit of chart No. 1131

Beyond this point, caution is the order of the day as there is no chart for this area.

After ⊕13, you enter a long bend and it is best to sail on the left-hand side of the river towards waypoints:

⊕ **14** • 14°03,58'S 038°58,75'W
⊕ **15** • 14°04,45'S 038°58,98'W
⊕ **16** • 14°05,38'S 038°00,45'W

Anchorage

It is possible to anchor near the floating pontoon:

⚓ ⊕ **17** • 14°06,01'S 039°01,09'W   Maraú anchorage

Quality of moorings ****

Excellent, with very good shelter and little current. Holding is very good in 4–5m of water on sand and mud.

Facilities – Services **

Post Office and telephone in Rua Beira Mar, which runs along the river.

For work or repairs on the boat, there is little available in the village; however, there is a mechanic (*badú*) and an auto electrician (*liliano*) who might be able to help with emergency repairs.

Water Tanks can be filled at the pontoon with water from the village, which is apparently treated; ask Ivó, who is in charge of the town pontoon.

Gas Sold in 13kg cylinders opposite the covered market, or at the top of Rua Lambada, in a small warehouse just before the chapel.

Maraú. Moored alongside with the fresco behind

Supplies **

The market is located on the riverbank and is limited to fruit, fish and crabs (*siri*), which are abundant in Maraú.

There are three mini-markets in the village where supplies are limited to a few basic products, and a bakery in Rua Lambada.

Location and surroundings ***

The anchorage is very calm, and only the music broadcast at high volume by the speakers at the market disturbs the quiet of this peaceful town.

The village is located on the Maraú peninsula, near the coast and the large tourist beaches, but the means of transport to reach it are very limited, on sandy, poorly-maintained tracks.

Playing dominoes

⚓ CACHOEIRA DE TREMENBÉ

If you want to head off the beaten track, leave the Rio Maraú and point your boat towards the waterfall at Tremembé, around six miles to the south of the village.

Let the boat thread its way through the mangrove roots and, as you round a bend, you will see the waterfall nestling amongst the greenery.

This is a site to visit before tourism takes over (facilities are being built)!

Warning

Access to the waterfall is strictly for shallow draught boats, dinghies, catamarans or motor boats only. It requires in-depth knowledge of the river in order to avoid the sandbanks and rocks that litter the route.

A series of waypoints can be used to reach it, but take into account the accuracy of the position of the GPS and keep a careful eye on the depth sounder at all times.

If you don't want to take your boat on this itinerary, you can always moor on the wider part of the river less than a mile from the waterfall and visit it in the tender.

Navigation

No DHN chart.

The best time to visit Tremembé is to leave the Maraú anchorage at the start of the rising tide.

Take into account the tide time lag, which is at least two hours behind the Salvador tide table (check locally).

To reach the waterfall, we were assisted by a local fisherman named Geraldo*, who guided us along the itinerary (*see Note opposite*).

From Maraú, steer towards the point that can be seen to port, opposite the Pedras da Baleia rocks, noticeable on the opposite bank.

⊕ 18 • 14°06,45′S 039°02,67′W Abeam Pedra da Baleia

Then head towards the other bank in order to avoid a shoal to port, covered from half-tide

⊕ 19 • 14°06,27′S 039°03,48′W Abeam Pedra Mole passing on the left-hand side, near the rocks

Then continue to:

⊕ 21 • 14°08,00′S 039°04,72′W

and:

⊕ 22 • 14°08,65′S 039°04,64′W

You can anchor near this waypoint and continue in the tender, as the channel leading to the waterfall is shallow and only accessible to shallow draught boats.

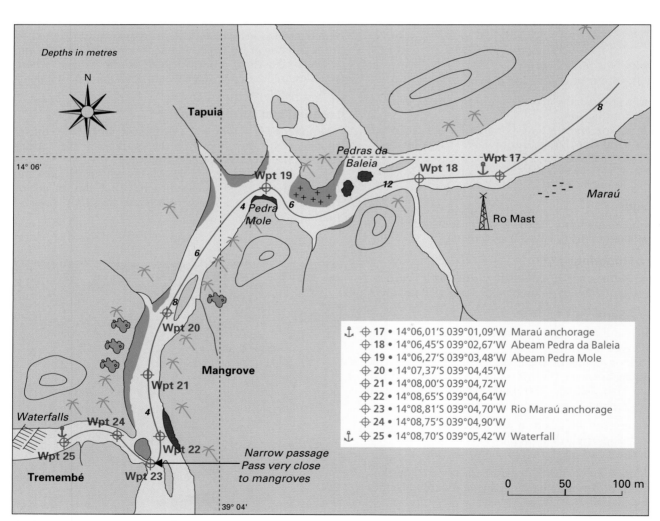

⚓ ⊕ 17 • 14°06,01′S 039°01,09′W Maraú anchorage
⊕ 18 • 14°06,45′S 039°02,67′W Abeam Pedra da Baleia
⊕ 19 • 14°06,27′S 039°03,48′W Abeam Pedra Mole
⊕ 20 • 14°07,37′S 039°04,45′W
⊕ 21 • 14°08,00′S 039°04,72′W
⊕ 22 • 14°08,65′S 039°04,64′W
⊕ 23 • 14°08,81′S 039°04,70′W Rio Maraú anchorage
⊕ 24 • 14°08,75′S 039°04,90′W
⚓ ⊕ 25 • 14°08,70′S 039°05,42′W Waterfall

CACHOEIRA DE TREMEMBÉ

An itinerary littered with rocks just above the surface of the water

The access channel

Access to Tremembé waterfall

To access the channel leading to the waterfall, go round the south end of a small islet. Enter a narrow passage, keeping close to the port-side bank, right against the mangroves, to stay in the deepest part of the channel.

We entered the channel on a rising half-tide, in spring tides, and the depth sounder showed 1.3m for most of the journey, our draught with centreboard raised being 1.1m.

⊕ 23 • 14°08,81'S 039°04,70'W Rio Maraú anchorage

Proceed slowly, watching out for the mangrove roots, which can jut out into the passage, and then turn to starboard, towards the opposite bank and a small stone breakwater.

⊕ 24 • 14°08,75'S 039°04,90'W

Coming out of a bend, a small overhang and an isolated palm tree can be seen on the bank. The mangrove then gives way to forest and the waterfall can be seen a little further on.

Anchor on the left-hand side near a small jetty, around 30m from the waterfall, in 2m on mud.

⊕ 25 • 14°08,70'S 039°05,42'W Waterfall

Maraú. Tremembé waterfall

Ilha Germana – Ilha dos Tubaroes – Ilha dos Tatus

These islands are located between the anchorages at Maraú and Campinho.

There are several anchorages in surroundings of tropical forest and small beaches.

Some mooring options:

⊕ 26 • 14°01,14'S 039°00,06'W Germana anchorage

Anchor in three metres of water on sand.

⊕ 27 • 14°00,49'S 039°00,05'W Tubaroés – Tatus

Anchor in two metres of water on sand, with deserted beach fringed with tropical vegetation.

Note

* Our guide Geraldo lives in the village of Maraú. He is an endearing man of around 60, with 10 children; he was born in Maraú and has spent his life on the river, where he fished from a dugout canoe to feed his large family.

Geraldo knows the tiniest details of the river better than anyone, the type of holding, the dangerous passages, the currents and, of course, the tide times and water depths, without ever having seen a tide table. His air of calm and the assurance with which he talked to me about the river, its dangerous areas, rocks and sandbanks, inspired me with great confidence. What's more, he doesn't smoke or drink and says very little – in short, he's the ideal autopilot, as he doesn't use electricity either!

Joking aside, I have the greatest respect for Geraldo and would recommend him highly to anyone who wants to make this trip.

You can ask for him or find him on the quay at Maraú, watching over his canoe or preparing for a day's fishing: Geraldo Alcibiades da Conceição.

Tremembé waterfall, manoeuvring close to the mangrove

Rio das Contas

⚓ ITACARÉ

25 miles to the south of Baía de Camamu, Rio das Contas shelters the small town of Itacaré, a charming stop on the Costa do Cacáo.

Due to its geographical location, with an entrance that is almost invisible from offshore, in days of old Rio das Contas was used as a hiding place for pirate ships, and it was said that fabulous treasures were buried beneath the waters of Itacaré.

This was doubtless true, but times have changed and pirates no longer come into Rio das Contas; the treasures of Itacaré are the beautiful beaches that stretch to the north of the river and especially to the south of the village.

Itacaré has branched out into tourism, offering experiences in the great outdoors and numerous routes through the immense forest surrounding it, still intact and with a number of waterfalls.

It is also one of the best surf spots in Brazil.

Despite the large number of tourists and the very cosmopolitan clientele wandering its lively streets, the village has retained its charm and the seafront area of the small bay has kept up its traditional fishing and boat repair activities.

Navigation

Brazilian Chart DHN No. 1100.

On leaving Baía de Camamu, stay well clear of Ponta Mutá, where the sea is always rough near the shoals that surround it, and steer a direct course of 192° in depths of around 25m.

Conspicuous landmarks

Taipus lighthouse, which can been seen to starboard as you leave Baía de Camamu.

Contas lighthouse, LpB.10s21m15M.

The antennae at the top of the hill overlooking the village, which can be seen from offshore.

Approach

Coming from either the north or the south, the tall white square tower of the Contas lighthouse, which marks the entrance to the Rio das Contas, can be seen from a long way off.

The village of Itacaré can be seen to the right of the lighthouse, at the foot of a hill topped by a group of antennae and a metal pylon painted red and white.

By navigating on the alignment of the lighthouse and the pylon, you will reach ⊕0, which is approximately half a mile from the entrance.

⊕ 0 • 14°16,00'S 038°58,75'W Landfall

Then head directly for the Contas lighthouse, located at the end of the breakwater.

⊕ 1 • 14°16,28'S 038°59,19'W Farol

Caution: the entrance to the Rio das Contas requires some attention, as the channel is narrow and the current is strong (around three knots). There have been several

The entrance to Itacaré with the Contas lighthouse and the antennae on the hill

groundings, fortunately not serious, on the Pontal sandbank at the north of the passage.

For a first visit to Itacaré, it is vital that you enter during the day, and the best time to cross the bar is on a rising half-tide.

Coming from offshore, the waves can be seen from a distance breaking on either side of the channel, on the sandbanks to the north and the rocks near the lighthouse to the south.

The lighthouse stands at the end of a breakwater; there are rocks off the end of this, with the sea breaking over them.

Pass close to the rocks and then turn slightly to port behind the lighthouse towards the beach, in order to avoid the sandbank on the northern tip (Pontal), which extends towards the middle of the channel.

Then head towards Ponta de Xareu, where again you pass very close to the protruding rocks (*see sketch*).

If in doubt, wait until a fishing boat arrives and ask for advice on entering the channel – it will be given gladly.

⊕ 2 • 14°16,45'S 038°59,47'W Ponta Xareu

Once past Ponta de Xareu, anchor approximately 200m further on to port,

⊕ 3 • 14°16,51'S 038°59,53'W Itacaré

Banc de sable

The entrance to the Rio das Contas from the northeast. Watch out for the end of the sandbank

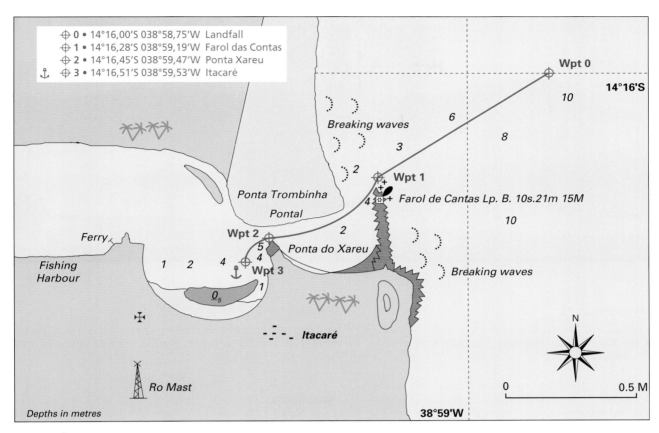

Legend on map:
⊕ 0 • 14°16,00'S 038°58,75'W Landfall
⊕ 1 • 14°16,28'S 038°59,19'W Farol das Contas
⊕ 2 • 14°16,45'S 038°59,47'W Ponta Xareu
⚓ ⊕ 3 • 14°16,51'S 038°59,53'W Itacaré

Wpt 0
14°16'S
10
Breaking waves
6
3
8
2
Wpt 1
Farol de Cantas Lp. B. 10s.21m 15M
4
10
Ponta Trombinha
Pontal
2
Wpt 2
Ferry
5
Ponta do Xareu
Fishing
Harbour
1   2   4   4
Wpt 3
1
0₅
Breaking waves
Itacaré
N
Ro Mast
0   0.5 M
Depths in metres
38°59'W

ITACARÉ

Anchorage

Quality of moorings ***

Anchor in 3.5m on sand. However, it is a good idea to put out a good length of chain (at least 30m) as the current in the river is relatively strong and can carry islands of floating vegetation that can get caught in the chain and cause the anchor to trip (see Note*).

The mooring area is generally well sheltered from the wind, but in strong northerly to northeasterly winds, it is a little choppier. In addition, at high tide, the sea partly covers the Pontal sandbank and a residual swell from offshore comes into the anchorage.

Tenders

Tenders can be left on a small patch of sand between the rocks at the end of Ponta de Xareu. They should be pulled well up onto the sand and then tied to the shore at the bows and anchored at the stern, as at high tide the surf tends to push them onto the rocks.

They can also be left opposite the village, but the sea falls a long way at low tide and they have to be pulled over a long distance to refloat.

The Pontal sandbank

The anchorage at Itacaré

The cove at Itacaré

Facilities – Services **

Buses to Ilhéus and Salvador.

Banco do Brasil, Rua Barbosa; withdrawals can be made with a bank card.

Post Office in the same street.

Several places in town have internet access.

Doctor: Dr Rodrigo ☎ (73) 9996 0371 (he owns the yacht *Trismus* anchored in the bay).

Public hospital ☎ (73) 3251 2034

Water, ice and fuel: ask at the fishing harbour at the end of the village.

There are no boat services locally, but a mechanic or auto electrician may be able to make emergency repairs.

Sol Auto Eletrica ☎ (73) 3251 2098.

The boat caught in the *baronesas* on the Rio das Contas

Supplies ***

Supplies are readily available; there are several mini-markets in the tourist quarter and larger supermarkets in the village.

Baronesas

After heavy rains, the Rio das Contas disgorges large quantities of vegetation, uprooted from the banks upstream, known as *baronesas* or *amazonas*.

Baronesas are veritable floating islands of entangled plants, which come down the river en masse; they can be 1m thick under the water, sometimes more, and depending on their size can weigh several tonnes.

Baronesas are dangerous for several reasons.

Carried by the current, they get caught on the anchor chain, accumulate on the bow and all around the boat, and can even clog the propeller; it is then impossible to raise the anchor and the captive boat can be dragged along by the significant additional weight, which causes it to trip the anchor.

This scenario is particularly dangerous on a falling tide, as the boat can be pushed towards rocks nearby or dragged into channels.

In addition, *baronesas* are colonised by all sorts of fauna (insects, spiders, toads and even snakes); these parasites can then climb onto the boat along branches reaching the bow, meaning that all the hatches need to be closed!

These large masses of vegetation have to be freed using a machete to cut them along the chain, in order to split them into two parts that can then escape along either side of the hull.

Don't hesitate to ask for help from locals in dugout canoes or fishing boats, who are of course used to this sort of situation and will assist willingly.

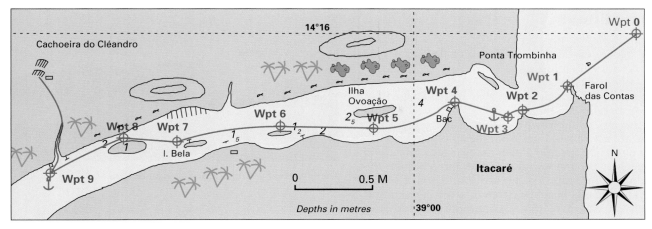

RIO DAS CONTAS

Location and surroundings ***

The village is pleasant, with a plethora of small restaurants and a vibrant nightlife.

Tourism

There are some beautiful beaches to the south of the village, the closest of which can be reached on foot: Praia da Concha, Praia Resende and Praia Tiririca, Praias da Costa and Ribeira, with long, regular waves for surfing; further south, the beaches of Jeribucaçu, Engenhoca and Havaizinho.

Inland, there are some lovely waterfalls in thick forest; some of them, such as Cachoeira do Cleandro and Cachoeira do Azevedo, can be reached along the Rio das Contas.

Neblina, a local fisherman, can take you up the river in his dugout canoe to experience life in the mangroves.

Several travel agencies in town also offer trips inland.

Cachoeira do Cleandro

Cachoeira Do Cleandro

Approximately five miles up the Rio das Contas there is access to a very beautiful waterfall in the middle of the tropical forest.

This itinerary is accessible by boat, but is mainly recommended for shallow draught boats, catamarans or dinghies.

Navigation

If you want to make the return trip in one day, you have to leave Itacaré right at the start of the rising tide so that you can come back before low tide.

Waypoint itinerary for travelling upriver:

⊕ 4 • 14°16,41'S 038°59,25'W The point near the ferry landing
⊕ 5 • 14°16,52'S 039°00,31'W Channel between land and Ilha Ovoação
⊕ 6 • 14°16,55'S 039°00,77'W
⊕ 7 • 14°16,60'S 038°01,31'W Off the Ilha Bela restaurant

Cross the river towards the opposite bank to go round a sandbank,

⊕ 8 • 14°16,50'S 039°01,78'W
⊕ 9 • 14°16,78'S 039°01,92'W Cléandro anchorage

Leave the boat on the anchor and take the tender up a narrow, shallow (0.5m to 0.8m) stream that snakes through the forest to the waterfall.

Tip: travel upstream silently using the paddle and you will spot all sorts of unexpected wildlife in the undergrowth.

The waterfall is reached after a 15 minute walk. Your efforts will be generously rewarded with a dip in the deliciously cool water, or a bracing shower on the various levels of the waterfall.

Note On the sides of the waterfall, avoid getting close to or touching the foliage tumbling down to the water, as it often hides nests of large flies (*marimbondos*) that sting like a wasp and cause painful swelling.

Porto de Ilhéus

In the 18th century the town was called São Jorge dos Ilhéus; it expanded rapidly as a result of cocoa farming on the large surrounding plantations.

Today, Ilhéus has become a major centre for tourism but despite this development, the town has retained all of the Bahian traditions.

There are several impressive 16th century monuments, as well as attractive buildings from the colonial period.

The countryside around Ilhéus is beautiful and there are numerous excursions and walks possible in the surrounding mountains. To the north and south of the town, magnificent beaches stretch over a hundred kilometres. It was here that the author Jorge Amado spent part of his life and wrote some of his well-known novels, such as *Pais do Carnaval*.

The port of Ilhéus-Malhado is located just 30 miles to the south of Itacaré and approximately 120 miles from Salvador.

It is easy to reach and can provide good shelter in bad weather from the southern sector.

Navigation

Brazilian Charts DHN No. 1100, No. 1210 and No. 1201.

Leaving Itacaré, steer a direct course of 185° in depths of 25m to Ilhéus. The coast is quite uniform with a series of relatively low hills, the highest point being Cabo Tromba Grande to the south of Itacaré.

The silos, clearly visible conspicuous landmarks

Approach

Conspicuous landmarks The buildings of the town and tall antennae on the hills can be seen from a long way offshore.

Head towards the imposing structure of the grain silos, which are painted white and located near the fishing harbour.

The Iate Clube de Ilhéus is located to the right of the silos, right next to the small line fishing harbour.

Approach by day Make landfall at:

⊕ 0 • 14°46,02'S 039°01,65'W Approach

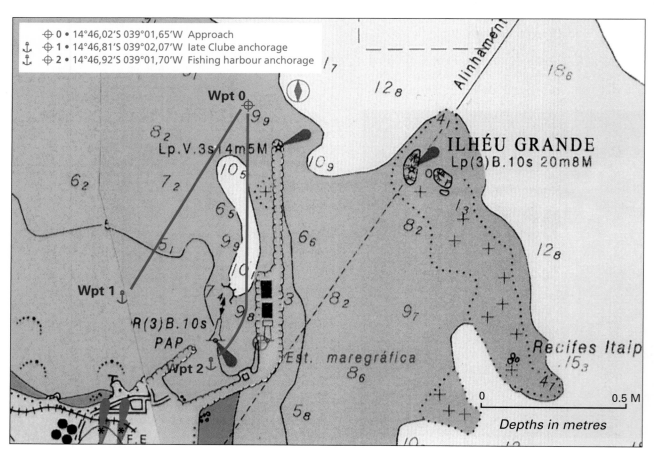

⊕ 0 • 14°46,02'S 039°01,65'W Approach
⊕ 1 • 14°46,81'S 039°02,07'W Iate Clube anchorage
⊕ 2 • 14°46,92'S 039°01,70'W Fishing harbour anchorage

Wpt 0

Lp.V.3s 4m 5M

ILHÉU GRANDE
Lp(3)B.10s 20m8M

Wpt 1

R(3)B.10s
PAP

Wpt 2

Est. maregráfica

Recifes Itaip

0   0.5 M

Depths in metres

F.E

PORTO DO MALHADO

Porto do Malhado. The riprap breakwater with the green tower at its end

From the north

There are no problems in entering the port of Ilhéus-Malhado, which has a long breakwater protecting the entrance. There is a green metal tower at the end of the breakwater that houses the facilities of Porto do

Ilhéus. The Iate Clube

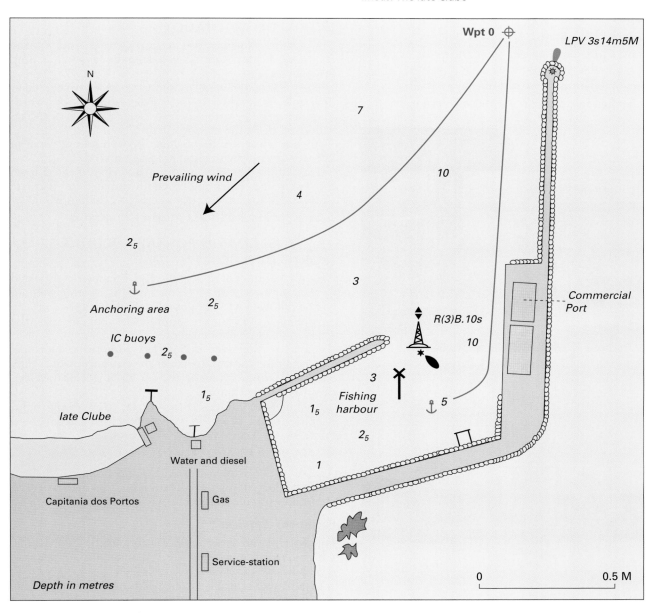

PORTO DO MALHADO

Malhado, the commercial port at Ilhéus, which takes large tonnage ships.

From the south

Approximately one mile from the entrance to the port, watch out for the Itaipins reefs, on which the sea breaks, extended to the north by a line of shoals to the rocks at Ilhéuzinho, and the island of Ilhéu Grande, which has a white tower.

Then head towards the end of the long riprap breakwater.

Go along the inside of the breakwater in depths of 10m, leaving it around a hundred metres to port, until you are level with the warehouses of the commercial port.

Approach by night Plot the light at Ilhéu Grande, Lp(3)B.10s20m8M.

There is a tower at the end of the breakwater protecting the entrance to Porto do Malhado with a green flashing light, Lp.V.3s14m5M.

Anchorages

There are several anchorage options at Ilhéus:

- the Iate Clube anchorage, which can be seen to starboard with several mooring buoys (paying),
- the anchorage inside the small fishing harbour,
- an anchorage further south, at the entrance to the Rio

The Iate Clube with the anchorage in the background

The fishing harbour cardinal buoy

Cachoeira, but accessing the river requires a degree of caution and good local knowledge.

Quality of moorings

A1 ⚓ IATE CLUBE ANCHORAGE **

The Iate Clube is located at the southern end of the beach, near a small riprap breakwater that is almost completely submerged at high tide. It has several mooring buoys located opposite its facilities and a boatman will ferry you to and from the shore.

It is also possible to anchor in 2.5–3m of water with good holding on sand.

When the wind is from the northern sector, this anchorage can become very choppy and uncomfortable, as it is largely open to the northeast and the swell comes into the mooring. However, it is well protected when the wind is from the southern sector.

⊕ 1 • 14°46,81'S 039°02,07'W Iate Clube anchorage

A2 ⚓ FISHING HARBOUR ANCHORAGE *** (PORTO DO MALHADO)

The fishing harbour is located at the end of the commercial port and is protected by a small riprap breakwater.

The breakwater, which is almost completely covered at high tide, is marked by an east cardinal buoy, which must be passed on the easterly side. There is a special yellow mark on the mooring area.

Anchor close to the fishing boat mooring area in 2.5–3m of water with good holding on sand.

The fishing harbour mooring is well protected from the swell and much more comfortable than the Iate Clube anchorage in a northeasterly (prevailing) wind.

⊕ 2 • 14°46,92'S 039°01,70'W Fishing harbour anchorage

A3 ⚓ ENSEADA DO PONTAL ANCHORAGE ** (PORTO DE ILHÉUS)

This further anchorage on the Rio Cachoeira is located in the southern part of town, but this itinerary should not be followed without good local knowledge.

Similarly, account should be taken of the approximately 2-knot current.

Access to the river is possible from rising half-tide; watch out for the sandbanks at the entrance, which only leave a narrow channel on the left-hand side of the river, towards the lighthouse.

Anchor after the first bend in the river on the right, near the small Praia do Cristo beach, located behind Ponta Maria Augusta.

⊕ 3 • 14°48,23'S 39°02,04'W Enseada do Pontal anchorage

Anchor in 3.5m of water with good holding on sand, near Condé Badaro, a small beach bar that also rents out chairs and sun umbrellas.

Facilities – Services **

For boat maintenance services, contact the Iate Clube, which has a list of repair and maintenance companies, mechanics, electricians, etc.

Ilhéus town centre is around 2km from the Iate Clube; it is made up of numerous pedestrian streets containing all the shops and services, such as banks, pharmacies, photo developers, travel agencies, internet cafés, etc.

Water The Iate Clube and fishing harbour pontoons have a tap for filling tanks (this is charged for at the fishing harbour, at a fixed price of R$5). To reach the pontoon, you have to drop an anchor and come stern to in depths of 2.5m to 3.5m at high tide.

Fuel There is a diesel pump on the pontoon at the fishing harbour.

Gas The *Petrogaz* plant is about 100m to the left of the Iate Clube, and cylinders can be refilled there.

Supplies ***

Supplies are readily available; there is a large *Itão* supermarket 300 metres to the right of the Iate Clube, and several mini-markets in the town centre.

Mooring fees **

Three days free of charge; thereafter the rate is R$1.50 to 1.80 per foot per day on a Iate Clube mooring buoy.

Location and surroundings ***

The Iate Clube has excellent facilities with a restaurant, a terrace overlooking the sea, swimming pools, toilets and showers. The bar and restaurant are open Tuesday, Wednesday, Thursday, Saturday and Sunday from 0900

Neptune stands guard over the Iate Clube

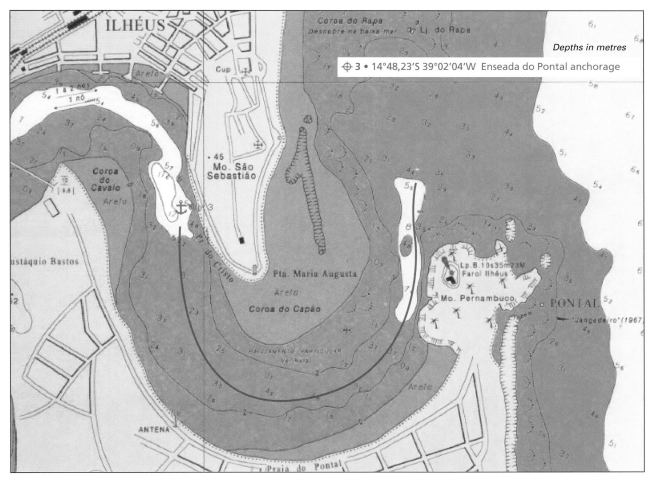

PORTO DE ILHÉUS - RIO CACHOEIRA

to 1800, Friday from 0900 to 1100, and closed Monday.

Security and access to the pontoon are provided 24 hours a day.

All of the facilities are available to visiting boats.

Tourism

Ilhéus has several historical buildings such as the church of Matriz de São Jorge de Ilhéus, which dates from the 16th century.

There is also the Museu de Arte Sacra, the Casa de Cultura Jorge Amado and the Museu do Cacau, which relates the history of cocoa farming, which is closely linked to the development of the town. The pedestrian streets of the town centre are very lively, and there is a huge market nearby.

The area around Ilhéus offers tens of kilometres of fantastic beaches, as well as tropical forest with numerous waterfalls.

Ilhéus Iate Clube, Rua Rotary s/n - Cidade Nova, CEP 45.650.000, ILHÉUS, Bahia
①/*Fax* (73) 3634 3560.

Security

When moored, either at the Iate Clube or the fishing harbour, it is wise to lock the boat and not leave anything desirable on deck.

There have been several reports of incidents during the night at the moorings.

The harbour is 15 minutes' walk from the town centre and is reached along an avenue that runs along the seafront. The road is not very busy in the evenings and although the area looks respectable, it does not have a very good reputation.

It is therefore advisable to return to the Iate Clube by taxi.

If you are moored in the fishing harbour, it is best to leave your tender at the Iate Clube pontoon at night; during the day you can leave it at the fishing harbour and pay a local youth a few R$ to watch it for you.

Useful telephone numbers

Area code ① (73)
Polícia Federal (Immigration), Avenida Roberto Santos
① (73) 3634 3771
Alfândega do porto, receta federal (Customs):
Praça Fermino Amaral, open 0800 to 1400.
① (73) 3231 2133
Capitania dos Portos (Port Captain's Office): located just next to the Iate Clube, open 1400 to 1700
① (73) 3634 1369
Banco do Brasil: Rua Marquês de Paranaguá
Correios (Post Office): Rua Marquês de Paranaguá
Tourist information: Rua Eustácio Bastos, 308, Centro
① (73) 3231 8679
Hospital Santa Isabel, Av. Osvaldo Cruz 205
① (73) 3231 1012.

Santo André – Santa Cruz Cabrália

90 miles to the south of Ilhéus and 20 miles to the north of Porto Seguro, Baía Cabrália shelters the village of Santo André and, a little further south, the small town of Santa Cruz Cabrália, behind a long barrier of reefs.

There is no direct access by sea to Santa Cruz Cabrália. The barrier of reefs extends right along the coast and you have to go through it at Santo André and then up the Rio João de Tiba to reach the town.

The geographical location of Santo André is advantageous as you can leave the boat in a calm anchorage and go on an excursion in the surrounding area or travel to nearby Porto Seguro by bus.

Navigation

Brazilian Charts DHN No. 1200 and No. 1205.

Coming from the north, a course of 255° leaves to starboard the reefs of Coroa Alta, which are uncovered at low tide, and allows for landfall at ⊕0.

⊕ 0 • 16°14,95'S 039°59,60'W Santo André landfall

Approach

It is advisable to enter Santo André during the day at the end of the rising tide, as the current is relatively strong, especially on the ebb.

Santo André is located on the Rio João de Tiba and the entrance to the river is protected by a double row of reefs that are very low to the water, but visible, and on which the sea breaks. The reefs are extended to the north by the Baixinha, submerged rocks just below the surface that form a hazard that is avoided by steering a course of 300° for 0.8 miles to the northwest, towards ⊕1.

⊕ 1 • 16°14,52'S 039°00,38'W

This waypoint is opposite the beach and allows you to stay well clear of the end of the reefs.

Turn 90° to port and sail along the beach to head

The double row of reefs at the entrance to Santo André

Santo André. Anchorage on the Rio João de Tiba

towards Ponta Santo André. A large sandbank extends beyond it and reduces the navigable width of the entrance to the river.

⊕ **2** • 16°14,82'S 039°00,61'W

Head back towards the inner reef and sail along it, leaving it about 15–20m to port, and then head towards the first houses in the village, opposite which you will see several boats on mooring buoys.

Anchor near the *Gaivota* restaurant.

⊕ **3** • 16°15,15'S 039°00,97'W Santo André anchorage

⚓ SANTO ANDRÉ ANCHORAGE

Quality of moorings ★★★

Holding is good in two metres of water on sand.

The mooring is completely calm and well-sheltered, and although there is always a current in the river, this doesn't affect the anchorage much.

Facilities – Services ★★

There are few facilities in Santo André.

Opposite the mooring area, the *Gaivota* restaurant offers visiting yachts a few services such as showers and emergency water, and tenders can be left safely near its entrance. The restaurant has a lovely terrace overlooking the river and serves excellent fish dishes.

Santa Cruz Cabrália, about one mile away, can easily be visited by tender from the Santo André anchorage. It is also possible to take a shared taxi to the ferry that crosses the river.

The village of Santa Cruz Cabrália, which is upstream on the opposite bank, provides almost every service, including a bank, Post Office, internet access, supermarkets, transport, fuel, etc.

For boat maintenance services, marine engineers and electricians are easy to find in Santa Cruz Cabrália given the large number of fishing and pleasure boats moored on the river.

Supplies ★★★

Supplies are very limited in Santo André, but there are several well-stocked supermarkets and numerous shops in Santa Cruz Cabrália.

Location and surroundings ★★★

This is the best place to leave your boat safely anchored to go to Porto Seguro, which is just 40 minutes away by bus.

Santa Cruz is very lively and numerous escunas and other trip boats take tourists out to sea daily to visit the offshore reefs.

⚓ ANCHORAGE ON THE RIO JOÃO DE TIBA

It is also possible to go upriver by boat to Santa Cruz Cabrália and anchor a little upstream of the Santo André ferry landing.

This itinerary is best suited to shallow draught boats, catamarans, dinghies or motor boats, and requires good local knowledge.

From the Santo André anchorage, sail along Ilha Paraíso, leaving it around 30–50m to port, and then cross to the right-hand side of the river, towards two wooden jetties.

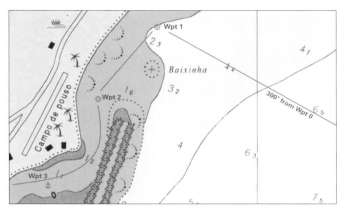

SANTO ANDRE LANDFALL

⊕**0** • 16°14,95'S 039°59,60'W Santo André landfall
⊕**1** • 16°14,52'S 039°00,38'W
⊕**2** • 16°14,82'S 039°00,61'W
⊕**3** • 16°15,15'S 039°00,97'W Santo André anchorage

Level with the jetties, turn to port, sail along the mangroves and then head back towards the reef.

Then turn to starboard and head for the church, which can be seen on the hill overlooking the village.

Near the Santa Cruz ferry landing, sail in the middle of the river to avoid a rock just under the surface to port.

Anchor a little further upstream in 2.5m of water, out of the path of the ferry.

During this journey a close eye should of course be kept on the depth sounder.

Santa Cruz Cabrália. Steer a course towards the church

Ilhota Paraíso on the Rio João de Tiba, surrounded by a large sandbank

Porto Seguro

Brasil nasceu aqui! Brazil began here!

On 22 April 1500, a Portuguese expedition made up of 13 ships, led by Pedro Alvarez Cabral, came in sight of land and, looking for a safe haven, made landfall to the north of modern-day Porto Seguro; their landing was officially seen as Portugal's first entry into Brazil.

This small town with a population of 5,000, at the mouth of the Rio Buranhém, retains all the charm of the period, traces of which can be found in the *cidade alta* (upper town) through several ancient buildings. The lower town houses all of the tourist-related business such as bars, restaurants and souvenir shops. The small streets are lined with colourful houses, and things get very lively in the evening. Street sellers arrive from all around and set out their stalls of local crafts, regional products and culinary specialities.

The carnival here is reputed to be the most authentic in the state of Bahia.

Porto Seguro is located approximately 220 miles south of Salvador on the *Costa do Descobrimento* (Coast of the Discovery). It is an interesting port of call for sailors, but does however present some difficulties in terms of entry and mooring.

There are several interesting sites around Porto Seguro, such as Santa Cruz Cabrália to the north and Arraial d'Ajuda and Trancoso to the south, with their beautiful beaches.

Navigation

Brazilian Charts DHN No. 1200 and No. 1205.

From Santo André, once you have passed Baixa de Coroa Vermelha, steer a course south to leave Pedra de Manguinhos and the Fora reef a good distance to starboard.

Then turn to starboard towards the town, leaving to starboard the Itassepocu reef, located around one mile from the entrance to the river.

⊕ 0 • 16°26,17'S 039°02,00'W Porto Seguro landfall

Conspicuous landmarks To the north of the town, the white tower of Porto Seguro lighthouse, BBE.30s57m26/21M.

To the left of the lighthouse, the church of Nossa Senhora da Pena.

The barrier of reefs, view from the entrance to the river to the east

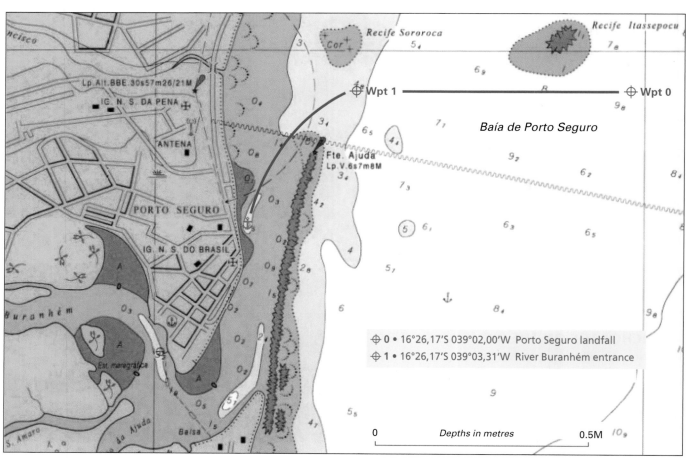

PORTO SEGURO

At the entrance to the river, the end of the reef, topped with a green tower with a green light Lp.V.6s7m8M.

Porto Seguro is accessible to shallow draught boats in general, catamarans and dinghies, and reaching it through a shoal area requires good local knowledge. It is advisable to enter by day only, from rising half-tide. This is a calm stretch of water and the obstacles in the channel can be seen clearly; keep a close eye on the depth sounder.

Approach

The entrance to the river can be seen from offshore, protected by a long barrier of reefs that are partly submerged at high tide, on which the sea breaks.

⊕ 1 • 16°26,17'S 039°03,31'W River Buranhém entrance

From this point, the depth decreases rapidly.

Go round the barrier of reefs staying well off, and enter the river, sailing along the channel well over to the right-hand side. To port is a large sandbank that extends almost right up to the first bend in the river, leaving only a narrow passage.

A jetty and several *escunas* at anchor can be seen; head towards these.

It is possible to anchor nearby, but space is limited and this is not the most comfortable of anchorages.

At high tide only, boats with a moderate draught can travel part way up the river, crossing over to the left-hand side, to the Porto da Quinta hotel, which has two pontoons near the ferry landing.

Quality of moorings *

The waters of the river are disturbed by the frequent passing of trip *escunas*, and the strong current must be taken into account, particularly on the ebb.

Facilities – Services **

There is every facility in town, banks, Post Office, communications, internet access, etc.

Porto Seguro is an official port of entry into Brazil.

Supplies ***

Supplies are readily available with a well-stocked supermarket, Avenida Getúlio Vargas, and several other shopping centres.

Mooring fees

The price at the hotel pontoon is R$60/day.

Location and surroundings ***

The town centre is pleasant and the seafront area with its colourful houses is always lively.

Long beaches protected by the barrier of reefs stretch to the north of the town along a coast dotted with *pousadas* and hotels to suit every budget.

To the south of the Rio Buranhém are the villages of Arraial d'Ajuda and Trancoso, two very touristy resorts.

There is a bus stop at the ferry landing.

Useful addresses in Porto Seguro

Polícia Federal (Immigration), Rua Pero Vaz de Caminha
DELTOUR. Polícia turística (Tourist police), Rua Itagiba
Alfândega do Porto (Customs) at the airport.
Capitania dos Portos (Port Captain's Office), Rua Viana Filho
☎ 288 1213
Tourist Office, Rua do Cáis Av. 22 Avril, 106, Vitoria Plaza Shopping Centre
International Airport
Rodoviaria (railway station), Rua do Aeroporto
Pronto socoro (emergency medecine), Rua da Feirinha
Hospital, Rua Cova do Moça
Correios (Post Office), Rua Itagiba
Internet access, Oceania Shopping Centre (2nd floor)
Most of these services are in the town centre.

The small streets with their colourful houses

Note

Porto Seguro is a charming little town but access and the precarious mooring conditions are the major problems with this port. A shallow draught boat can enter without any trouble but many yachts will prefer not to call here.

For this reason, it might be better to call in around fifteen miles to the north at Santo André – Santa Cruz Cabrália, from where a regular bus link to Porto Seguro runs several times a day (*see the section on Santo André*).

Caravelas

The first Portuguese presence in Caravelas dates from 1503, in the very early days following the discovery of Brazil.

Amerigo Vespuci discovered the entrance to the river during a reconnaissance expedition in the region. A short time later the town of Santo Antônio do Rio das Caravelas, now known as Caravelas, was founded.

Located 80 miles south of Porto Seguro, the town itself is of no particular interest but is a good starting point for visiting the Abrolhos archipelago.

In addition, the offices of IBAMA (the Brazilian Institute of Environment and Renewable Natural Resources) are located nearby; IBAMA is the body that issues information and permits for visiting the Abrolhos islands, which are covered by a very strict environmental protection scheme.

Navigation

Brazilian Charts DHN No. 1205, 1300, 1310 and 1312.

From Porto Seguro or Santo André, steer a course south in depths of 25 to 30 metres.

Off Caravelas, the chart shows a large area of reefs and this should be approached with caution, monitoring progress carefully. It is preferable to approach by day at the start of the rising tide, as this allows you to see some uncovered reefs and, above all, to spot rocks just on the surface on which the sea can break or, in calm seas, create significant surface eddies.

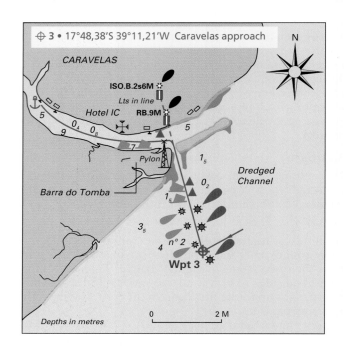

Conspicuous landmarks

To the north of Caravelas, the lighthouse at Ponta da Baleia, Lp.B.5s19m14M.

The white pylon of the Barra do Tomba lighthouse, followed by the Projeto Baleia observation tower (the organisation spots and counts dolphins and whales).

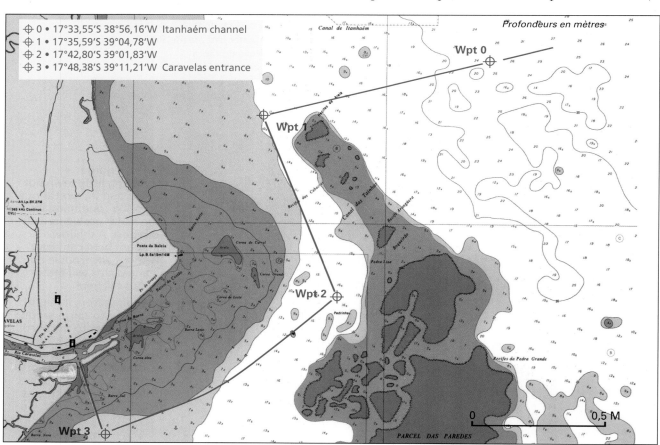

CARAVELAS

Buoy No. 2 in the approach channel

The Barra do Tomba range markers

The Barra do Tomba pylon, which can be seen to port on entering the channel

Approach

Itinerary from the north
From the north, access to Caravelas is through the Canal dos Abrolhos, which is extended to port by the Canal de Itanhaem, in a maze of shoals that are hidden at high tide but some of which are uncovered at low water.

⊕ 0 • 17°33,55'S 38°56,16'W Itanhaém channel

This waypoint is located to the southeast of the Timbebas reefs and allows for entry into the canal; a course of 256° then leads to ⊕1, which avoids the Areia reefs.

⊕ 1 • 17°35,59'S 39°04,78'W

Then steer a course of 160°, leaving to port the reefs of Caboclas and Aranguera, to the Pedra Lixa reef.

⊕ 2 • 17°42,80'S 39°01,83'W

then head towards

⊕ 3 • 17°48,38'S 39°11,21'W Caravelas entrance

This waypoint is level with green buoy No. 2 of the marked channel leading to Barra do Tomba and the entrance to the Rio Caravelas.

Itinerary from the south
From the south, enter the Canal de Sueste, which passes between the Sebastião Gomes and Parcel das Paredes reefs, and which presents no particular difficulties; then head for ⊕3, at the entrance to the marked channel.

Entrance to the Rio Caravelas
The Rio Caravelas is entered through a well-marked channel that is dredged regularly to allow large tonnage ships to enter.

However, depending on the state of the tide, there is a relatively strong side current that carries you southwest.

Entry is possible in just about all weather conditions, which means you can call at Caravelas when waiting for favourable conditions to reach the Abrolhos archipelago.

Approximately 2.5 miles into the channel, you enter the Rio Caravelas through a narrow passage, the Barra do Tomba.

Two range markers (two vertical red stripes and one white stripe) can be seen above the vegetation.

Navigation on the Rio Caravelas
Navigation on the river is easy and most of the time you are sailing in depths of seven to 10 metres. The current is strong, around three to four knots in spring tides, and it is of course advisable to enter on the flood current from rising half-tide.

To reach Caravelas, go approximately four miles upriver, sailing on the left-hand side of the river, to a clearly visible concrete jetty to starboard.

You can come alongside the jetty or moor on buoys nearby.

The jetty at Caravelas

Alongside the jetty at Caravelas

In port

Quality of moorings ***
The mooring area is calm; the mooring on the jetty is slightly affected by the tidal current.

Facilities – Services ***
The jetty is located opposite the town and is just a few minutes' walk from the central square.

All facilities are available in town, including bank, Post Office, internet access and tourist office.

It is important that you go to the offices of IBAMA to obtain information about visiting the Abrolhos islands; they are around 3km away (take a bus heading for 'Praia' in the central square).

IBAMA, Rua Praia do Kitongo s/n°,
CARAVELAS, BA., CEP 45 900 00
☎ (73) 3297 1111, 297 1270
Email abrolhos.ba@ibama.gov.br

Supplies ***
Supplies are readily available; there are well-stocked supermarkets in town, as well as several mini-markets.

Water Taps on the jetty.

Fuel Diesel pump on the jetty.

Location and surroundings ***
This is a quiet town; upstream there is a small fishing harbour with brightly-coloured boats.

Fishing boats moored on the river

Note
Caravelas is a starting point for visiting the Abrolhos Marine National Park, and a great number of trip boats go to the islands every day (*see pousada Iate Clube*).

The interest of the archipelago lies in underwater exploration, but diving enthusiasts should note that diving alone is strictly prohibited. You can join a diving group leaving from Base Abrolhos (located in Caravelas) as exploration of the underwater environment is tightly controlled.

If you want to visit the islands with your boat, you must first obtain a permit to land from the Brazilian Navy, 2nd Naval District, in Salvador (*see next section, Abrolhos*).

Arquipélago dos Abrolhos

In days gone by, some charts bore the inscription '*abra los oyos*' near reef areas that might put the ship in danger; this was a warning to sailors, and means 'open your eyes'.

The Abrolhos archipelago comprises a vast area of rocky shoals that stretch over a large area around a small group of islands. There have unfortunately been several accidents and shipwrecks on these shoals, which can also cause very rough seas in bad weather.

In these waters, you too should '*abra los oyos*'.

Navigation
Brazilian Charts DHN No. 1300, 1310 and 1311.

The Abrolhos archipelago is approximately 90 miles from Porto Seguro, 35 miles from Caravelas and 170 miles from Vitoria.

Before going to the Abrolhos, it is a good idea to stop in Caravelas to gather together all of the information and permits necessary to visit the islands.

Conspicuous landmark The Abrolhos lighthouse, a tall black and white striped cylindrical tower, stands at the top of Ilha Santa Bárbara, the largest in the archipelago.

At night, its light Lp.B.6s60m20M can be seen 20 miles away.

Abrolhos. Approach from the west

Note on the Abrolhos Archipelago
These islands form part of a National Park, and there are tight controls on visiting them.

The main island of Santa Bárbara is occupied by a Brazilian Naval base and it can only be accessed with a permit issued by the 2nd Naval District in Salvador. You cannot therefore land on the island's only beach without such a permit.

In addition, access to the other islands is also prohibited, apart from Ilha Siriba, which can be visited with prior permission from IBAMA. An IBAMA representative will accompany you on your visit.

Permits can be obtained in Caravelas and also once you are there by contacting IBAMA Abrolhos on VHF Channel 16.

A contribution of R$10 is requested for each person landing on the archipelago.

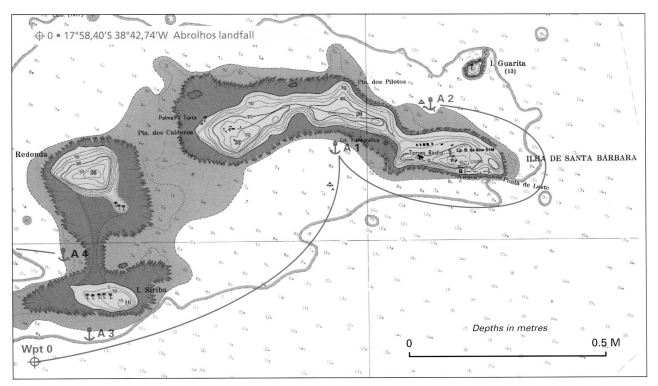

Within the chart image (labels):
⊕ 0 • 17°58,40'S 38°42,74'W Abrolhos landfall

I. Guarita (13)

Pta. dos Pilotos

A 2

Palmeira Torta

Pta. dos Calderos

A 1

Est. marégrafica

Torres Rádio

Lp. B. 6s 60m 51M

ILHA DE SANTA BÁRBARA

Redonda

36

Ponta de Leste

A 4

I. Siriba

A 3

Wpt 0

Depths in metres

0   0.5 M

ARQUIPÉLAGO DOS ABROLHOS

Approach

From the north or from Caravelas, make landfall at

⊕ 0 • 17°58,40'S 38°42,74'W Abrolhos landfall

which is at the entrance to the archipelago through the channel between Ilha Siriba and Ilha Sueste.

Anchorages

Yellow mooring buoys have been installed for tourist and visiting boats to moor on, to the south of Ilha Santa Bárbara and to the north and south of Ilha Siriba.

- In northerly and northeasterly winds, pick up a buoy to the south of Ilha Santa Bárbara, anchorage ⚓A1, or to the south of Ilha Siriba, anchorage ⚓A3.

Note

A strip of sand and rocks links the islands of Redonda and Siriba and can only be seen at low tide.

These rocks are completely covered at high tide and are difficult to see coming from the west, with the sun in your face.

Boats cannot pass between the two islands.

- In easterly and southeasterly winds, the swell coming into the islands makes these anchorages very uncomfortable and it is best to pick up a buoy between Ilha Redonda and Ilha Siriba, anchorage ⚓A4.

- In a southerly wind, moor to the north of Ilha Santa Bárbara at anchorage ⚓A2.

Ilha Siriba

Between the islands of Redonda and Siriba, the strip of rocks and anchorage A4

Ilha Redonda

Quality of moorings ***

The moorings are frequented depending on the wind conditions and the state of the sea, and for the sake of comfort you should have no hesitation in changing anchorage when the wind changes direction.

Facilities – Services *

The Brazilian naval base provides radio cover and can be contacted on VHF Channel 16, call sign *Farol Abrolhos*, if you need assistance or want to request a recent weather forecast.

Supplies

None available on the islands; even fishing is prohibited.

Location and surroundings ***

The archipelago is a haven of peace and tranquillity, and the waters are particularly clear.

However, draconian conditions are imposed on visitors to protect nature and the environment, and it is advisable to contact IBAMA before you go:
☏ (73) 3297 11 11, (73) 297 12 70, Caravelas base.
Email abrolhos.ba@ibama.gov.br

The Abrolhos archipelago is also a centre for monitoring and counting whales, which are numerous in this area.

Whales coming from the Antarctic head for warmer waters up to the Abrolhos, where they gather together, sometimes providing an amazing spectacle for visitors.

For the best chance of seeing whales in the archipelago, visit between July and September.

The Brazilian Naval base

Ilha Santa Bárbara and the Abrolhos lighthouse

Whale spotting

STATE OF ESPÍRITO SANTO

It was the Jesuits, led by Father José de Anchieta, who were behind the founding in 1551 of Espírito Santo, one of the smallest states in Brazil.

The proximity of Minas Gerais with its underground riches on the one hand, and coffee growing on the other, contributed significantly to the rapid development of the region.

Ore still passes through its major ports today, and the enormous mineral complex at Tubarão is the second largest in the world.

The coast offers beautiful beaches and the mountainous hinterland boasts summits at altitudes of 1,000 to 1,500 metres.

Vitória. General view

Barra do Riacho

The port of Barra do Riacho is approximately 30 miles to the north of the ports of Tubarão and Vitória. The port is visited by large ships loaded with wood, which is used as a raw material at the cellulose factories in the region.

It provides good shelter in bad weather and there are no problems on entry, by day or night.

Navigation

Brazilian Charts DHN No. 1400 and No. 1420A.

Conspicuous landmarks

The white smoke from the cellulose factories can be seen from a long way offshore.

The Barra do Riacho lighthouse, a 25m high white cylindrical tower.

⊕ 0 • 20°19,33'S 040°14,56'W Vitória landfall

Then head towards the end of the northern breakwater to enter the waters of the commercial port, and then towards Praia das Conchas.

Approach

Approach by day The entrance to the port can be seen clearly between the northern and southern breakwaters, and the marked approach channel enables large ships to dock at the quay on the northern apron.

Approach by night Make out the Barra do Riacho lighthouse: Lp(2)B.10s30m14M.

Barra do Riacho. The port takes large tonnage ships, loaded with wood

From ⊕0 steer a course of 249.5° towards two range lights located on land, R.B.8m6M and Oc.B.4s10m6M.

This brings you to the end of the northern breakwater, which has a tower with a red light, Lp.E.5s10m8M.

Anchorage

It is possible to anchor off Praia da Concha, in the northwestern section of the port. Anchor in three to four metres of water on sand; the anchorage is well-sheltered from winds from the northern sector and well-protected from the swell.

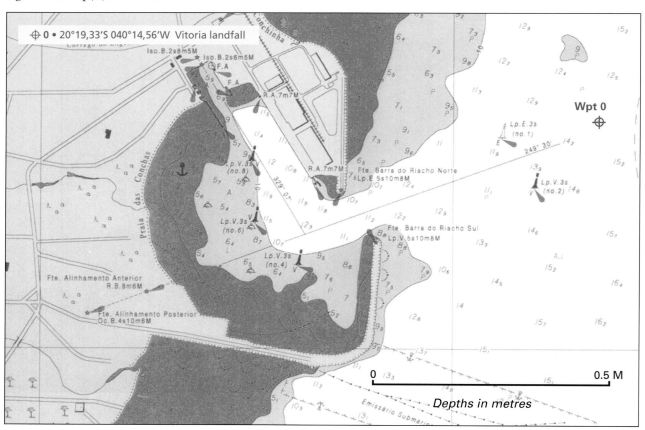

BARRA DO RIACHO

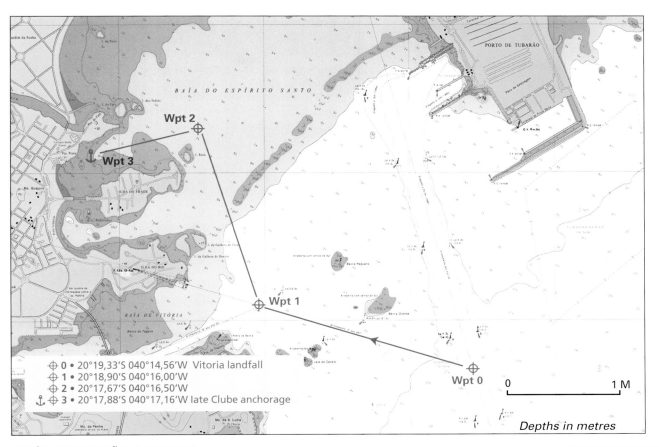

0 • 20°19,33'S 040°14,56'W Vitoria landfall
1 • 20°18,90'S 040°16,00'W
2 • 20°17,67'S 040°16,50'W
3 • 20°17,88'S 040°17,16'W Iate Clube anchorage

0   1 M

Depths in metres

VITÓRIA-TUBARÃO LANDFALL

Baía do Espírito Santo
Vitória – Tubarão

The town of Vitória was founded in 1551, shortly after the discovery of Brazil.

The old town was built on an island and the old quarters overlooking the bay have kept their colonial character. There are still a few vestiges of the period and some old buildings.

This entire region developed due to coffee growing, which was for many years the main activity and is still big business.

It has however been overtaken by the mining industry. The commercial ports of Tubarão and Vitória form a very large port complex and enormous ships call daily at Tubarão, the second largest mineral port in the world.

The expansion of industrial and port activity has led to the growth of the town off the island, with the creation of new districts along the shore. The island is now linked to the mainland by a series of bridges of resolutely modern design.

Vitória, the capital of the state of Espírito Santo, also makes an interesting stop from the point of view of tourism. Located two-thirds of the way between Salvador and Rio de Janeiro, Baía do Espírito Santo houses an easily-accessed marina and the Iate Clube makes for an excellent stopover.

Navigation

Brazilian Charts DHN No. 1300, 1310 and 1401.

The cranes at the port of Tubarão, the second largest mineral port in the world, can be seen from a long way off

Tubarão. The tower to starboard at the entrance to the port of Tubarão

Conspicuous landmarks

By day The facilities of Companhia Vale do Rio Doce, a huge industrial complex that stretches to the northeast of the town, extending beyond the port of Tubarão, can be seen from a long way offshore.

By night The Morro do Frade Leopardo lighthouse, Iso.B.2s208m20M, behind the town. The Ponta Santa Luzia lighthouse to the southeast of the entrance to the port can be seen clearly from offshore Lp(4)B.12s29m34M.

Landfall

Go along the long riprap breakwater that protects the port, staying well off, to make landfall at

⊕ 0 • 20°19,33'S 040°14,56'W Vitoria landfall

Approach

⊕0 is located on the entrance channel to the port of Tubarão, approximately one mile from the end of the southern breakwater, which has a red and white striped cylindrical tower at its end (RE.14m6M).

Tide and currents

The tide is semi-diurnal with a mean level of 0.8m above the chart datum and a maximum amplitude of around 1.7m.

The two to three knot tidal current on the ebb is particularly noticeable in the approach channel to the port of Vitória.

Entrance fairway

The traffic in the port of Tubarão is particularly heavy, and the approach channel is used by very large tonnage ore carriers, which manoeuvre a little further north of the channel to enter the docks.

It is never enjoyable being in a channel faced with a huge ship manoeuvring with the help of three or four tugs; it is therefore better to leave the Tubarão channel and head for the Vitória channel, on a bearing of 287°, towards Ilha do Boi,

⊕ 1 • 20°18,90'S 040°16,00'W

Go towards

⊕ 2 • 20°17,67'S 040°16,50'W

Abeam to port, the Iate Clube do Espírito Santo marina can be seen at the far end of the bay, sheltered by a riprap jetty.

IATE CLUBE MARINA

There are several options available to visitors:

- moor on one of the buoys set aside for visitors (blue and orange painted buoys),
- come alongside inside the marina,
- anchor nearby.

For the first two options, contact the club on VHF Channel 16/69 Foxtrot 23.

⊕ 3 • 20°17,88'S 040°17,16'W Iate Clube anchorage

Note The direct route from ⊕2 towards the marina entrance goes over a shoal marked at 0.8m on the chart. To avoid the shoal, round the route slightly northwards to head towards a yellow buoy set aside for pilot launches, located to the right of the marina entrance, ⊕3.

APPROACH TO THE MARINA

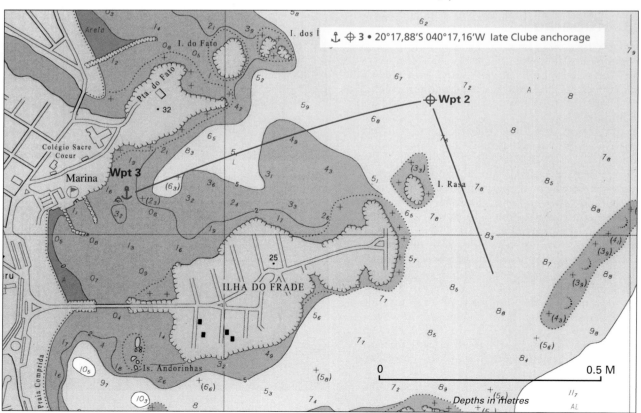

Quality of moorings ***

Anchorage

The mooring area is in four to 5m of water on sand and mud.

The club has installed mooring buoys near the marina and these are available for use by visiting boats free of charge.

The mooring is generally well-protected from the wind, but there is a slight undertow that disturbs the water and makes the anchorage a little rolly.

However, the biggest nuisance comes from the frequent comings and goings of the pilot launches, which pass close to the moored boats at full throttle, with little respect for the tranquillity of the mooring area.

IATE CLUBE MARINA

The marina is mainly occupied by motor boats, most of which are used for big-game fishing, and a few small and medium-sized yachts.

There are a few spaces available for visiting boats on the southern jetty, inside and outside the marina.

Moor bow or stern to, picking up a mooring buoy.

Inside the marina, the spaces near the entrance on the left are however a little rough, and depending on availability, it is best to choose a mooring on the other side of the quay, outside the marina.

Facilities – Services ***

Vitória is an official port of entry into Brazil; contact the marina office for formalities.

The boatyard is located inside the marina complex and there are offices, a dry storage area, a chandlery, and a slipway that can be used to take boats weighing up to around 12 tonnes out of the water.

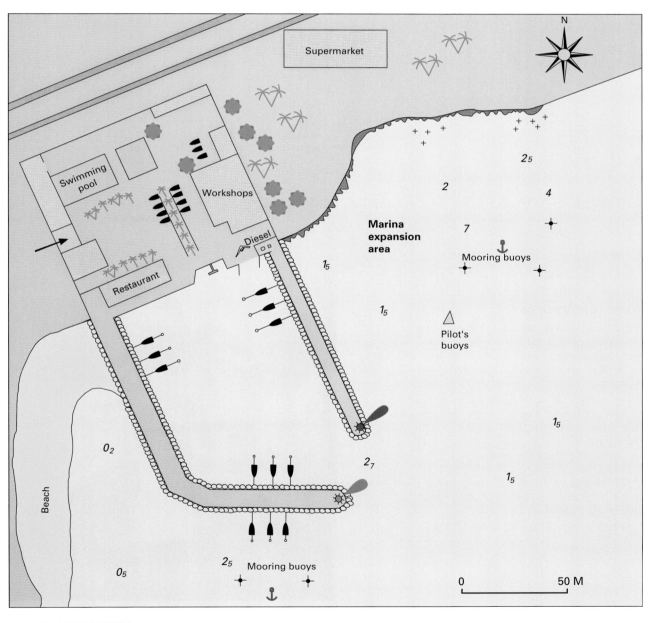

IATE CLUBE MARINA

Vitória. The marina and the buoy reserved for pilot launches

Vitória. A colonial building in the town centre

There are personnel on site to carry out general maintenance work; for more technical operations, the marina has a list of businesses that normally work on the boats at the club.

Water The quays have a good number of taps.

Electricity 110 volt (blue) and 220 volt (red) outlets on the quay.

Fuel There is a service station on the quay, near the boat repair shed.

Supplies ***

There is a large well-stocked supermarket on the right, 300m from the entrance to the Iate Clube; supplies can be delivered directly to the boat. It is an easy 20 minute walk from the Iate Clube to Shopping Vitória, which is the largest shopping centre in town.

Mooring fees **

Three days free of charge; thereafter R$50 per day, for a 45' boat.

Location and surroundings ***

Iate Clube do Espírito Santo is located on the island of *Vitória*. It has excellent facilities and offers everything you might need in a stopover: a warm welcome, assistance, toilets and showers, electricity, fuel, a good restaurant, etc.

At the back there is a large pool with sun deck, a paddling pool and a children's play area. Several bus routes run from near the Iate Clube to the various districts of the town.

Security

There is a 24-hour surveillance service, and to date there have been no incidents or thefts within the marina.

The town itself seems very peaceful.

Iate Clube do Espírito Santo, Praia do Canto, Vitória, ES
☎/ *Fax* (27) 3225 0422
Email iateclube@ebr.com.br

Tourism

Although it is rarely mentioned in lists of tourist destinations, Vitória and its environs are particularly interesting from the point of view of tourism.

Vitória is an island, and the surrounding countryside is strewn with granite peaks that emerge out of luxuriant vegetation.

For keen walkers, there are a great many excellent hikes in the mountains that start from Vitória.

Make sure you walk up through the forest to the Convente de São Francisco, founded by Frei Pedro Palácio, which has panoramic views of the whole town.

The old town is home to several impressive monuments and colonial buildings.

Above all, don't miss a trip to the Garoto complex, one of the largest chocolate manufacturers in Brazil (guided tour and tasting).

Vitória. The monastery of São Francisco above the town

Vitória. The Hotel do Boi pontoon

Useful telephone numbers

Area code ☎ (27)
Polícia Féderal (Immigration) ☎ 3331 8000
Polícia Civil (Civilian Police) ☎ 147
Tourist protection ☎ 3137 9117
Tourist information ☎ 3382 6363
Shopping Vitória ☎ 3382 6364
Vitória Airport ☎ 3235 6300
São Lucas Hospital ☎ 3381 3385

HOTEL ILHA DO BOI MARINA

In order to promote its luxurious hotel complex, the Hotel Ilha do Boi has very recently built a jetty that can hold around a dozen 10–15m boats.

The pontoons are equipped with water and electricity, and provide access to the hotel and its various services.

The jetty is located on the north of Ilha do Boi, and is reached from the Iate Clube by going around Ilha do Frade in depths of 3.5–8m, without any obstacles.

Information: Hotel Ilha do Boi
☎ (27) 3345 0111 *Fax* (27) 3345 0115
www.hotelilhadoboi.com.br

Enseada de Guarapari

See plan page 123

Just 40 miles south of Vitória, Enseada de Guarapari shelters the largest resort in the state of Espírito Santo.

Along with neighbouring Enseada de Perocão, it forms a very pleasant site, with several anchorages in well-sheltered inlets.

Navigation

Brazilian Charts DHN No. 1400, 1402 and 1404.

Landfall

From the north, make landfall at
⊕ 0 • 20°40,70′S 040°28,65′W Guarapari landfall

This waypoint is located approximately one mile from the entrance to the bay, to the south of Ilha Raposa.

Approach

From ⊕0 steer a course of 340° towards the beach until you reach:
⊕ 1 • 20°39,97′S 040°29,00′W

Be sure to pass between Baixa Grande de Boqueirão and Baixa de Ipanema where, in winds from the southern to eastern sector, the sea can be rough with breaking waves.

Anchorages

There are two possible anchorages at Guarapari:
• on the river, near the old town,
• off the beach.

From ⊕1, to go to the old town of Guarapari on the banks of the river to the left of the beach, head west towards the church of São Pedro until you reach
⊕ 2 • 20°39,75′S 040°29,56′W

Bridge
Entrance to the river

The entrance to the river can then be seen, with the bridge in the background.

Take care, as there is not much room to manoeuvre in this narrow channel.

A few trip *escunas* are moored on a small jetty and, as long as they are not leaving port, you can raft onto them for a limited time, with the consent of the owner or skipper.

Another fair weather option is to anchor off the long beach of Morro da Pescaria.

However, if the wind is from the southern to eastern sector, the swell makes this anchorage untenable. The right-hand end of the beach, where a few boats can be seen on mooring buoys, is more sheltered from easterly winds.

You can anchor in this area around
⊕ 3 • 20°39,27′S 040°28,58′W Guarapari

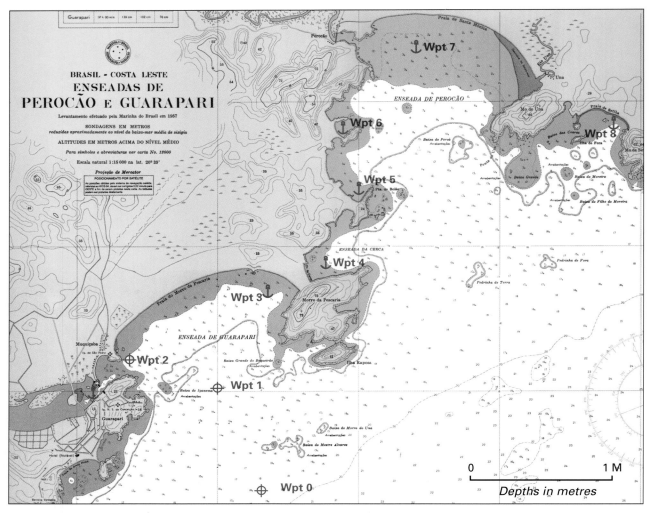

ENSEADA DE GUARAPARI ET PEROCÃO

Quality of moorings ***

River anchorage

It is possible to anchor in the river with bow and stern anchors, as swinging space can cause problems in this relatively narrow channel.

A not insignificant tidal current should be taken into account.

Beach anchorage

It is possible to anchor all along the beach in three to four metres of water, over the whole bay.

On the right-hand section of the beach, the smooth rocks of Morro da Pescaria protrude a long way into the bay, and anchor holding on these rocks, which have a thin covering of sand, can be patchy; it is preferable to stay around ⊕3 where the bottom is sandy, beyond the rocks.

Facilities – Services **

All facilities are available in Guarapari: banks, Post Office, internet access, etc.

Boat maintenance services are however more limited.

There is a service station on the jetty, near the bridge at the entrance to the river.

Supplies ***

There is no problem finding supplies and there are several well-stocked supermarkets in town.

Location and surroundings ***

Guarapari is a large, very touristy seaside resort and numerous hotels and holiday houses have been built along its beaches on either side of the old town.

It is the destination of choice for the inhabitants of Vitória, who regularly spend weekends and summer holidays here.

The seafront is of course very lively with a pleasant holiday atmosphere, especially at the weekend.

Right next door is Enseada de Perocão, which is an attractive extension to the bay with lovely beaches in well-sheltered inlets.

Enseada de Perocão

Slightly northeast of Enseada de Guarapari and only separated from it by Morro da Pescaria, is Enseada de Perocão, which offers a few pleasant inlets and several possible anchorages. The cove is littered with rocks just above the surface of the water and vigilance is the order of the day in this area.

Guarapari. *Escunas* moored at the jetty on the river

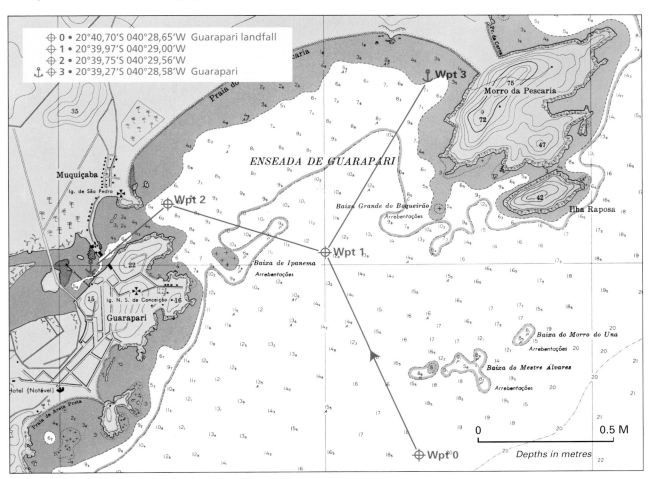

ENSEADA DE GUARAPARI

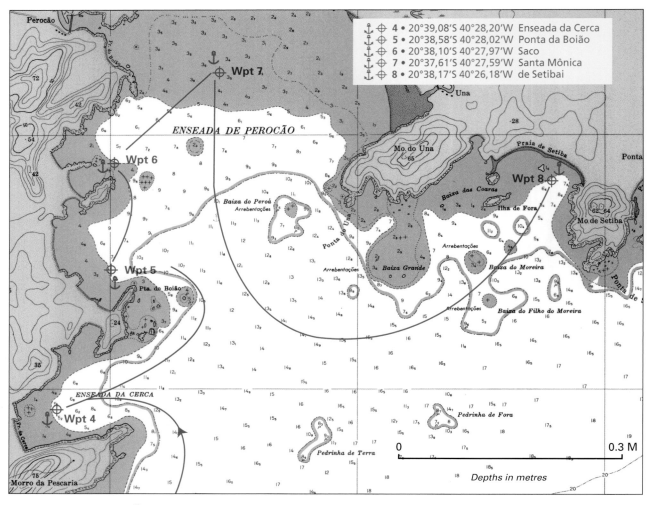

⚓⊕	4 • 20°39,08'S 40°28,20'W	Enseada da Cerca
⚓⊕	5 • 20°38,58'S 40°28,02'W	Ponta da Boião
⚓⊕	6 • 20°38,10'S 40°27,97'W	Saco
⚓⊕	7 • 20°37,61'S 40°27,59'W	Santa Mônica
⚓⊕	8 • 20°38,17'S 40°26,18'W	de Setibai

ENSEADA DE PEROCÃO

Enseada de Perocão. The anchorage at ⊕6, a quiet beach

Anchorages

⚓ ENSEADA DA CERCA

This is a pretty inlet in the northern part of the cove, but the anchorage is not always comfortable due to the swell.
  Anchor off Praia da Cerca

⊕ 4 • 20°39,08'S 40°28,20'W Enseada da Cerca

The surroundings are unexceptional, with the backs of the buildings on the beach in Guarapari in the background.

A huge area is set aside for fish farming in the more sheltered southern section, and you cannot moor here.

⚓ PONTA DO BOIÃO ANCHORAGE

This is one of the most pleasant anchorages in Enseada do Perocão. It is well-sheltered from the swell and from winds from the northern to western sector.

⊕ 5 • 20°38,58'S 40°28,02'W Ponta da Boião

The water is calm and clear and the beautiful backdrop is made up of greenery, a white sandy beach and a chaos of granitic rocks.

⚓ SACO ANCHORAGE

A pleasant cul-de-sac reached through a narrow entrance between two rocks:

⊕ **6** • 20°38,10'S 40°27,97'W Saco

You can anchor inside in a rather small, but very calm, mooring area.

Depending on the season it might be besieged by *escunas* packed with tourists and blaring out loud music, which temporarily disturbs the peace of this pretty anchorage.

⚓ PRAIA DE SANTA MÓNICA ANCHORAGE

Anchor in three meters of water off the beach, opposite the *Cabana Tropical* restaurant.

⊕ **7** • 20°37,61'S 40°27,59'W Santa Mônica

The anchorage is well-protected from winds from the northern to eastern sector, but if you want to go ashore, it is a little far off the beach.

Very exposed to winds from the southern sector.

⚓ SETIBA ANCHORAGE

A good anchorage, well-sheltered from northeasterly winds by Ponta de Setiba.

⊕ **8** • 20°38,17'S 40°26,18'W de Setibai

However, in southwesterly to southeasterly winds, the sea breaks on the shoals between Ponta de Una and Ponta de Setiba, and the anchorage can quickly become insecure. It is therefore only recommended if the weather forecast is good.

Porto de Ubu

30 miles to the south of Vitória, on the route to Rio de Janeiro, Porto de Ubu provides good shelter in strong winds from the southern sector.

The entrance to the port is approximately five miles from the coast to the southwest of Ilha Escalvada, and commercial ships can be seen anchored offshore, waiting to enter the port.

Navigation

Brazilian Chart DHN No. 1402.

Approach

The port takes large tonnage ships and is approached along a well-marked channel.

Approach by day Make landfall at ⊕0, which is in the centre of the channel slightly to the west of beacons No. 1 and No. 2.

⊕ **0** • 20°46,90'S 040°33,45'W Ubu approach

Approach by night By night, a transit of 270° on the two towers located on land, R.B.26m10M and Iso.B.2s30m10M allows easy entry into the port.

Anchorage

Anchor inside the breakwater in three to four metres of water, with good holding on sand and mud.

On entering the port, watch out for large tonnage ships manoeuvring. The area is large enough to stay well clear of them and not hinder their manoeuvres.

Quality of moorings **

The mooring area is well-sheltered from winds from the southern sector, but very exposed to winds from the northern sector. Porto de Ubu is only of little interest as a port of call, but it provides shelter when there is a cold front coming in. This is the main advantage of this port, whilst waiting for more favourable weather conditions to continue the route southward towards Rio de Janeiro.

PORTO DE UBU

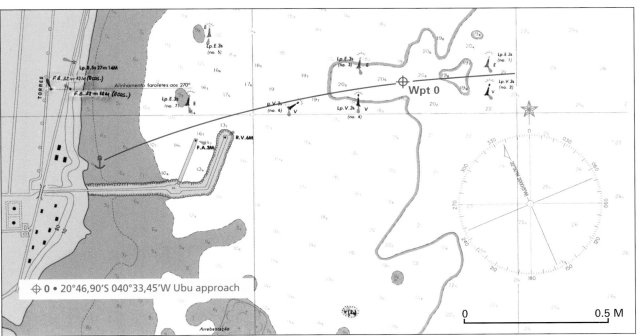

⊕ 0 • 20°46,90'S 040°33,45'W Ubu approach

STATE OF RIO DE JANEIRO

Although the state of Rio de Janeiro is one of the smallest in the area, it is without doubt the largest in terms of its dedication to tourism. The capital, Rio, known as the *cidade marvilhosa*, is located in the centre of the state. Sugarloaf Mountain (*Pão de Açúcar*) stands proudly above the city and the statue of Christ the Redeemer at the summit of Corcovado Mountain keeps watch over the people below.

For yachting, the state of Rio de Janeiro offers three main centres of interest:

- to the north, Búzios, one of the most attractive tourist resorts, and nearby Cabo Frio represent a significant coastal route,
- in the middle, Baía de Guanabara and Rio de Janeiro,
- to the south, Baía da Ilha Grande and its 250 islands form a sailor's paradise.

It's a delicious cocktail to be drunk in copious amounts, with a bit of samba thrown in for good measure!

Rio de Janeiro bay

Cabo de São Tomé

Vitória to Cabo de São Tomé

Navigation

Brazilian Charts DHN No. 1400 and 1403.

On leaving Vitória, the coast offers only a few possibilities of shelter before Cabo Búzios around 200 miles away, so this leg should be undertaken on a good weather forecast.

The port of Ubu, approximately 40 miles from Vitória, can be used as a refuge whilst waiting for more favourable sailing conditions if a cold front comes in. Sailing in this area does not pose any particular problems, apart from rounding Cabo São Tomé, where locally the winds can be changeable in both direction and strength. Southerly and easterly winds make the sea rough near the cape in a shoal area that extends over 10 miles from the coast. Further to the east, a large oil exploration area stretches over 40 to 50 miles offshore.

It is therefore preferable to round the cape a good distance from the coast, around 20 to 25 miles in depths of 30 to 40 metres, between the Banco de São Tomé shoal area and the oil exploration fields.

At night, an attentive watch must be kept as a great many fishing boats operate in the cape area and their course, which depends on the demands of fishing, frequently changes.

Cabo de São Tomé to Cabo Frio

Beyond Cabo de São Tomé, the uniformly sandy coast stretches up to Macaé and Imbetiba, which are used as a logistics base for the oil platforms.

Further southwest, the coast becomes rocky and jagged, with numerous coves hiding beautiful beaches. Cabo Búzios and Cabo Frio stand out from the coast and provide several excellent anchorages and good shelter depending on the wind direction.

Enseada de Búzios

Búzios used to be a peaceful, picturesque little fishing village; Brigitte Bardot often stayed here in the 1960s, unintentionally transforming this small fishing harbour into one of the most high profile and popular tourist resorts in Brazil.

The memory of Bardot's time here is omnipresent in the resort and in the minds of its inhabitants, and numerous monuments, engravings and signs recall the period in various locations around town.

The population of the town increases tenfold in the summer season, and there are no fewer than twenty beaches stretching to the north and south of the peninsula, which is where the longest are to be found.

Although it receives a great many visitors in the form of tourists and the people of Rio, the town retains a natural charm. Its streets are well-kept and there is art everywhere in the form of statues, fountains, mosaics, small squares, and so on.

It is an unmissable stop for visiting boats on the route from Salvador to Rio de Janeiro.

The town is at its liveliest in the summer season and the vibrant nightlife draws large numbers of holidaymakers and tourists.

For sailors dreaming of unspoilt coves and deserted beaches, an out of season visit might be a good compromise; the town enjoys a little respite and the anchorages are peaceful once more.

Navigation

Brazilian Charts DHN No. 1504 and 1505.

Approach

Conspicuous landmarks To the north of Búzios, Ilha Branca, which is left to port.

Approach by day Approximately 75 miles from Cabo de São Tomé on a course of 240°, make landfall at ⊕0, which is located around one mile off Enseada de Búzios.

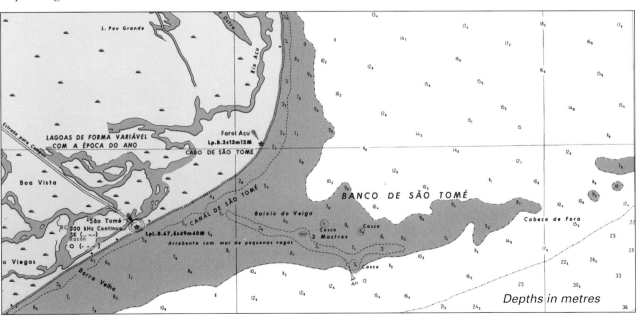

CABO DE SÃO TOMÉ

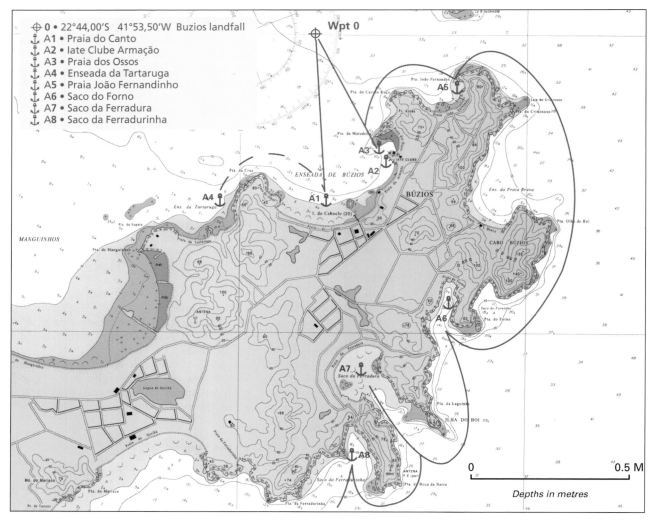

- ⊕ **0** • 22°44,00'S 41°53,50'W Buzios landfall
- ⚓ **A1** • Praia do Canto
- ⚓ **A2** • Iate Clube Armação
- ⚓ **A3** • Praia dos Ossos
- ⚓ **A4** • Enseada da Tartaruga
- ⚓ **A5** • Praia João Fernandinho
- ⚓ **A6** • Saco do Forno
- ⚓ **A7** • Saco da Ferradura
- ⚓ **A8** • Saco da Ferradurinha

CABO BÚZIOS

⊕ **0** • 22°44,00'S 41°53,50'W Buzios landfall

Approach by night The light on Ilha Branca, Lp.B.5s38m8M.

In port

There is no yacht harbour in Búzios, which is nonetheless heavily frequented by yachts from Rio de Janeiro and visiting boats travelling south. However, you will be spoilt for choice for anchorages:
- near the lively, touristy centre,
- off the beautiful sandy beaches,
- in peaceful inlets.

Anchorages

The winds in Enseada de Búzios can change in strength and direction several times a day, and the calmness of the water is affected accordingly.

The anchorages are generally fairly comfortable apart from when the wind is from the northern to eastern sector, when several areas can become choppy.

Quality of moorings ★★★

⚓ A1 PRAIA DO CANTO

The anchorage is off Praia do Canto, to the west of Ilha do Caboclo facing the town. This is the anchorage to choose if you arrive at night as it is a huge area that is generally not too busy, and can be used as a waiting anchorage by staying slightly offshore; you can always choose another option in the morning.

Anchor in four to five metres on sand.

This anchorage is well-sheltered from southerly to easterly winds, but exposed to northeasterly winds, and the swell can make it uncomfortable.

⚓ A2 IATE CLUBE ARMAÇÃO DE BÚZIOS

Iate Clube Armação de Búzios is a sailing club, and above all a competitive sailing club, as it is where the Brazilian Olympic team trains. The club is run by an affable Frenchman, Alain Joullié, Commodore and experienced sailor.

The club is very involved in teaching, with a good sailing school.

It also performs very well in regattas and every April organises Búzios Sailing Week, which is attended by numerous boats from other Brazilian clubs.

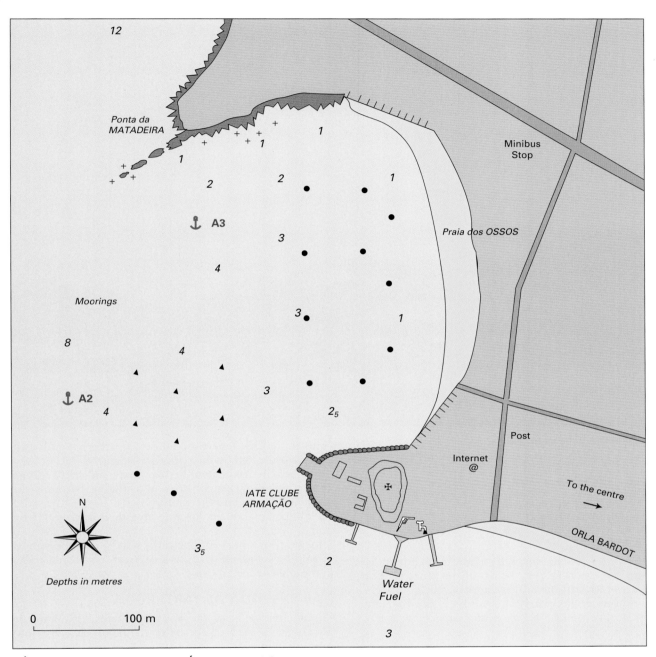

12

Ponta da
MATADEIRA

1

Minibus
Stop

1

2   2   1

⚓ A3

3

Praia dos OSSOS

4

Moorings

3

1

8

4

⚓ A2

4

3

1

3

2₅

Post

Internet
@

IATE CLUBE
ARMAÇÃO

To the centre
→

N

ORLA BARDOT

3₅

2

Water
Fuel

Depths in metres

0   100 m

3

BÚZIOS. IATE CLUBE ARMACÁO DE BUZIOS

The jetty and Praia do Canto

Its members include several Olympic sailors, such as gold medallists Robert Scheidt in the Laser class and Torben Grael and Marcelo Ferreira in the Star class, with creditable results in the Tornado, 470 and Mistral classes (Seoul 1990, Atlanta 1996 and Athens 2004).

The yacht club has a mooring area with several mooring buoys, some of which can be used by visiting boats.

The rate of R$50 per day gives access to the club and all of its amenities, including toilets, shower, restaurant, etc.

The anchorage is safe and generally well-sheltered, but westerly to northerly winds make the water quite choppy.

It is very well-located near the town centre, and is the best and most convenient place if you are spending several days in Búzios.

Búzios. The Iate Clube anchorage and facilities

Iate Clube Armação de Búzios, Praía dos Ossos, 28 900 Armação de Búzios, RJ
☏ (22) 2623 1493, 2220 2966 in Rio
VHF Channel 68, call sign *Echo 43*

⚓ A3 PRAIA DOS OSSOS

This is located between the Iate Clube and Ponta da Matadeira, and the rocks off the tip of the point form a natural barrier against the northeasterly swell.

It is without doubt the best position. Like the Iate Clube anchorage, it can be uncomfortable in westerly winds but a little less troubled by a northerly wind, as it is better protected by the rocks off the point.

It is heavily frequented by trip boats and small fishing craft; a relatively small area is available between the yacht club buoys and the shore.

Holding is good in three to five metres of water on sand.

In westerly and southwesterly winds, attention must be paid to swinging space as there are submerged rocks on the edge of the mooring area.

⚓ A4 ENSEADA DE TARTARUGA

This anchorage is to the west of Búzios, off Praia de Tartaruga, and is well-sheltered from easterly and southerly winds.

It is a good day-time anchorage, but it is quite far away from the town centre and therefore not very convenient.

Anchor on the left-hand side of the beach in 3–4m of water on sand.

Praia dos Ossos anchorage

Praia de João Fernandinho

⚓ A5 PRAIA JOÃO FERNANDINHO

Another good anchorage and one of the prettiest, to the left of the main beach, sheltered by Ponta João Fernandes. Anchor in three to four metres off a gorgeous little beach, in clear water with a particularly pleasant wooded backdrop.

⚓ A6 SACO DO FORNO

To the south of Cabo Búzios behind Ponta do Forno is a small inlet with a narrow entrance between two walls of rock. You have to go through the mouth of the inlet before you see a pretty little beach at the end of the cul-de-sac. The anchorage is well-protected from westerly to northeasterly winds.

⚓ A7 SACO DA FERRADURA

Also to the south of the headland, behind Ilha do Boi, another cul-de-sac hides Praia da Ferradura. The entrance to the inlet, between two steep rock faces, is more open than the previous inlet. Holding is good in four to five metres of water on sand off the beach.

⚓ A8 SACO DA FERRADURINHA

This cul-de-sac is also surrounded by steep rocks; you can anchor on the right at the entrance to the inlet, in five to six metres of water. It is a good dive site.

Note on Anchorages ⚓A5, ⚓A6 and ⚓A7
These last three anchorages should only be used in good weather; they provide good protection in westerly to northeasterly winds, but in easterly to southerly winds the sea comes violently into the coves and they soon become uncomfortable.

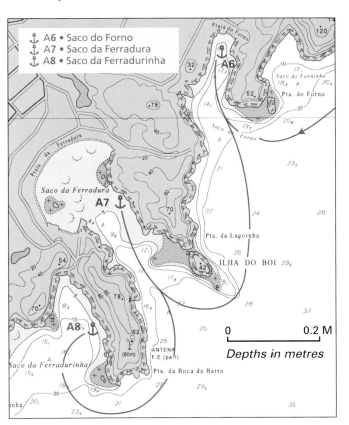

Facilities – Services **

All facilities are available in the Armação quarter: banks, Post Office, several internet access points, shops, travel agency, car hire, etc.
Tourist office: Praça Santos Dumont (open from 0900 to 2100)
☎ (22) 2623 20 99
Transport: Rodoviária (bus station) Estrada da Usina Velha, N° 444
☎ (22) 2623 20 50

Buses to Cabo Frio leave from the bus station (these run every ½ hour).
Buses for Rio de Janeiro also leave from here; first departures at 0700 and 0900.
Shared taxis can be caught 200 metres to the left of the small square, near the Iate Clube entrance.

Supplies ***

Supplies are readily available in town, which has several well-stocked supermarkets in the Manguinhos district.

Fuel There is a marine service station with diesel and petrol (*gasolina*) pumps on the jetty near the Iate Clube.

Water The town is faced with a water shortage every summer; additional water is delivered by tanker and water must therefore be paid for.
You can fill your tanks at the marine service station.

Gas At the Minasgas - Télégas station
Estrada J.B. Ribeiro Dantas (Cabo Frio Road) ☎ (22) 2623 6969.

Location and surroundings ***

The town of Búzios is very spread out and split into several districts:

• the oldest, Praia dos Ossos, near the Iate Clube, is the most attractive; the mooring area is nearby.

• Armação is the fishing harbour and town centre district where all the bars, restaurants, banks, Post Office, etc., can be found.
   This is where the mythical Orla Bardot is located, an almost obligatory walk along Praia da Armação that continues into town along the lively Rua das Pedras.

• Manguinhos to the east of the town is the non-touristy district with all sorts of shops, supermarkets and everyday supplies.

Fishermen on Orla Bardot (bronze statues)

An anchorage with crystal-clear waters, near Praia João Fernandinho

Entertainment

By day The beaches to the south of Búzios, such as Praia de Geribá, are good for surfing, with long, even, moderately powerful waves. For diving enthusiasts, the crystal waters of the inlets and the diversity of seabed are particularly favourable for underwater exploration.

By night Nightlife guaranteed. Every evening, the unavoidable Rua das Pedras is crowded with people out for a stroll; the eclectic, sophisticated restaurants and bars stay open until dawn.

Useful telephone numbers

Area code ☎ (22)
24-hour Emergency Services ☎ 2623 2919
Capitania dos Portos (Port Captain's Office) ☎ 2643 2840
Polícia Féderal (Immigration) ☎ 2629 1281
Tourist Office ☎ 2623 2099.

Cabo Frio

The Cabo Frio region was discovered in 1503 by Amerigo Vespucci; it was coveted by the Dutch and French in turn before being taken back by the Portuguese in 1615.

The town, which was previously known as Santa Helena de Cabo Frio, was built on the banks of the Rio Itajuru, at the mouth of which the Portuguese built Forte de São Mateus in 1620. Subsequently, the town developed towards the seashore; it now has a population of fifty thousand, but this triples in the summer season.

The Costa do Sol starts at Cabo Frio. Its beautiful white sandy beaches and cool, clear waters attract increasing numbers of water sports-loving holidaymakers and tourists.

Just 14 miles from Búzios, it is an interesting port of call, and can also be used while waiting for favourable weather conditions to round Cabo Frio and reach Rio de Janeiro.

Navigation

Brazilian Charts DHN No. 1503 and No. 1505.

Leaving Búzios, you sail along a jagged coastline with alternating hills and beaches, some of which are well-protected up rocky inlets.

You then enter the Canal de Papagaios, travelling past a group of rocky islets to port, whilst a very long white sandy beach fringed with dunes stretches out to starboard, followed by a rocky outcrop. This route brings you to:

⊕ **0** • 22°53,47'S 042°00,16'W Cabo Frio landfall

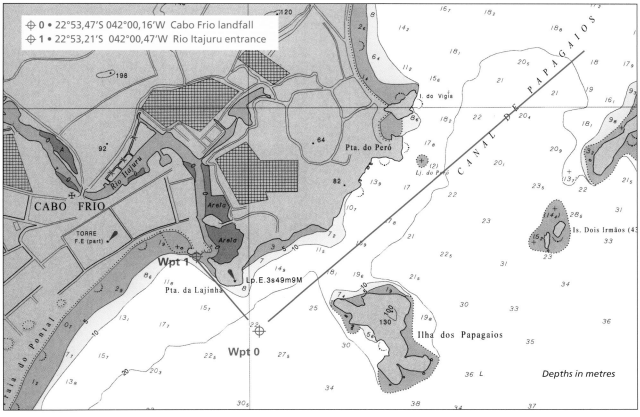

0 • 22°53,47'S 042°00,16'W Cabo Frio landfall
1 • 22°53,21'S 042°00,47'W Rio Itajuru entrance

CABO FRIO LANDFALL

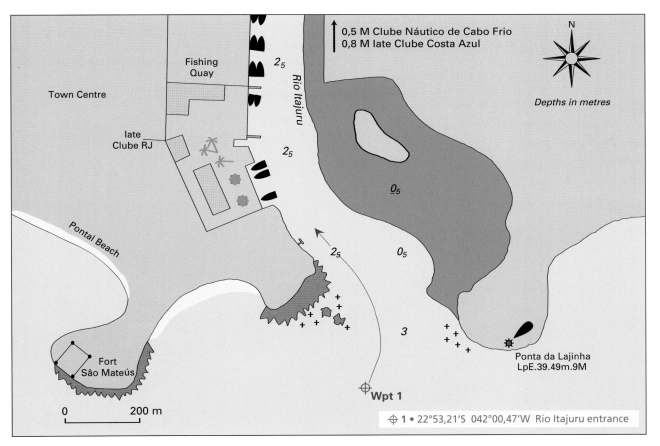

0,5 M Clube Náutico de Cabo Frio
0,8 M Iate Clube Costa Azul

Ponta da Lajinha
LpE.39.49m.9M

1 • 22°53,21'S 042°00,47'W Rio Itajuru entrance

ENTRANCE TO THE RIO ITAJURU

The entrance to the Rio Itajuru between two walls of steep rocks

Approach

It is best to enter Cabo Frio by day, from rising half-tide. ⊕0 is around half a mile to the south of Ponta da Laginha, which hides the entrance to the Rio Itajuru and the town of Cabo Frio. On rounding the point, Forte de São Mateus can be seen, located on a rocky promontory; head towards this. The entrance to the river can then be seen between two walls of steep rocks.

⊕ 1 • 22°53,21'S 042°00,47'W Rio Itajuru entrance

The passage is narrow, but the depth allows yachts to enter without any trouble, on a rising tide. Stay in the middle of the river, as a few isolated rocks jut out to port. Also watch out for a large sand bank to starboard, which is covered at high tide.

Once past the entrance, the river immediately bends to the left and just after this the Iate Clube do Rio de Janeiro annex and the fishing harbour can be seen.

There are three mooring options in the Rio Itajuru:
• Iate Clube do Rio de Janeiro,
• Clube Náutico de Cabo Frio,
• Iate Clube Costa Azul.

Access to the latter two is only possible for shallow draught boats (1.5m maximum), catamarans, dinghies or motor boats.

The riverbed is narrow and littered with sand banks that cannot be seen at high tide. If you have any doubts about entering the channel or going upriver, ask for help from a local boatman.

The trip boats moor at the quay near the town centre, just before the bridge.

IATE CLUBE DO RIO DE JANEIRO CABO FRIO ANNEX

This is located immediately on the left at the mouth of the river, just after the first bend.

The club is annex of the Iate Clube do Rio de Janeiro and has about a dozen berths. Depending on the space available, you can moor alongside the quay or drop an anchor and come stern to.

Quality of moorings ***

This is the most convenient mooring for yachts with a draught of more than 2m. The water is calm but slightly affected by the frequent comings and goings of fishing boats, as the fishing harbour is upstream, just after the Iate Clube.

Facilities – Services ***

All facilities are available in Cabo Frio.
Post Office: Largo de Santo Antônio.
Banco do Brasil: Praça Porto Rocha.
Tourist office: Praça do Contorno, Praia do Forte
℡ (021) 647 16 89.

For boat maintenance services, there are several businesses attached to the Iate Clube that can work on site. You can let them know you are coming by calling on VHF Channel 68.

Water Directly on the club quay.

Electricity 110V and 220V on the quay.

Fuel Petrol and diesel on the club quay.

The trip boat quay on the river

The Iate Clube do Rio de Janeiro annex, at the entrance to the river

Supplies ***

Supplies are easily available in town, where there are several well-stocked supermarkets, as well as all sorts of other shops.

Mooring fees ***

The Iate Clube gives visitors two days free of charge.

Thereafter, the price is R$70 per day, plus R$15 per crew member.

Location and surroundings ***

The location of the Iate Clube makes it a very convenient stop. It is a 15-minute walk from the town centre and right next to Praia do Pontal, the beautiful, long white sandy beach on the edge of the town.

Iate Clube do Rio de Janeiro, Rua Amirante Barrosso 1141, Bairo Oasage, Cabo Frio
☎/*Fax* (22) 2643 34 32, 2643 08 36
Email carlos.jjs@uol.com.br
VHF Channel 68, call sign *Echo 23*

CLUBE NÁUTICO DE CABO FRIO

CNCF is a private club with around 500 members, half of whom own boats, all motor boats.

It is also home to a large number of diving enthusiasts; there is a laudatory record of its achievements on display in the club restaurant.

The sailing club is located less than one mile upstream of the mouth of the Rio Itajuru; its facilities can be seen to starboard at the end of a long straight line.

It gladly welcomes visiting boats if there is space available.

Mooring is on buoys, bows or stern to the quay.

Quality of moorings ***

Completely calm.

Facilities – Services ***

You can let them know you are coming by calling on VHF Channel 16/31.

All facilities are available in town (*see previous section*).

For boat maintenance services, the club has maintenance, painting, engineering, electrical and sun canopy making services on site; these businesses all have workshops in the club's boatyard.

There is a slipway on which small and medium-sized boats (max. 38') can be taken out of the water.

Water Taps on the pontoons.

Electricity 110V and 220V outlets on the pontoons.

Supplies ***

There are several well-stocked supermarkets and numerous shops in town.

Mooring fees **

As a guide, the price is R$40 per day for a 45' boat, including water and electricity; the price is very reasonable for the quality of the services offered by the club.

Club Náutico de Cabo Frio and the visitors' pontoon

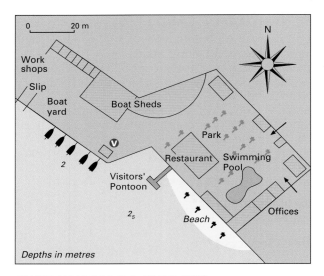

CLUBE NAUTICO DO CABO FRIO

Location and surroundings ***

The club is opposite the town centre on the other bank of the river, which makes it a bit far from the beach. However, it is one of the nicest due to the friendly welcome and the quality of the surroundings.

The facilities are comfortable and luxurious, and include toilets and showers, swimming pool, sauna, solarium, restaurant, volleyball court, basketball court, small private beach, etc., all in attractive gardens planted with coconut palms, swathes of flowers and decorative shrubs.

Clube Náutico de Cabo Frio, Avenida dos Meros, s/n, Ogiva, CABO FRIO CEP 28 960- 140
☏ (22) 2596 0140, (21) 2509 0764 Rio de Janeiro
Email CNCFRIO@uol.com.br

Iate Clube Costa Azul

IATE CLUBE COSTA AZUL

This Iate Clube is located on the river, just before the bridge, after the Capitania dos Portos.

It has some 600 members but only around sixty boats, all motor boats. The club mainly operates in the summer, and is only open part-time the rest of the year.

Clube Náutico de Cabo Frio, swimming pool and gardens

Quality of moorings **

There is around 2m of water along the quay, but the depth decreases significantly towards the middle of the river and this should be taken into account during approach manoeuvres. Mooring is on buoys, bows or stern to the quay.

The water is calm but there is a slight current.

Facilities – Services **

Identical to the other clubs in Cabo Frio.

However, the pool and some other services are for members only and visiting boats do not generally have access to them.

Water Taps on the quay.

Electricity 110 volt outlets on the quay.

Supplies ***

There are several well-stocked supermarkets and numerous shops in town.

Mooring fees **

As a guide, the price is between R$50 per day for a 45′ boat, including water and electricity.

Location and surroundings **

A major road bridge overlooks the club facilities, which makes the surroundings rather noisy.

Iate Clube Costa Azul, Rua José Rodrigues Povoas, 02, Gamboa, CABO FRIO, RJ
℡ (22) 2645 5474
Email costazul@uol.com.

The greatest concentration of small fishing boats in the region

Arraial do Cabo

Located just behind Ilha do Cabo Frio, the small town of Arraial do Cabo is the last port of call before you round Cabo Frio, heading for Rio de Janeiro.

The town stretches right along the long beach of Enseada dos Anjos, with some industrial activity, including a large chemicals factory, a short distance to the north of the town.

However, the main activity in Arraial do Cabo is small-scale fishing, and it has the greatest concentration of small fishing boats in the region.

In terms of tourism, the white sandy beaches are amongst the most beautiful in Brazil, and there are some excellent dive sites here, in waters of amazing clarity.

Navigation

Brazilian Chart DHN No. 1505.

On leaving the river from Cabo Frio, steer a course of 165° towards the tip of Ilha dos Porcos to

⊕ 0 • 22°57,35′S 041°59,15′W Arraial approach

You can go round Ilha dos Porcos or take a narrow channel between the island and the coast; this option gives direct access to Enseada dos Anjos.

Approach

Conspicuous landmarks

- As you approach Arraial do Cabo, a riprap breakwater can be seen to starboard; this shelters a large dock where commercial ships, oil platform support boats and Capitania dos Portos launches moor.
- At the end is the fishing harbour, where a whole flotilla of fishing boats of all sizes is moored on three concrete jetties.

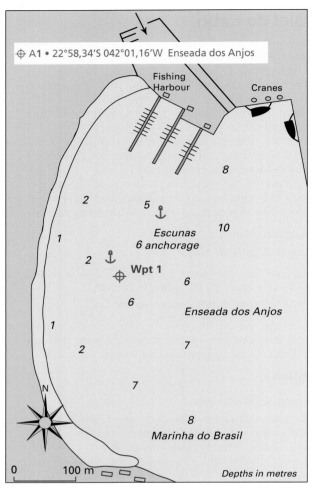

A1 • 22°58,34'S 042°01,16'W Enseada dos Anjos

Fishing Harbour

Cranes

8

2

5

Escunas
6 anchorage

10

2

Wpt 1

6

6

Enseada dos Anjos

1

1

2

7

7

8

Marinha do Brasil

N

0   100 m

Depths in metres

ARRAIAL DO CABO

Anchorages

South of the jetties and in the middle of the cove is a mooring area where *escunas* and other trip boats are anchored off the beach.

⚓ A1 ENSEADA DOS ANJOS

You can anchor level with this area, in four metres of water on sand.

⊕ A1 • 22°58,34'S 042°01,16'W Enseada dos Anjos

This anchorage is convenient as it is near the fishing harbour. It allows you to go ashore in the tender and get into town easily.

It is however a little rolly and open to easterly winds and the offshore swell.

⚓ A2 ENSEADA DO FORNO

Slightly to the northeast of the port, this small inlet, with a beach at the end, forms a peaceful anchorage in three to four metres of completely calm water.

⊕ A2 • 22°57,95'S 042°00,77'W Praia do Forno

⚓ A3 ILHA DO CABO FRIO

This is the most attractive anchorage at Arraial do Cabo and is well-sheltered by Ilha do Cabo Frio. The water is a

Ilha do Cabo Frio. The anchorage

Arraial do Cabo, the *Boqueirão* channel from the northeast

beautifully clear turquoise colour, with a white sandy seabed.

This anchorage is reached over a sandy shoal, and this itinerary is best taken at high tide; depth readings show a depth of 10m that rapidly drops to 2.5m.

The point at which the deep water meets the sandbank can be seen clearly in the difference in the colour of the water, which becomes turquoise in the space of a few metres.

Then head southward towards Ponta Maramutá. A large white sand dune can then be seen behind the point to port; anchor opposite this, near the beach.

⊕ A3 • 22°59,96'S 042°00,23'W Boqueirão

Caution There is a fish farming area level with this anchorage, protected by a special yellow marker.

A small building and a jetty can be seen at the end of the cove; these are occupied by the Brazilian Navy, which patrols this sector.

There is a narrow passage between tall rocks on the right which leads directly towards Rio.

Note

Ilha do Cabo Frio is a Brazilian Navy military zone; landing on the island is monitored and a permit must be obtained in advance from the Capitania do Porto do Cabo Frio. You might be asked for your permit by members of the Brazilian Navy once on the island; if you forget to request a permit, there might however be a little leeway for a short stay.

The Cabo Frio lighthouse, seen from the east

Cabo Frio

The Cabo Frio lighthouse is on the south of the island, on a rocky promontory, and its tall white tower is clearly visible LpB.10s140m49M.

The cape should be rounded a good distance offshore, as the sea is often rough around the island.

⚓ ⊕ 4 • 22°59,89'S 042°00,77'W
    Boqueirão channel

The back of Cabo Frio

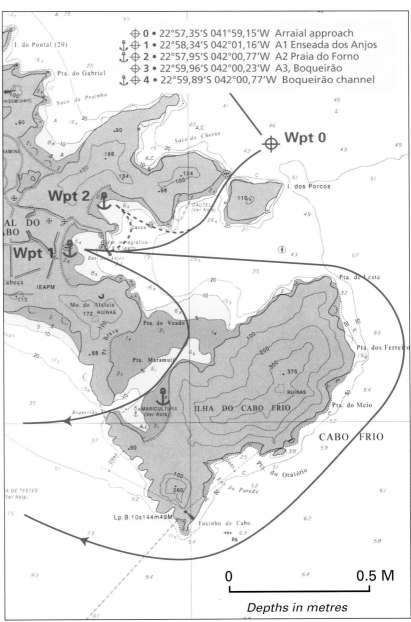

⊕ **0** • 22°57,35'S 041°59,15'W Arraial approach
⚓⊕ **1** • 22°58,34'S 042°01,16'W A1 Enseada dos Anjos
⚓⊕ **2** • 22°57,95'S 042°00,77'W A2 Praia do Forno
⊕ **3** • 22°59,96'S 042°00,23'W A3, Boqueirão
⚓⊕ **4** • 22°59,89'S 042°00,77'W Boqueirão channel

Wpt 0

Wpt 2

Wpt 1

0   0.5 M

Depths in metres

ARRAIL DO CABO

Rio de Janeiro – Baía de Guanabara

On 1 January 1502, a Portuguese expedition made up of a number of ships led by André Gonçalves discovered the mouth of a river that they named Rio de Janeiro. The river was in fact an enormous 250km² arm of the sea, and the Tamoios Indians who inhabited the region called it Baía de Guanabara.

The French already knew of the existence of the bay as they had started trading wood inland.

Several years later, under the guidance of Nicolas Durand de Villegagnon, they mounted an expedition to attempt to create 'Antarctic France', but the Portuguese would not tolerate their presence and chased them from the area following a series of bloody battles.

The city of Rio was then founded, and soon prospered due to the sugar cane plantations that developed across the entire region. The Portuguese built several fortifications to protect the entrance to the bay and at the beginning of the 17th century, the discovery of gold in Minas Gerais radically changed the town of Rio, which became an important port through which the precious metal passed before being transported to Portugal.

Its rapid expansion made it the foremost town in Brazil to the detriment of the capital, Salvador de Bahia.

By the 1920s and 30s, Rio had become a modern capital, frequented by people from the world of show business, artists, writers and members of high society, who found in Brazil a magical destination full of the exotic and … the samba.

Rio is no longer the political capital, but it has always remained the tourist capital of Brazil.

Just like André Gonçalves and his expedition, and following the same route, you are now entering Rio de Janeiro, in Baía de Guanabara.

Navigation

Brazilian Charts DHN No. 1501 and No. 1511.

Once past Cabo Frio and its lighthouse FE.LpB.10s144m49M, the coast is oriented east-west and is made up of an immense beach with a mountain chain in the background.

Half way between Cabo Frio and Rio de Janeiro, the lighthouse at Ponta Negra Lp(2).B.10s71m21M can be seen to starboard, and further on is Ilha Maricás, LpFi.15s80m11M, which is left to port; these are the only conspicuous landmarks on this featureless coast.

Approach

A course of 270° on the parallel 23° south leads directly to the entrance of Baía de Guanabara.

Tide and current

Baía de Guanabara has an irregular semi-diurnal tide.

Mean sea level is 0.7m above the chart datum, with a maximum amplitude of approximately 1.05m.

The speed of the flood and ebb currents varies between 0.2 and 1.5 knots, but in the narrow passage between Ilha de Laje and Ponta São João, the current can reach 2.5 knots or more in spring tides, depending on the weather conditions (heavy rain).

Winds

See also *Navigation aids and information – Climate and weather.*

Winds from the southern sector generated by cold fronts can make Baía de Guanabara very rough, and the offshore swell that comes violently into the bay forms 2–2.5m waves at the entrance. Under these circumstances, it is unadvisable to take the passage between Ilha de Laje and Ponta São João, which can be difficult and even dangerous. Similarly, after very hot days in the summer, there can be violent storms accompanied by heavy rain and gusty winds. During these gales, it is a good idea to ensure that you are securely moored.

Rio de Janeiro. General view

Rio de Janeiro landfall

Conspicuous landmarks A higher group of mountains becomes visible as you approach Rio, and the familiar silhouette of Sugarloaf Mountain (*Pão de Açúcar*) overlooking Baía de Guanabara can be seen in the distance.

At the entrance to the bay, Ponta de Santa Cruz and its fortress can be seen to starboard; it is an imposing building occupied by the Brazilian navy.

To port, Ilha de Laje, which is quite low to the water, is topped by a clearly visible green tower.

Landfall

From the east Once past Ilha do Pai and Ilha da Mãe, make landfall at:

⊕ 0 • 23°00,00'S 043°06,00'W Rio East landfall

The fortress of Santa Cruz to starboard, at the entrance to Baía de Guanabara

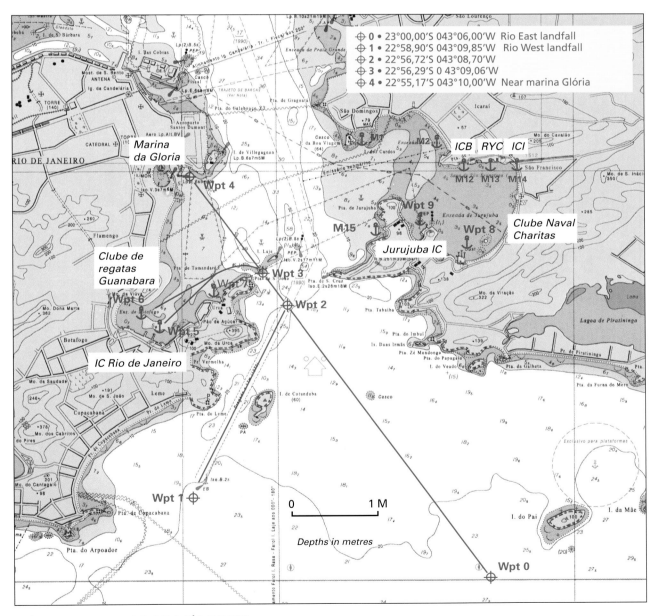

⊕ 0 • 23°00,00'S 043°06,00'W Rio East landfall
⊕ 1 • 22°58,90'S 043°09,85'W Rio West landfall
⊕ 2 • 22°56,72'S 043°08,70'W
⊕ 3 • 22°56,29'S 0 43°09,06'W
⊕ 4 • 22°55,17'S 043°10,00'W Near marina Glória

BAÍA DE GUANABARA OR BAÍA DE RIO

Baía de Guanabara. The passage between Ilha de Laje and Ponta São João

Baía de Guanabara. The isolated danger buoy near Ilha de Laje

From the west Make landfall directly on the buoy (Iso.B.2s)

⊕ **1** • 22°58,90'S 043°09,85'W Rio West landfall

that marks the entrance to the marked channel for commercial ships off Copacabana beach.

Follow this channel, which passes between Ponta de Leme to port and Ilha de Cotunduba to starboard.

For both landfalls, head towards ⊕**2** and ⊕**3**.

⊕ **2** • 22°56,76'S 043°08,70'W

⊕ **3** • 22°56,29'S 043°09,06'W

Ilha de Laje is an elongated rock, relatively low to the water, on which a bunker topped with pieces of artillery has been built; the tapered green tower at the northeastern end of the rock can be seen from a long way off.

You can pass between the island and Ponta São João by sailing on the left of the passage, the point side. However, account must be taken of the tidal currents, which can be around 2.5 knots or more in this passage, both on the flood and on the ebb.

Approach by night At night, the lights of the town in the background make the itinerary more difficult to identify.

Ponta Santa Cruz and the green light on Ilha de Laje, LpV.2s17m11M are clearly visible, but in misty weather, the passage between the island and Ponta São João, which is not marked, can be a little unclear.

In this case, or if you are in any doubt, follow the entrance channel to the commercial ports of Rio, and after Ilha de Laje, go around the isolated danger mark Lp(2)B.5s to the north, towards Enseada de Botafogo.

There are two options when calling at Rio de Janeiro:
• Marina da Glória, 1.5 miles to the northwest,
• a mooring area to the west, in Enseada de Botafogo.

⊕ **4** • 22°55,17'S 043°10,00'W Near marina Glória

Baía de Guanabara. Ilha de Laje, seen from the east

MARINA DA GLÓRIA

This is the only marina in Rio de Janeiro and definitely the best place for a stopover in Baía de Guanabara.

It is very well located not far from the centres of interest of Rio, and the nearby districts of Glória, Catete and Flamengo provide all the facilities you will need.

Furthermore, both boat and crew will be completely safe.

The marina is around 100,000m² in size and can hold 400 boats, with a few berths available for visiting boats.

The new management envisage the marina as being a base for the 2016 Olympic Games.

In port

Report to the marina office with the boat's papers and, if you have them, your Brazilian entry and visitor's permits, stamped by the authorities.

Quality of moorings ***

Moor on the pontoon or quay, bows to on a buoy.

The mooring is well protected, but unfortunately, as with many locations in Rio bay, the quality of the water is far from good and there is considerable pollution.

Facilities – Services ***

There are several boat maintenance businesses attached to the marina, some of which are located in the boatyard behind the marina offices and shops.

There are chandleries within the marina.

There is a slipway on which boats up to 35′ only can be lifted out of the water; it is a shame that a marina of this size doesn't have a travel lift or other heavy-duty lifting equipment for taking larger boats out of the water.

Water Taps on the pontoons.

Electricity 110V and 220V power on the pontoons; the installation is a bit dodgy and could do with overhauling!

Fuel Service station on the right at the entrance to the marina.

Supplies ***

Supplies are readily available. Rio has one of the largest shopping centres in Brazil, Shopping Barra, with a large Carrefour supermarket and hundreds of shops in the mall. There are also numerous more modestly sized supermarkets in each district.

Glória: Mercadez, Rua da Glória; Ultra, Rua Candido Mendes (will deliver shopping direct to the boat).

Catete: Large Sendas supermarket on Largo do Machado.

Botafogo: Shopping Rio Sul shopping centre; reached on the Copacabana-Rio Sul bus.

Mooring fees ****

As a guide, the price for mooring on the pontoon is R$4 per foot per day, including water and electricity.

A 3-month contract is considerably more expensive.

However, in the festive period and the summer season, the prices increase dramatically and it is advisable to check at the marina office.

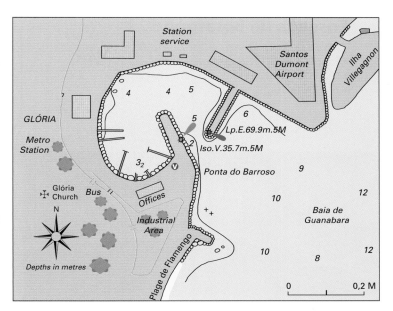

MARINA DA GLORIA

Location and surroundings ***

The marina is very well located near the Centro district, and not far from Copacabana and Ipanema beaches by bus. There is a bus and metro stop opposite the marina.

24-hour security service.

All around the marina there are numerous parks that are heavily frequented by joggers from first light. However, after dark, despite the paths being well-lit, it is unadvisable to cross these parks on foot as attacks have taken place. It is vital that you take a taxi to return to the marina in the evening.

Marina da Glória, Av. Infante Dom Henrique s/n°, CEP 20 021-140, RIO DE JANEIRO
☎ (21) 2205 6716, *Fax* (21) 2285 4558
VHF Channel 68, call sign *Echo 37*
Email marinadagloria@marinadagloria.com.br
www.marinadagloria.com.br

Rio de Janeiro. Marina da Glória, the best location in Baía de Guanabara

Enseada de Botafogo

There are three mooring options in Enseada de Botafogo:
- Iate Clube do Rio de Janeiro (ICRJ),
- Clube de Regatas Guanabara (CRG),
- the Urca anchorage.

Rio de Janeiro. Enseada de Botafogo anchorage

Note on the anchorages in Baía de Guanabara

The anchorages in Enseada de Botafogo are located near the *Urca* district and a small fishing harbour close to the Iate Clube do Rio de Janeiro.

In your absence at night, beware of break-ins and thefts of inflatable tenders and outboard motors in the mooring area.

There have been several robberies at night from visiting boats when the owner wasn't there, and a similar attempt was made on my boat, even though the tender was raised on davits and padlocked.

A word of advice: secure the whole thing with a large cable or chain, fitted with a strong padlock, or even better, pull your tender up on deck.

The same rules of caution apply to the other moorings in Baía de Guanabara.

IATE CLUBE DO RIO DE JANEIRO (ICRJ)

Iate Clube do Rio de Janeiro is one of the largest clubs in Brazil and its members own both sailing and motor boats.

The buildings are imposing and the facilities luxurious, especially the lounges, restaurant and swimming pool. It is the preferred meeting place of the well-heeled of Rio, sailors or otherwise.

Unfortunately it does not have a marina, and the majority of the boats are moored in the bay on mooring buoys.

If you want to stop over at the yacht club, bear in mind that it is a private club and entry is only for

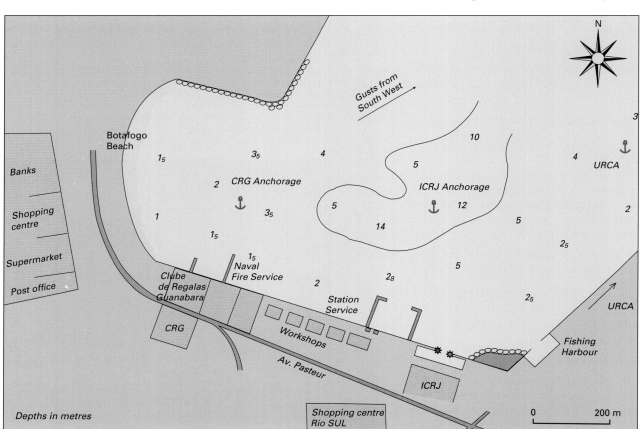

ENSEADA DE BOTAFOGO

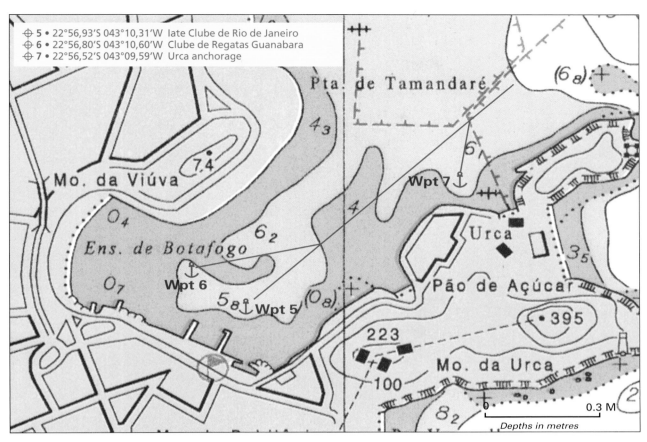

⊕ 5 • 22°56,93'S 043°10,31'W Iate Clube de Rio de Janeiro
⊕ 6 • 22°56,80'S 043°10,60'W Clube de Regatas Guanabara
⊕ 7 • 22°56,52'S 043°09,59'W Urca anchorage

Depths in metres

ENSEADA DE BOTAFOGO

members, the members of affiliated Brazilian clubs and members of a number of foreign clubs; the European clubs listed include the Paris Country Club in France, the Clube Naval de Cascais in Portugal and the Real Sociedade Bilbaina in Bilbao, Spain. It's a short list!

However, you can be invited by a member (*sócio*) who will sponsor you during your stay.

In any event, your application will have to go through the directors, or Diretoria de Administração Náutica (DIRAN).

When you arrive, you should report with, of course, all your papers and, if you have them, your Brazilian entry and visitor's permits duly stamped by the authorities. Whether or not you are allowed to stay at the club will depend on the goodwill of the DIRAN.

⊕ 5 • 22°56,93'S 043°10,31'W Iate Clube de Rio de Janeiro

Quality of moorings ***

There are two mooring options at the Iate Clube.

You can either pick up a club mooring buoy or moor on the jetty:

- on the mooring buoys, the water is relatively calm but disturbed by passing motor boats, often travelling at high speeds with no respect for the boats anchored nearby,
- on the jetty: stern to the jetty with a bow anchor.

Getting ashore is rather difficult, as a considerable undertow, especially in spring tides, means that you have

Arriving at the Iate Clube do Rio de Janeiro, towards the tall building in the background

to stay well off the quay; it is highly advisable to double your mooring lines. Watch out also for the swell and for anchor holding during gales.

Facilities – Services ***

The club has toilet and shower facilities and a snack bar for visiting boats.

The lounges, restaurants and pool are as a rule for members only.

Rio de Janeiro. Botafogo anchorage at the CRG

If you are moored off, a boatman will ferry you to and from the shore day and night; he can be contacted by VHF Channel 67. All types of boat maintenance service are available at the Iate Clube, which has several businesses on site, including maintenance, repair, engineering, electrics, a refrigeration specialist, an upholsterer, a sail loft, and so on.

Contact the office to be put in touch with the relevant business.

Water Taps on the quay and pontoons.

Electricity 220V on the quay and pontoons.

Fuel Fuel pump on the quay, which can be used even by visiting boats and non-members of the club.

Boat lifting facilities

The club has two 35-tonne travel lifts for taking boats out of the water.

This equipment is for members only and as a rule cannot be used by non-members.

Supplies ***

Supplies are readily available in town and in the Botafogo district, where there is a Mundial supermarket. Cash payment only – bank cards are not accepted.

Mooring fees ****

The club offers three days free of charge.

Thereafter, there is a fixed price for a mooring buoy of R$30 per day whatever the size of boat.

Location and surroundings ***

The Iate Clube is well located between the Urca and Botafogo districts, on a pleasant site near Sugarloaf Mountain; unfortunately, there is considerable water pollution, as is the case in most of the other locations in the bay.

It is also possible to anchor near the club mooring area, but you can only go ashore in your tender at the club if you are registered there. If you do go ashore at the Iate Clube and leave the grounds to go into town, you will not be able to get back in and will come up against an intransigent security service.

Iate Clube do Rio de Janeiro, Av. Pasteur, 333, Urca, Rio de Janeiro, RJ, CEP/22290-40
☎ (21) 2543 1244
VHF Channel 68, call sign *Echo 21*
www.icrj.com

CLUBE DE REGATAS GUANABARA (CRG)

This club has over 3,500 members and is located between Iate Clube do Rio de Janeiro and Praia de Botafogo. It is a private club but is absolutely nothing like its elegant neighbour. It has basic facilities; there is no luxury here but a very friendly atmosphere and non-members are accepted.

The club has a mooring area and a small jetty where tenders can be left in complete safety. The water is not very deep at the end of the jetty (1.6m), but you can moor nearby.

The facilities are reasonable (restaurants, bar, two swimming pools) and there are numerous other activities (tennis, fitness room, snooker tables, sailing school, etc.). The infrastructure is rather old and could do with renovation to make the surroundings a little more pleasant. For access to the club and its services, contact it by VHF or report with a form of identification (formalities are limited).

⊕ 6 • 22°56,80'S 043°10,60'W Clube de Regatas Guanabara

Praia de Botafogo is just nearby, but it is unadvisable to leave your tender on the beach to go to town.

Quality of moorings ***

Clube de Regatas Guanabara has several buoys in the mooring area, but check the condition of the buoy and the rope.

You can anchor near the buoys in 3–4m of water on mud, and the mooring area is generally calm.

With regard to the cleanliness of the water, the same comments apply here as for the other locations in Baía de Guanabara.

Facilities – Services **

Toilets and showers, bar and restaurant.

There are some boat services on site with a mechanic, an electrician and a carpenter, but you can also call on external contractors.

The club has a boatman to ferry you to shore.

Water Taps at the end of the jetty but the water is shallow (approximately 1.6m) and it is best to wait for high tide to approach (or use jerry cans).

Fuel You can fill up with fuel at the nearby ICRJ pump, or at the Esso Service station (with jerry cans), which is 50m down the road to the right as you leave the club (through the boatyard).

Enseada de Botafogo. Clube de Regatas de Guanabara

Supplies ***

Supplies are readily available in town and in the Botafogo district; there is a Mundial supermarket on the other side of the square. They can deliver to the boat.

Mooring fees **

Contact the office or talk directly to João Enrique, the Chairman of the club.

A fixed price of $50 per day is requested for mooring and access to the club's services.

Location and surroundings ***

Very well located with a magnificent view of Rio, Sugarloaf Mountain and the tall silhouette of Christ the Redeemer, which towers over the town and is illuminated at night.

Entertainment

Two evenings a week, it's party time at Clube de Regatas Guanabara!

On Wednesday and Friday evenings there is an extremely lively atmosphere at Bar da Rampa, which hosts local bands and singers, much to the delight of the clientele.

Clube de Regatas Guanabara, Av. Reporter Nestor Moreira, 42, Botafogo, Rio de Janeiro
☎ (21) 2295 2647, 2295 2597, *Fax* (21) 2275 1796
VHF Channel 68, call sign *Echo 25*
www.crguanabara.com.br

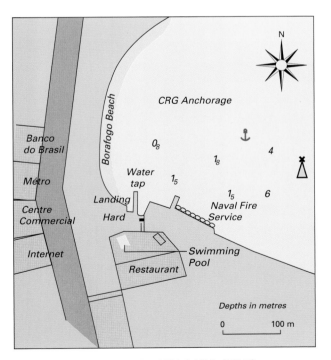

CLUBE DE REGATAS GUANABARA (CRG)

Enseada de Botafogo. The Urca anchorage

Urca Anchorage

This anchorage is located in the Urca district, to the left of the Iate Clube, opposite a small beach and some Brazilian Navy buildings.

⊕ 7 • 22°56,55'S 043°09,56'W Urca anchorage

Quality of moorings ***

Anchor in 3–4m of water on sand off the beach.

This is a peaceful anchorage and the water is calm, apart from when fishing boats pass close by.

Location and surroundings ***

It is nonetheless a convenient anchorage, free of charge, and there is a supermarket in the Urca district.

However, it is a little far away from the Botafogo district and transport by bus and metro.

In terms of floating debris, the water pollution is a little less apparent here than elsewhere in the bay. Avoid leaving the tender unattended on the beach.

It may be moored to the right of the beach or landed on the quay near the steps. Watch out for pilot boats berthing alongside.

Niterói

The town of Niterói is also located in Baía de Guanabara, facing Rio de Janeiro, on the opposite shore of Enseada de Botafogo. It is a lively town and nearby are beaches and Icarai, São Francisco and Charitas.

Clube Naval Charitas, in Enseada de Jurujuba, has an excellent marina and it is without a doubt one of the best places to stay on a boat.

CLUBE NAVAL CHARITAS (CNC)

CNC is at the south of Baía de Guanabara opposite Rio and is the preferred choice of cruising yachts.

The marina has five pontoons and its facilities are well-maintained with all the usual amenities found at the Brazilian clubs, such as lounges, restaurant, swimming pool, etc.

The club is partly run by Brazilian Navy officers; of course, nautical traditions are *de rigueur*, and it is to the club's credit. Its members include a great many racing enthusiasts, and a sailing school teaches the youngest of children in Optimists and Lasers.

⊕ Clube Naval

Quality of moorings ***

The mooring area is calm, but occasionally disturbed by passing fast catamarans heading for Rio.

Mooring is on buoys, bows or stern to the pontoon. There are around 200 berths. It is possible to anchor off the marina depending on the weather but watch out for gusts from the SW and during storms. The winds can be strong and variable. A good line is therefore strongly recommended.

The water is similar to the other locations in Baía de Guanabara, but seems a little less polluted.

Clube Naval Charitas with Rio in the background

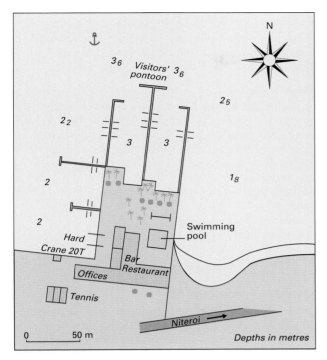

CLUBE NAVAL CHARITAS

Facilities – Services ✱✱✱

The club takes visiting boats up to 50′ in length, depending on the berths available, of which there are around a dozen.

There is a 20-tonne crane and a slipway for lifting boats out in the boatyard.

Clube Naval Charitas

For boat maintenance services, the club has several businesses that can work on site. Ask at the marina office.

Wi-Fi internet connection.

Water Taps on the pontoons.

Electricity 110/220 volts

Supplies ✱✱✱

Readily available; all types of supplies around São Francisco and in Niterói in the town centre. There is a well-stocked Carrefour and Sendas supermarket.

⊕ **8** • 22°55,97′S 43°06,48′W   Clube Naval Charitos
⊕ **9** • 22°55,64′S 43°06,92′W   Jurujuba Iate Clube
⚓**A15** • 22°55,25′S 43°07,47′W Praia de Adão Eva

ENSEADA DE JURUJUBA

Mooring fees **

The longer you stay in the marina, the more it costs; this is the club's way of encouraging the turnover of visiting boats in the marina.

However, the prices are reasonable and the club is well-organised with qualified staff.

Rates for guidance:

3 days	R$17 per day
4 to 15 days	R$34
16 to 30 days	R$51
31 to 60 days	R$66
61 to 90 days	R$101

You can anchor off the marina and use all of the club's facilities for a price of R$12 per day.

Location and surroundings ***

The club is located in Charitas, a small town a few kilometres from the centre of Niterói.

The facilities are of a high standard, in a pleasant setting with attractive gardens.

There is an efficient caretaking and security service operating 24 hours a day. Tenders with outboard motors should be lifted at night.

The No. 33 bus for the town centre stops opposite the entrance. There is a fast catamaran service between Charitas and Rio that takes 20 minutes, and in the summer holiday period, there is a direct service between Rio and Charitas. Embarkation and disembarkation are at the ferry terminal, Praca XV in Rio, and 500m from the Clube Naval.

Clube Naval Charitas, Charitas, Niterói
☎ (21) 2109 8100, *Fax* (21) 2109 8199
VHF Channel 68 or 69, call sign *Echo 30*
Email nautica@cncharitas.com.br
www.cncharitas.com.br

JURUJUBA IATE CLUBE (JIC)

This Iate Clube is at the entrance to the small fishing village of Jurujuba, which is approximately half a mile from Clube Naval Charitas.

Approach

The entrance to the Iate Clube marina does not pose any particular problems, but account must be taken of two obstacles marked with isolated danger marks. Avoid passing between the first mark and the club as the water depth decreases rapidly. Pass between the two marks or go around the westerly buoy. The Iate Clube allows visiting boats. Report with your passport and the boat's papers.

⊕ 9 • 22°55,64'S 43°06,92'W Jurujuba Iate Clube
JURUJUBA Iate Clube, Charitas, Rio de Janeiro
☎/*Fax* (21) 2714 8875
Email jicclube@ig.com.br
VHF Channel 69, call sign *Echo 45*

Quality of moorings ***

The mooring area is calm and well-sheltered; it is however slightly disturbed by passing fast catamarans on the Rio-Charitas line and by the fishing boats that come into this small cove, often without slowing down.

Facilities – Services ***

As part of its extension, the Iate Clube has built three new pontoons, which gives it good capacity.

JIC has toilets, showers, restaurant, pool, etc.

There are a few businesses on site that work on the club's yachts (engineering, electrics), but external contractors can also be brought in; contact the marina office.

There is a slipway for lifting out boats up to around 15 tonnes, but sailing boats with a deep draught will have some difficulties with the marina forklift, which is more suitable for shallow draughts.

Anchorage in front of Clube Naval Charitas

View of Jurujuba Iate Clube

Water Taps on the pontoons.

Electricity 110V and 220V outlets on the pontoons.

Mooring fees **

As a guide, the price is between R$20 and 25 per day for a 45' boat.

Location and surroundings ***

The Iate Clube is in the small fishing port of Jurujuba, about 10km from Niterói. The setting is very pleasant, in a small cove where local fishermen anchor their boats. The water quality is poor.

There is little by way of entertainment in the village; a few kilometres away, Forte de Santa Cruz, which marks the entrance to Baía de Guanabara, is worth a visit.

JIC has a 24-hour security and surveillance service.

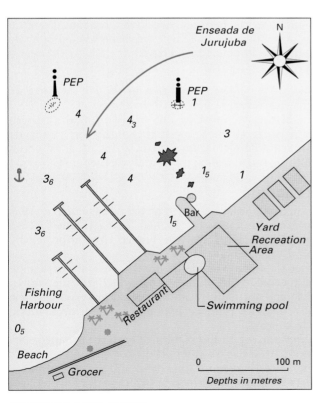

JURUJUBA IATE CLUBE

The Boa Viagem anchorage, near the contemporary art museum

Other anchorages and yacht clubs in Baía de Guanabara

⚓ PRAIA DE BOA VIAGEM ANCHORAGE

Anchor in 3.5m of water on sand. This is an unusual setting near the jagged rocks of Ilha dos Cardos.

The anchorage faces the modern flying saucer building of the contemporary art museum, designed by the architect Oscar Niemeyer.

Unfortunately, in certain wind directions the inlet is littered with floating debris, which is a shame as this could be a very nice anchorage.

⚓ **A10** • 22°54,56'S 043°07,74'W Boa Viagem

⚓ PRAIA DE ICARAÍ ANCHORAGE

Anchor on the right-hand side of the beach in 4m of water.

⚓ **A11** • 22°55,97'S 043°06,48'W Praia de Icaraíi

With regard to the water quality, the same comment applies as to the previous anchorage, particularly on the left-hand side of the beach, where there is all sorts of floating debris.

Yacht clubs

There are numerous yacht clubs in Baía de Guanabara. These offer a variety of nautical activities; all of them have excellent facilities, with pools, sauna, fitness room, sports ground, television room, bar, restaurant, etc. They are a place for the members and their friends to meet up for a meal at the weekend. Some of these private clubs might be of interest to visiting sailors.

⚓ IATE CLUBE BRASILEIRO (ICB)

The oldest Clube Náutico in Brazil (1906).

The anchorage off the club is free of charge, and you can use the club's facilities (apart from the pool, which is for members only).

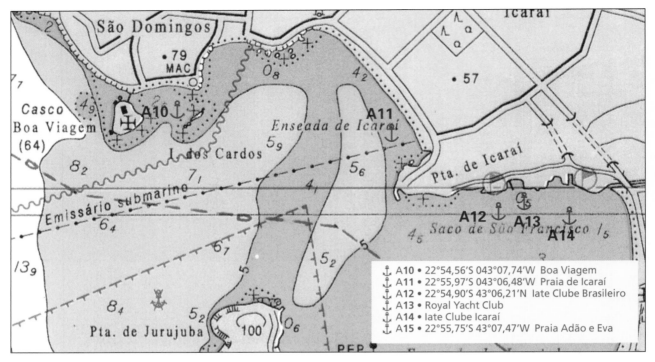

⚓ A10 • 22°54,56′S 043°07,74′W	Boa Viagem
⚓ A11 • 22°55,97′S 043°06,48′W	Praia de Icaraí
⚓ A12 • 22°54,90′S 43°06,21′N	Iate Clube Brasileiro
⚓ A13 • Royal Yacht Club	
⚓ A14 • Iate Clube Icaraí	
⚓ A15 • 22°55,75′S 43°07,47′W	Praia Adão e Eva

ENSEADA DE ICARAÍ

Mooring alongside: R$60/day, for a maximum of five days.

Has a fuel pump but it is not easily accessible. VHF call sign *Echo 20*.

⚓ **A12** • 22°54,90′N 43°06,21′N Iate Clube Brasileiro

⚓ ROYAL YACHT CLUB (RYC)

Mooring on buoys: 15 days free of charge, and you can use the club's facilities. 10-tonne crane.

⚓ **A13** • Royal Yacht Club

Iate Clube Icaraí, a club with a big-game fishing tradition

⚓ IATE CLUBE ICARAÍ (ICI)

This is a private Iate Clube with a big-game fishing and scuba diving tradition. 20-tonne crane.

⚓ **A14** • Iate Clube Icaraí

⚓ PRAIA ADÃO E EVA ANCHORAGE

This anchorage is between two lovely beaches, Praia de Adão and Praia de Eva, in a cove between Ponta de Jurujuba and Ponta de Santa Cruz.

⚓ **A15** • 22°55,75′S 43°07,47′W Praia Adão e Eva

Anchor in four metres of water, to the left of Forte de Santa Cruz, which houses the Brazilian Navy.

The setting is pleasant, but winds from the eastern sector rush over the smooth rock faces of Morro de Macaco and accelerate into the mooring area; however, it's nothing too alarming in normal weather conditions.

Ilha Paquetá

This small island in the north of Baía de Guanabara was discovered in 1556 by French cartographer André Thevet, who was part of the French expedition led by Admiral Villegagnon.

After the expulsion of the French, several Portuguese families came to live on the island, which became known for fishing, horticulture and its natural resources; the island's quarries produce lime and granite for building and decorating.

Luxuriant vegetation combined with the granite rocks forms an attractive, restful backdrop.

There are no cars on the island and you travel along its dirty roads by foot, bicycle or horse-drawn carriage. At the weekend, the natives of Rio (who are known as

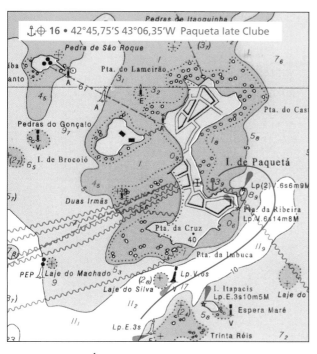

ILHA PAQUETÁ

cariocas) descend on the island in large numbers on the passenger boats that run regularly from Rio in less than an hour.

There are several beaches and the quality of the water for swimming seems better than in the rest of the bay.

Approach

Situated approximately 10 miles from Rio in the northeast of Baía de Guanabara, this is a particularly good destination on leaving Rio, and it is easy to reach.

Approaching the island, make sure that you leave to starboard the rocks of Pedra Rachada, marked by a beacon, LpE.3s.

The anchorage is reached on the eastern side of the island.

Ponta da Ribeira can be seen to port, with its white tower LpV.6s14m8M, and a breakwater behind which a few fishing boats are moored, and you then go around the small Ilha dos Lobos, Lp(2)V.6s6m9M.

Anchor off Praia Grossa, between the ferry terminal and the Iate Clube, which is to the left of the beach.

⊕ 16 • 42°45,75′S 43°06,35′W Paqueta Iate Clube

Anchorage. Praias Adão e Eva

PAQUETÁ IATE CLUBE (PIC)

Paquetá Iate Clube is the only one on the island. It is a modest club that willingly takes visiting boats.

Quality of moorings ***

The mooring area is calm, but slightly affected by northwesterly winds, which cause a slight chop.

You can come stern to the club's quay, dropping a bow anchor, in 5m of water.

Facilities – Services **

The club has toilets and showers, a restaurant, a fitness room and a pool, and for a small contribution you can use all of the facilities and services.

Ilha Paquetá. Ponta da Ribeira

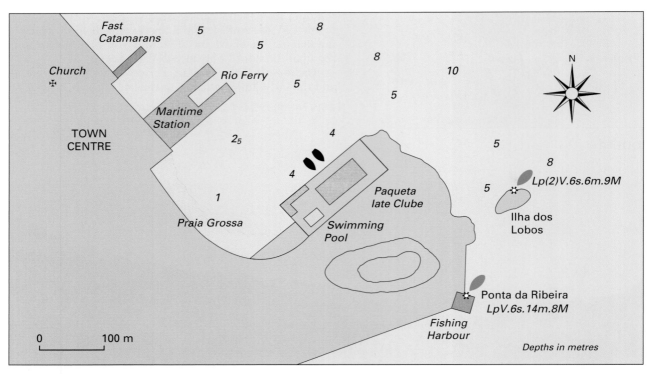

PAQUETÁ IATE CLUBE (PIC)

Paquetá Iate Clube, on the left

Beach on Ilha Paquetá

You can also become a member by paying a membership fee of approximately R$150 and a monthly subscription of R$60.

Water No taps on the quay, but you can collect water from the club in jerry cans.

Electricity No electricity on the quay.

Location and surroundings ***
The Iate Clube is well-located near the centre of the village and the passenger boat terminal, from where boats run regularly to Rio.

The village is very pleasant with its central square and quiet streets, and the setting is exceptional.

Paquetá Iate Clube, Praia das Gaivotas, Paquetá, CEP 20396-060
③ (21) 3397 0113
Email pic@paquetaiateclube.com.br
VHF Channel 69, call sign *Echo 44*
Office: Baiano.

Rio de Janeiro

Useful Information
For arrival by sea, the immigration, customs and port captain's office formalities must be carried out in the same way as for the other states. (*See chapter entitled Entering Brazil by Boat at the start of this book*).

Entering Rio de Janeiro by boat
(*see also chapter entitled Entering Brazil by Boat*).

The formalities must be carried out in the following order:

Polícia Féderal (Immigration)
Praça Mauá, Avenida Alfred Agache, Armazem 13,
Porto de Rio de Janeiro ③ (21) 2291 2142, extension 1106.

The Polícia Féderal offices are located in the first building on the port in the passenger terminal.

To extend your stay, you have to go to the immigration office at the airport.

Offices open from 0800 to 1800.

Alfândega dos Portos (Customs)
Av. Rodrigues Alves, Armazem 13, Door 1 and Door 2
③ (21) 2263 1386.
Offices open from 0900 to 1630.

Ministério da Saúde (Health department)
Av. Rodrigues Alves, Armazem 18, Centro
③ (21) 2516 4445.
You only need to go to the health department if this is the first time you have entered Brazil and you have come from a foreign country.

If you are arriving from another state in Brazil, you do not need a health check.

Capitania dos Portos do Rio de Janeiro
(State of Rio Port Captain's Office)
Av. Alfred Agache s/n°, Centro ③ (21) 3870 5313, 2104 5308.
Offices open from 0900 to 1100.

Useful addresses and telephone numbers

Communications
• Rio area code: ③ (21).
• Domestic calls are made using a 'DDD' phone card.
• International calls are made using a 'DDI' phone card (cards can be purchased at the post office or a variety of shops displaying a *Cartãos telefônicas* sign).
• To call the UK dial ③ 00 44 + area code without the 0 + telephone number.
• From a mobile dial ③ 00 44 + telephone number without the 0.
• To call from the UK dial ③ + 55 21 + telephone number.

Tourist office
• RIOTUR, Rua da Assembléia, 10-9°, Centro, Rio
③ (21) 217 7575.
• Avenida Princesa Isabel, 183, Copacabana, Rio
③ (21) 2542 8080.
• Alô Rio, an information service in several languages, including English. ③ 2542 8080.

• Request a *Nomad Guide*, a very comprehensive small catalogue of information.
Email nomad@nomad.com.br

Travel agencies

There are of course many of these in Rio, including:
• Bon Voyage, Maison de France, Av. Presidente Antônio Carlos, n° 56/10th floor ☎ (21) 2532 2866.
• Rio Voyage Turismo, Avenida Calogeras, 06, Sala 508, Rio ☎ (21) 2544 1350.

Public transport

Very convenient and reasonably priced (R$2 to 2.50).
   Check the destination and the number of the bus, and if you are in any doubt, ask the driver.

Buses for excursions

Terminal Rodoviário (bus station), Central do Brasil district ☎ 3213 1800.

Metro

Price R$3, very convenient and safe.
   Line 1 runs from Copacabana and crosses Rio, towards Botafogo, Flamengo, Glória, etc.
   Last train at 2300.

• There is a stop in the Botafogo district, not far from Clube de Regatas Guanabara.
• There is a stop in the Glória district in the square near the marina.
• Line 2 serves the northern suburbs from Estácio station.

Air transport

• British Airways, Alameda Santos, 745, cj 71, 7th floor, 01419 001, São Paulo, SP ☎ 0800 761 0885 (0900–1800 Monday–Friday).
• TAM, Praça Floriani, 19/28, Rio ☎ (21) 2524 1717
Av. Jurandir, 856, lote 4, São Paulo ☎ (11) 5582 8811.

Further information can be obtained from the offices at Antônio Carlos Jobim international airport on Ilha do Governador, or at Santos-Dumont domestic airport.

Post office (correios)

There are Post Offices in every district of Rio.
• In Glória, opposite the marina.
• In Botafogo (300m down from Clube de Regatas Guanabara).

Money

You can change or withdraw money with a bank card in several institutions, which can be found easily in every district, including:
• Banco do Brasil, rua Augusto Severo, Glória (opposite the marina).
• Banco do Brasil, Praia de Botafogo. ☎ 2537 2755.
• Bradesco: same address, opposite Clube de Regatas Guanabara, next to the Shopping Botafogo shopping centre.

HSBC bank is however one of the most convenient for bank card withdrawals from an ATM.

Consumer protection

• PROCON, Rio. ☎ 15 21.
• APADIC, Av. Erasmo Braga, 255, sala 1104. Rio ☎ 2533 4417.

Diplomatic representations

• British Consulate General, Praia do Flamengo 284/2nd Floor, Rio de Janeiro, RJ, CEP 22210-030
☎ +55 (21) 2555 9600, *Fax* +55 (21) 2555 9671
Email bcg.rj@fco.gov.uk

Emergency medicine

• Pronto socorro Rio ☎ 192 and 2273 0846.

Health

• Hospital Samaritaino, rua Bambina, 98, Botafogo ☎ 2537 9722.

Boat maintenance services

• Iate Clube
There are several businesses attached to Iate Clube do Rio de Janeiro, with their workshops in the club's boatyard.
   To contact them, you have to call the office on ☎ 5432 1244, and they will put you through to the correct extension (if you have permission to access the Iate Clube, *see ICRJ*).

• Marina da Glória
Electrics: Guiseppe Miceli, Loja A21 ☎ (021) 9919 7328.
Engineering. Maintenance, painting, sail loft.
   Contact the marina office.

• Clube de Regatas de Guanabara.
Enquire at the boatyard (José).

Batteries

• Poli-bateria
Rua General Polidaro, 183 6 Botafogo, Rio ☎ 2541 4466, 2275 4948

Refrigeration specialist

• Julio Refrigeração, rua das Laranjeiras, 336/74 ☎ 2225 2710.
Reliable tradesman who is happy to come to your boat. *Mobile* 9703 5867.

Ice

• Flor real ☎ 2539 5422.
Delivers ice and mineral water to CRG.

Chandleries

• Real Marina
Marina da Glória, Rio ☎ 2483 9704.

• West-Marine
Rua Gildásio Amado, 55 – sala 608, Rio ☎ 2493 0875.

Rigging

• Náutos
Marina da Glória, Rio ☎ 2205 9509.

Hull maintenance

• Diver (*mergulhador*) Anisio ☎ 8183 3819.
• Jacaré, diver, Marina da Glória.

Charts

These can be purchased at:
• Marinha do Brasil, rua Barão de Jaceguay s/n°, Niterói ☎ 2613 8316
www.mar.mil.br

• O VELEIRO, Ed. Maritimas – Jacques Mille (all charts with updates) Rua Theofilo Otoni, 48, Centro, Rio ☎ 2233 3025.

Life raft overhaul

Carlinho ☎ 2270 057-314 2936

Photocopying

There are many options in every district of Rio.

• **Opposite Marina da Glória:**
Papeleria, Rua da Glória, Rio

• **Opposite Clube de Regatas Guanabara:**
Copiadora Novo Horizonte, Rua Volontários da Pàtria, 45, Botafogo.

• Near the Rio Sul shopping centre:
Copylite, Rua Lauro Müller, 16, Botafogo, Rio
☎ 2543 0720.
Can also produce large format prints.

Rio de Janeiro, tourism and culture

With a population of six million, and over 10 million in the entire conurbation, Rio de Janeiro extends over 15,000m², from the immense Baía de Guanabara to Barra de Tijuca.

The beauty of the landscapes, the exuberance of its parks, its rich heritage, the *joie de vivre* of its inhabitants, and quite simply the insolent charm of the *cidade maravilhosa* (marvellous city) are irresistible.

You can explore the older districts such as São Cristovão or the heights of Santa Tereza, or stroll through Centro, buzzing with activity during the day but quiet at night and deserted on Sundays.

Centro is Rio's business district, home to shops, administrative services, banks, and so on.

Stop off in Uruguaiana with its popular market, where you can find anything and everything in the maze of countless stalls. Nearby Saara is the biggest shopping district in the city, with over 1,200 shops selling clothes, jewellery, interior design products, beauty products, toys, Carnival items, bars, and more. There's something for everyone, at low prices.

The church of Nossa Senhora da Candelária with its imposing dome stands at the top of Avenida Presidente Vargas.

Despite the construction of modern buildings, Carioca and Cinelândia still boast some beautiful colonial architecture and numerous museums, such as the Museo Histórico Nacional (National History Museum), the Teatro Municipal (Municipal Theatre), the Museo Nacional de Belas Artes (National Museum of Fine Arts) and the Museo Naval e Oceanográfico (Naval and Oceanographic Museum), to name but a few.

There is also the enormous Catedral Metropolitana; a modern cone-shaped building, 83m tall with a base diameter of 95m, it can hold 96,000 people!

Santa Tereza is an old district and one of the most picturesque in Rio; it is also the artists' quarter.

A small train known as the *bondinho* will take you around this old part of town, with its variety of boutiques and unusual art studios; you can have lunch in a traditional restaurant or buy kebabs in the street to eat on the move. There is a magnificent view over Baía de Guanabara from here.

Christ the Redeemer on Corcovado Mountain

As you head back towards the seafront you will come across the district of Glória; its 18th century church overlooks Marina da Glória and the surrounding parks.

Flamengo and Botafogo are two districts whose names evoke famous Rio football clubs more than anything else; their white sandy beaches are very popular, but unfortunately the water quality is poor.

In the middle of this part of the bay, the majestic Sugarloaf Mountain (Pão de Açúcar) rises 400m above the town, overlooking the waters of Enseada de Botafogo; you will easily be able to spot your boat anchored in the cove from the summit.

Further away is the statue of Christ the Redeemer on Corcovado mountain, casting its tall shadow from an altitude of 700m; it is magnificently lit at night and visible from all over Rio.

Don't miss a hike in the Tijuca National Park and Forest, above which Pico de Tijuca rises to 1,010m. It's a beautiful walk through thick tropical forest with fantastic waterfalls.

For a change of scene, visit the legendary Copacabana district!

Its very name evokes all the splendour of Rio's past and the myth of the present.

This is Rio's most touristy area, with its large luxury hotels, organised tour parties, bars, restaurants and ladies of the night (and day...).

All of the cross streets lead onto Avenida Altántica, which is always bustling and in itself represents the spectacle that is Copacabana. It runs along 4km of beautiful, wide, crowded beach; the waves come in as powerful rollers and swimming isn't always easy. When the beach empties, the crowds sadly give way to a devastating scene of waste – paper, plastic, *canudos* (drinking straws), bottles and packaging of all sorts.

Half of the beach is occupied by a large number of sandy football pitches. The goalposts are permanently in place for Brazil's favourite sport. In the evening, and far into the night, you can watch any number of amateur matches, loudly accompanied by shouts, cries and applause and punctuated by the whistle.

Continuing on your route, you come to Ipanema, a more chic district that also has a beautiful beach. This is where the young people of Rio congregate, to play volleyball and footvolley, at which Brazilians excel.

The most beautiful girls in Rio gather on one part of the beach, wearing the skimpiest of swimming costumes; on another part of the beach are the most handsome male specimens, also wearing the skimpiest of swimming costumes; this is the area frequented by Ipanema's gays and transvestites. Don't get mixed up!

Still further along the sea front is Leblon. This is a chic, modern residential district; it's very lively and attractive with numerous shops, bars and restaurants, and a vibrant nightlife.

Just behind Leblon and Ipanema is Lagoa Rodrigo de Freitas, a huge lake connected to the ocean by a canal.

All around the lake there are parks, playing fields, a cycle track, a race course and the helicopter pad that is the departure point for magical flights over Rio. It's quite expensive but worth it!

Just nearby is the Jardim Botânico, marvellous gardens that contain specimens of almost every plant in the Brazilian forests. Spectacular!

Further west the new district of Barra de Tijuca forms an extension to Rio with its huge complex of modern buildings; it is of little tourist interest but has the largest shopping centre in Brazil.

All of these districts, from the oldest to the most modern, are backed by a series of hills known as *morros*. Slum dwellings cling to the slopes of the hills in the most precarious of surroundings. These are the *favelas*, where the disadvantaged of the northern districts live in close quarters; they stretch from Nova Brasília to the large *favelas* of Mangueira to Canoa and Rocinha, which houses over 50,000 people.

This is the darker side of the *cidade maravilhosa*.

Rio Carnival. Banda d'Ipanema

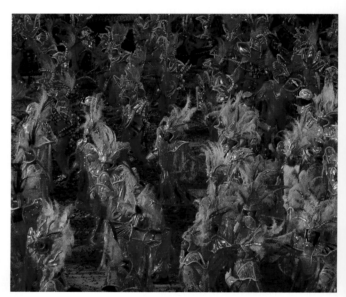

Rio Carnival

Carnival

Rio carnival is held 50 days before Good Friday and lasts for four days.

They are four days of intense madness during which the town becomes one huge show, with parties in the various districts.

Although some *cariocas* leave town during carnival, the rest of the population actively participates in the festivities.

There are two ways of experiencing carnival: the street carnival and the samba schools parade.

Street carnival

Each district pulsates to the samba beat. The *bandas*, accompanied by their orchestra, perched on the flatbed of a lorry, ply the streets escorted by the crowd. Don't miss the parades in Ipanema on Saturday and Sunday afternoons, when the party continues well into the night.

The botanical gardens in Rio

Banda de Ipanema is one of the oldest and its parade is among the most spectacular. The *bandas* generally parade along Avenue Vieira Souto, which runs along the beach, from 1700 onwards.

The samba schools parade

From its inception, carnival has been a big popular festival and the numerous samba schools engage in fierce competition to win a place in the special group of 14 schools that are given the honour of parading in the Sambódromo.

The Sambódromo is the stadium where the competition takes place; a long avenue lined with stalls and stands, it holds no fewer than 90,000 people.

The best samba schools (those in the special group) parade in the Sambódromo.

The parade takes place on Sunday and Monday evenings. Each display is carefully timed and must not last longer than one hour. The show starts at 2100 and ends the next morning after dawn.

On average, a single samba school enters around 10 floats accompanied by four to five thousand participants, split into several groups wearing different costumes. Each school chooses a theme and the floats, costumes and choreography are based on the theme. A samba song, specially composed for the event and performed by as many as 250 musicians, forms the musical background for the school's parade.

The Reina da Bateria (always beautiful and scantily-clad) leads the way, followed by the musicians and the first float; this is impressive, monumental, brightly-lit, glittering with gold and silver decoration and accompanied by similarly scantily-clad ravishingly beautiful dancers perched on their stilettos. The dancers follow behind; each group is made up of around one hundred participants of all ages, wearing sumptuous costumes in shimmering colours covered in sparkling sequins, and headdresses that are as enormous as they are extravagant.

The whole thing is a gigantic ballet, sometimes swaying, sometimes stamping, dominated of course by the frenetic rhythm of the samba.

The crowd of spectators in the stands accompanies the procession by singing along to the school's samba song as it passes.

But this impressive display cannot distract from the fact that the samba schools parade is first and foremost a competition!

A very strict panel scores each performance on 10 specific categories.

Preparations for the parade take all year, and the schools try to outdo each other in imagination and resources. They redouble their training efforts during the last few weeks before the final, when the winner receives the supreme title.

How to take part in and watch the samba schools parade

You can take part in the parade by going to a samba school and choosing a costume (*fantasia*) from around ten offered by the school. After one or two fittings you'll look amazing!

This gives you a place in a group. You will attend rehearsals on the school's premises and, being a sailor accustomed to balancing against a rolling, pitching boat, you'll be a natural at the samba!

The samba schools parade at the Sambódromo

Price: A costume for the parade comes to around R$300 at a modest school and R$800 or more at a school at the top of the ranking.

How to watch the parade in the stands (*arquibancada*) at the Sambódromo.

The best places are in sectors five, seven and nine, with nine being the very best.

The price of tickets at travel agencies varies from R$450 to R$1,000 in the stands; places on the side of the samba avenue cost between R$1,700 and R$2,200.

Tip: don't buy tickets from a travel agency! On the evening of the parade, numerous touts sell tickets on the black market, near the entrances to the Sambódromo; you can negotiate them down to R$150 to R$200 for places in sector five.

If that seems too expensive, wait until the show has started and once the third school has been through, you'll be able to buy tickets from around R$50.

Check the sector number on the entry stub and the date on the reverse of the magnetic card that should come with it.

If you are passing through Rio, don't miss this amazing spectacle, and above all, join a samba school!

Information

Associação das Escolas de Samba da Cidade do Rio de Janeiro,
Rua Jacinto, 67, Méier, Rio
② (21) 2596 1127
www.aescrj.com.br
LIESA – Liga Independente das Escolas de Samba do Grupo
Especial, Av. Rio Branco, 4/18°, Centro, Rio
② (21) 2253 7676
www.liesa.com.br
Sambódromo
Passarela Professor Darcy Ribeiro, Av. Marquês de Sapucai, Cidade Nova, Rio
② 3985 3000
Metro: get off at Central or Praça XI.

The national sport

Yes, you guessed it, it's football!

From the very youngest age, all Brazilians can kick a ball, and every football club has a nursery of champions. Even if you aren't a football fan, it is worth going to watch a match at the Mário Filho Maracanã stadium while you are in Rio.

Maracanã is the largest stadium in the world, with a capacity of 120,000.

That many overexcited people makes an impressive sight! Fans wave club flags and banners, shout, cry, sing and chant slogans, and fire crackers and smoke bombs in the team colours fly through the crowd. It's madness!

Your position in the stadium is important, but in any event you will be alone in the middle of a group of fans. Tip: make sure you're shouting for the same team as your neighbours.

Don't applaud any good shots by the opposing team, or you might find yourself being manhandled.

Other sports

Frescobol, which is played on the beach at the water's edge. Two players face each other with large racquets and hit a ball back and forth with surprising force and speed.

Volleyball, which is also played by numerous people at the beach.

Footvolley, which is also played on the beach, on a volleyball court but with the feet. It is very widely played and the Brazilians are extremely good at it.

Nautical events

January: Regata Almirante Tamandaré – CNC
April: Regata Comodoro – ICRJ
May: Regata Aniversário – JIC
May: Regata Aniversário do RYC
May: Regata Karl Heinrich Baddener – ICB
June: Regata Rio Boat Show, Marina Glória
August: Regata Aniversário – PCSF
October: Regata – DPC-ICI
October: Regata Prefeitura Municipal de Niterói – RYC
October: Regata Aniversário – ICB
November: Regata Força Aérea Brasileira – ICJG
November: Regata– CIAGA EFOMM/ICI
Regata Escola Naval – GVEN

Maracanã stadium, a temple to Brazilian football

Baía da Ilha Grande

Leave Rio de Janeiro and the bustle of a large city with its hectic pace of life behind, and head west, where less than 100 miles to the southwest you will find the Costa Verde and the idyllic anchorages of Baía da Ilha Grande.

This is the destination of choice for the people of Rio and São Paulo, who spend their weekends and holidays here; it is also one of the most beautiful tourist areas on the Brazilian coast.

From Mangaratiba through Angra dos Reis to Paraty, discover dozens of islands and inlets, glorious sheltered anchorages and long beaches beside limpid waters.

Navigation

Brazilian Charts DHN No. 1621, 1631, 1632 and 1633.

Baía da Ilha Grande is approximately 80 miles away from Rio de Janeiro, and the coastline has three distinct sets of feature on the way:

- From Rio to Ponta do Marisco, the beaches of Rio unfold one after the other, with the hills of the town, overlooked by Christ the Redeemer, in the background. At 850m, Pedra da Gávea with its flat top towers over Barra de Tijuca and the islands of the same name.
- The second section of coast is uniformly low and made up of an endless beach.

  The beach is a narrow strip of sand 40 miles long, which shelters Baía de Sepetiba.
- Further on, the mountains reappear; Ponta de Marambaía and the hills of Ilha Grande mark the entrance to the bay.

Conspicuous landmarks

On leaving Rio, Ilha das Palmas is left to port, Lp.BE.6s32m10/7M.

Further on, to starboard, are the Ilhas de Tijuca, Lp.BE.10s11M and the light on Ilha Rasa de Guaratiba LpB.6s42m18M.

Lage de Marambaía Lp(2)B.10s24m18M is a small rocky island just on the route, located around 15 miles from the entrance to Baía da Ilha Grande.

The lighthouse on Ponta de Castelhanos, a white square tower Gr.Oc(3)B.10s121m27M, is clearly visible from offshore, and marks the entrance to the bay.

Tide and current

Mean sea level is 0.7m above the chart datum, with a maximum amplitude of 1.2m.

The current is relatively weak and depends on the winds, which are sometimes strong in the bay.

Weather

Compared with Rio de Janeiro, which has relatively consistent weather, there are some notable differences in the weather in Baía da Ilha Grande.

Generally there is more frequent and heavier rain in summer (December and January).

In settled good weather, this entire area is generally characterised by close heat and little or no wind at night and for a good part of the morning.

Clouds form on the summits in the middle of the day and the wind gets up; the winds are northeasterly to southeasterly and in general rarely exceed a Force 3.

Baía da Ilha Grande, islands as far as the eye can see

Further inside the bay, the clouds gather on the hills and the overcast sky often brings rain in the late afternoon, sometimes with isolated storms.

The atmosphere becomes very close with maximum humidity.

Cold fronts can occasionally bring strong south and southwesterly winds, with gusts of up to 40 knots.

Entrance to Baía da Ilha Grande

The bay is approached through a marked channel for large commercial ships, and the mooring area, where huge container ships and oil tankers are often anchored, can be seen offshore.

The entrance is five miles wide and should preferably be approached on a rising tide as the ebb current, although weak, when running against a strong south easterly wind can make the entrance to the bay rather rough.

It is a good idea to enter Baía da Ilha Grande by day, at the end of the rising tide, so that you can choose an anchorage before nightfall.

Where to sail

Absolutely everywhere! However, watch out for rocks just above the surface of the water on numerous itineraries and around the islands.

Baía da Ilha Grande can be broken down as follows:

- **Ilha Grande, the largest island**
- **Angra dos Reis, the main town**
- **East of Angra dos Reis**
  Baía de Jacuacanga
  Baía de Mangaratiba with its beautiful inlets
  Baía de Sepetiba further east at the end of the bay, which houses a large commercial port.
- **West of Angra dos Reis**
  Baía da Ribeira
  Baía de Paraty with the village of Paraty, the most traditional and most touristy in the entire region.

Apart from Baía de Sepetiba, all of these locations are very popular with yachts.

In addition, this enormous body of water contains no fewer than 250 islands and islets, providing good shelter in extremely calm, clear waters. The islands, along with the entire coastline, are covered in thick tropical forest, the *mata atlántica*, which tumbles into the sea. It's an ecotourist's paradise!

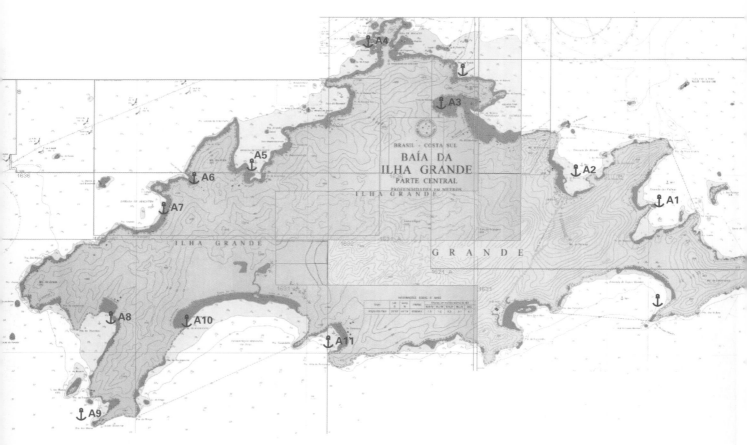

BAÍA DA ILHA GRANDE

Ilha Grande

This is the largest island in the archipelago, and the most visited by tourists and yachtsmen.

It offers numerous lovely beaches, and the small town of Abraão has several *pousadas*, campsites, restaurants and crafts and souvenir vendors.

There are no cars on the island and transport between beaches is by trip boat, often as part of a tour organised by the travel agencies.

Sailing is of course the best way to explore the island's anchorages, which are many and varied, and we will only look at a few of them here.

There are paths linking the beaches, providing beautiful walks through the tropical forest or up to spectacular waterfalls.

It's a different way of seeing the island on foot!

Quality of moorings ***

The anchorages on Ilha Grande are generally excellent or slightly choppy on the northern part of the island. The water is calm and clear everywhere, and the perfect temperature for swimming.

The southern part of the island is more exposed to the swell and the mooring areas are choppier.

The scenery of Baía da Ilha Grande

Facilities – Services *

You can only count on yourself on Ilha Grande, as you won't even be able to find a litre of petrol for your outboard motor; there is no service station as there are no cars, and most of the boat maintenance services are on the mainland.

There is however a ferry that runs regularly between the village of Abraão and Angra dos Reis or Mangaratiba, as well as numerous passenger boats.

There are however some basic services for simple suplies like bread water, drinks etc. and a few satellite internet access points.

Supplies **

Supplies are minimal on the island, with a few small mini-markets; there are numerous bars and restaurants dotted around the village of Abraão.

However, you will find a phenomenal selection of t-shirts, swimming costumes, shorts, sarongs and craft items in general.

Location and surroundings ****

The island is a perfect ecological unit with mountains covered in thick forest that stretches right down to the sea; its dozens of white sandy beaches slope into water that is sometimes green, sometimes turquoise, against a landscape littered with blocks of granite. There are a great many scuba diving sites all around the island.

Anchorages

Ilha Grande has a wide variety of isolated inlets in deep coves, and you will always be able to find a safe anchorage to suit the weather conditions. The anchorages are best on the northeastern and northwestern shores of the island. The southern part also has some anchorages, but they are very exposed to the offshore swell and should preferably be used in the day and in good weather.

⚓ A1 - ENSEADA DAS PALMAS

⊕ **1** • 23°08,65'S 44°07,50'W Palmas

There are two beautiful beaches in this large cove:

- Praia dos Mangues is in the deepest part of the cove; the water is calm but there are a lot of trip boats during the day.

  There is a small path leading around 2.5km from this beach through the forest to the southern part of the island, on the ocean side. The magnificent Praia Lopes Mendes can be reached along this path, with its clear waters and excellent waves for surfing.

- Further north, Praia Grande das Palmas is longer and has a pretty mooring area; it is also less crowded and disturbed by the comings and goings of trip boats. There are a few small bars that also serve food on these beaches.

Praia dos Mangues

Praia Grande das Palmas

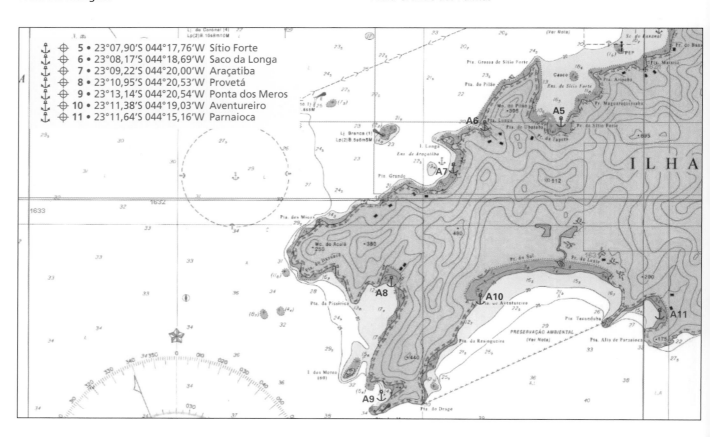

⚓ ⊕ **5** • 23°07,90'S 044°17,76'W Sítio Forte
⚓ ⊕ **6** • 23°08,17'S 044°18,69'W Saco da Longa
⚓ ⊕ **7** • 23°09,22'S 044°20,00'W Araçatiba
⚓ ⊕ **8** • 23°10,95'S 044°20,53'W Provetá
⚓ ⊕ **9** • 23°13,14'S 044°20,54'W Ponta dos Meros
⚓ ⊕ **10** • 23°11,38'S 044°19,03'W Aventureiro
⚓ ⊕ **11** • 23°11,64'S 044°15,16'W Parnaioca

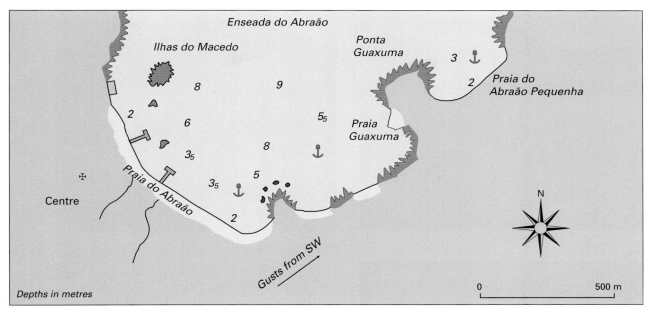

ILHA GRANDE, ABRAÃO

Abraão village

⚓ A2 - ENSEADA DE ABRAÃO

This is the tourist centre of Ilha Grande and numerous passenger boats bring tourists to the island every day.

It is possible to anchor to the left of the jetties, but during the day the anchorage is rather disturbed by the comings and goings of the trip boats.

⚓ ⊕ **2** • 23°08,33'S 44°09,95'W Abraão

There is another anchorage off Praia de Abraão Pequenha, on the left of the bay.

⚓ A3 - SACO DO CEU

The water is so calm that on a clear night, the stars are reflected in it, hence the name of this anchorage. A veritable millpond!

Even in bad weather, whatever the wind direction, this anchorage is completely protected.

When entering or leaving Saco do Ceu, stay well clear of Ponta Rapozinho, as the sand bank off its tip extends a long way into the channel. Watch out for the rocks that obstruct the middle part of the cove, and are shown by an isolated danger mark.

It is possible to anchor at the entrance to the inlet, on the right opposite a *pousada*, where the water is very clear.

Saco do Ceu anchorage

The anchorage of Sitio Forte with the water supply point on the rock

The rocks in the middle of Saco do Ceu

There is another anchorage at the end of the cul-de-sac, where several buoys have been installed near another very pretty *pousada*.

⚓ ✛ 3 • 23°06,58'S 44°12,19'W Saco de Ceu

⚓ A4 - ILHA DE MACACOS

This anchorage, also known as Lagoa Azul, is located on the northwestern part of Ilha Grande, behind Ilha de Macacos.

Ilha de Macacos

It offers an excellent mooring area and can be used to visit nearby beaches.

The waters are amazingly clear and, depending on the season, you can see large numbers of sea turtles.

⚓ ✛ 4 • 23°04,98'S 44°14,23'W I. Macacos

⚓ A5 - ENSEADA DE SÍTIO FORTE

There are numerous anchorages off the beaches of Sitio Forte, Tapera and Ubatuba at the head of this wide enseada. These attractive anchorages are much used by yachts.Off the beach at Tapera is a rock which has a water pipe on it. By night take care as this rock is not clearly visible. You anchor at the end of the cove and it's a pleasant anchorage, much used by yachts. The small bar to the right of the beach has installed a few mooring buoys for visiting boats. Great atmosphere!

✛ 5 •23°08,15'S 044°17,35'W Sítio Forte, Praia de Tapera

Scuba diving enthusiasts can dive on the wreck of the Panamaian ship *Pingüino*, which sank in 1967. The 66m carcass lies in 18m of water.

✛ wreck 23°07,07'S 044°16,92'W

⚓ A6 - SACO DA LONGA

This is a little fishing village nestled at the end of a cul-de-sac. It is also an excellent, completely sheltered anchorage but a little narrow, as a number of mooring buoys have been installed for the fishing boats. The jetty on the right is for unloading the boats only, but you can anchor on the left-hand side in 5m of water.

✛ 6 •23°08,17'S 044°18,69'W Saco da Longa

Another option is to pick up a mooring buoy temporarily in the absence of a fishing boat. This is a good place to buy fresh fish! Sheltered by Ilha Longa is another anchorage which is very nearby, but because it is relatively narrow it becomes congested very quickly. Depths of 10m require a long length of chain which makes avoiding action difficult when crowded.

⚓ A7 - ENSEADA DE ARAÇATIBA

The anchorage is on the right-hand side of the cove, off a small beach.

✛ 7 •23°09,22'S 044°20,00'W Araçatiba

The Sítio Forte anchorage

There are other possibilities and I favour a small beach between rocks in front of Praía Vermelha. Use with care.
⊕ **7 bis** •23°09,50'S 044°20,83'W near Praía Vermelha

⚓ A8 - PRAIA PROVETÁ

This anchorage is rather exposed to the offshore swell and should only be used in the day in good weather. At the head of the bay is a small fishing village where boats use the left side of the beach.
⊕ **8** • 23°10,95'S 044°20,53'W Provetá

⚓ A9 - PONTA DOS MEROS

This very pleasant anchorage is however open to the southwest, and a cold front coming in can make this cul-de-sac uncomfortable very quickly.
⊕ **9** • 23°13,14'S 044°20,54'W Ponta dos Meros

⚓ A10 - PRAIA DO AVENTUREIRO

This area is a State Marine Park and therefore protected. Any fishing, underwater hunting or other sport that might damage the environment is strictly forbidden. It is possible to anchor in the small cove, on the very left-hand side of the beach.
⊕ **10** • 23°11,38'S 044°19,03'W Aventureiro

Caution: this beach is open to winds from the southern sector and the offshore swell!

⚓ A11 - PRAIA PARNAIOCA

Located just next to Praia do Aventureiro, this pleasant inlet is also open to the southwest and you should always be on the look-out for an approaching cold front.
⊕ **11** • 23°11,64'S 044°15,16'W Parnaioca

⚓ A12 - PRAIA LOPES MENDES

Already mentioned under anchorage one, most of the time this beautiful beach is hard to reach because of the waves, which make landing difficult. It is best to walk to it from anchorage one, Enseada das Palmas, described above.

The small fishing harbour at Saco da Longa

Praia Lopes Mendes

Angra dos Reis

The largest town in Baía da Ilha Grande is Angra dos Reis, with a population of 115,000.

It is a commercial port and a logistics base for the offshore oil exploration companies; there are large shipbuilding and repair yards nearby. It is also the main tourist centre in the region. Most of the trip boats that visit the numerous islands in the bay leave from the port, which is always a hive of activity in the summer season.

Although this is a historical town, there is little of any particular interest apart from its two churches, Nossa Senhora de Conceição and Convento do Carmo, both built in the 17th century. However, the bustling town centre on the edge of the harbour is very traditional, with numerous small shops along its crowded pavements.

The town is concentrated on the seafront and surrounded by steep mountains covered with thick tropical forest. In the surrounding area, this jagged coast is home to several yacht clubs and marinas of varying sizes.

There are three marinas with decent infrastructures that are worth mentioning, located in the immediate vicinity of the town centre.

⊕ 0 • 23°00,18'S 044°18,10'W Near the marinas

MARINA PIRATAS

This is a modern marina that is home to sailing boats and motor boats, some very large. It has 150 berths spread over four pontoons with catwalks, which can take boats up to 120' long. The small and medium-sized motor boats are stored on land in immense storage sheds.

The marina is located at the end of the bay, at the northern tip of the town; it is approached along a marked channel and the entrance is regularly dredged to a depth of 2m at low tide.

Marina Piratas

Angra dos Reis. The fishing and trip boat harbour

Angra dos Reis. General view of Marina Piratas

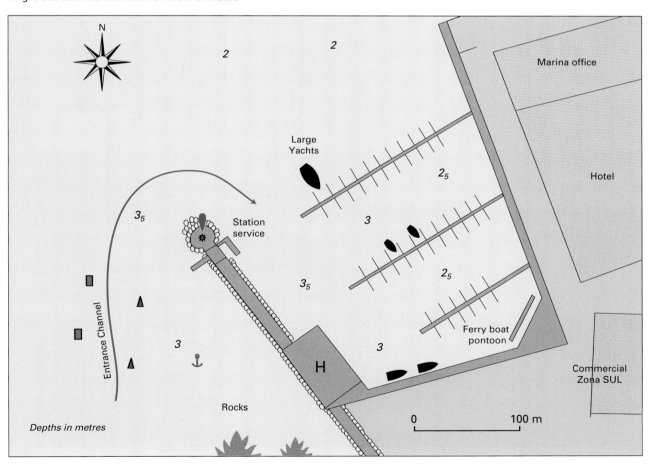

MARINA PIRATAS

Quality of moorings ***

The mooring area is calm inside the dock, but the water is unfortunately often strewn with floating debris.

Facilities – Services ***

Water and 110/220 volt electricity on the pontoons.

Service station with diesel, petrol, oil and ice in bags made with filtered water (*gelo filtrado*).

Engineer, electrician and boat maintenance and repair services on site.

No travel lift; 12-tonne forklift for lifting out small motor boats.

Heliport.

Angradiesel in the fishing harbour, near the ice factory.

Supplies ****

There is a shopping centre within the marina grounds with a Zona Sul supermarket; very convenient for supplies.

Mooring fees ****

As a guide, the price is R$8 to 10 per day. However, the price can be negotiated depending on the length of stay.

Location and surroundings ***

The marina is located approximately 2km from the town centre, and there is a regular bus service from the marina.

24-hour surveillance.

The bus station is very nearby, with buses for Rio, Paraty, São Paulo, etc.

VHF Channel 68, call sign *Echo 62*
☎/*Fax* (24) 3365 4089
Email mpiratas@marinapiratas.com.br
www.marinapiratas.com.br

IATE CLUBE AQUIDABÃ

This club is just before Marina Piratas, to the left of it.

It is a very pleasant, well-organised Iate Clube with 1,800 members and excellent facilities. The club accepts visiting boats if there is space available, but limits any stay to one week to encourage the turnover of boats, depending on demand.

Quality of moorings ***

Very calm; there are around one hundred berths on a quay or pontoons, 54 with catwalks.

Can take boats up to 70'.

Water depth three to four metres.

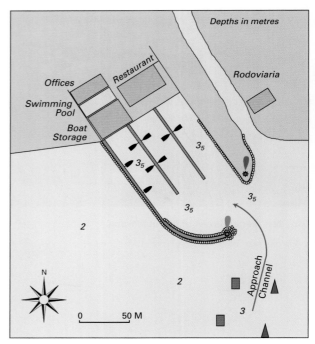

IATE CLUBE AQUIDABÃ

Angra dos Reis. The Iate Clube Aquidabã marina

Facilities – Services ★★★

There is a whole range of facilities on site. The club has all the normal amenities of the large Brazilian clubs, including bar, restaurant, swimming pool, tennis courts, fitness room, etc.

Water and 110/220 volt electricity on the pontoons. No service station. Repair and maintenance service provided by specialist businesses (engineering, electrics, electronics, etc.). The club has a slipway for lifting out boats up to 50'.

Supplies ★★★

There are two supermarkets nearby.

Mooring fees ★★★★

At the Club's discretion.

Location and surroundings ★★★

Very well located near the town centre and the bus station. 24-hour video surveillance and security service.

Iate Clube Aquidabã, Angra dos Reis
VHF Channel 68, call sign *Echo 29*
℡ (24) 3365 1343
Email clubeaquidaba@uol.com.br

ANGRA DOS REIS MARINA CLUBE

This marina is located opposite the town of Angra dos Reis, to the northeast, not far from Ponta da Cidade. It can be seen to starboard at the end of the bay, with a large number of moored boats. It has excellent facilities and accepts visiting boats.

Quality of moorings

The mooring area is very calm and the water is clear, with no pollution from floating debris. The marina has 40 berths on a single pontoon, and around one hundred mooring buoys. Watch the water depth, which decreases significantly on the left-hand side of the mooring area.

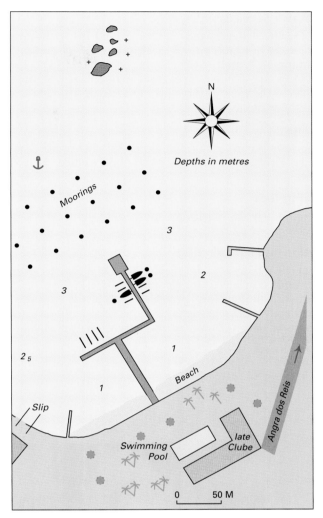

ANGRA DOS REIS MARINA CLUBE

Angra dos Reis Marina Clube and the mooring area

Facilities – Services

The marina offers every comfort and its on-shore facilities are outstanding, with bar, very good restaurant, swimming pool, etc.

Services are limited to general maintenance, with a slipway on the right of the mooring area for lifting boats out of the water.

Supplies

In the town centre or at the Zona Sul supermarket at Marina Piratas, which can easily be reached in the tender.

Mooring fees

Approximately R$30 per day on the pontoon, and R$20 on a club mooring buoy.

Location and surroundings

The marina is a little far from the town centre, with rather limited means of transport.

The surroundings are beautiful with shady greenery and perfectly tended gardens.

Angra dos Reis Marina Clube, Saco da Cacheira – Marinas, Angra dos Reis, RJ, CEP 23900-000
☎ (24) 3365 0444
VHF Channel 68, call sign *Echo 34*
Email armclube@uol.com.br

Anchorages

It is also possible to anchor off Angra dos Reis Marina Clube or outside Marina Piratas and Iate Clube Aquidabã, on the edge of the marked channel in depths of 2–3m. The latter anchorage is however greatly disturbed by the incessant comings and goings of the motor boats entering and leaving the marinas.

It is however quite convenient, as you can easily go into Marina Piratas in the tender, where a floating pontoon is set aside for tying up small boats and visiting the shopping centre.

Inside Marina Piratas, you can also moor the boat alongside the quay on the right-hand side of the marina, but only for short periods. The quay is reserved for trip boats taking on or letting off tourists. Mooring here is permitted and free of charge for the time it takes to do some shopping in the mall or supermarket.

Many visiting boats abuse the permission granted to use this quay by staying too long, and it would be a shame if this very convenient mooring was to become more strictly regulated or charged for.

Outside these marinas, there are a few possible anchorages near the fishing harbour or the Capitania dos Portos.

However, near the town there are two peaceful anchorages in pleasant surroundings:

- Praia do Bomfim
- Praia Grande

Angra dos Reis Marina Clube. The swimming pool with the mooring area in the background

Praia do Bomfim anchorage

⚓ PRAIA DO BOMFIM ANCHORAGE

This is located in a small cove just after the Colégio Naval.

An excellent anchorage near an island on which the church of Nosso Senhor do Bomfim stands, and very close to a small district of Angra dos Reis.

Anchor in three to 4m of water off the beach in a very calm mooring area. The tender can be tied up to the jetty in the middle of the beach.

This small district, around 2.5km from the centre of Angra dos Reis, is served by a regular bus link.

⊕ 1 • 23°01,30′S 044°19,86′W

⚓ PRAIA GRANDE ANCHORAGE

Another very calm anchorage in the cove after the previous anchorage.

Anchor off the beach, where holding is good in three to four metres of water on sand.

⊕ 2 • 23°01,46′S 044°20,40′W

Praia Grande anchorage

East of Angra dos Reis

Baía de Jacuacanga

On this part of the coast, the most noticeable feature is the large shipyard at Verolme; the yard builds and reconditions large vessels and can be seen from a long way off at the end of the bay, with its jib cranes, bridge cranes and scaffolding shrouding the huge hulls of ships under construction or repair.

This is the site of Marina Verolme, one of the largest marinas in the region.

MARINA VEROLME

Located in a huge, mainly marine, industrial zone, this marina is not the most pleasant in terms of surroundings, but it is certainly ideal for yacht maintenance services.

Marina Verolme

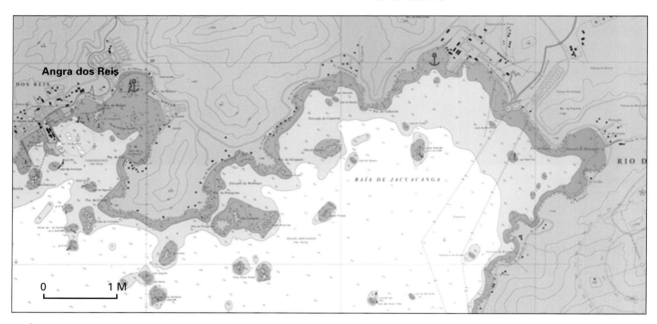
BAÍA DE JACUANGA

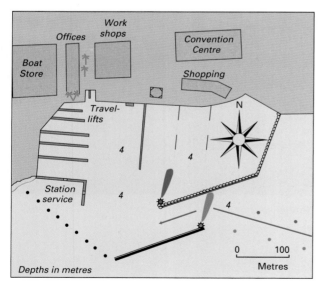
MARINA VEROLME

It is approached along a marked channel that is lit at night and was dredged when it was created to ensure a depth of 5m at low tide at the marina entrance.
⊕ 22°59,52'S 044°14,59'W

Quality of moorings **

Very calm, with a water depth of 3.5–4m in the dock.
Well-protected from the winds in general.
120 berths on well-equipped pontoons.

Facilities – Services ***

Water and 110/220 volt electricity on the pontoons. Service station.
Every kind of boat repair and maintenance service is available on site and in the industrial zone.
Three travel lifts: 35-, 70- and 100-tonne.
Bus stop at the entrance to the industrial zone.
Heliport.

Mooring fees ****

As a guide, R$10 per foot per day.
Electricity is paid for separately at 58cts/kW.

Location and surroundings *

Approximately 15km from Angra dos Reis, but there is a regular bus service.

Although the services at the marina are comprehensive, the surroundings have been sacrificed somewhat; but it might be difficult to do any better in this enormous industrial complex.

A huge dry storage area, with boats stored in sheds over several levels, but it is little used by visiting boats apart from when major repairs are needed.

24-hour video surveillance.

☎ (24) 34214090, *Fax* (24) 3361 3101
VHF Channel 68
Email marinaverolme@uol.com.br
www.marinaverolme.com.br

Baía de Mangaratiba

Baía de Mangaratiba offers a large number of anchorages in tranquil coves. Near the bay, there are also a few marinas incorporated into luxury housing developments. Some of these marinas can be used by visiting boats, but the prices do of course match the standing of the condominium.

MARINA PORTO REAL

The surroundings are not great on this concrete development, but it is good to know that this marina has a slipway for lifting out boats weighing up to 30 tonnes.

⊕ 23°02,07'S 044°09,45'W Porto Real

Marina Porto Real

Mooring fees

Around R$150 to 180 per day for a 45' boat.
VHF Channel 68, call sign *Foxtrot 97*
☎ 21 2685 7080
Email marina.portoreal@terra.com.br

Just next door, Praia de Sororoca provides a good anchorage. Service station nearby.

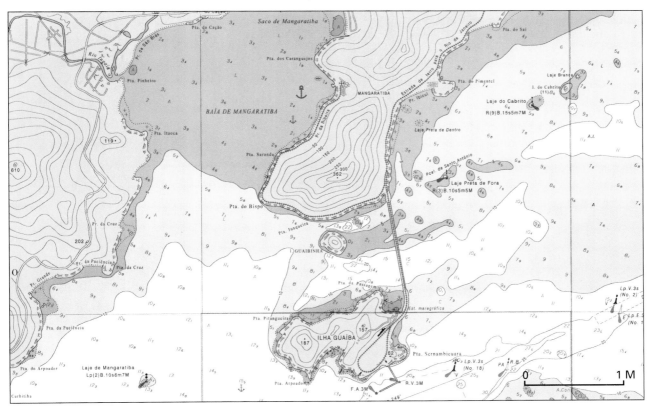

BAÍA DE MANGARATIBA

Marina Portogalo

MARINA PORTOGALO

This small marina is located in a large condominium built on the mountainside, forming a pleasant site with luxury residences.

⊕ 23°02,34'S 044°12,20'W Portogalo

Facilities – Services

Crane: 5-tonne capacity. Water, 110/220V electricity.
 Service station with diesel, petrol and boat maintenance services.

Mooring fees

As a guide, the price is between R$180 and 200 per day for a 45' boat.
VHF Channel 68, call sign *Echo 34*
☎ (24)3361 4343

Mangaratiba

This is a sprawling town with an old part and a more modern part opposite a long beach. It is however preferable to anchor near the old town, which has a busy town centre with numerous facilities.

⊕ 22°57,70'S 044°02,65'W Near Mangaratiba

Baía de Sepetiba

Although less frequently visited by passing boats than other locations in Baía da Ilha Grande, Baía de Sepetiba has several good anchorages and interesting dive sites such as those to the west of Ilha de Itacuruçá and to the north of Ilha de Jaguanum.

Mangaratiba

Quality of moorings **

A tranquil anchorage and berths for 132 boats on three pontoons.

Facilities – Services

Possible mooring for boats up to 80'. Petrol and diesel at the service station. Bar/restaurant.
VHF canal 68 / Foxtrott 22
☎ (21) 2680 7437 / 7551
Email marinaitacuruca@uol.com.br
www.marinaportoitacuruca.com.br

West of Angra dos Reis

Baía da Ribeira

Baía da Ribeira is located to the northwest of Angra dos Reis and there are several good marinas here.

IATE CLUBE DE ANGRA DOS REIS

This Iate Clube has 350 members and is located in Baía da Ribeira. It does not have a floating pontoon, but around thirty mooring buoys.
 There is a boatyard for general maintenance work.
 It is a pleasant Iate Clube, with a dynamic racing section.
☎ (24) 3377 2506
VHF Channel 68, call sign *Echo 27*

Iate Clube de Angra dos Reis (ICAR)

Angra dos Reis. Porto Marina 1

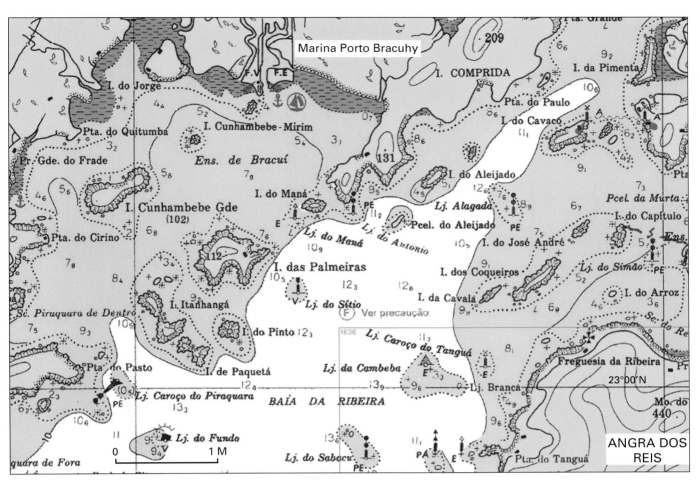

PORTO MARINA 1

This marina is made up of three pontoons with catwalks and can hold 140 boats.

The 20-tonne crane can only be used by motor boats (there is no cradle for sailing boats).

There is a plan to build a slipway for lifting out larger boats.

Service station with petrol and diesel.

⊕ 22°56,44'S 044°19,63'W

Mooring fees ***

As a guide, R$4.50 per foot per day; R$20 per foot per month.

① (24) 3367 0050, *Fax* (24) 3367 0055
Email marina@portomarina1.com.br

There are also two other marinas at the end of the bay, Porto Marina Bracuhy and Marina Porto Frade.

These marinas were built as part of large housing developments and the marina at Bracuhy is one of the best stopovers in the bay.

MARINA PORTO BRACUHY

This marina is easily reached coming from Angra dos Reis, and is one of the largest in the region; you can leave your boat here completely safely for long periods without any problems.

⊕ 22°57,35'S 044°23,77'W Bracuhy

Quality of moorings ****

The enormous mooring area is completely calm with no undertow or current.

600 berths spread over eight pontoons.

Facilities – Services ***

There are numerous facilities in the marina, with bars, restaurants, a pool at the hotel next door, etc.

A multi-service company, Estaleiro Boat Service, is located within the marina itself.

Marina Porto Bracuhy, to the northwest of Angra dos Reis

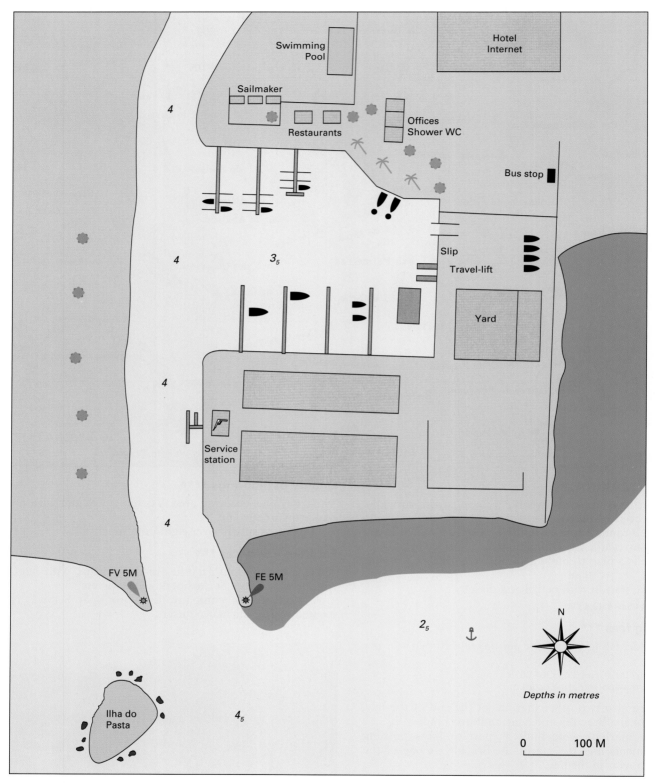

MARINA PORTO BRACUHY

A whole range of services is available on site: engineering, electrics, service station, sail loft, laminating, careening, painting, etc.

There is a travel lift for lifting out boats but it is unfortunately rather old and limited to 10 tonnes.

There is also a slipway for lifting out larger vessels.

Supplies **

There is a small supermarket near the marina in the village of Bracuhy, around 4km from the marina, or the Zona Sul shopping centre in Angra dos Reis.

Mooring fees ***

As a guide, the price is between R$2 per foot per day. For long stays, the marina offers attractive rates.

Location and surroundings ***

The surroundings are pleasant, with large, well-tended gardens.

The marina is a half-hour bus journey away from Angra dos Reis, and the buses stop inside the marina (Angra-Frade line via Bracuhy).

24-hour security service.

VHF Channel 68, call sign *Echo 62*

MARINA PORTO FRADE

⊕ 22°58,29'S 044°26,00'W Frade

Quality of moorings ***

Completely sheltered, calm mooring area.

The entrance is through a marked channel to the marina, as the water is shallow nearby. Boats are moored on pontoons or on buoys outside the marina.

Facilities – Services **

Several boat maintenance businesses operate within the marina.

Water and 110 and 220V electricity on the pontoons.

Supplies **

There is a supermarket in the nearby village of Frade.

Mooring fees ****

As a guide, the price on the pontoon is between R$9 per foot per day.

Location and surroundings ***

The marina is on the site of a luxury condominium, with a small beach nearby, all in very pleasant surroundings.

Marina Porto Frade
Angra dos Reis ☏ (24) 3369 0431
VHF Channel 68, call sign *Echo 47*
Email marinapfrade@uol.com.br

Just next to the marina, Iate Clube de Santos has set up an annex in equally exceptional surroundings.

☏/*Fax* (24) 3369 0100
Email isar@icsantos.com.br

Angra dos Reis to Paraty

The coast from Angra dos Reis to Paraty also provides a wide variety of anchorages, near beaches, in isolated inlets or on the islands that punctuate the entire coastline.

* The Ilhas Botinhas, off Angra dos Reis
* Ilha Itananguá, with a lovely viewpoint at its summit.
* Ilha Gipóia and the anchorage at the beautiful Praia do Dentista, unfortunately all too often crowded.
* Ilha Comprida, Saco de Tarituba and dozens of other anchorages depending on your wants and needs.

Near Angra dos Reis

Saco de Tarituba

Entrance to Marina Porto Frade

Baía de Paraty

This region was originally inhabited by the Goianás and Tamoios Indians, and the Portuguese arrived at the beginning of the 16th century.

The town of Paraty soon became an important port and a vital port of call, as this was where the slaves were brought off ships to work on the surrounding plantations; the boats returned to Europe laden with gold and gemstones.

These treasures were transported from Minas Gerais to Paraty along the Camino do Ouro, a track across the mountain paved with huge blocks; at the time it was the fastest and safest route for the convoys.

However, around the beginning of the 18th century, the abolition of slavery and the creation of new routes for transporting gold resulted in the decline of the rich city of Paraty, and its status gradually waned.

Today, the town's colonial architecture remains intact and it has successfully diversified into tourism; it is a Brazilian Heritage site and is one of the destinations most frequently visited by Brazilian and foreign tourists.

Tourism

Paraty is an excellent tourist destination, near Ilha Grande, and the shores of the bay form an uninterrupted series of beautiful inlets and beaches with warm, clear waters. The surrounding mountains also offer some good hikes through thick tropical forest. In addition, the town of Paraty is a veritable historical monument in itself, which you can explore by foot on its narrow streets paved with large, uneven blocks of granite (watch your step!).

The old city was built at sea level; it is partly flooded during big tides, and almost completely flooded in spring tides. Previously, the receding waters on the falling tide were used to clean the streets and acted as a sanitation system, with the slope of the ground being carefully calculated so that there isn't even the slightest puddle at low tide.

The houses were also built raised up by two steps, so that the water didn't run inside.

This is one of the great curiosities of Paraty.

Santa Rita church on a big tide day

Navigation

Brazilian Charts DHN No. 1633 and No. 1633A.

Baía de Paraty is located in the very western part of Baía da Ilha Grande.

Navigation in the bay is easy, and there are several islands and numerous inlets that are well-protected from the ocean swell.

The winds are generally fairly moderate but after a very hot day, there can be short gales, often accompanied by rain and sometimes by violent storms.

From the north, head towards Ilha de Mantimento, leaving to port Ilha dos Ganchos, on which there is a tall white building with large picture windows.

Make landfall at

⊕ **0** • 23°10,62'S 44°38,70'W Paraty approach

This waypoint is between Ilha de Mantimento and Ponta Grossa de Paraty, near the Laje de Moleques shoal, which must be pinpointed (danger buoy, topped with a white light).

Continue towards Ilha da Bexiga, which is left to starboard.

Paraty, the historical centre, flooded during big tides

The marinas at the end of Baía de Paraty

Paraty marinas

Steer a course southwest and once you have passed Ilha da Bexiga to starboard, the marinas are concentrated on the left-hand side at the end of the bay. Along what was Praia Boa Vista, there are no fewer than seven marinas.

⊕ 1 • 23°13,57'S 44°41,80'W Near the marinas

MARINA DO ENGENHO

This small marina was built in 2004 by Amyr Klink, a Brazilian sailor famous for his polar expeditions.

This is the first marina you come to after entering Baía de Paraty. There are a few large motor boats, but mainly sailing boats of all sizes, and this is the stop favoured by visiting boats.

Quality of moorings ★★★

The mooring area is well-sheltered, but slightly disturbed by the large motor boats passing in the bay, paying no attention to the 5-knot speed limit.

Moor stern or bows to, picking up a mooring buoy, on two sturdily-built floating pontoons. The marina can hold around one hundred boats on pontoons and a dozen on mooring buoys.

Facilities – Services ★★★

Taps on the pontoons.
110/220 volt electricity.

The pontoons at Marina do Engenho

New toilet and shower facilities comprising six separate cubicles (each with basin, toilet and hot shower).

Washing machine.

Free internet access.

It is also possible to anchor near the marina and use the marina services (water, toilets and showers, etc.) for a small charge.

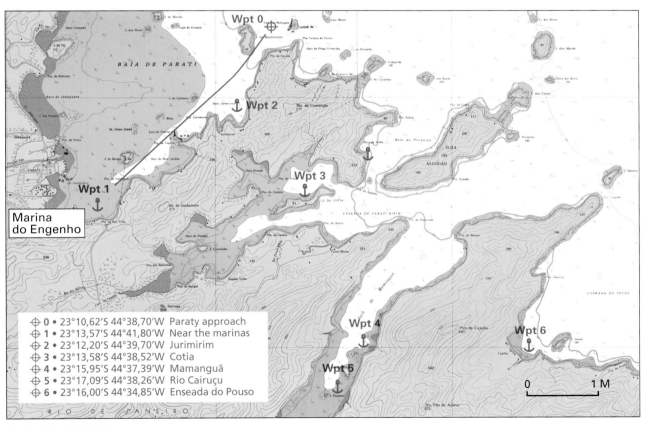

⊕ 0 • 23°10,62'S 44°38,70'W Paraty approach
⊕ 1 • 23°13,57'S 44°41,80'W Near the marinas
⊕ 2 • 23°12,20'S 44°39,70'W Jurimirim
⊕ 3 • 23°13,58'S 44°38,52'W Cotia
⊕ 4 • 23°15,95'S 44°37,39'W Mamanguã
⊕ 5 • 23°17,09'S 44°38,26'W Rio Cairuçu
⊕ 6 • 23°16,00'S 44°34,85'W Enseada do Pouso

BAIA DE PARATY

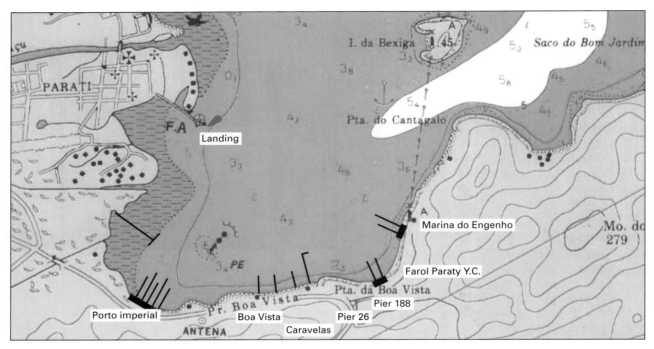

I. da Bexiga 45

Saco do Bom Jardim

PARATI

FA

Landing

Pta. do Cantagalo

PE

Marina do Engenho

Mo. do
279

Farol Paraty Y.C.

Pta. da Boa Vista

Pier 188

Porto imperial

Pr. Boa Vista

Boa Vista

Pier 26

Caravelas

ANTENA

PARATY MARINAS

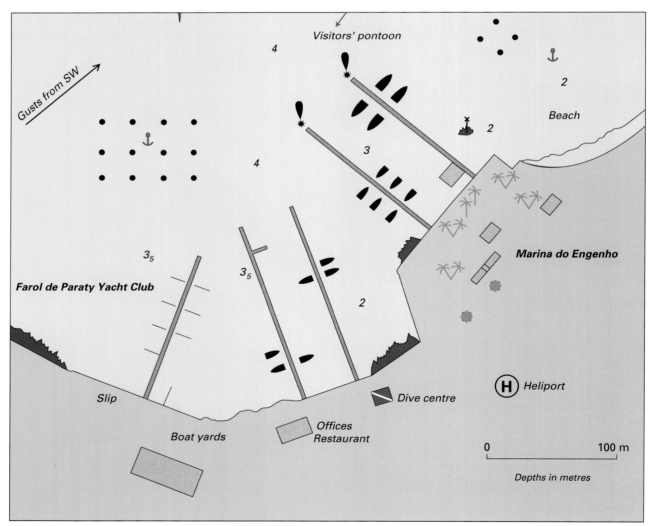

Visitors' pontoon

4

Gusts from SW

2

Beach

3

2

4

Marina do Engenho

3₅

Farol de Paraty Yacht Club

3₅

2

H Heliport

Slip

Dive centre

Boat yards

Offices
Restaurant

0   100 m

Depths in metres

MARINA DO ENGENHO AND MARINA FAROL DE PARATY YACHT CLUB

Marina do Engenho, the most welcoming in the bay

The dynamic manager Luiz, an experienced sailor, and his assistant Thalita are always at the marina, and this is doubtless one of the reasons why the service is second to none.

He and his team will do everything in their power to help, advise and meet visiting boats' every need, which gives this marina a very welcoming atmosphere.

Mooring fees **

As a guide, R$2.50 per foot per day on the pontoon, and R$40 on a mooring buoy.

Special rates for long stays.

The schooner *Paraty II*. Destination Antarctic

The first of Amyr Klink's many achievements took place in 1984 when he rowed from Namibia to Brazil (Salvador) in 100 days and six hours.

He then had two sailing boats built, *Paraty I* in which he wintered in the Antarctic for the first time, and *Paraty II*, a 75-foot schooner in which he spent several more Antarctic winters and completed other polar expeditions.

An explorer, photographer and writer, he is one of Brazil's best-known sailors.

Location and surroundings ***

Completely peaceful marina, recently built near the former home of German novelist Thomas Mann, which is a National Heritage site.

24-hour surveillance.

Amyr Klink, Caixa postal 74.805, Paraty, RJ, CEP 23.970-000
☎ (24) 3371 1260, *Mobile* (24) 9999 9957
VHF Channel 68
Email marinadoengenho@amyrklink.com.br
www.marinadoengenho.com.br

FAROL DE PARATY YACHT-CLUB

This marina is next door to the previous marina and undergoing alterations.

The plans show 120 berths spread over three pontoons, one with catwalks, and 30 mooring buoys.

Quality of moorings ***

Completely calm.

Facilities – Services ***

Water and 110/220 volt electricity on the pontoons.
Excellent toilet and shower facilities.
Slipway for lifting out boats.
Service and maintenance area on site.
A 50-tonne travel lift is planned.
Bar, restaurant.
Heliport.

Farol de Paraty Yacht Club

Mooring fees ***

As a guide:
R$8 per foot per day on the pontoon.
R$22 to 25 per foot per month for a 34′ to 45′ boat.

Location and surroundings ***

Pleasant, well-protected site.
    24-hour video surveillance.
① (24) 3371 1933, *Mobile* (24) 9217 1633
Email contact@faroldeparaty.com.br
www.faroldeparaty.com.br
VHF Channel 16.
Wi-Fi.

MARINA 188

This marina has 85 berths on one sturdily-built pontoon.

Quality of moorings **

The mooring area is quite calm, but the berths on the end of the pontoon are exposed to the chop in winds from the northern sector.

Facilities – Services ***

Water and 110/220V electricity on the pontoons.
    50 mooring buoys.
    Slipway for lifting out boats up to 20 tonnes, but the cradles belong to the owners. Boatyard, engineering, electrics and maintenance services on site.
    Shell service station. Gaz.
    Bar, restaurant, mini-market, shop.

Mooring fees **

As a guide, the price is between R$6–8 per foot per day on the pontoon.
    R$50 per day on a mooring buoy.

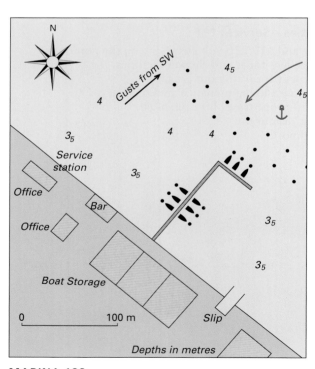

MARINA 188

Marina 188

Location and surroundings ***

Near the bus stop for Paraty.
    24-hour surveillance.
①/*Fax* (24) 3371 2362
Email marina188@marina188.com.br
www.marina188.com.br
VHF Channel 16

MARINA PIER 46

This small marina has 50 berths on two pontoons, for small and medium-sized boats and room for 37 on buoys. It is welcoming, but the mooring installations and pontoons seem a little unstable.

Quality of moorings **

Around twenty berths on a slightly unstable-looking pontoon. 37 mooring buoys.
    In strong winds, it is definitely more comfortable on a mooring buoy than on the pontoon.

Facilities – Services ***

Water and 110/220 volt electricity at the top of the pontoon.
    Slipway for lifting out boats up to 30 tonnes.
    Engineering and maintenance services on site.
    Scuba diving base.
    Shell service station.

Mooring fees **

As a guide, the price is about R$22 per foot per month.

Marina Pier 46

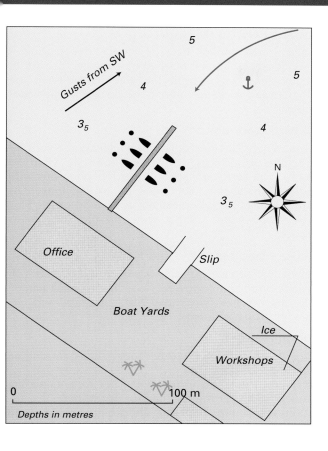

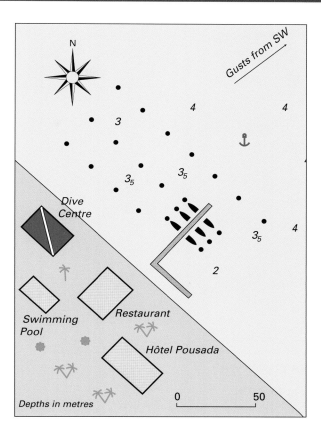

REFUGIO DAS CARAVELAS

Location and surroundings ***

Near the bus stop for Paraty, which is 4km away.
24-hour surveillance.
☎/*Fax* (24) 3371 1150
Email pier46@uol.com.br
VHF Channel 16

REFUGIO DAS CARAVELAS

30 berths on one pontoon for small and medium-sized boats, and 30 mooring buoys.

Quality of moorings ***

As at the two neighbouring marinas, the mooring buoys are more comfortable than the pontoon.

Facilities – Services **

Water and 110/220 volt electricity on the pontoon.

Mooring fees *

As a guide, the price is between R$2.50–3.00 per foot per day on the pontoon.
R$2.00 per foot per day on a mooring buoy.

Location and surroundings ***

This small marina has a *pousada* with restaurant and swimming pool and a diving base, all in very pleasant, tasteful surroundings.
☎/*Fax* (24) 3371 1270
Email refugiocaravelas@paratyinfo.com.br
www.paraty.com.br/caravela.htm
VHF Channel 16

Refugio das Caravelas

MARINA BOA VISTA

This is a small boat storage and maintenance company with around twenty buoys in a mooring area.
The small floating pontoon is only used for coming ashore and filling up with fuel and water.

Quality of moorings ***

Generally calm mooring area in 4–5m.

Facilities – Services ***

Water and electricity on the pontoon. Service station.
Maintenance, engineering and repair service on site.
Service station, fuel. Snack bar

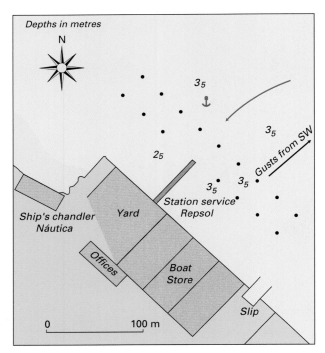

Depths in metres

N

Gusts from SW

Ship's chandler Náutica

Yard

Offices

Station service Repsol

Boat Store

Slip

0   100 m

MARINA BOA VISTA

Mooring fees **

As a guide, the price is between R$90 per day, or R$350 per month for a 45′ boat.

Location and surroundings **

The marina is located right on the road between Paraty and Santos, and near a bus stop.
☎/Fax (24) 3371 1381
www.paraty.com/boavista.htm

MARINA PORTO IMPERIAL

Located at the end of Baía de Paraty, this marina is reached along a channel marked by beacons that are lit at night. Stay well within the channel as there are sandbanks and rocks just above the surface of the water on either side.

Quality of moorings ***

Approximately 200 berths, half of which are reserved for Iate Clube de Santos and Iate Clube de Ubatuba (private). The berths are spread over five pontoons with catwalks, which can take boats up to 50′ long. The mooring area is calm because it's at the end of the bay; however, the quality of the water in the dock looks mediocre.

Facilities – Services ***

Maintenance service on site. Water and 110/220 volt electricity on the pontoons. Service station. Snack bar.

The marina has two travel lifts (20-, 50- and 75-tonne) for lifting out boats.

Mooring fees ***

As a guide, the price is R$10 per foot per day, depending on the length of stay.

Lifting out with travel lift: R$25 per foot, including re-launch + R$3 per foot per day for dry storage.

Additional lump sum for chocking, cleaning and application of two coats of anti-foul (anti-foul not included): R$20 per foot per day.

Location and surroundings ***

This marina is located around 5km from Paraty, beside the main road. It is surrounded by sheds and a dry storage area for boats on chocks, and the section

Note

All these marinas are near the BR-101 highway which is a few kilometres from the centre of Paraty.

There is a bus every half hour to the town centre.

It is about a mile by dinghy to the landing at Paraty but it is not advisable to leave the boat there after dark.

Approach channel to Marina Porto Imperial

Marina Porto Imperial

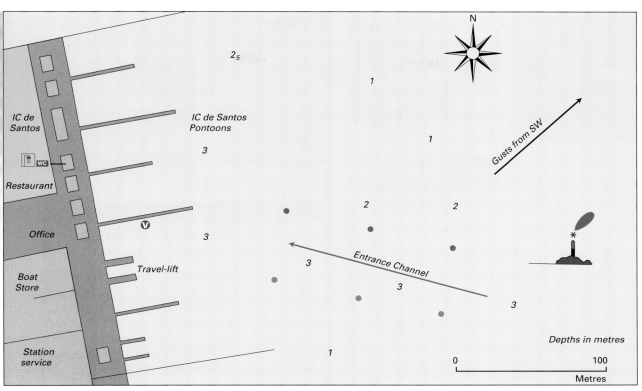

MARINA PORTO IMPERIAL

The 50-tonne travel lift at Marina Porto Imperial

alongside the dock has some garden areas. 24-hour video surveillance. Wi-Fi.
☎/*Fax* (24) 3371 6022
Email adm@marinaportoimperial.com.br
www.marinaportoimperial.com.br
VHF Channel 16, call sign *Echo 37*

A few anchorages around Paraty

⚓ ILHA DO CEDRO

A good anchorage north of Paraty. Sheltered, with bars and restaurants. Popular during the holidays.

⊕ 23°04,18'S 044°38,64'W Ilha do Cedro

⚓ SACO JURIMIRIM

This cove at the entrance to the bay provides two possible anchorages, one of which is at the end of a narrow cul-de-sac. They offer good shelter in northeasterly to southwesterly winds.

Holding is excellent in 4m of water on mud.

⊕ **2** • 23°12,40'S 044°39,60'W Jurimirim

The Ilha da Cotía anchorage

The small beach bar (Cotía)

Baía de Paraty. The Saco de Mamanguá anchorage

⚓ ILHA DA COTÍA

To the northeast outside the bay is Enseada de Paraty-mirim. Ilha da Cotía can be seen to starboard; go around the north of the island. This anchorage is very safe in all weathers, and the surroundings are pleasant.

⊕ 3 • 23°13,58'S 044°38,52'W Ilha da Cotía

⚓ SACO DO MAMANGUÁ

This is reached through a deep passageway between two rows of steep wooded mountains.

In the middle of the cul-de-sac to port is a small village, with a few moored fishing boats; you can drop anchor opposite the church, in three to 4m of clear water.

The village can only be reached by sea and is completely isolated with no land access; only those with a small generator have electricity.

SACO DE MAMANGUÁ

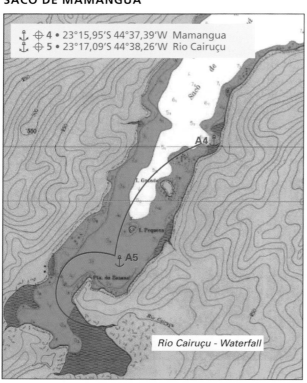

⚓ ⊕ 4 • 23°15,95'S 44°37,39'W Mamangua
⚓ ⊕ 5 • 23°17,09'S 44°38,26'W Rio Cairuçu

A4

I. Grande

I. Pequena

A5

Pta. do Bananal

Rio Cairuçu

Rio Cairuçu - Waterfall

On the other hand, the water from the waterfall above the village is abundantly available; it is delicious, cool, clear and free.

The village lives at an old-fashioned pace; the men go fishing and the women look after the house, the children, the cooking and crafts. The inhabitants are happy to welcome the rare boats that call here.

They take it as an opportunity to meet outsiders, and open their doors wide to show you their village, the surroundings and their way of life.

Walking around the village, you may meet Hélio, the old fisherman who now has a small sailing boat, Ivaniudo, the young carpenter who repairs boats, or Osana who will wait on you hand and foot; he is a virtuoso behind his stove and will cook you an excellent fish fresh from the water.

After a while you'll be a member of AMAM, Associação de Moradores e Amigos do Mamanguá (the Association of Inhabitants and Friends of Mamanguá).

⚓ ⊕ 4 • 23°15,95'S 44°37,39'W Mamangua

⚓ RIO CAIRUÇU

At the end of Saco de Mamanguá, the river enters the tropical forest and after a short walk, a small track leads to a beautiful waterfall.

Go to the end of Saco de Mamanguá and leave the boat anchored to the south of Ilha Pequenha, near Ponta do Bananul.

⚓ ⊕ 5 • 23°17,09'S 044°38,26'W Vers rio Cairuçu

Beyond this point, the water depth decreases rapidly towards the end of the cul-de-sac, and it is best to use the tender to go around Ponta do Bananal and thus reach the mouth of the Rio Cairuçu.

Go slowly up the small river, which snakes its way through an enormous mangrove swamp; the average depth is 0.5m and the bottom is sandy with a few rocks or tree branches, which you should look out for.

After about one mile, the mangrove gives way to beautiful tropical forest.

Leave the tender and head through the jungle along a small track, using the sound of the waterfalls coming down the mountain as a guide.

The cool waters of the waterfall on the Rio Cairuçu

The water is clear and cool and, after a little hesitation, you can dive into the natural pools.

No special equipment is required for this hike – just sturdy shoes, a stick to make noise with to scare off any snakes, and, most importantly, mosquito repellent. Duration: two to three hours.

A few Tamoios Indians still live discreetly in this region, where they farm on small plots of land and produce handicrafts.

⚓ ENSEADA DO POUSO

This cove, located east of Baía de Paraty, is surrounded by mountains that come straight down into the sea. On a low section in the middle of the cove is the beautiful Praia de Cajaiba, which can only be reached by sea; the water is clear and warm.

⊕ 6 • 23°16,00'S 044°34,85'W Praia Grande-Cajaibá

⚓ ENSEADA DO SONO

A long sandy beach at the end of the cove, which is home to a fishing community.

Leaving Baía da Ilha Grande, once past Cabo Juatinga, the coast is jagged, with deep coves and beautiful beaches, some of which are often deserted as they can only be reached by sea.

These coves are partly open to the southeast, but in good weather and sea conditions they provide some good anchorages.

Enseada de Trindade

⚓ ENSEADA DA TRINDADE

Although it is outside Baía da Ilha Grande and 35 miles from Paraty, this cove is worth a visit, but only in good weather. The beaches are beautiful but very exposed to the offshore swell, and popular with surfers.

When the sea is calm, you can anchor for the day in a small inlet located at the entrance to the cove off the small Praia Brava. Watch out however for the rocks on either side of the beach, only some of which are visible.

A few good scuba diving sites

There is good diving throughout the region and below is a selection of locations:
- Ilha dos Ganchos
- Praía Vermelha
- Ilha Comprida
- Saco da Velha
- Ilha and Laje dos Meros
- Ilha Deserta
- Enseada do Pouso

Useful addresses and telephone numbers for Baia de Paraty

Treating diving accidents
First Aid ☎ 192
Hospital Naval Marcílio Dias Rio de Janeiro ☎ (21) 2599 5599
Centro medico hiperbárico São Paulo ☎ (11) 3815 6067
Salvamar Sueste Rio ☎ (21) 2104 6119
Polícia Féderal Angra Dos Reis ☎ (24) 3365 5060
Receta Féderal Angra Dos Reis ☎ (24) 3364 8252
Capitania dos Portos Angra dos Reis ☎ (24) 3365 0365

Services

For all equipment maintenance and good contacts with local specialists ☎ (024) 9229 7322.

Electricity

Nardo - Paraty
☎ (024) 9913 4858, 3371 6483
Email nardomalo@yahoo.com.br

Refrigeration

Aquino refrigeração (Tadeu)
☎ (24) 3365 2883, *Mobile* (24) 7834 3695

Chandlery

Companhia da pesca, rue da praia, loja 01 (near the landing)
☎ (24) 3371 2210
Email ciadapesca@paratyinfo.com.br
Ship's Chandler Nautica, Boa Vista, Paraty, RJ
☎/*Fax* (24) 3371 3123, 9213 0347
Email benoit@shipnautica.com.br

Sailmaker, covers

Tlaloc - Porto Marina Bracuhy ☎ (24) 3363 1024, 9226 4580
Email tlaloc@tlaloc.com.br
Professional well-supervised work

Porto Imperial Travel-lift

The only travel-lift in the Baia. Rather expensive. Parking available. Prior to launching handling and strapping need supervision.

Painting/antifouling

Benoit ☎ (24) 9213 0347
Eduardo ☎ (24) 9999 7176

STATE OF SÃO PAULO

This is the richest state in South America and the most industrialised state in Brazil; there are only superlatives to describe it.

The capital, São Paulo, is the largest city in Brazil and Latin America; its population of 18 million makes it the second biggest city in the world.

The people are the most cosmopolitan in Brazil, the descendants of millions of immigrants – European in the 1800s, Japanese in the 1900s – and Brazilians from other states.

The port of Santos is the largest in Brazil and the north coast is also one of the most beautiful areas in the country.

The coast is split into two sections:

- the northern section, which is beautiful, wild, jagged and made up of both beautiful beaches and numerous islands as far as São Sebastião and Ilhabela.
- the southern section, which is relatively flat and more uniform, with long beaches stretching as far as Paraná.

There are some beautiful coves in the area around Ubatuba

Ubatuba

Approximately 50 miles from Ilha Grande, Ubatuba, with a population of 65,000, is the largest built-up area on this part of the coast.

It is a very touristy region, and makes a close and particularly pleasant holiday destination for the inhabitants of São Paulo.

The interest of Ubatuba lies in water sports in general – sailing, scuba diving and surfing. To the northeast of Ubatuba, the coast is jagged, forming coves at the end of which stretch wild, almost deserted beaches, some only accessible by boat. The coastline is littered with a great many islands and is of course a popular location for sailing.

On the coast to the south of Ubatuba, the long beaches exposed to the offshore swell are ideal for surfing.

Cabo Juatinga to Ubatuba

Navigation

Brazilian Chart DHN No. 1635.

From Ilha Grande, the coast is made up of a group of mountains, the highest peaks of which are no more than 600m. These hills drop straight into the sea, forming numerous coves and beautiful beaches at their feet.

Between Ponta Juatinga LpB.10s175m17M and Ponta Grossa, Lp(3)B.10s65m16M, it is possible to anchor off some of these beaches, but although these anchorages are well-sheltered from winds from the northern sector, all of

Saco da Ribeira. Bringing in the day's catch of marlin

Ubatuba. The Voga Marina mooring basin with the town quay in the foreground

The town quay. Marina Pier Saco da Ribeira

these bays and coves are open to winds from the southern and eastern sectors, which quickly make the mooring areas uncomfortable. There are however a few good anchorages, and one of the best shelters in bad weather is Ilha Anchieta, to the north of Ubatuba.

⚓ PICINGUABA

Once past Ponta da Trinidade heading eastwards, you come to a small group of islands, the largest of which are Ilha das Couves and Ilha Comprida.

By passing between Ilha Comprida and the coast, you reach the small fishing village of Picinguaba, located to port after Ponta da Cruz.

⊕ 23°22,72'S 044°50,31'W Picinguaba

It is well-sheltered from winds from the eastern sector; it is possible to anchor on the right of the beach, beyond the fishing boats. The mooring area is very calm and only disturbed by passing fishing boats.

There are few supplies available in the village apart from, of course, a whole range of fresh fish.

⚓ ILHA ANCHIETA

15 miles further to the southwest, sailing through a string of islands and islets, you will see Ilha Anchieta; this is one of the best shelters in bad weather. The island used to house a penitentiary, which has now been abandoned but remains a curiosity. It is classified as a protected area, and there are numerous walks on marked routes through the thick tropical forest.

There is a good anchorage on the north of the island, in Enseada das Palmas, off Praia do Presidio:

⊕ 0 • 23°32,20'S 045°07,30'W Ilha Anchieta

Anchor near this waypoint, where holding is good in 3m of water on sand. The anchorage is open to the north, but the mooring area is generally calm and it is an excellent shelter in northeasterly, southerly and westerly winds.

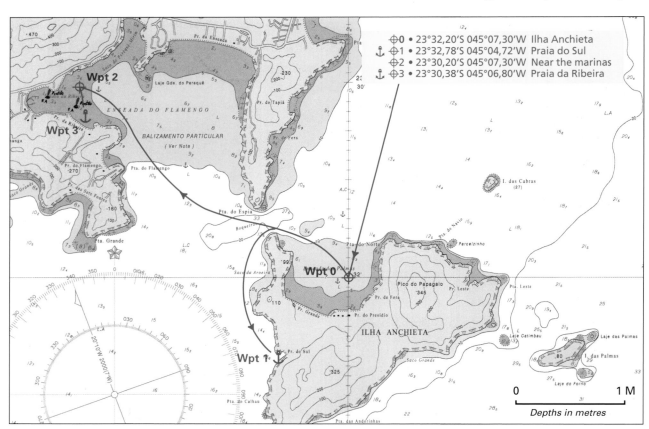

⊕0 • 23°32,20'S 045°07,30'W Ilha Anchieta
⚓ ⊕1 • 23°32,78'S 045°04,72'W Praia do Sul
⊕2 • 23°30,20'S 045°07,30'W Near the marinas
⚓ ⊕3 • 23°30,38'S 045°06,80'W Praia da Ribeira

Depths in metres

UBATUBA

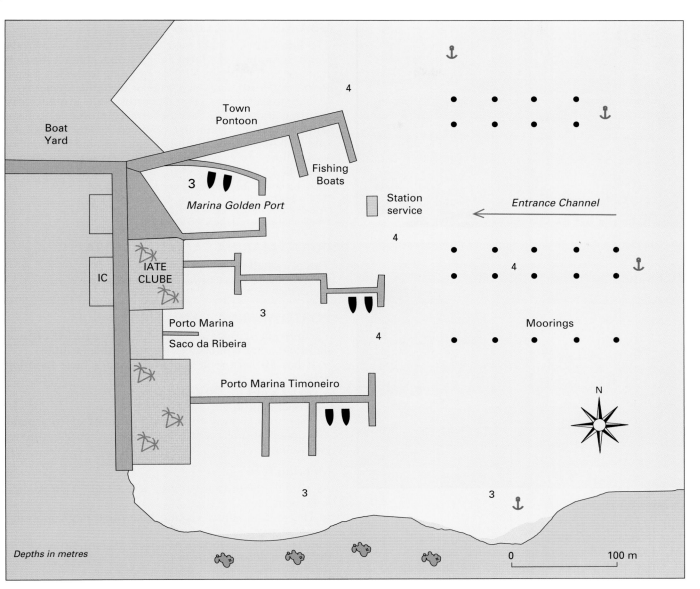

UBATUBA - SACO DE RIBEIRA

⚓ PRAIA DO SUL

At the end of a cul-de-sac, this small beach, which is less popular than the previous anchorage, is without doubt one of the most beautiful on the island, with calm, clear water.

⊕ **1** • 23°32,78'S 045°04,72'W Praia do Sul

Anchor on the left-hand side in 3m of water on sand.

Saco da Ribeira

There are a great many boats in Ubatuba, including numerous yachts, which congregate in the marinas located in Saco da Ribeira, at the end of Enseada do Flamengo.

⊕ **2** • 23°30,20'S 045°07,30'W Near the marinas

MARINA PIER SACO DA RIBEIRA

This is the town quay, where fishing boats and yachts moor alongside in depths of 3m.

It is possible to moor against the quay but fishing boats use it continuously and yachts must leave if necessary. It is advisable to leave a crew member on board.

Mooring fees

As a guide, the price is between R\$25 per day for a 45' boat.

You can also anchor near the marina and then go ashore in the tender, leaving it on the town quay.

Marina Pier Saco da Ribeira, Ubatuba, SP, CEP 11680-000
☎/Fax (12) 3842 1231
VHF Channel 73

The Iate Clube pontoon in the foreground with Porto Marina Timoneiro in the background

Ubatuba. The mooring area

Just next door, to the right of the quay, is a boatyard, AUMAR, for all types of maintenance work.

There is a slipway for lifting out boats up to 20 tonnes; there are plans to alter it soon to improve the lifting out facilities.

Water and 110/220V electricity on the quay.

VOGA MARINA

This is one of the largest marinas in Saco da Ribeira; it has 96 berths on floating pontoons and good facilities.

The water depth is around 3.5m in the dock.

Facilities – Services

Water and 110/220 volt electricity.
   Service station.
   Slipway for lifting out boats up to 35 tonnes.

Mooring fees

As a guide, the price is between R$6 per foot per day.
   Monthly rate on application.
Voga Marina , Saco da Ribeira
① /Fax (12) 3842 2000
VHF Channel 68
Email edna@vogamarine.com.br
www.vogamarina.com.br

UBATUBA IATE CLUBE

The Iate Clube is right next door, to the left of Marina Voga. To moor in the Iate Clube marina, contact the club manager first either by VHF or by going to the Iate Clube in the tender from an anchorage or from the town quay.

The marina has several berths and around fifty mooring buoys. The facilities are comfortable (toilets, bar, restaurant, swimming pool, etc.). The Iate Clube offers all of the services and amenities found at Brazilian yacht clubs, but as with all of them, access to it is strictly controlled.

Ubatuba Iate Clube, Saco da Ribeira, Ubatuba, SP
① (12) 3842 8080
VHF Channel 68, call sign Delta 30
Email ubatubaiateclube@terra.com.br

PORTO MARINA SACO DA RIBEIRA

This is a small private marina.
Porto Marina Saco da Ribeira, Saco da Ribeira
① (12) 3842 1017

PORTO MARINA TIMONEIRO

This private marina, located on the extreme left of Saco da Ribeira, has faultless, very comfortable facilities.

It has 80 berths on a pontoon and a huge mooring area.

Water and 110/220V electricity.
   Service station.
   There is a slipway for lifting out boats up to around 20 tonnes. Inside there is a bar, restaurant, barbecue, swimming pool, etc.

Mooring fees

As a guide, the price is between R$65 and 70 per day for a 45' boat.

The marina offers visiting boats one day's mooring free of charge.

Porto Marina Timoneiro, Saco da Ribeira, Ubatuba, SP.
VHF Channel 68, call sign Delta 41
①/Fax (12) 3842 1122
Email timoneiro@timoneiroclub.com.br

Anchorages

All of these marinas are reached along a channel inside the mooring area.

Before choosing one of them, a good solution is to anchor outside and visit each one in the tender.

It is also possible to anchor on the right-hand side of the mooring area or, if you want a more peaceful location, anchor off Praia da Ribeira, on the left of Saco da Ribeira.

Holding is good in 3.5m of water on sand, and the anchorage is well-sheltered.

⊕ 3 • 23°30,38'S 045°06,80'W Praia da Ribeira

Ilha de São Sebastião (Ilhabela)

Ilhabela (or Ilha de São Sebastião) is one of the largest islands in Brazil, with an area of 750km².

This charming, very touristy island has a population of just 20,000, but this increases fivefold in the summer season.

The island is mountainous; its highest point is 1,375m and two other peaks are over 1,300m. The mountains have steep sides covered in thick tropical forest (*mata Atlântica*).

However, the tourists are not the only inhabitants of the island; the most numerous and most aggressive tenants are the mosquitoes and the fearsome hordes of *borrachudos*. These bloodthirsty warriors are always ready for action, spare no-one and attack at any time, day or night! Sailors are fortunately slightly protected from this scourge, as they prefer the tropical forest to the open sea. Still, take a good stock of insect repellent, which you will need along this whole stretch of coastline.

Navigation

Brazilian Charts DHN No. 1614, 1641 and 1645.

From Ubatuba, the coast is jagged and made up of coves and beautiful beaches with the high mountains of the Serra do Mar in the background.

There are several potential anchorages along this stretch, but most of the coves are open to the offshore swell and the weather conditions must always be taken into account. The port of São Sebastião is approximately 25 miles from Ubatuba.

Conspicuous landmark

On the northern tip of the island, the cylindrical tower of Ponta das Canas, with horizontal red and white stripes, LpB.6s13m9M, visible sector 211°.

Tide and current

The tide has a mean level of 0.66m above the chart datum and a mean amplitude of 1.2m.

The current generally carries you southwest, but under the influence of winds from the southern sector, which rush forcefully into the channel, it reverses and carries you northeast.

It is normally 1.5–2 knots, but can reach four knots in strong winds.

Winds

The winds around the island generally blow from the northern sector and the eastern sector in summer.

In July and August there can be strong northeasterly gales reaching 50 knots, but these are generally short-lived.

Similarly, a cold front coming in causes a particularly strong southwesterly wind between Ilhabela and the mainland. A good strong mooring line is advisable on this part of the Canal de São Sebastião.

Approach

Day and night, from the north, make landfall at

⊕ **0** • 23°42,50'S 045°20,51'W Ilhabela landfall

approximately one mile from the entrance to the Canal de São Sebastião, to the north of Ponta das Canas.

The entrance channel is northeast – south-west oriented and well marked as it takes large petrol tankers that dock at the São Sebastião terminal.

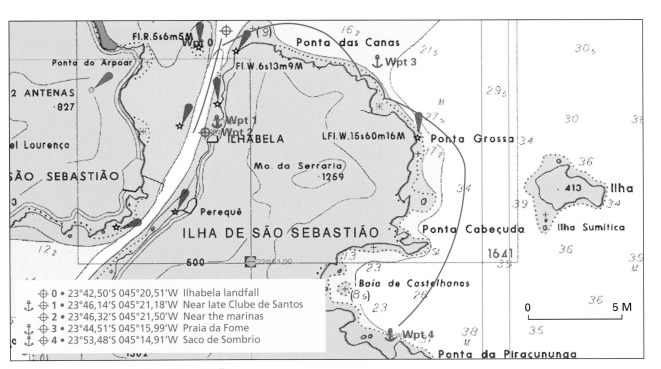

⊕ **0** • 23°42,50'S 045°20,51'W Ilhabela landfall
⚓ ⊕ **1** • 23°46,14'S 045°21,18'W Near late Clube de Santos
⊕ **2** • 23°46,32'S 045°21,50'W Near the marinas
⚓ ⊕ **3** • 23°44,51'S 045°15,99'W Praia da Fome
⚓ ⊕ **4** • 23°53,48'S 045°14,91'W Saco de Sombrio

ILHABELA - ILHA DE SÃO SEBASTIÃO

São Sebastião. The old quarter

Ilhabela. The Iate Clube de Santos pontoon

IATE CLUBE DE SANTOS (ANNEX)

The club is located to the north of the town and has excellent facilities on the shores of the Canal de São Sebastião. Once past Ponta das Canas, it is the first set of mooring buoys that can be seen to port after 2.5 miles, near a jetty.

The mooring area contains 64 mooring buoys and the club accepts visiting boats; there is a boatman to ferry you between the mooring and the club.

On site there is a bar, restaurant, lounge, swimming pool, etc.

⊕ 1 • 23°46,14'S 045°21,18'W Near Iate Clube de Santos
Iate Clube de Santos (annex), Av. Luiz Massa, 201, Ponta do Barreiro, Ilhabela, SP
℡ (12) 3896 4348

Ilhabela marinas

The geographical location of Ilhabela and the winds that blow plentifully in the Canal de São Sebastião mean that the island is famous for sailing.

This is why there are two more yacht clubs in Saco da Indaiá.

⊕ 2 • 23°46,32'S 045° 21,50'W Near the marinas

YACHT-CLUB DE ILHABELA

The Yacht Club is home to a large number of sailing boats and for several years has organised the *Semana Internacional de Vela de Ilhabela* (Ilhabela International Sailing Week), one of the largest sailing events in Brazil.

It is a private club with luxurious facilities; it accepts visiting boats either on the pontoon depending on the availability of berths, or on buoys in the mooring area.

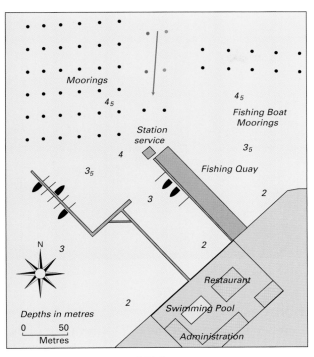

The pontoons are currently being extended.
24-hour boatman.
Lifting out facilities for boats up to 50 tonnes.

Facilities – Services ***

Impeccable toilet and shower facilities, beautiful pool, bar, restaurant, etc.

Every type of service is available at the Yacht Club, and contractors can be brought in (engineering, electrics, sail loft, general maintenance).

The club has a boatyard and a slipway for lifting out boats up to 45′.

Water as well as 110 and 220V electricity on the pontoons.

Service station on the town quay where the fishing boats moor, right next to the Yacht Club.

Supplies ***

Supplies are readily available in the nearby town centre.

Mooring fees **

The club gives visitors four days free of charge; thereafter, the price is around R$120 per day.

Location and surroundings ***

Very well-located near the lively town centre.

Yacht-Club de Ilhabela, Av. Força Expedicionaria Brasileira, 299-Centro. Ilhabela, SP
① (12) 3896 2300, *Fax* (12) 3896 1748
VHF Channel 68, call sign *Delta 24*
Email sec-ilha@yci.com.br

Administrative headquarters in São Paulo
Av. Angélica, 2503/45, São Paulo
① (11) 3151 3616, *Fax* 3259 8299
Email sec-sp@yci.com.br
www.yci.com.br

YACHT-CLUB DE ILHABELA

It is also possible to anchor nearby and use some of the club's services after contacting the club office.

Quality of moorings **

In northeasterly winds, the mooring area is a little rough. Cold fronts bring southwesterly winds that blow in gusts and make the Canal de São Sebastião very choppy.

The marina has 120 berths on pontoons and the mooring area is equipped with 150 mooring buoys.

The reception pontoon and mooring area at Yacht Club de Ilhabela

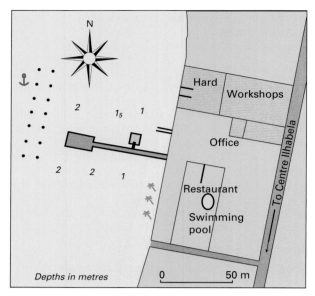

PINDA IATE CLUBE

Pinda Iate Clube

PINDA IATE CLUBE

This is a private club with around 200 members. It is not far from the Yacht Club, and right next to the town centre.

It has around one hundred mooring buoys and accepts visiting boats.

Quality of moorings ***

The mooring area is generally calm, apart from in southwesterly winds.

Facilities – Services ***

The welcome is very warm and the club allows visiting boats to use all of the facilities (toilets and showers, restaurant, swimming pool, etc.).

Slipway for lifting out boats up to 20 tonnes.

There is a boatyard adjacent to the Iate Clube where all types of repairs and maintenance work can be carried out.
Mauricio ☎ (3896 1580).

Supplies

Supplies are readily available in town.

Mooring fees

Three days free of charge; thereafter a fixed rate of R$60 per day.

Location and surroundings

Very well-located, with a small adjoining beach, very close to the square in Ilhabela.
Pinda Iate Clube
☎ (12) 3896 1580
VHF Channel 16, call sign *Delta 56*
Email pinda3@telefonica.com.br
www.pindaiateclube.com.br

Anchorages

There are several anchorages on the northern side of the island, such as the one at Praia de Jabaquara, which is very busy in the high season. Praia da Fome, at the end of a cul-de-sac, and further on Praia do Poço, where there is a waterfall, provide more peaceful anchorages. However, watch out for the rocks that litter the surrounding area.

⊕ **3** • 23°44,51′S 045°15,99′W Praia da Fome

On the part of the island exposed to the east, the offshore swell comes directly in, but in Baía de Castelhanos, Saco de Sombrio at the end of the bay provides good shelter in the south of the cove. Holding is good in 4m of water on sand, near the Iate Clube de Santos pontoon.

⊕ **4** • 23°53,48′S 045°14,91′W Entrance to Saco de Sombrio

Useful telephone numbers

Area code ☎ (012).
Polícia Féderal (Immigration) ☎ 3895 8564.
Capitania dos Portos (Port Captain's Office) ☎ 3892 1555.
Tourist office ☎ 3896 1091.

Tourism

Ilhabela is a large tourist centre, and very lively in summer.

Its mountains provide numerous activities, such as hiking (there is a multitude of paths) and 4x4 trips (there is a track over the top of the mountain to the other side of the island).

To the north of the bay, there is an interesting walk through the forest to Cachoeira do Gato, one of the most beautiful waterfalls on the island. On all of these trips in the forest, don't forget your insect repellent.

For scuba diving enthusiasts, the waters are very clear and the area around the island contains 21 shipwrecks, some of which make interesting dives.

On the other side of the channel, the town of São Sebastião is also very touristy and has an interesting history.

There are several ferries that cross regularly between the island and the mainland.

Santos – Guarujá – Bertioga

Ilha de Santo Amaro

Located approximately 150 miles from Baía da Ilha Grande, and 70 miles from Ilhabela, Santos is the largest commercial port in Brazil.

Its geographical location places it just 80km from São Paulo, which is also the largest town in Brazil.

The port is located on the river that separates Santos from Ilha de Santo Amaro, on which the main town is Guarujá.

The port of Santos is approached along a marked S-shaped channel that is dredged regularly so that it can take large tonnage ships.

For yachts, Santos can be a worthwhile technical stop-off on the southern route, both in terms of boat maintenance and repairs and in terms of life raft overhaul.

With regard to tourism, the town of Guarujá is a well-known seaside resort popular with the inhabitants of São Paulo at the weekend and during the summer. It is connected to Santos by a car ferry.

Navigation

Brazilian Charts DHN No. 1701 and No. 1711.

Coming from São Sebastião, the coast is jagged and fringed with the mountains of the Serra do Mar. These mountains, which are around 1,000m high, drop straight down into the sea and are covered in thick tropical forest, the *mata Atlântica*.

Once past the southern tip of Ilha de São Sebastião, leave well to port the archipelago of Alcatrazes, identifiable by its lighthouse, a white tapered tower, LpB.6s24m15M. The archipelago is made up of a dozen islands with a rocky main island standing at 316m.

It is a military manoeuvres and firing area and it is advisable to consult the Capitania dos Portos and notices to mariners before going there.

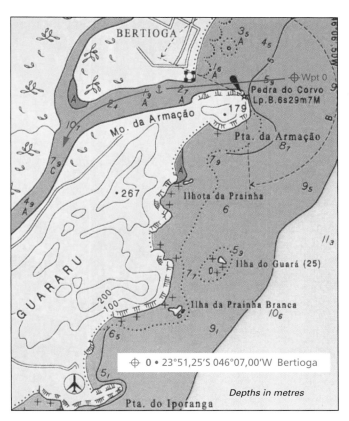

SANTOS BERTIOGA

Approaching Santos, the coast becomes lower and fringed with long beaches up to Ilha de Santo Amaro.

Tide and current

The tide is semi-diurnal with a mean level of 0.7m above the chart datum and a maximum amplitude of around 2.5m. The tidal current in the river is no more than 1.5 knots on the ebb.

Near Santos

Santos Marinas

There are two marina areas in Santos:
Guarujá-Bertioga on the north of Ilha de Santo Amaro
Guarujá, on the south of the island, opposite Santos.

GUARUJÁ – BERTIOGA

Enseada de Bertioga opens up 20 miles to the north of Ilha de Santo Amaro.

The marinas are located on the Canal da Bertioga, a long way from the centre of Guarujá, but near to the town of Bertioga.

The town is pleasant and very lively, and a few boats moor in the mouth of the river; there is a regular ferry between the island and the mainland.

These marinas are mainly used by local boats, and are on a canal that disappears into the interior of the island, in the middle of thick tropical forest. They are well-equipped but, for a visiting boat, the main disadvantage of these marinas is their distance from Guarujá.

ENSEADA DE BERTIOGA

To reach Bertioga, make landfall at

⊕ 0 • 23°51,25'S 046°07,00'W Bertioga landfall

which is opposite the entrance channel and Ponta do Armação.

Conspicuous landmarks

The tower of Pedra do Corvo, LpB.6s29m7M to port, and Forte de Bertioga to starboard.

The entrance to the river does not pose any problems with a depth of 3.5–4m in the middle of the channel; sail preferably in the left-hand half of the channel, as Praia do Forte São João extends a long way into the mouth of the river.

It is possible to anchor on the right-hand side of the river, before or after the landing stage for the ferry that links Bertioga and Ilha de Santo Amaro; this anchorage has the advantage of being near the town centre.

Holding is good in 2.5–3m of water on sand.

The town is pleasant and there is a regular bus service to the centre of Guarujá.

Heading upriver poses no particular problems as there are no obstacles and a depth of 3–10m, always more than enough. The current in the channel can reach a speed of two knots on the ebb. Going up the channel, there are five marinas to port over a distance of around six miles. It is however preferable to go up the channel during the day so that you can see the pontoons and mooring buoys, which are sometimes hard to see at night.

The fort at the entrance to the channel, a very conspicuous landmark

MARINA PORTO DO SOL

This is the first marina you see to port on the first bend in the river.

The mooring is completely calm and the facilities are adequate. You can easily reach the village of Bertioga in the tender, or take the ferry, which is a 10 minute walk away.

Marina Porto do Sol, Guarujá-Bertioga, SP
☎ (13) 3305 1588, *Fax* (13) 3305 1584
Email marinaportodosol@uol.com.br

MARINAS NACIONAIS

This luxuriously-appointed marina is mainly home to motor boats, some of which are very large. There is every boat maintenance service on site, and all the comforts offered by Brazilian clubs such as restaurant, swimming pool, etc. It has a service station and a 50-tonne travel lift.

Mooring fees

R$80 per day, or approximately R$2,000 per month, for a 45' boat.

Marinas Nacionais, Guarujá-Bertioga, SP
☎/*Fax* (13) 3305 1421
VHF Channel 68, call sign *Delta 45*
Email marina@marinasnacionais.com.br

MARINA VIM DO MAR

This marina is also located after the first bend in the river, after Marinas Nacionais.

Marina Vim do Mar, Guarujá-Bertioga, SP
☎ (13) 3305 1235

MARINA TCHABUM

Another small marina on the Canal de Bertioga.

Marina Tchabum, Guarujá-Bertioga, SP
☎ (13) 3305 1232

MARINA TROPICAL

This well-kept 128-berth marina is very well equipped and extends a warm welcome.

The mooring area is completely calm. It is around five miles from the entrance to the channel.

Mooring fees

R$60 per day for a 45' boat.

Marina Tropical, Guarujá-Bertioga, SP
☎/*Fax* (13) 3305 1321
Email marinatropical@ig.com.br
VHF Channel 68, call sign *Delta 42*.

Guarujá-Bertioga. Marina Tropical

Santos – Guarujá

Approach

Conspicuous landmarks

Coming from offshore, around six miles from the entrance to Santos, leave to starboard Ilha da Moela, which has a white lighthouse on its summit, Oc.Alt.BBE.60s110m40/39M.

By day and night, a number of commercial ships can be seen anchored in the mouth of the bay, waiting for a pilot. Landfall can be made at ⊕0, on a bearing of 21°5 on the entrance channel.

⊕ **0** • 24°00,80'S 046°20,40'W Santos landfall

Complexo industrial naval do guarujá

This enormous industrial zone on Ilha de Santo Amaro is home to half a dozen marinas of varying sizes, all grouped in the same sector. Each of them offers more or less comprehensive services and charges different mooring fees at their discretion.

They all have one thing in common: they are a long way from the centre of Guarujá or Santos, which is after all a disadvantage for visiting yacht crews.

Before you choose one, it can be a good idea to anchor at a waiting anchorage on the right-hand side of the river, at the entrance to the approach channel to the port of Santos, around 0.5 mile after Ponta da Fortaleza. This enables you to visit the marinas one by one in the tender and make a decision about their location, the ease of access in terms of the size of your boat, and the various services they offer.

The mooring areas in these marinas are generally calm, as they are all located on rivers and only strong winds might bring some disturbance.

Clube International de Regatas

CLUBE INTERNATIONAL DE REGATAS

This is the first marina you come to on entering Canal de Santos, on the right, at the mouth of the small Rio Icanhema.

⊕ **1** • 23°59,69'S 046°18,00'W Rio Icanhema entrance

It is located in the Santa Cruz dos Navegantes district and generally takes small boats. Its facilities are old and there is little room for manoeuvre in the dock. This marina has the advantage of being on the edge of the Canal de Santos and you can easily reach Santos in the tender by crossing the 800m-wide channel.

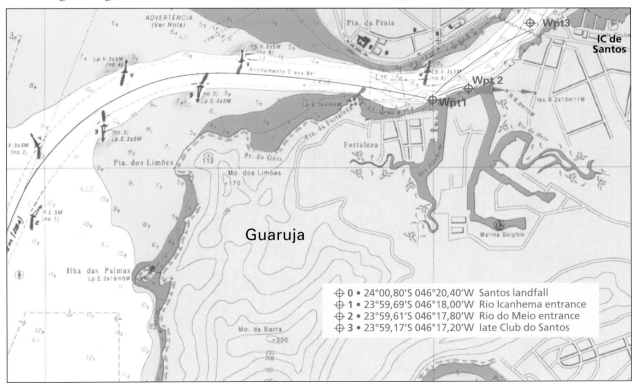

⊕ **0** • 24°00,80'S 046°20,40'W Santos landfall
⊕ **1** • 23°59,69'S 046°18,00'W Rio Icanhema entrance
⊕ **2** • 23°59,61'S 046°17,80'W Rio do Meio entrance
⊕ **3** • 23°59,17'S 046°17,20'W Iate Club do Santos

SANTOS-GUARUJÁ

Clube International de Regatas, Santa Cruz dos Navegantes, Guarujá, SP
☎ (13) 3261 5711, *Fax* (13) 3261 5162
VHF Channel 68
Email informatica@intersantos.com.br

The other marinas on Ilha de Santo Amaro are located along Rio do Meio in the industrial complex.

⊕ **2** • 23°59,61'S 046°17,80'W Rio do Meio entrance

To reach them from the main channel, turn to starboard before the fishing harbour and the marina is on the bend in the river 0.8 miles further on, on the right. A little further upstream on the main Santos channel, the entrance to Rio do Meio is to starboard, just before the fishing boat quay. This river houses several marinas and shipyards.

MARINA HIFLY

This is a small marina on Rio do Meio, with 30 berths on a pontoon and a whole range of services.

There is a slipway for lifting out boats up to 40'.

Marina HIFLY, Complexo Industrial Naval do Guarujá, Guarujá, SP
☎/*Fax* (13) 3354 3506
VHF Channel 68
Email marina@hifly.com.br

MARINA PIER 26

24°00,16'S 046°17,58'W

This well-organised marina neighbours the previous one; it has a pontoon with 40 berths equipped with taps and 110 and 220 volt power outlets.

For lifting out, it has a 30-tonne travel lift and a huge, well-equipped boatyard.

Bar and cafeteria on site.

No service station.

Mooring fees

R$75 to 80 per day, or R$1,500 per month, for a 45' boat.

Marina PIER 26, Complexo Industrial Naval do Guarujá, Guarujá, SP
☎/*Fax* (13) 3354 3306
VHF Channel 68, call sign *India 95*
Email pier@pier26.com.br

SUPMAR

This marina, which is larger than the previous two, is also located on Rio do Meio and has 45 berths on a floating pontoon with water and 110 and 220 volt electricity.

It offers every service you need for boat maintenance and even for more significant boat repairs (polyester, steel welding, aluminium, etc.).

It has a huge, well-designed boatyard; its efficient organisation demonstrates the professionalism of this marina.

Santos–Guarujá. Marina SUPMAR

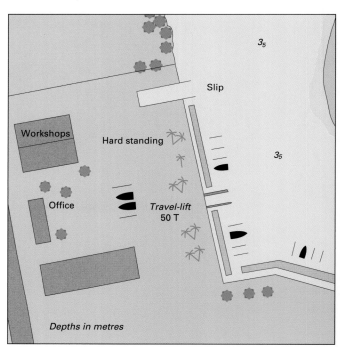

SUPMAR

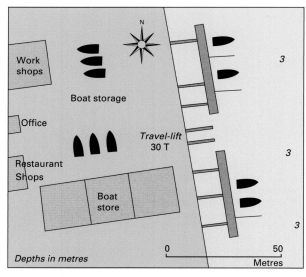

MARINA PIER 26

Mooring fees

Around R$2 per foot, per day.

This is a good choice for a technical stop-off.

SUPMAR – Suprimentos Marítimos, Complexo Industrial Naval do Guarujá, Guarujá, SP
☎/*Fax* (13) 3354 2859
Email supmar@uol.com.br
VHF Channel 68

PORTO MARINA ASTÚRIAS

This is a luxurious marina that offers every possible comfort and service. It is mainly home to large motor boats.

The mooring area is calm and well-sheltered from the winds in general. There is a depth of 1.8–2m in the dock at low tide.

There is a 50-tonne travel lift but the cradles are individually owned. The mooring fees are high and reflect the standing of the marina: R$180 per day, and R$2,600 per month, for a 45' boat.

Porto Marina Astúrias Serviços Navais, Complexo Industrial Naval do Guarujá, Guarujá, SP
☎/*Fax* (13) 3354 3888
VHF Channel 68, call sign *Zulu 60*
Email porto@marinasasturias.com.br

IATE CLUBE DE SANTOS

⊕ 3 • 23°59,17'S 046°17,20'W Iate Club do Santos

This is the largest Iate Clube in Brazil. Its headquarters are in São Paulo and it has annexes at Santos-Guarujá, Frade, near Angra dos Reis, Paraty and Ilhabela.

The marina at Guarujá is without a shadow of a doubt one of the largest and most impressive in Brazil, and it gladly welcomes visiting boats that are non-members.

You can feel the dynamism injected into this club by its managers, and behind the strict organisation lies a refreshing simplicity and friendliness.

It runs numerous activities, among which deep sea fishing and sailing are important nautical events; there is great participation in fishing competitions and regattas.

The Iate Clube is on the shore of the Canal de Santos, to starboard, after the ferry terminal.

Its facilities are impeccable and luxurious, and as the largest club in Brazil, it offers every comfort and amenity imaginable.

Facilities – Services ★★★

Visiting boats are accepted at the club and crews can use the facilities and services without any restrictions. It has a 50-tonne travel lift for lifting boats out of the water into the boatyard.

Service station with diesel and petrol.

The ferry terminal for ferries to Santos is 500m to the right of the Iate Clube.

Mooring fees ★★

The club offers visiting boats two days free of charge. Thereafter, there is a fixed rate of R$100 per day.

Iate Clube de Santos – Guarujá
☎ (13) 3348 4000, *Fax* (13) 3358 2873
VHF Channel 68–74

Iate Clube de Santos; top left, the mouth of the river.
Photo Marco Yamin. ILHABELA

Headquarters in São Paulo
Av. República do Libano, 315, IBIRAPUERA, CEP 04501-000
☎ (11) 3887 0406, *Fax* (11) 3885 0419
Email ics@icsantos.com.br

Anchorages around Santos

There are some beautiful beaches on the southern and southeastern sides of Ilha de Santo Amaro, and it is possible to anchor near some of them.

⚓A1, Saco do Major

⚓A2, to the east of Praia do Guaiúba

⚓A3, Praia das Pitangueiras

⚓A4, to the east of Praia da Enseada

These anchorages should be used in good weather conditions because in southerly to easterly winds, the mooring areas soon become rough and uncomfortable.

Useful telephone numbers

Area code ☎ (13).
Policía Féderal (Immigration), Praça da República ☎ 3224 2701.
Police Headquarters ☎ (13) 3201 5000.
Tourist office ☎ (13) 3201 8000.
Pronto Socorro (Emergency Medicine) ☎ (13) 3222 7342.
Capitania dos Portos de Santos (Port Captain's Office), Cais da Marinha, Armazem 27/29, Barrio Macuco, Santos, SP.
☎ (13) 3221 3454
www.santos.sp.gov.br

Life raft overhaul

Artigas e Salvatagem náuticos, Av. dos Caiçaras, 1485, Jd. Las Palmas, Guarujá, SP, CEP 11420 440
☎ (13) 3386 3065, 3383 1828.

STATE OF PARANÁ

Paraná is one of the largest States in the southern region, and its population is mainly made up of the descendants of German, Italian and Polish immigrants. You will see another side of Brazil here, with people from diverse backgrounds and different traditions.

The terrain is more mountainous with its highest point at 1,500m; there are pine and fir forests, chalet-style buildings and a significantly cooler climate.

The rich soil lends itself well to agriculture, particularly corn, wheat, soya, coffee and fruit farming, and there are large banana plantations.

Huge industrial projects have been undertaken for the development of the state, one of the most important of which is the enormous Itaipu dam.

Tourism

The coastal area is relatively narrow, with 100km of long beaches. In terms of tourism, the interior offers some interesting excursions:

- The train journey from Curitiba to Paranaguá, through the mountains covered in tropical forest; the trip is spectacular and rather vertiginous in places, as the track clings to the rock face!
- The geological curiosities of the region.
- On the borders with Uruguay and Argentina, the spectacular falls at Foz de Iguaçu.

Foz de Iguaçu. The spectacular Igauçu falls

Baía de Paranaguá

Baía de Paranaguá is a huge stretch of water 700km^2 in area, made up of several secondary bays strewn with numerous islands. At the end of the bay are the ports of Antonina and Paranaguá, the third largest port complex in Brazil.

The town has a population of around 120,000 and stretches out around the commercial port. The historic centre on the banks of the Rio Iberé is interesting, with several colonial buildings with attractive coloured façades.

Fishing is also an important activity in the region and there are numerous boats moored alongside the quays on the river.

For yachts, Paranaguá and its environs make a good stop on the southern route.

Navigation

Brazilian Charts DHN No. 1700, 1703, 1820, 1821 and 1822.

From Santos to São Francisco do Sul, the coast is uniformly low, made up of long beaches with mountains in the background.

There are two large bays along this stretch of coast:

- Baía de Paranaguá, the largest,
- the smaller Baía de Guaratuba; its bar, obstructed by large sandbanks, is tricky to cross.

Apart from Ilha do Bom Abrigo, it must be noted that in bad weather, there is no shelter on the 220 mile stretch between Santos and Ilha de São Francisco do Sul in the

The old town

neighbouring state, and Paranaguá cannot be seen as a refuge as it is hard to enter in poor weather. A good weather forecast is therefore necessary when undertaking this passage. It is 145 miles from Santos to Baía de Paranaguá, which is reached by steering an almost direct course between Ilha Queimada Grande and Ilha Queimada Pequenha.

Watch out however for a shoal, Laje de Pedro II, where the chart shows a depth of 1.7m.

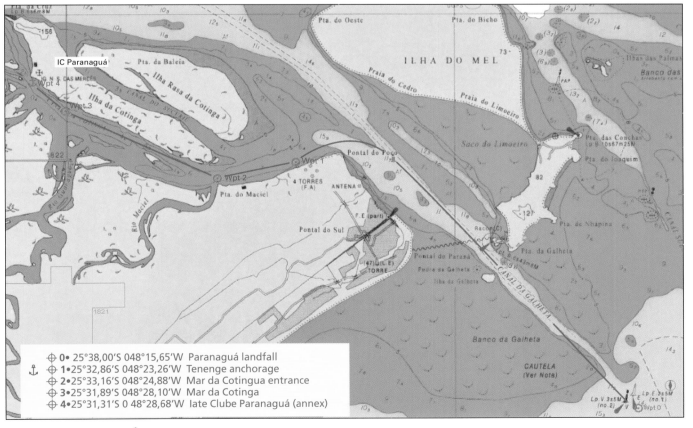

⊕ 0• 25°38,00'S 048°15,65'W Paranaguá landfall
⚓ ⊕ 1•25°32,86'S 048°23,26'W Tenenge anchorage
⊕ 2•25°33,16'S 048°24,88'W Mar da Cotingua entrance
⊕ 3•25°31,89'S 048°28,10'W Mar da Cotinga
⊕ 4•25°31,31'S 0 48°28,68'W Iate Clube Paranaguá (annex)

BAIA DE PARANAGUÁ

Conspicuous landmarks

There is a succession of islands on this route:
Laje de Conceição, Lp(2)BE.12s34m6/17M
Ilha Queimada Pequenha
Ilha Queimada Grande, LpB.10s83m23M
Ilha do Bom Abrigo, which has a white tower Lp.Alt.BBE.30s146m28/23M; it is located 110 miles southwest of Santos, and is the only shelter in strong winds from the southern sector.

⊕ 25°07,14'S 047°51,69'W Ilha do Bom Abrigo

Ilha do Castelo and Ilha Figueira, on the approach to Paranaguá.
Ilha do Mel with the Ponta das Conchas lighthouse, a tapered white metal tower.

Tide and current

Mean tide level is 0.84m above the chart datum, with a maximum amplitude of approximately 1.6m.

The tidal current is strong and can reach 4.5 knots on the ebb in spring tides, which makes the bar particularly rough.

Entry on the end of the rising tide is therefore strongly recommended.

Winds

In strong winds from the northern, western and southern sectors, the sea breaks dangerously on the shoals and the Paranguá bar becomes impracticable.

Approach

Approach by day Coming from offshore, the Ponta das Conchas lighthouse can be seen from a long way off on Ilha do Mel, together with the anchored commercial ships awaiting a pilot.

A series of breaking waves can be seen on either side of the approach channel to Baía de Paranaguá and it is vital that you take the marked channel that crosses the bar and leads to the port of Paranguá.

Approach by night For a first visit, entry by night is unadvisable but if this is necessary, take a bearing on the Ponta das Conchas lighthouse, Lp(3)B.10s67m25M and, to starboard at the entrance to the channel, the light on the southern point of Ilha do Mel, LpL.6s43m8M. The channel is straight and well-marked and the lights on the entrance buoys have a luminous range of five miles.

Paranaguá landfall

⊕ 0 • 25°38,00'S 048°15,65'W Paranaguá landfall

This waypoint is approximately one mile from the entrance to Canal da Galheta. A course of 316° leads to the channel, which is marked with buoys carrying lights Lp.E to starboard and Lp.V to port, to the commercial port approximately 15 miles from the open sea.

IATE CLUBE DE PARANAGUÁ

Iate Clube de Paranaguá is located to the south of the town, on one of the many channels that empty into the bay.

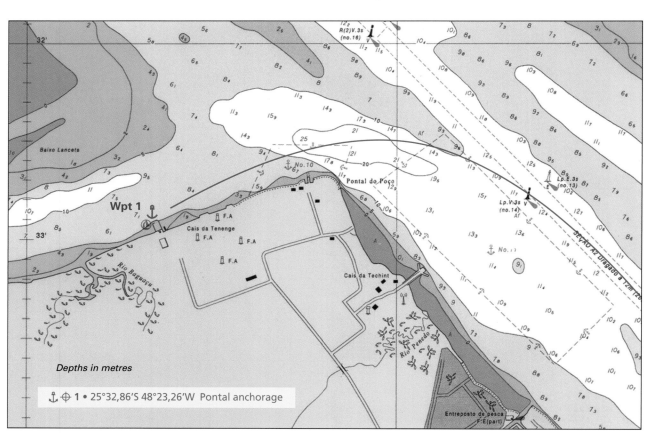

Depths in metres

⚓⊕ 1 • 25°32,86'S 48°23,26'W Pontal anchorage

PONTAL DO POÇO

The club can be reached along the main Canal da Galheta by following it to buoy No. 30; then head to the north of Ilha da Cotinga, with the Canal do Furado to port and the Rio Iberé to starboard.

This itinerary is relatively long and to reach the Iate Clube it is better to go through the Mar da Cotinga, but only in daylight.

This shorter, more pleasant route takes you through mangroves littered with small islets, and avoids the main channel with its large commercial ships.

Follow the marked channel to green buoy No. 13. Then leave the channel and turn to port, towards Pontal do Poço, which is rather low to the water but can be identified by four large pylons standing out on its tip.

Once past the point, there is a pontoon to port and, further on, the concrete structures of a private dock housing several motor boats.

It is possible to anchor nearby while waiting for good conditions to either go up to the Iate Clube in daylight or wait for the right state of the tide to leave Baía de Paranaguá.

The Iate Clube annex anchorage

⊕ 1 A good anchorage while waiting for favourable conditions

⊕ **1** • 25°32,86'S 048°23,26'W Tenenge anchorage

From this waypoint, follow the coast to
⊕ **2** • 25°33,16'S 048°24,88'W Mar da Cotingua entrance

which is level with the southeastern tip of Ilha da Cotinga. Leave to port Ilha do Papaguayo and go along Ilha da Cotinga, keeping to the right-hand section of the channel.

Head towards a huge grain silo, partly hidden by vegetation, to:
⊕ **3** • 25°31,89'S 048°28,10'W Mar da Cotinga

The facilities of the Iate Clube annex (*Sub Sede*) can be seen to starboard on the island.
⊕ **4** • 25°31,31'S 048°28,68'W Iate Clube Paranaguá (annexe)

The annex does not have any pontoons, but several buoys and a few anchored boats.

On first entry, it is preferable to anchor off the Iate Clube annex, where a boatman ferries people between the club and the annex. You can then go to the marina to enquire about mooring on the pontoon.

It is best to take this itinerary during the day. By night, without good local knowledge, it is advisable to anchor behind Pontal do Poço, near ⊕1, until morning.

Going along the river leading to the old quarters, you will see in succession the buildings of three private marinas, Port Marina Océania, Marina Velha Marujo and Marina Marlin Azul.

Just after these is the Iate Clube de Paranaguá marina.

The club has around 500 members and has 46 berths on the inside of its two pontoons for boats up to 40'; larger boats have to moor on the outside of the pontoons.

Visiting boats are accepted if there is space available, and this is relatively limited; however, there is always the option of staying at the Ilha da Cotinga annex, which has 18 mooring buoys, or anchoring nearby.

Iate Clube de Paranaguá

The Iate Clube de Paranaguá marina

Quality of moorings ***

The water in the marina is calm, but the berths on the outside of the pontoons are disturbed by the current of the river, which is relatively strong, and by passing fishing boats and trip boats.

The depth is 4m on the outside of the pontoons.

Facilities – Services **

The Iate Clube has a list of boat repair and maintenance contractors. These can work in the club's boatyard or at the annex.

There is a slipway for lifting out boats up to around 15 tonnes; there is also one at the club's annex.

Water At each berth there are two taps on the pontoon, one for boat washing and one for drinking water.

Electricity 110 and 220 volts on the pontoons.

Fuel The Palanganá service station has diesel and petrol, right next to the Iate Clube.

There is a ferry service from the club's annex from 0800 to 1100 and 1330 to 1800.

Supplies ***

The Iate Clube is located right next to the town centre, where there are several supermarkets, including one near the station, which is very well stocked.

Mooring fees **

The club offers visitors two days free of charge.

As a guide, a fixed price of R$65 to R$70 per day is then charged, whatever the size of the boat.

Location and surroundings **

The marina is well-located near the old quarter of Paranaguá.

24-hour security service.

Iate Clube de Paranaguá, Rua Benjamin Constant, 423, Paranaguá, CEP 83203-4506, PARANÁ
☎/*Fax* (41) 3422 5622
VHF Channel 68
Email icpgua@pop.com.br
www.icpgua.com.br

Useful telephone numbers

Area code ☎ (41).
Polícia Federal (Immigration) ☎ (41) 3422 2033.
Receita Federal (Customs) ☎ (41) 3423 1277.
Capitania dos Portos (Port Captain's Office) ☎ (41) 3422 3033 (near the Iate Clube).
Procon (Consumer Protection) ☎ (41) 3422 5433.
Pronto Socorro (Emergency Medicine) ☎ (41) 3423 1422.
Prefeitura (Town Hall) ☎ (41) 3420 2700.
IBAMA (Brazilian Institute of Environment and Renewable Natural Resources) ☎ (41) 3423 1818.
Tourist information ☎ (41) 3420 2700.
Hospital ☎ (41) 3423 3466.

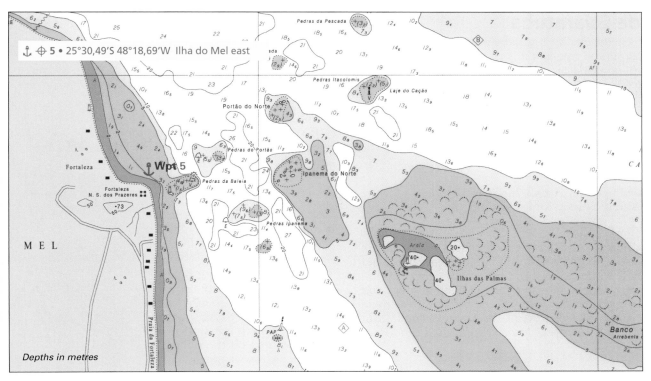

⚓ ⊕ 5 • 25°30,49'S 48°18,69'W Ilha do Mel east

Depths in metres

ILHA DO MEL

Ilha do Mel

Ilha do Mel is located to starboard at the entrance to Baía de Paranaguá.

In order to protect the bay and the ports from Spanish and French incursions, the Portuguese built a fort on the northeastern part of the island in 1767.

There are no roads on the island; its long sandy beaches, beautiful forest walks and the fortress of Nossa Senhora dos Prazeres are all tourist attractions that make this a popular location, and it is particularly busy during holiday periods.

In good weather with winds from the northern sector, it is possible to anchor near the southern tip of the island.

⊕ 4 • 25°34,30'S 048°18,95'W Ilha do Mel south

This anchorage is at the end of a long beach and is well-sheltered from the southwesterly winds generated by cold fronts. However, if there is a low, the more exposed surrounding waters will be particularly rough, making departure difficult.

If a front is forecast, it might be better to look for an anchorage on the northeastern shore of the island, not far from the fortress of NS dos Prazeres, to the northwest of the Pedras da Baleia rocks (marked by a tower).

⊕ 5 • 25°30,49'S 48°18,69'W Ilha do Mel northeast

Ilha das Peças

This island is located to the north of Ilha do Mel and there is a small fishing community behind the point.

This is a pleasant fair weather anchorage, near Pedra da Galiça.

⊕ 6 • 25°28,63'S 048°18,99'W Ilha das Peças

The fortress of Nossa Senhora dos Prazeres

The fishermen of Ilha das Peças

Baía de Guaratuba

Baía de Guaratuba is located around 25 miles from Paranaguá and is reached by steering a direct course of 222°, with no obstacles.

The town itself is of no particular interest. Unless absolutely necessary, this port of call can be avoided as access to the bay is particularly difficult.

Navigation

Brazilian Chart DHN No. 1803.

Conspicuous landmark

The Caiobá lighthouse, LpB.7s27m15M, a tapered white metal tower, is clearly visible from offshore.

Approach

The entrance to the bay is best suited to moderate draught boats, motor boats, catamarans or dinghies, and good local knowledge is vital when crossing this bar.

Despite the apparent tranquillity in good weather and calm seas, the entrance poses several difficulties as there are large sandbanks obstructing the passage. The sea can break violently on these shoals, and their uncertain

position varies depending on the weather conditions and currents.

The depth is between 1.8m and 2m at most on the bar, at mean low water.

The current is relatively strong and can exceed three knots in spring tides.

It is therefore vital to enter by day, in good weather, on the end of the rising tide with a high tidal coefficient.

If you are in any doubt, wait for a local boat, which will be able to give you advice about this difficult approach.

⊕ 0 • 25°51,67'S 048°31,00'W Guaratuba landfall

⊕ 1 • 25°51,55'S 048°33,80'W Entrance to Baía de Guaratuba

There are several marinas in Guaratuba but few sailing boats; the difficult bar could be the reason behind this.

IATE CLUBE DE CAIOBÁ

This is one of the largest Brazilian sailing clubs and it has a beautiful marina with impeccable facilities.

There are 367 berths spread over six pontoons, together with all possible amenities, but it is a long way from the town. It is mainly used by motor boats.

It is located on the right-hand side of the bay at the end of a narrow channel.

⊕ 2 • 25°50,70'S 048°34,88'W Iate Clube de Caiobá

Iate Clube de Caiobá, Estrada do Cabaraquara, MATINHOS, PR
☎ (041) 452 1645
Email iatecaioba@ves.com.br

Guaratuba. Worrying breakers on the bar

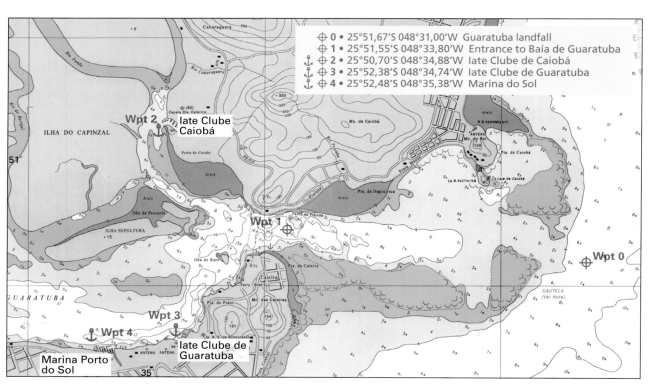

⊕ 0 • 25°51,67'S 048°31,00'W Guaratuba landfall
⊕ 1 • 25°51,55'S 048°33,80'W Entrance to Baía de Guaratuba
⚓ ⊕ 2 • 25°50,70'S 048°34,88'W Iate Clube de Caiobá
⚓ ⊕ 3 • 25°52,38'S 048°34,74'W Iate Clube de Guaratuba
⚓ ⊕ 4 • 25°52,48'S 048°35,38'W Marina do Sol

GUARATUBA

Guaratuba. Iate Clube de Caiobá

IATE CLUBE DE GUARATUBA

The Iate Clube is located on the left of the bay; it has a full range of boat maintenance services.

However, the pontoons were designed to take relatively small boats.

⊕ 3 • 25°52,38′S 048°34,74′W Iate Clube de Guaratuba

Headquarters: Iate Clube de Guaratuba, Rua Professor Fernando Moreira, 784, Curitiba, PR
☏ (41) 3222 6813, *Fax* (41) 3224 3482;

in Guaratuba, Rua José Bonifácio
☏ (41) 3442 1535
VHF Channel 68, call sign *Charlie 20*

Iate Clube de Guaratuba

MARINA DO SOL

This marina is located around two miles from the entrance to the bay, on the left after Iate Clube de Guaratuba.

Marina do Sol

It willingly accepts visiting boats and is well-organised to take larger boats, above 32′. It has 60 berths spread over five pontoons.

⊕ 4 • 25°52,48′S 048°35,38′W Marina do Sol

Quality of moorings

The mooring area is calm, well-protected from the winds in general and only slightly affected by the current.

Facilities – Services

There is every amenity at this well-kept marina – bar, restaurant, swimming pool, etc.

The marina also has a range of boat maintenance services and a slipway for lifting out boats up to 30 tonnes.

Mooring fees

Two days free of charge; thereafter R$68 per day for a 45′ boat.

Location and surroundings

The marina is not far from the town centre and has a 24-hour security service.

Marina Porto do Sol, Rua União da Vitória, 100, GUARATUBA, PR
☏ (41) 3442 1178
VHF Channel 68, call sign *Charlie 27*
Email Marinadosol@terra.com.br

Marina do Sol *Photo Castro*

STATE OF SANTA CATARINA

The State of Santa Catarina is without doubt the most European of the Brazilian states, as its population is mainly made up of the descendants of German and Italian immigrants who settled here in the 19th century. This is a prosperous region and there are numerous very diverse farms, as well as some medium-sized industrial firms.

The majority of the population is white, and the difference between social classes is much less marked than in many other Brazilian states.

The two largest towns are São Francisco do Sul, which is a major commercial port, and the capital Florianópolis, which is on Ilha Santa Catarina. The island is home to considerable tourist and commercial activity. Its varied landscape, with mountains, lakes and beaches, are of particular tourist interest.

The climate in this region is clearly differentiated: hot in summer, cooler and windier in winter, with invasions of cold air from Argentina.

São Francisco do Sul

It was French mariner Binot Palmier de Gonneville who first discovered these lands in 1504. One and a half centuries later, Portuguese Manoel Lourenço de Andrade settled in the region and the town of São Francisco do Sul was founded in 1660.

A port soon grew up with the arrival of the Portuguese, whalers from the Azores who found excellent fishing grounds here. Much later, in March 1851, it was the port of entry for German, Swiss and Norwegian immigrants on board the Colón; they arrived in large numbers to settle in the Joinville area, and founded the Colonia Dona Francisca.

São Francisco makes an interesting stop, and there are numerous vestiges of this period in the seafront area and old streets of the town; the historic centre, which is undergoing restoration, is now classified as a UNESCO World Heritage Site.

The area around São Francisco is also very touristy and renowned for its beautiful long beaches, which stretch to the north and south of the entrance to the bay.

Navigation

Brazilian Charts DHN No. 1804, 1804A and 1805.

São Francisco is a large commercial port for container ships. It is 40 miles from Paranaguá, and reached on a direct course of 203°.

The coast is low, uniform and featureless, with no shelter, and mainly made up of long straight beaches open to the offshore swell.

The Rio São Francisco, which has a well-marked southeast-northwest oriented approach channel, allows large ships to enter the port. For yachts, the port can be a good stopover while waiting for a cold front to pass.

Tide and current

Mean tide level is 0.8m above the chart datum, with a maximum amplitude of approximately 1.7m.

Depending on the tidal coefficient, there is a current of 2–4 knots in the channel, which is a little stronger on the ebb.

The historic centre on the shores of the bay

Winds

The strong winds from the southern sector that accompany cold fronts whip up 2.5m waves on the bar.

Approach

Given the strong current in the channel, it is highly recommended that you enter São Francisco do Sul on a rising tide.

Conspicuous landmarks

The lighthouse on Ilha da Paz, LpB.20s84m26M, is clearly visible from offshore.
Cabo João Dias, LpB.6s8m7M.
At the mouth of the Rio São Francisco, Ponta do Sumidouro to port, LpB.10s15m8M and Pontal to starboard, LpE.6s9m10M.
At night, the channel is well-marked with buoys carrying by lights LpV.3s5M to port and LpE.3s5M to starboard.

Landfall

From the north

Make landfall at:

⊕ 0 • 26°08,50'S 048°32,00'W   North landfall

From this waypoint, you can directly enter the marked approach channel, red buoy No. 7, LpE.3s3M, to the north of Ilha da Paz. This itinerary can be taken in good weather. In strong winds from the southern to eastern sectors, the offshore swell breaks on the shoals of Banco João Dias, which is left to port.

From the south

Enter directly along the marked channel, to the south of Ilha da Paz:

⊕ 1 • 26°11,32'S 048°29,40'W   South landfall

There are no marinas near the town of São Francisco, but it is possible to call at the small Capri Iate Clube marina near the entrance to the bay, to port.

It is also possible to anchor near the town centre, off the old quarter, where the trip boats are anchored near the jetty. This is the most convenient anchorage for visiting the town with its lively old quarter.

CAPRI IATE CLUBE

Located on Ilha de São Francisco, this is the first marina that you come to, to port near the open sea.

Once past Ponta do Sumidouro, a white cylindrical tower can be seen to port, FA.7m5M. Go along the coast to the tip of a long strip of sand that ends after 2.5 miles at Ponta das Galinhas.

⊕ 2 • 26°11,20'S 048°34,63'W   Off Capri channel

This waypoint is slightly north of the red and green beacons of the approach channel to the Iate Clube.

Beaconage has been installed by the Iate Clube and allows for the marina to be approached along a channel. Make sure to follow the beacons, as the water depth decreases very quickly on the left-hand side of the channel. Ponta das Galinhas is also extended by a large sandbank, which you must go around.

Immediately after the point to port, the mouth of a small river can be seen; enter this through a narrow passage between two sandy banks.

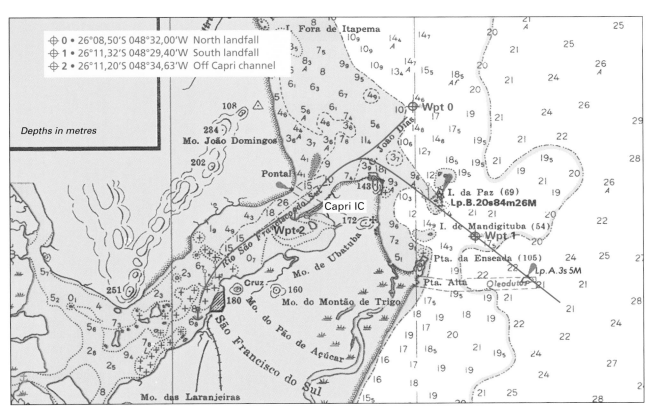

SÃO FRANSISCO DO SUL

The entrance to Capri Iate Clube. A narrow channel between two sandbanks (*Photo IC Capri*)

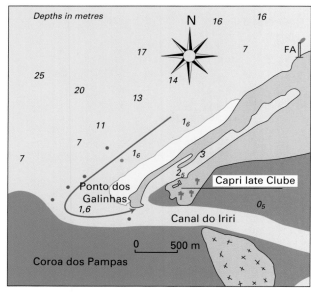

IATE CLUBE CAPRI

A transit can be taken on two white poles on land, and on the right there is a tower marking the Capri Iate Clube facilities.

If you are in any doubt about this channel, call the club on VHF Channel 16 and they will guide you in.

It is best to enter during the day at high tide to reach the Iate Clube, as the entrance is narrow with a depth of 2m at low tide; the depth then increases to 3.5m near the pontoons.

It is also possible to anchor near the Capri Iate Clube entrance channel and reach the facilities in the tender.

Quality of moorings ***

The river is narrow, well-sheltered from the wind and has no current.

The marina has two pontoons, one on each bank, with a total capacity of 38 berths.

There is a ferry between the far bank and the club.

Facilities – Services ***

The facilities are comfortable with good amenities (toilets and showers, bar, restaurant, etc.).

All the necessary services are on site and external contractors can be brought in for repairs.

Capri Iate Clube Marina

The marina has a 25-tonne travel lift, which should be operational soon.

There is also a slipway for lifting out boats up to 40 tonnes.

Water Taps on the pontoons.

Electricity 110 and 220 volts on the pontoons.

Fuel Service station with diesel and petrol on site.

Supplies **

These are available some distance away, around 5km, at the resort of Ubatuba.

Mooring fees **

The first day is free of charge; thereafter the price is R$60 per day for a 45' boat.

Location and surroundings

The marina is well-located at the entrance to Baía de São Francisco, in an attractive setting with beautiful beaches nearby. However, due to its position at the tip of the island, it is unfortunately a very long way from the town of São Francisco and rather isolated in a large condominium, offering little by way of communications facilities.

The club is pleasant though, and very lively at the weekend and during the holiday season.

24-hour security service.

Capri Iate Clube, Balneário de Capri, São Francisco do Sul, SC
☎/*Fax* (47) 442 7247
VHF Channel 16/68, call sign *Bravo 23*
Email capri-iate-clube@ilhanet.com.br
www.capriateclub.cm.br

JOINVILLE IATE CLUBE

Joinville Iate Clube is located around 12 miles from the entrance to Baía de São Francisco, and is reached along a marked channel through a string of islands dotted around the northwestern part of the bay. Although there are no problems in terms of depth for most of the journey, after red buoy No. 1 the last few miles are only accessible for moderate draught boats as the depth drops rapidly from 4m to 2m at low tide. If you are in any doubt, it might be preferable to request assistance in approaching the marina (Channel 68, call sign *Bravo 21*).

The Iate Clube has two pontoons and around 20 berths, but there are plans to enlarge and modernise the club, doubling the moorings available. It is in the Espinheiros district, which is unfortunately quite a distance from the town centre (6km), but there is a bus stop nearby.

The town is modern and very 'European' with flower-lined streets on the outskirts and all the necessary amenities in the centre, such as banks, supplies, health care, travel agencies, etc.

Joinville Iate Clube, Rua Pref. Baltazar Bushie, No. 2850, Espinheiros, Joinville, SC
☎/*Fax* (47) 434 1744
Email Jic@joinvilleiareclube.com.br
VHF Channel 68, call sign *Bravo 27*

Useful telephone numbers

Area code ☎ (47).

Capitania dos Portos do Estado de Santa Catarina (State of Santa Catarina Port Captain's Office), rua Dr Lauro Muller, 138 ☎ (47) 0204 0205.

Polícia Federal (Immigration) ☎ 431 6800.

Polícia Civil (Civilian Police), Alameda Ipiranga, 250 ☎ 440 2594.

Pronto Socorro (Emergency Medicine) ☎ 192.

Hospital São José ☎ 441 6666.

Promo-TUR Tourist Office ☎ 454 2644.

The pontoon at Iate Clube de Joinville

São Francisco do Sul to Ilha Santa Catarina

Navigation

Brazilian Charts DHN No. 1809, 1810 and 1800A.

Ilha Santa Catarina is approximately 75 miles from São Francisco do Sul.

The coast is low at first, made up of long beaches with mountains in the background. Around 40 miles to the south, it becomes hillier again, with rocky outcrops forming several coves sheltering beautiful beaches:

Enseada de Itapocorói
Enseada de Camboriú
Enseada de Porto Belo
Baía das Tijucas

There are also several islands: the Ilhas Tanboretes, Ilhas dos Remedios and Ilhas dos Lobos, which are left to starboard, and the Ilhas Itacolomis and Ilhas Feias in Enseada de Itapocorói.

Further south, on the approach to Santa Catarina, are the Ilhas de Galé, Calhau São Pedro, Ilha Deserta and Ilha do Arvoredo.

Enseada de Itapocorói

This cove, made up of a long beach, is well-sheltered from winds from the southern sector by Ponta do Vigia, and you can anchor at the southern end.

⊕ 26°45,78′S 048°36,54′W Itapocorói landfall

Enseada de Camboriú

The town of Camboriú spreads out from its long beach and has a population of 60,000 that increases five-fold in the summer season. It is a large seaside resort with the seafront lined with large buildings; there are some interesting places to visit and pleasant anchorages in the surrounding area.

General view of Enseada de Camboriú

Camboriú. The mouth of the river

Approach

⊕ 27°00,12′S 048°36,43′W Camboriú landfall

A riprap breakwater, which protects the mouth of the Rio Camboriú, can be seen at the southern end of the beach.

To gain access to the river, go along the breakwater on the right-hand side of the channel, then move over to the left-hand side as the sandbank off the point extends a long way into the mouth of the river.

There are several fishing boats and pleasure boats (reproductions of old sailing boats) anchored in the river. It is possible to anchor nearby or a little further upstream on the left-hand side.

TEDESCO MARINA GARDEN PLAZA

This recently opened marina is located on the right at the mouth of the river.

⊕ 27°00,28′S 048°36,20′W

The quay is fitted out to take motor boats and sailing boats on floating pontoons.

It is a modern marina with a restaurant, swimming pool, tennis court, etc.

There are numerous facilities on site, including a 50-tonne travel lift.

Mooring fees

R$140 per day for a 36′ to 48′ boat.

Tedesco Marina Garden Plaza, Av. Normando Tedesco 1350, Barra Sul, Balneário Camboriú
℗ (47) 3361 1420.

Only motor boats, dinghies, catamarans and other moderate-draught boats can negotiate the Rio Camboriú. It should preferably be entered by day, at high tide.

Boats with a deeper draught can anchor in the cove in good weather, near the breakwater in 2.5–3m of water.

The Praia de Laranjeiras anchorage

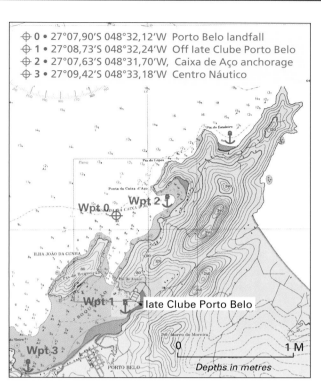

⊕ 0 • 27°07,90'S 048°32,12'W Porto Belo landfall
⊕ 1 • 27°08,73'S 048°32,24'W Off late Clube Porto Belo
⊕ 2 • 27°07,63'S 048°31,70'W, Caixa de Aço anchorage
⊕ 3 • 27°09,42'S 048°33,18'W Centro Náutico

Wpt 0
Wpt 2
Wpt 1 late Clube Porto Belo
Wpt 3
0   1 M
Depths in metres

ENSEADA DE PORTO BELO

Praia de Laranjeiras

There is another possible mooring outside the town, behind Morro da Aguada, off Praia de Laranjeiras. Approximately two miles from Camboriú at Ponta das Laranjeiras, a small beach, well-sheltered from the south and surrounded by hills covered in a mixture of tropical forest and pine, provides a peaceful anchorage.

This is a popular tourist location for holidaymakers and the beach is often very crowded. However, it is a pleasant anchorage in clear waters.

Anchor off the beach, away from the buoys marking a marine farm. The part near the jetty is more disturbed by passing trip boats.

⊕ 26°59,64'S 48°35,33'W Praia de Laranjeiras

Tourism

- There is an excellent dive site near Ponta das Laranjeiras.
- There is a good walk in the Morro da Aguada ecology park along a well-marked route through the *mata Atlántica*.
- The cable car between the town and Praia de Laranjeiras provides a panoramic view over the cove.

There is a stop halfway at the top of Morro da Aguada, where you can get off to visit the ecology park.

Enseada de Porto Belo

Porto Belo is approximately 60 miles south of São Francisco do Sul.

Enseada das Garoupas, as Baía de Porto Belo was formerly known, was colonised two and a half centuries ago by a community of immigrants from the Azores. These whalers found that there were well-stocked fishing grounds and good sailing conditions in this part of Brazil, and the town of Porto Belo was founded in 1832.

It is one of the busiest fishing harbours in the region and there are several fish canneries around the bay. The town stretches out along a huge sandy beach, and its charming surroundings make it a popular holiday resort.

Navigation

Brazilian Charts DHN no. 1810 and no. 1902.

⊕ 0 • 27°07,90'S 048°32,12'W Porto Belo landfall

Enseada de Porto Belo. General view

Porto Belo. The Iate Clube marina

IATE CLUBE PORTO BELO

This club is located at the end of a cul-de-sac that is well-protected from winds from the northern to southern sectors, but open to the southwest; it is reached by going between Ponta do Caixa de Aço and Ilha João da Cunha, which is left to starboard. You then head southwest into a narrow channel between Ponta do Boqueirão and Ponta de Araújo. This leads to a very large inlet with several anchored fishing boats, and the Iate Clube facilities can be seen at the end of the cul-de-sac to port.

The marina houses around 150 boats on sturdily-built pontoons. The club is luxurious, with impeccable, well-kept facilities, including toilets and showers, a restaurant, swimming pool, etc.

⊕ **1** • 27°08,73'S 048°32,24'W Off Iate Clube Porto Belo

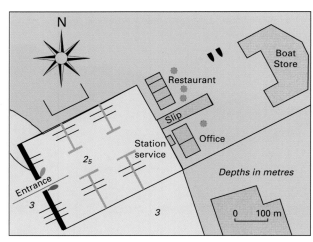

IATE CLUBE DE PORTO BELO

Quality of moorings ★★★

The marina is well-protected and houses around 150 boats on sturdily-built pontoons.

Facilities – Services ★★★

There are several businesses that work in the Iate Clube's boatyard and there is no problem arranging mechanical, electrical or refrigeration repairs. The marina has a slipway for lifting out boats up to around 20 tonnes, but this service is for members only and as a rule is not available to visiting boats apart from in an emergency.

Water There are sufficient taps on the pontoons.

Electricity 110 and 220 volts on the pontoons.

Fuel Service station with diesel and petrol. Visitors have to pay a surcharge on fuel of 15% for diesel and 30% for petrol – very odd!

Supplies ★★

There are several shops, supermarkets and businesses in the town centre.

Mooring fees ★★★

Guide prices:

Low season prices for 33' to 42' boats:
R$50 per day for the 1st week
R$100 per day for the 2nd week
R$150 per day for the 3rd week

Above 42':
R$80 per day for the 1st week
R$160 per day for the 2nd week
R$240 per day for the 3rd week

The longer you stay in the marina, the higher the price; it seems that the Iate Clube prefers to keep up the turnover on the berths available for visiting boats.

These prices double in the high season.

Location and surroundings ***

The marina is located at the end of town, slightly hemmed in at the end of the cul-de-sac; its facilities are luxurious with attractive gardens.

The town centre is 4km away and there is a bus stop near the club.

Iate Clube Porto Belo, Rua Pedro Jacinto Dias, 281, Caixa postal 24, Porto Belo, SC
☎/*Fax* (47) 369 4333
Email icpb@terra.com.br
VHF Channel 68, call sign *Bravo 23*

MARINA ATLÂNTIDA

This is not a marina, but a boatyard that houses a few small local vessels in a narrow channel unsuitable for cruisers.

It is located in the town centre, at the northeastern end of Praia do Baixo.

It might however be of interest to visiting yachtsmen as it offers a number of boat repair and maintenance services.

Marina Atlântida, Portobelo, SC
☎ (47) 3369 5665
www.marinatlantida.com.br

PORTO BELO ANCHORAGES

The bay is open to winds from the northern sector, but these hardly affect the anchorages; it is well-sheltered from winds from the southern and eastern sectors.

There are several possible anchorages in the cove:

- off the beaches in good weather, or to the south of Ilha João da Cunha,
- at the northern tip, off the small Praia do Estaleiro,
- there is a good anchorage in Enseada do Caixa de Aço, off a lovely beach. If a cold front comes through, check that the anchor is holding well as the anchorage is open to the southwest,

⊕ **2** • 27°07,63′S 048°31,70′W, Caixa de Aço anchorage

- opposite the church in Porto Belo, the Centro Náutico where you can come ashore in the tender and leave it on the jetty.
    The centre is planning to restructure its site in the near future and build a new jetty on the site of the existing one.

⊕ **3** • 27°09,42′S 048°33,18′W Centro Náutico

The centre allows visiting yachts to use its toilet and shower facilities and services.

Centro Náutico de Porto Belo,
Centro, Porto Belo, SC
☎ (47) 369 4361
Email c.npbelo@ig.com.br

Baía das Tijucas

Go around Ponta de Porto Belo to the southeast, where there are several coves providing excellent, well-protected anchorages:

- Enseada de Mariscal,
- behind Ponta de Zimbros, opposite the church, is an anchorage off some beautiful beaches that provides good shelter in northerly winds.

⊕ **4** • 22°11,18′S 048°32,14′W Zimbros

Enseada de Ganchos

See plan page 220

At the south of Baía das Tijucas, Enseada de Ganchos is a large cove made up of three inlets, with an attractive fishing village at the end.

Anchor in the second inlet, Ganchos do Meio, opposite the jetty at the Iate Clube de Caiobá annex.

It is possible to reach the club's pontoon and use some of the services, such as water, electricity, bar, restaurant, tender watching, etc.

⊕ **5** • 27°18,66′S 48°33,36′W Ganchos

This is an excellent anchorage that is recommended if a cold front arrives; it is completely sheltered from winds from the southern and eastern sectors.

⊕ **6** • 27°18,91′S 048°33,66′W Iate Clube de Caiobá (annex)

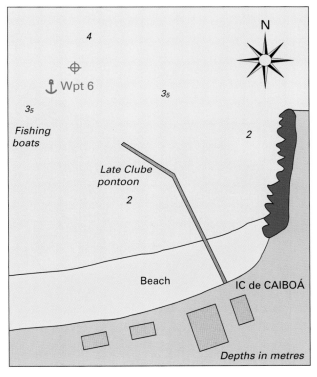

ENSEADA DE GANCHOS

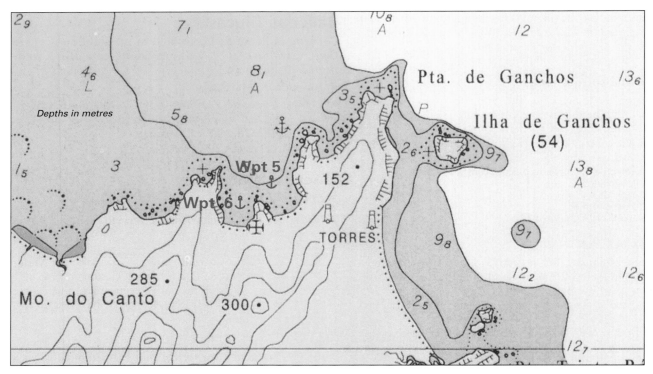

ENSEADA DE GANCHOS

An excellent anchorage near the late Clube de Caiobá annex

Ilha Santa Catarina. The suspension bridge from the north with the new bridge in the background

Ilha Santa Catarina – Florianópolis

Ilha Santa Catarina is separated from the mainland by a channel and the state capital, Florianópolis, population 350,000, is split between the two sides of the channel. The bridge connecting the island to the mainland divides the channel into two parts, Baía Norte and Baía Sul.

The northern part of the island is very touristy, with residential areas and beautiful beaches.

The south of the island is less populated and all along the southwestern section of the coast there are numerous oyster farms, where the regional gastronomic speciality is gathered.

The central section is mountainous, and the thickly forested eastern slope drops down into a large expanse of water, Lago da Conceição.

The eastern coast is home to beautiful long beaches that are open to the offshore swell and ideal for surfing.

There are various industries on the mainland, which is of no particular tourist interest.

Navigation

Brazilian Charts DHN No. 1902, 1903 (north) and 1904 (south).

The coastline of the State of Santa Catarina is made up of alternating rocky outcrops and long beaches, with some low hills in the background that are rarely over 500m.

Conspicuous landmarks

From the north

From Porto Belo, go round Ponta de Bombas staying well off, and then steer a course south to Ilha Santa Catarina.

The following are left to port in succession:
Ilha da Galé, LpB.10s78m8M.
Calhau de São Pedro, LpB.3s19m8M.
Ilha do Arvoredo, Oc(4)60s90m24M.

From the south

Leave to port Ilha do Coral, LpB.3s81m14M and head towards Ponta dos Naufragados, Lp(2)B.15s43m18M.

Tide and current

Mean tide level is 0.4m above the chart datum, with a maximum amplitude of 0.9m.

The tidal current in the channel is 1.5 knots, and can reach three knots in spring tides.

Winds

With regard to the wind conditions, there are two tendencies:
- winds from the northern sector, which generally blow from October to March, and are sometimes strong,
- winds from the southern sector, which generally blow from March to September and are generated by cold fronts formed in Argentina.

These violent winds, the *Pampeiros*, blow in strong gusts of 40 knots or more between Ilha Santa Catarina and the mainland. The current in the channel depends directly on the winds and can reach speeds of three knots or more (*see Rio Grande do Sul, Winds*).

In winter, and more particularly in August, there are often morning mists on this coast.

Approach

From the north, there are two options for stopping on the island:
- an anchorage to the north of the island, off the Iate Clube de Santa Catarina annex,
- the marina at Iate Clube de Santa Catarina – Veleiros da Ilha, in Florianópolis.

The best and most convenient option is to anchor on the northern part of the island, near the Iate Clube de Santa Catarina annex, off the lovely Praia de Jureré.

There are other possible anchorages in good weather, both on the northwestern side and the east coast.

The centre of Florianópolis is around 20km away, and there are several means of transport available for visiting the state capital.

You can also reach the Iate Clube marina by going down the Canal de Santa Catarina, but there are two bridges over the channel. There is approximately 25m

North
⊕ **0** 27°24,00'S 048°29,80'W North landfall
⊕ **1** 27°25,76'S 048°29,05'W Off Iate Clube
⊕ **2** 27°30,53'S 048°31,34'W Santo Antônio de Lisboa
⊕ **3** 27°22,81'S 048°32,15'W Praia do Fagundes

South
⊕ **0** 27°50,82'S 048°33,85'W South entrance landfall
⊕ **1** 27°36,32'S 048°33,00'W Near Iate Clube

ILHA SANTA CATARINA

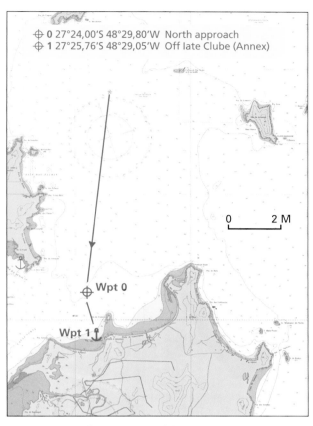

⊕ **0** 27°24,00'S 48°29,80'W North approach
⊕ **1** 27°25,76'S 48°29,05'W Off Iate Clube (Annex)

0   2 M

Wpt 0

Wpt 1

ILHA SANTA CATARINA NORD

Jureré. Iate Clube de Santa Catarina, a good anchorage on the north of the island

under the deck of the old Hercilio Luz suspension bridge, and the central section of the new bridge is only 17m above the water.

The passage from the north to the south of the island therefore depends on this bridge, and sailing boats with mast heights of 17m or more will be obliged to go round the southern tip of the island.

Crossing the southern bar can pose real problems in the Banco dos Naufragados channel, where the waves break in bad weather; if the weather conditions are unfavourable, it is best to avoid this passage. Similarly, great care is required when navigating in the southern channel of the island, in order to avoid the sandbank areas and rocks that litter the route.

Baía Norte

The Iate Clube de Santa Catarina marina is located in Florianópolis, but its Jureré annex on the north of the island makes a very good stopover.

IATE CLUBE DE SANTA CATARINA (JURERÉ ANNEX)

From the north, make landfall at

⊕ **0** • North • 27°24,00'S 048°29,80'W   North landfall
Anchor near the Iate Clube annex's long jetty.

⊕ **1** • 27°25,76'S 048°29,05'W   Off Iate Clube

This anchorage is located at the end of Praia de Jureré, which is overlooked by Igreja São Francisco on the one hand and Fortaleza São José da Ponta Grossa, built by the Portuguese in 1740, on the other.

The Iate Clube de Santa Catarina jetty

Quality of moorings ***

Holding is good in 2.5–3m of water on sand. The mooring area is completely sheltered from westerly to easterly winds, but winds from the northern sector, which are sometimes strong, make it particularly rough.

Facilities – Services **

There are around twenty buoys available for visiting boats.

Water and electricity at the end of the jetty.

The club has a slipway, but it is only used for lifting out small tonnage boats.

The toilets and showers are decent and the bar/restaurant is laid out in pleasant surroundings with a very relaxed atmosphere.

Supplies ***

Supplies are readily available in town at several supermarkets.

Fuel has to be obtained in jerry cans.

Mooring fees **

The club offers visitors two days free of charge; thereafter, the price on a buoy is around R$50 per day for a 45' boat.

Location and surroundings ***

Excellent; pleasant surroundings off a beautiful sandy beach, with a very warm welcome at the Iate Clube annex.

Iate Clube de Santa Catarina, Praia de Jureré
☎/Fax (48) 266 1280
Email jurere@icsc.com.br
VHF Channel 16, call sign *Bravo 26*

Other anchorages

In strong winds from the northern sector, it is best to leave the Iate Clube anchorage, as it quickly becomes uncomfortable, and head for another better protected anchorage further south in the channel, off the beach and church of Santo Antônio de Lisboa.

⊕ 2 • 27°30,53'S 048°31,34'W Santo Antônio de Lisboa

Shelter can also be found to the northwest, inside the coves on the mainland.

To the west of Ponta de Armação there is an anchorage that is well-sheltered from the north, off Praia do Fagundes.

⊕ 3 • 27°22,81'S 048°32,15'W Praia do Fagundes

The winds from the southern sector that accompany cold fronts blow violently between the island and the mainland. There are several sheltered anchorages on the northeastern part of the island.

Similarly, eight miles to the north on the mainland, Enseada de Ganchos provides excellent shelter (anchorage described in the previous section).

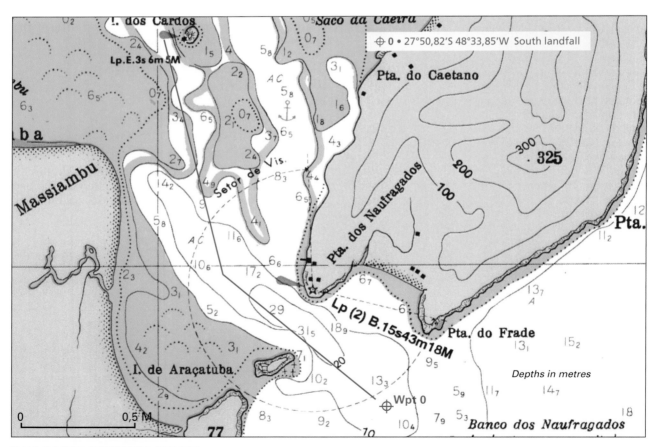

ILHA SANTA CATARINA SOUTH

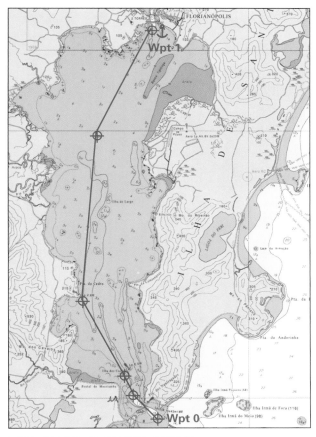

ILHA SANTA CATARINA SOUTH

Baía Sul

The southern part of the island is much less developed than the northern part, and heading up the Canal de Santa Catarina towards the bridge you come to Iate Clube de Santa Catarina – Veleiros da Ilha, which is near the centre of Florianópolis.

IATE CLUBE DE SANTA CATARINA (FLORIANÓPOLIS)

The Iate Clube headquarters and the marina are located on the southern part of Ilha Santa Catarina.

To reach it in a sailing boat, pay attention to the height of the bridge (*see Note in Navigation – Approach*) and if you have a boat with a tall mast, you will have to go around the south of the island.

However, you should only sail along this part of the island in good weather, as the straight coastline made up of long beaches offers little by way of safe shelter.

To reach the southern channel from the north, go around Ponta do Frade staying well off, and head towards Ponta dos Naufragados with its lighthouse (Lp(2)B.15s43m18M).

From the south, make landfall at ⊕0, located approximately 1.5 miles from the entrance channel.

⊕ 0 • 27°50,82'S 048°33,85'W South entrance landfall

Caution: in bad weather, the sea breaks violently on Banco dos Naufragados, making this area dangerous.

The narrow channel of the southern entrance to the island can be seen between Ponta dos Naufragados and Ilha de Araçatuba.

Then head towards Ilha do Cardos, going along it close to its west coast, around the end of the Coroa de Massiambu sandbank.

Steer along Canal do Meio towards Ponta de Enseada (LpV.10s8m8M), around three miles to the northwest, and then turn to starboard.

The Iate Clube de Santa Catarina - Veleiros da Ilha marina

Six miles further north, Ilha do Largo and the shoals surrounding it are left to starboard.

Then head towards the bridge between Ilha Santa Catarina and the mainland, leaving Banco de Tipitinga, a shoal that shows on the surface and is uncovered at low tide, a good distance to starboard.

The Iate Clube facilities can then be seen.

⊕ 1 • 27°36,32'S 048°33,00'W Near Iate Clube

The club accepts visiting boats if there is space available.

However, it is possible to wait on the anchor in a small cove housing a few fishing boats to the north of the marina entrance.

Quality of moorings **

Moor bows or stern to the pontoon, with lines to two posts.

The mooring area is generally calm, and more disturbed in winds from the southern sector and when the *Pampeiro* is blowing in strong gusts.

Facilities – Services **

The club has all the comforts offered by the Brazilian clubs, including bar, restaurant, television room, internet access, toilets and showers, etc.

There is a boatyard where electrical, engineering, refrigeration and maintenance contractors in general can work on site.

Slipway for lifting out boats up to around 10 tonnes.

Water Taps on the pontoons.

Electricity 220 volts on the pontoons.

Fuel Service station with diesel and petrol on site.

Supplies ***

All types of supplies are available in town, where there are several supermarkets.

Mooring fees ***

The price is calculated depending on the area of the boat (lxb), on a basis of approximately R$65 per day for a 45' boat.

Location and surroundings **

A good location near the centre of Florianópolis, with a bus stop nearby.

24-hour security service.

Florianópolis. Moored on the Iate Clube pontoon

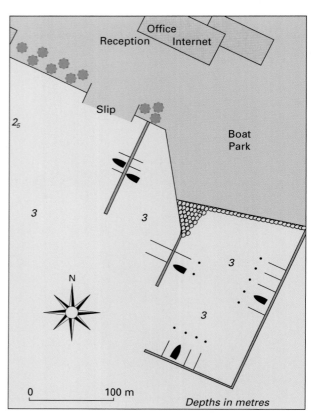
Depths in metres

IATE CLUBE DE SANTA CATARINA – VELEIROS DA ILHA

Iate Clube de Santa Catarina – Veleiros da Ilha, Rua Silva Jardim, 212, Praina, Florianópolis, SC
☎/Fax (48) 266 1260, 225 7799
Email iscs@iscs.com.br
VHF Channel 16, call sign *Bravo 20*. 0900–1900.

Useful addresses and telephone numbers

Area code ☎ (48).

Polícia Federal (Immigration), Av. Beira Mar Norte (next to the Casa do Governador (Governor's Residence), Florianópolis ☎ 281 6500 (0800 to 1700).

Receita Federal (Customs), Rua Tenente Silveira, n° 229, Edificio Reflex ☎ 222 6033 (near the Biblioteca Pública (public library), Florianópolis (0900 to 1130 and 1300 to 1630).

Capitania dos Portos (Port Captain's Office), Rua 14 de Julho, n° 440 ☎ 258 5500 (opposite bank to the Iate Clube).

Vigilância Sanitária (Health Surveillance), Praça Pereira Olivera, 6e (opposite the Alvaro de Carvalho theatre), Bairro Estreito ☎ 244 1176 (0830 to 1130).

Rodoviária (Bus Station), Av. Paulo Fontes ☎ 212 3100.

Tourist Office, Av. Paulo Fontes ☎ 271 7000.

Pronto Socorro (Emergency Medicine) ☎ 192.

Celsio Ramos Hospital ☎ 251 7000.

Department of Tourism, Av. Eng. Max de Souza, 236, Coqueiros.

ENSEADA DA PINHEIRA

An excellent, well-sheltered anchorage on the south of the island which can be used whilst waiting for favourable conditions on the route north or south.

⊕ 25°52,02'S 048°35,16'W Enseada da Pinheira

This waypoint is in the entrance to the bay, slightly west of a rock which breaks in bad weather. Depending on the wind find a sheltered anchorage in the north or south of the bay.

I

STATE OF RIO GRANDE DO SUL

The State of Rio Grande do Sul is located at the southern tip of Brazil; it shares borders with Uruguay on the coast, and Argentina inland.

The region was colonised in the 18th century by the Portuguese and later, in the 19th century, large numbers of immigrants from Germany, Italy and Eastern Europe settled here. The huge *pampas* that stretch to the west, such as Serra Iguriaça and Serra das Encantadas are particularly good for animal husbandry and agriculture, which are the main activities in the region.

The state capital, Porto Alegre, population 1.3 million, lies to the north of Lagoa dos Patos, a vast inland body of water.

On the northern section of the coast are two ports, Imbituba and Laguna.

Once past Cabo de Santa Marta Grande, the coastline is one long beach; there is nothing on this sandy shore other than small holiday resorts and, further south, the large port of Rio Grande.

Imbituba

Brazilian Chart DHN No. 1908.

This medium-sized commercial port, which mainly takes container ships, is located approximately 55 miles from the northern tip of Ilha Santa Catarina.

There is no particular interest in calling at Imbituba, but this easily-reached port can serve as a refuge for boats caught by surprise by the arrival of a cold front. It is well-sheltered from winds from the southern sector by Ponta de Imbituba, which has a lighthouse Lp(3)B.15s69m21M, clearly visible from offshore. Two radio masts in the background can also be used to pinpoint the port. There is a long riprap breakwater protecting the entrance, with a white and green striped tower at its end.

Take note however that 0.5 mile to the northeast of the protective breakwater there are two shoals, Pedras de Imbituba, marked by a north cardinal buoy, and Pedras de Aracaju, marked by a south cardinal buoy. The swell breaks on these shoals in bad weather.

Make landfall at:

⊕ 28°12,62'S 048°39,00'W Near Imbituba

Laguna

Brazilian Chart DHN No. 1901.

Around 60 miles south from Santa Catarina, the fishing port of Laguna is located on the channel linking Lago Santo Antônio to the sea, three miles from Ilha dos Lobos, Lp.B.5s50m11M and eight miles from Cabo Santa Marta Grande, Oc(3)BE.30s74m46/39M.

The entrance, between two lines of breaking waves, requires caution and excellent local knowledge of the position of the sandbanks and the depth, which both change frequently. The bar can be crossed in good weather by moderate-draught boats, but soon becomes very rough in strong breezes from the northern and eastern sectors.

Laguna must not be seen as a refuge.

Rio Grande

The port of Rio Grande was created to enable the development of this southern region of Brazil. It is located on a long channel that links Lago dos Patos to the ocean.

To allow for easy access to the port, significant work was carried out on the entrance bar in 1908, with the construction of two breakwaters that stretch 2km out to sea. A 130km railway line was built specially to bring riprap from the quarries at Capão de Leão, near Pelotas, to the entrance to the port. The work was completed in 1915 and enabled the expansion of the port of Rio Grande, which is now one of the largest ports in South America. 120 miles to the south, the large lighthouse of Arroio Chui (a tapered tower with red and white stripes Lp(2)35s43m46M) marks the border between Brazil and Uruguay.

Navigation

Brazilian Charts DHN No. 90, 2101 and 2110.

Between Ilha Santa Catarina and Cabo de Santa Marta Grande, the coastline is jagged and made up of alternating points, islands and beaches against a

The long breakwater protecting the port of Imbituba

backdrop of mountains, the highest peaks of which are below 1,000m.

After the cape, the coast is uniformly low and formed of a string of long beaches with just a few sand dunes.

There is no shelter in the 350 miles between Santa Catarina and Rio Grande (apart from Imbituba) and it is recommended that you stay well offshore (at least 50 miles) if bad weather is forecast. A good 3-day forecast is preferable, as the approach to the port of Rio Grande can be difficult, or even impracticable, in bad weather.

Tide and current

Mean tide level is 0.22m above the chart datum, with a maximum amplitude of approximately 0.6m.

At the entrance to Rio Grande, the tide and current are strongly influenced by the wind strength and direction, particularly in southeasterly winds.

In winds from the southern sector, the flood current can reach three knots, and in a northerly wind, the ebb current can reach five knots on the falling tide.

Crossing the bar will therefore depend on these factors, and on sufficient engine power for sailing boats. If you enter on a rising half-tide, you will be able to go up the channel, which is over 12 miles long, with the help of the flood current.

Watch out in the channel for large merchant ships and a considerable flotilla of fishing boats that move around and moor on the river.

Winds

Winds from the northern sector, which generally blow from November to March, make sailing down this coast easy. However, the cold fronts that form in Argentina bring a particularly fearsome southwesterly wind, the *Pampeiro*, which blows in strong gusts. This wind is characterised by sudden anti-clockwise changes of direction (*see Navigation aids and information – Weather forecasts*). It is generally followed by another

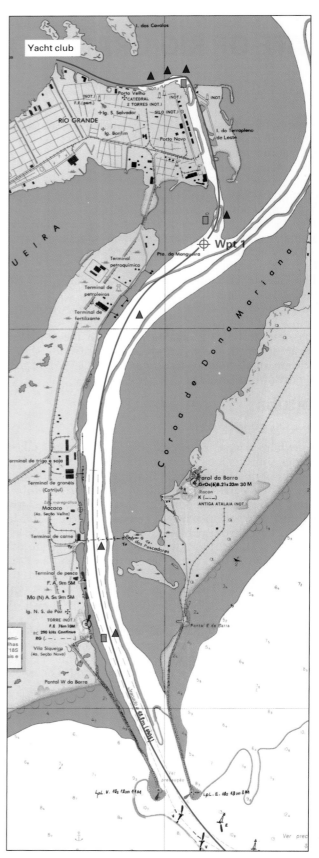

RIO GRANDE CHANNEL

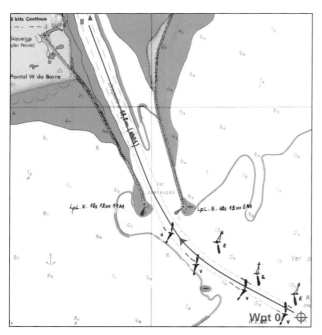

RIO GRANDE LANDFALL

Rio Grande Yacht Club. The buoys of the approach channel and the RGYC tower, which can be seen to port

equally fearsome wind, the *Carpinteiro*, which blows from the southeast and whips up a rough sea that dangerously pushes boats towards the coast.

Approach

Conspicuous landmarks

By day Farol da Barra, a black and white striped tapered metal tower.

The channel entrance towers, at the ends of the riprap breakwaters.

By night Farol da Barra, Oc(6)B.21s32m30M.
The tower on the East mole LpL.E.10s13m8M.
The lighthouse on the West mole LpL.V.10s12m11M.

The port facilities are located on the left-hand side, all along the channel.

The entrance channel, which is southeast/northwest oriented, is well marked and extends a long way out to sea, beyond the two riprap breakwaters. From the north or the south, make landfall at

⊕ **0** • 32°12,30'S 052°03,24'W

In good weather and calm seas, it is possible to enter the channel directly at beacon No. 5. Then follow the marked channel, alongside the port facilities, towards the petrochemicals terminal and red buoy No. 17

⊕ **1** • 32°04,00'S 052°04,50'W

The channel then splits into two parts: the starboard channel towards Lagoa dos Patos, and the port channel, which is marked and leads to the town of Rio Grande. Follow this channel which has the port installations along its porthand side to Porto Novo.

⊕ **2** • 32°01,78'S 052°04,74'W

Turn 90° to west (buoy no. 2) and follow the shore and quays towards the fishing harbour. Afte about 1.5 nautical miles the Oceanographic Museum will be seen. It is possible to wait for the tide on the museum pontoon (with permission) before entering the Yacht Club Marina (with its own buoyage)

⊕ **3** • 32°01,56'S 052°06,37'W oceanographic museum pontoon, near the Yacht Club

Rio Grande Yacht Club

Founded in 1934, Rio Grande Yacht Club is one of the oldest in Brazil.

The friendliness of a yacht club is a reflection of the people running it, and Rio Grande Yacht Club is certainly one of the finest examples in Brazil.

The club has 400 members and is remarkably well-organised. The particularly friendly welcome confirms the traditional hospitality of *gaucho* country, and the dynamic Vice Commodore Guto and his colleagues contribute greatly to this.

RGYC is approximately 14 miles from the open sea at the western end of town, after the oceanographic museum. It has a marina, the entrance to which is marked by the red and green buoys of a regularly-dredged channel. The marina can however only be accessed by shallow-draught boats (no more than 2m), and must be entered at high tide.

Quality of moorings

The water is calm and hardly affected by the current.

Facilities – Services

The club's facilities are impeccable, with bar, restaurant, swimming pool, tennis court, etc.

For boat maintenance – marine engineering, electrics, refrigeration, etc. – there are all types of service in Rio Grande, where numerous businesses are used to working on fishing boats and commercial ships; ask Jesé at the Yacht Club office.

There is a slipway for lifting out boats up to 20 tonnes.

Water Taps with drinking water on the pontoons.

Electricity 110 and 220 volts on the pontoons.

Fuel At the Ipiranga service station in the fishing harbour.

Supplies

Supplies are available at the Guanabara supermarket (a 15-minute walk away), which can deliver.

Mooring fees

As a guide, the price is between R$1.50 per foot per day, with one day free of charge.

The Rio Grande Yacht Club marina *Photo Guto, RGYC*

Rio Grande Yacht Club *Photo Guto, RGYC*

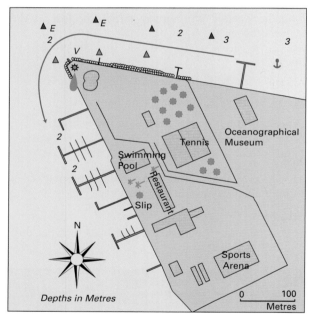

RIO GRANDE YACHT CLUB

Excellent leisure facilities

Location and surroundings

Very well-located in attractive surroundings, with shady gardens and beautiful parks; everything is impeccably kept.

Rio Grande Yacht Club, Rua Capitan Heitor Perdigão, Rio Grande do Sul, CEP 96200-580
☎ (53) 3232 7196
Email rgyc@rgyc.com.br
VHF Channel 16

Useful telephone numbers

Area code ☎ (53).

Polícia Federal (Immigration), Av Presidente Vargas, 888 ☎ 32 1433.

Comando 5° Distrito Naval (5th Naval District Command), same address ☎ 32 1433.

Receita Federal (Customs), Rua Marechal Floriano, 300 ☎ 32 3616.

Ministério da Saúde (Health Department), Rua Marechal Floriano, 300 ☎ 32 3916.

Capitania dos Portos (Port Captain's Office), Av. Almirante Cerqueira e Souza, 198 ☎ 3233 6168.

Note

If you are entering or leaving Brazil, you must complete the regulatory formalities:

Polícia Federal (Immigration)

Alfândega dos Portos (Customs)

Ministério da Saúde (Health Department)

Capitania dos Portos (Port Captain's Office) (*see sections entitled Introduction – Entering Brazil by boat – Entry formalities/Departure formalities*)

II. Northwards from Salvador de Bahia to Belém

Fernando de Noronha

STATE OF ALAGOAS

In the 17th century, the region of Maceió was mainly agricultural, with large sugar cane plantations. The creation of the first sugar cane processing plant led to the rapid expansion of the town. The Jesuits built a church, and then a lighthouse was erected, which allowed for the creation of a port, which soon prospered with the sugar trade.

Today, the town has a population of 750,000 and is the capital of the State of Alagoas. It is a modern town, mainly given over to tourism; large modern buildings line the seafront, leaving little room for the historic quarter, where there are still some beautiful colonial buildings.

There are several fishing villages on the neighbouring coastline, where fishing is still carried out as in the past from *jangadas*, small traditional sailing craft.

Maceió. *Jangadas,* the traditional fishing vessels of the northeast

Maceió

Navigation

Brazilian Chart DHN No. 901.

Maceió is located around 265 miles north of Salvador and 120 miles south of Recife.

There are few ports of call on this stretch of coast, with the port and town of Aracaju which, apart from the beaches, offers nothing of particular tourist interest, and the Rio São Francisco do Norte. Caution should be exercised at the latter, where entry can be problematic with a difficult bar, strewn with shifting sandbanks; there have been several accidents on this bar, which requires good local knowledge.

Approach

Maceió is a medium-sized commercial port that does not present any particular problems on entry day or night, sheltering a mooring area occupied by a large number of fishing boats behind its inner breakwater. It can be a good rest stop when heading north, to break up the leg between Salvador and Recife, which can be hard work against the wind and current.

Conspicuous landmarks

From the south, the buildings of the town stand out clearly against this low, uniform coast.

The radio and television antennae and the Maceió lighthouse, a tapered tower with black and white diamonds, Lp.Alt.BE.20s68m43/36M, can be seen at the top of the town.

The quay at the Salgema mineral terminal protrudes at the left-hand end of the beach and has a light Lp.RE.5M. From the north, the Ponta Verde lighthouse, Lp.B.10s13m13M, stands in front of a reef ledge to the north of the commercial port.

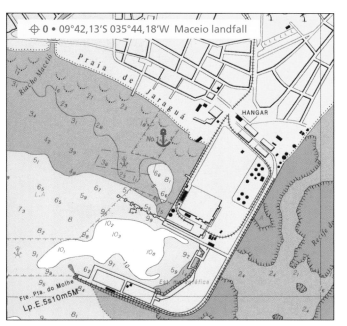

PORT DE MACEIÓ

Ponta Verde lighthouse

Tide and current

Mean tide level is 1.1m above the chart datum, with a maximum amplitude of 2.3m in spring tides.

The current, which is above all generated by the winds, is relatively weak near the coast.

Winds

The prevailing winds are northeasterly during the dry season, which runs from August to April, and easterly to southeasterly the rest of the year.

Landfall

Make landfall on red buoy Lp.E.3s.

⊕ 0 • 09°42,13'S 035°44,18'W Maceio landfall

Then head towards the commercial port, the facilities of which can be seen half a mile to the north, behind the riprap breakwater (Ponta do Molhe, LpE.5s10m5M).

A second quay is used by commercial ships and just behind it, a large number of anchored fishing boats can be seen.

Anchor between the quay and the beach, on the edge of the area occupied by the fishing boats. The facilities of the Federação Alagoana de Vela e Motor can be seen near this mooring area, on the right-hand part of the beach.

Federação Alagoana de Vela e Motor

This yacht club is located at the northern end of Praia de Jaraguá, and you can easily go ashore in the tender near the slipway and the sea access gate.

Quality of moorings ***

Holding is good in 2.5–3m of water on sand.

The mooring area is completely sheltered from the prevailing northeasterly winds.

In winds from the southern sector, the anchorage is very uncomfortable, with swell and a significant undertow in the mooring area.

Facilities – Services ✱✱✱

The club is welcoming and well-located in the seafront district; there is a bus stop nearby for buses to the town centre.

For services, ask for 'Bira', who can solve all of the little problems encountered by yachtsmen – maintenance, miscellaneous repairs, water, fuel, ice, etc.

Supplies ✱✱✱

These are readily available and there are several supermarkets in town.

Location and surroundings ✱✱

The town does not have a bad reputation in relation to safety or theft, but it is however necessary to take the usual precautions and not leave anything unnecessary on deck when you are absent.

There are some beautiful beaches with clear waters around Maceió, such as Praia do Francés, Praia de Maragori, Praia de Cururipe and Barra de São Miguel to the south. At low tide, the barrier of rocks that runs along the coast forms wonderful natural pools and makes for some interesting scuba dives.

Some of the beaches can also be reached by boat, but it is advisable to seek guidance from a trustworthy local boatman, as these itineraries are littered with rocks on the surface of the water that become invisible as soon as there is a slight chop.

Federação Alagoana de Vela e Motor, Av. Cicero Toledo, 330, Jaraguá, Maceió, AL
☎ (82) 3223 4344
Email favm-al@afm.com.br

Alagoas Iate Clube

This Iate Clube now only exists in name and in the form of its former facilities between Praia de Jaraguá and Praia de Pajussara.

It was founded in 1952 but is soon to be closed by court order.

Useful telephone numbers

Area code ☎ (82).
Polícia Federal (Immigration) ☎ 216 6700, 214 4094.
Receita Federal, Rua Sá e Albuquerque ☎ 216 9100.
Capitania dos Portos do Estado do Alagoas (State of Alagoas Port Captain's Office), Rua Uruguay, 44, Maceió
☎ 3336 4004.
Pronto Socorro (Emergency Medicine) ☎ 3221 5939.
Hospital Santa Casa de Misericordia ☎ 217 6000, 3326 6816.

Tourism

The beaches of Ponta Verde and Sete Coqueiros with their beautiful natural pools on the reefs at low tide.

The Maceió Festa festival, which takes place over several days at the beginning of December; think floats with music, samba, etc.

Setur, Tourist Information, Av. Antônio Gouveia ☎ 315 1601.

Maceió. The mooring area

II

STATE OF PERNAMBUCO

Recife-Olinda

In the 17th century, the sugar trade was flourishing and the rich sugar cane plantations that stretch as far as the eye can see in this area contributed significantly to the rapid expansion of the towns of Olinda and Recife.

However, it was at Recife that a commercial port was established, enabling the town to become the economic and commercial centre of the region.

With a population of 1,500,000, *Recife*, the capital of the State of Pernambuco, is today one of the largest cities in the northeast of Brazil.

This historic quarter of Olinda boasts some beautiful colonial buildings, immortalising its prestigious past.

For the yachtsman, Recife is an unmissable stop, and one of the best locations on the northeast coast.

The annual Recife – Fernando de Noronha race brings together over 100 sailing vessels of all types and nationalities, and racing crews and cruisers alike take part in a competition which, despite its formal aspects, remains very relaxed.

Navigation

Brazilian Charts DHN No. 906, 902 and 930.

From Maceió to Recife the coast is low and made up of long beaches, with a mountain chain in the background

and a few peaks that are clearly visible from offshore. A long line of coral reefs, which is uncovered at low tide, forms an almost uninterrupted barrier along most of this coastline.

There are three lighthouses: Porto das Pedras, Lp(2)B.15s90m24M, a black and white striped tower, Tamandaré, a white cylindrical tower Lp(3)B.10s27m18M, and Santo Agostinho, LpB.10s91m22M.

Porto de Suape

22 miles from Recife, to the south of the lighthouse on Cabo Santo Agostinho (LpB.10s91m22M), Porto de Suape provides good shelter and is completely protected in bad weather.

⊕ 0 • 08°23,60'S 034°55,80'W Suape landfall

The port is formed by a long riprap breakwater and the port area is entirely open to the northeast. Inside the port, at the end of the barrier of reefs, there is an entrance to starboard that leads to a completely calm area of water. Anchor between Ilha dos Franceses and the reef, where holding is good in 3.5m of water on sand against an attractive backdrop of beaches fringed with coconut palms. This area is uncharted, but it is possible

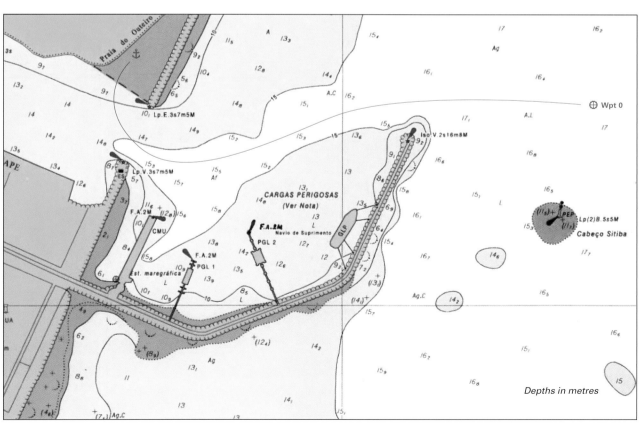

PORTO DE SUAPE

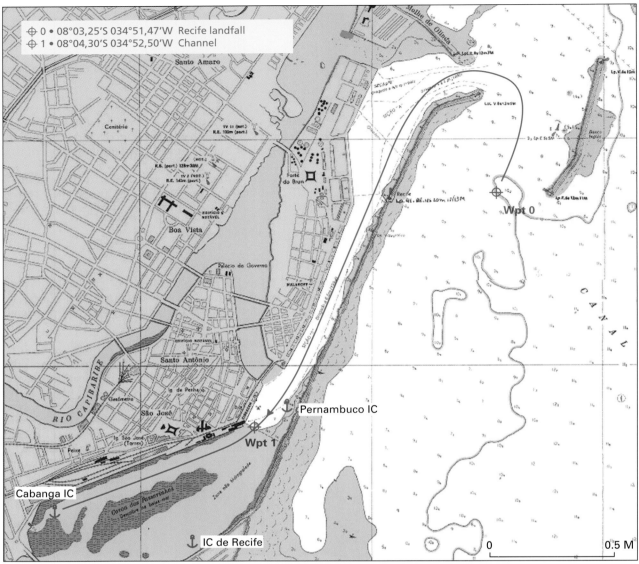

⊕ 0 • 08°03,25'S 034°51,47'W Recife landfall
⊕ 1 • 08°04,30'S 034°52,50'W Channel

Wpt 0

Pernambuco IC

Wpt 1

Cabanga IC

IC de Recife

0   0.5 M

PORTO DE RECIFE

to reach Vila de Suape by going along the reef towards the Rio Massangana and around Ilha de Tatuoca. However, watch out for a large sandbank to the north of Ilha dos Franceses, and another off Praia de Suape, which extends a long way beyond the Pontal.

Porto de Recife

Approach

The coastline leading up to Recife is low and uniform, without any geographical features of note, and is made up of a series of long, beautiful beaches.

Conspicuous landmarks

By day From the south, the tall buildings of Recife are visible from a long way offshore.

On approaching the port, a curious collection of art installations (cylindrical columns, statues, etc.) can be seen, and on the long riprap breakwater, the white and red striped tower of Recife lighthouse.

Strange columns in front of the lighthouse

Recife lighthouse, built on a long breakwater

From the north, Olinda lighthouse, a 42m tapered black and white striped tower, is located to the north of the town, at an altitude of 90m on Morro de Serapião.

By night Recife lighthouse, Lp.Alt.BE.12s20m17M. Olinda lighthouse, Lp(2)B.35s90m46M.

The entrance to the port of Recife is protected by a long riprap breakwater with a light at either end: LpE.6s12m11M to the south and LpV.6s12m11M to the north.

Tide and current

Mean tide height is 1.14m above the chart datum, with a maximum amplitude of 2.6m in spring tides.

The tidal current is normally three knots, but in spring tides it can reach four knots on the flood and five knots on the ebb, and is at its strongest at the entrance to the port.

Landfall

Make landfall at ⊕0,

⊕ 0 • 08°03,25'S 034°51,47'W Recife landfall

Brazilian Navy training ship the *Cisné Branco* leaving the port of Recife, and the port entrance tower at the end of the breakwater

which is short distance south of the breakwater. The port is reached by going between Molhe de Olinda to the north, LpL.E.8s12m7M, and the end of the long Recife breakwater, LpL.V.8s12m5M, to the south.

Go along the quays of the port to starboard, where the commercial ships are moored, to ⊕1:

⊕ 1 • 08°04,30'S 034°52,50'W Harbour channel

There are three options available to visitors:

* Pernambuco Iate Clube, to port,
* Iate Clube de Recife, half a mile further on to port, heading towards the bridge,
* Cabanga Iate Clube, to starboard, after the commercial port.

PERNAMBUCO IATE CLUBE

The Iate Clube can be seen approximately one mile ahead to port on entering the port channel.

It has a floating pontoon and a few mooring buoys.

The 3–4m water depth in the mooring area means that you can wait for high tide if you want to go to Cabanga Iate Clube.

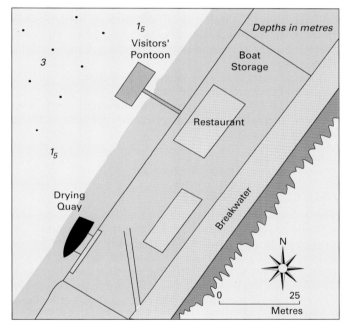

PERNANBUCO IATE CLUBE

Pernambuco Iate Clube

Pernambuco Iate Clube. The grounding jetty

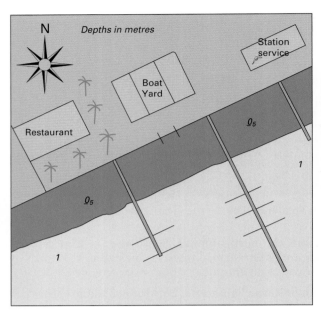

IATE CLUBE DE RECIFE

This club is modest but welcoming, with decent facilities (toilets and showers, bar, restaurant, etc.) and there is a ferry between boats on mooring buoys and the club.

One advantage worthy of mention is that it is possible to ground boats against the jetty.

The club offers three days on a mooring buoy free of charge; thereafter a fixed price of R$5 to R$6 is requested per day.

VHF Channel 16
☎ (081) 3465 0847
Email pernambucoiateclube@bol.com.br

IATE CLUBE DE RECIFE

This is located to port, after Pernambuco Iate Clube, and is home to motor boats only. The depth at the end of the pontoons is just 1m at low tide, and around fifteen mooring buoys have been installed for mooring off the club. There is a slipway for lifting out boats up to around 15 tonnes in the boatyard, which has three vast sheds for dry storage of motor boats. Service station with diesel and petrol.

The daily rate is R$6 per metre.

VHF Channel 68
☎ (081) 3326 3327

Iate Clube de Recife

CABANGA IATE CLUBE

This is the largest Iate Clube in Recife, and its marina holds around one hundred boats, both sailing and motor vessels. It is a welcoming club that willingly accepts visiting boats if there is space available.

It is approximately one mile from ⊕1.

Go along the quays to starboard until you see the entrance to the marina at the end of a channel marked with wooden poles painted red with green tips.

> **Note**
> This last section passes between two sandbanks where the depth decreases rapidly; boats with a draught of more than 1.6m will have to wait for high tide to enter the Iate Clube mooring basin.

Cabanga Iate Clube, Av. Jose Estelita, Recife
☎ (81) 3428 4277
Email secretaria@cabanga.com.br or cicero@cabanga.com.br
VHF Ch 9
www.cabanga.com.br

Quality of moorings ***

The club has around one hundred berths, with just a few pontoons or rather catwalks.

Moor bows to the jetty with a stern mooring buoy; access to the jetty located near the entrance is inconvenient. The mooring area is completely calm with a depth of around 2.5m at low tide.

Facilities – Services ***

The club's facilities are of an excellent standard, with toilets and showers, bar, restaurants, two swimming pools, etc., together with all of the comfort offered by the Brazilian clubs.

With regard to services, all types of repair work can be carried out on site by contractors; contact the office for information.

There is a slipway for lifting out boats up to 35'.

Water On the pontoon, one tap shared between several boats.

Electricity 220 volt power outlets.

Supplies ***

Supplies are readily available in town, where there are several Bompreço supermarkets and hypermarkets, the Shopping Recife shopping centre to the north of town or, closer by, Shopping Tacaruna between Recife and Olinda.

Mooring fees ***

As a guide, the price is between US$7 per day, with two days free of charge.

Location and surroundings **

The town centre is a little far away, but there is a bus stop nearby.

You can also go to nearby Olinda.

24-hour security service.

Note These three Iate Clubes are located near the port area, and despite the fact that Recife doesn't really have a bad reputation in terms of safety, it is preferable to take a taxi for trips or if you are coming back to the club late at night.

Useful telephone numbers

Area code ☎ (81).

Polícia Federal (Immigration), Armazém 10, Cais do Porto ☎ 3424 1539.

Vigilância Sanitária (Health Surveillance), Av. Alfredo Lisboa ☎ 3424 0217.

Receita Federal (Customs), Av. Alfredo Lisboa ☎ 3424 2536.

Capitania dos Portos de Pernambuco (Pernambuco Port Captain's Office), Rua São Jorge, 25, Bairro Antigo do Recife ☎ 3424 7111.

Hospital Portugais, Avenida Agamenon Magalhães ☎ 3416 1122.

British Honorary Consulate in Recife ☎ +55 (11) 3094 2700 *Email* hc.recife@fco.gov.uk

Tourist Department – Town Hall ☎ 3425 8000.

Tourism

When approaching Recife, sailors are met by the sight of a collection of strange statues surrounding a tall column

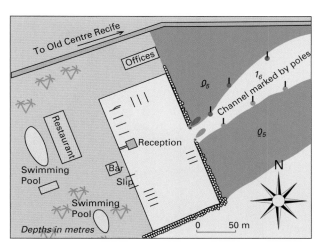

CABANGUA IATE CLUBE

The mooring basin at Cabanga Iate Clube

on the breakwater. This work by local artist Francico Brennar is Recife's way of demonstrating its interest in the arts.

In the historic centre, the beautiful old buildings include Capella Dourada, one of the finest Baroque churches in Brazil.

Recife is also a shopper's paradise, with a wide variety of local crafts on sale in its winding streets.

Cabanga Iate Clube. The entrance to the marina at low tide

Cabanga Iate Clube. The entrance to the marina at high tide

Fernando de Noronha. Morro do Pico, the highest point on the island, a conspicuous landmark from a long way off, looking southeast

Recife –
Fernando de Noronha Regatta

In September, Recife puts on the biggest sailing festival in the northeast, and possibly Brazil, with over 100 boats in attendance. Argentine and Brazilian crews happily travel hundreds of miles to be on the start line.

Olinda

In 2006, the Cidade dos Artes (city of the arts) as it is known received the honorary title of Brazilian Capital of Culture, awarded by Culture Minister Gilberto Gil, himself a singer.

Its historic centre is home to a wide variety of art installations, and the old stone buildings of Rua Amparo house numerous art studios, galleries, museums, etc.

In the old quarters, there are many old buildings and traditional bars and restaurants.

Have a drink at Bodega do Véio, a curious, bustling shop that sells everything from chewing gum to works by local artists. If you can manage to fight your way to the miniscule counter, crammed with bottles, jars of sweetmeats and other miscellany, they serve excellent *caipirinha* and ice-cold beer.

Olinda carnival in February has a reputation as one of the most authentic street carnivals in Brazil.

Fernando de Noronha

There is a great deal of controversy over the discovery of the Fernando de Noronha archipelago.

It was apparently discovered for the first time in 1492 by Spanish explorer Juan de la Costa, who mentioned the islands in his log.

Several Portuguese expeditions then followed and in 1502, the charts showed an archipelago the main island of which was called Ilha da Quaresma. Some historians attribute its discovery to Gaspar de Lemos, one of the commanders of Francisco Cabral's fleet, but the first to describe the island with any accuracy was Amerigo Vespucci, who formed part of Gonçalvo Coelho's 1503 expedition.

Later, the islands were held in turn by the English in 1534, the French in 1556 and the Dutch in 1628, finally returning in 1737 to the Portuguese, who occupied the main island and built three fortresses, Nossa Senhora dos Remédios, Nossa Senhora da Conceição and Santo Antônio.

In 1938, the island was used to isolate political prisoners and then, in 1942, it became a military base during the Second World War.

This volcanically-formed archipelago is made up of around twenty islands, islets and isolated rocks, and at 17km^2, the island of Fernando de Noronha is the largest.

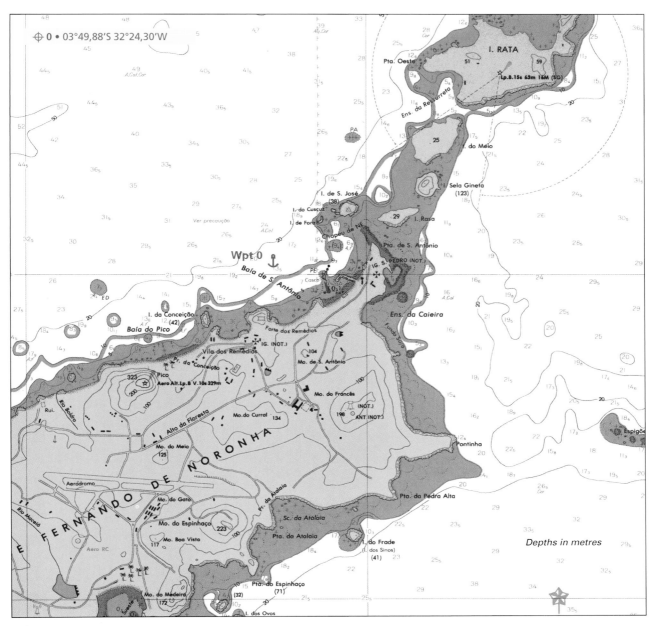

FERNANDO DE NORONHA

It is an important ecological centre and the Marine National Park is very strictly monitored by IBAMA (the Brazilian Institute of Environment and Renewable Natural Resources).

Its numerous inlets are home to a wide variety of fish, sea turtles and a large number of dolphins, which can be watched daily. There are also several species of birds that have taken up residence in this chaotic landscape and nest in the trees by the sea.

The tiny population of around 1,600 is concentrated on the main island, in the village of Vila dos Remédios, which is a district of the State of Pernambuco.

Visiting formalities

For boats flying foreign flags, Fernando de Noronha is not an official port of entry into Brazil (*see section entitled Entering Brazil by Boat – Entry formalities*).

Fernando de Noronha. Praia do Meio

However, contrary to certain rumours on the pontoons, it is not necessary to clear through an official Brazilian port of entry before visiting the island. A degree of tolerance is shown for short stays, and the skipper of a visiting boat can use the excuse of technical problems or tiredness on the part of the crew after a difficult passage to obtain permission to stay for a limited period. Report to the port authority, which represents the government of the State of Pernambuco, and has its offices in the first building on the right as you go ashore, near the breakwater.

Time spent on Fernando de Noronha is not normally included in the length of stay granted in Brazil, and the *Capitania dos Portos de Pernambuco* (Pernambuco Port Captain's Office) in Recife is simply informed of the presence of the boat and crew.

Porto de Santo Antônio Authority
☎/*Fax* (081) 3619 1744
VHF Channel 16
Email teles@noronha.pe.gov.br

Navigation

Brazilian Chart DHN No. 52.

Fernando de Noronha is located approximately 300 miles northeast of Recife and the local time in the archipelago is two hours behind GMT.

Conspicuous landmarks

By day The distinctive steep-sided form of the highest peak on the island, Morro do Pico, which rises to 323m, can be seen from a long way off.

On the southwestern tip of the island, at the summit of Morro Alto da Bandeira, the white tower of the Fernando de Noronha lighthouse.

By night From the northeast, the lighthouse on Ilha Rata, LpB.15s63m16M (SG).

The aviation radio beacon on Morro do Pico has a clearly visible white and green alternating light, Lp.Alt.B.V.10s329m.

From the southwest, the first light is the Fernando de Noronha lighthouse at the summit of Morro do Alto da Bandeira, Lp.Alt.BBE.30s203m28/24M.

The breakwater with the mooring area in the background

Charge

A fixed charge of R$180 per day is requested for mooring a boat over 10m in length; the first day is free of charge.
Do not try to evade this formality, as your arrival will be noted by an official monitoring the mooring area.

Taxa de Preservação Ambiental (TPA, Environmental Preservation Tax)

Boats arriving at the island must make contact on VHF Channel 16, and pay the Environmental Preservation Tax to the Distrito Estadual de Fernando de Noronha (Fernando de Noronha State District) for each person on board.
The tax is R$32 per day for any person landing on the island, and reduces slightly the longer the stay.

Climate

There are two clearly defined seasons, with a rainy season from February to July (with maximum rainfall in March/April) and a dry season for the rest of the year.

The prevailing winds are southeasterly to easterly, with an average speed of Force 4.

A 1–1.5 knot current flows west.

The average air temperature is around 27°C and the average water temperature is 24°C.

Approach

The only place on the island where anchoring is permitted is Baía de Santo Antônio, on the northeast of the island. At the end of the bay, a small L-shaped jetty on the riprap breakwater is reserved for boats bringing supplies to the island and for tourists boarding trip boats or dive boats.

Make landfall at:
⊕ **0** • 03°49,88'S 32°24,30'W

And anchor nearby.

Quality of moorings **

Holding is good on sand. The water in the bay is completely clear, but the anchorage is rough and sometimes very rough as the islets to the northeast of the tip of the island provide little protection. In addition, depending on the season and weather conditions, the offshore swell comes in strongly and getting in and out of the tender is an operation that requires skill and good judgment of the waves in this particularly exposed anchorage.

Facilities – Services – Supplies *

There are few boat maintenance services on site. For practical reasons, it is best to arrive in Fernando de Noronha with your own supplies; there is however a supermarket and a few shops selling everyday goods.

Tourism

The island has a large number of magnificent beaches with clear waters, including Praia da Conceição, one of the most beautiful.

You can rent a buggy or motorbike to tour the island on tracks that lead to the shore; leave the vehicle at the end of the track and continue on foot into the forest on paths that run along the coast and provide spectacular views of the marine park.

Festivals

10 August, festival to celebrate the founding of Fernando de Noronha.
29 August, festival of *Nossa Senhora dos Remédios* (Our Lady of the Remedies), patron saint of the island.

The Marine National Park

This is of course the main interest of the island. The National Park is marked with a dotted line on the charts. It comprises a protected area around the island, leaving an area clear to the northeast of the island between Baía de Santo Antônio and the Ilhas Dois Irmãos. The park is controlled by IBAMA, the aim of which is to protect the terrestrial and marine ecosystem; this involves conservation of the fauna, flora, natural resources and historic sites.

Note

The following activities are banned in the Marine National Park:

- Anchoring in the protected area and landing around the island.
- Underwater hunting and fishing, as well as carrying any equipment relating to these activities.
  Swimming, diving or stopping the boat near Baía dos Golfinhos.
- Visiting Praia Leão and Praia do Sancho at night between 1800 and 0600 from January to June during the sea turtles' egg laying and hatching period.
- Collecting shells, pebbles, plants, fruit, etc.
- Visiting areas off-limits to the public without permission.

As a general rule, visitors must respect the environment and avoid causing any damage, and must not drop litter or make fires.

For scuba diving, contact one of the specialist diving clubs that organise daily dives on the best sites around the island.

Fernando de Noronha. Praia da Conceição

STATE OF PARAÍBA

João Pessoa – Cabedelo

The State of Paraíba is one of the smallest in Brazil, and its capital, João Pessoa, has a population of 600,000.

The main interest of this region centres on its coastline.

It is the most easterly point on the Brazilian coast, and heading north, the town is located a short distance beyond Cabo Branco.

Today, seashore activities are tourism-related, making the most of the long white sandy beaches that stretch the length of this beautiful coast.

There are large sugar cane plantations in the coastal belt south of João Pessoa, whilst inland the landscape is arid and sparsely populated. Approximately fifteen miles to the north, the Rio Paraíba houses the commercial port of Cabedelo, and there is a mooring area for yachts upriver.

Navigation

Brazilian Chart DHN No. 830.
Cabedelo – Rio Paraíba Chart.

The port of Cabedelo is located approximately 80 miles from Recife, on the Rio Paraíba estuary. For yachts heading north, often against the NE Trade Winds, Jacaré provides a break on the route.

Tide and current

Mean tide level is 1.3m above the chart datum, with a maximum amplitude of approximately 2.6m in spring tides.

The tidal currents are strong in the Rio Paraíba, generally 2.5–3 knots, and they can reach 5–6 knots in spring tides.

It is therefore best to enter the river on a rising tide.

Winds

The winds generally blow from the south/southeastern from March to September and from the northeastern/east from October to February.

Approach

Conspicuous landmarks

From the south, once past Cabo Branco and its lighthouse LpB.10s13m13M, the tall buildings of João Pessoa can be seen.

10 miles to the north, the Pedra Seca lighthouse, a white tapered tower, Lp(3)B.10s16m16M, stands out slightly east of the entrance to Cabedelo, at the tip of a long line of reefs running parallel to the coast.

Cabedelo is used by large ships and is approached along a marked channel, with landfall at:

⊕ **0** • 06°56,32'S 034°49,00'W Cabedelo landfall

This waypoint is located near port buoy No. 4, two miles offshore from the mouth of the river.

Leave to starboard a line of shoals, Banco de Tabuleira and Pedra Nova, on which the sea breaks.

Follow the channel towards the end of the riprap breakwater, LpV.6s8m7M.

Once you have crossed the bar, continue with the commercial port facilities to port, to:

⊕ **1** • 06°58,95'S 034°50,18'W

From this point, head to the opposite side of the channel towards Ilha da Restinga to avoid the Coroa Taquarua shoal to port, which extends a long way into the inside of the bend in the river. The shoal is uncovered at low tide but is an invisible obstacle when the water rises, and it is a good idea to stay well off, keeping an eye on the depth sounder and any drift due to the current.

Then sail in the middle of the river along Ilha da Restinga, staying in depths of 5–6m, to

⊕ **2** • 07°00,92'S 034°50,22'W Near S point of Ilha Restingha

Rio Paraíba fishing boats. In the background, the Pedra Seca lighthouse from the west

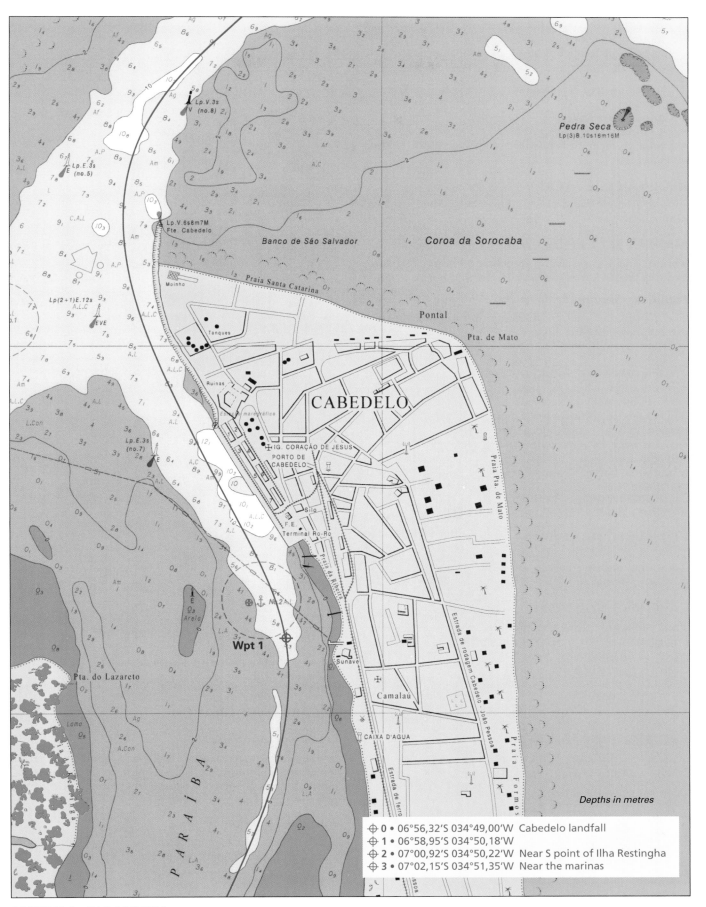

Depths in metres

⊕ 0 • 06°56,32'S 034°49,00'W	Cabedelo landfall
⊕ 1 • 06°58,95'S 034°50,18'W	
⊕ 2 • 07°00,92'S 034°50,22'W	Near S point of Ilha Restingha
⊕ 3 • 07°02,15'S 034°51,35'W	Near the marinas

CABEDELO - RIO PARAIBA

Approximately two miles after the southern tip of the island, the village of Jacaré lies to port.

It is possible to anchor at ⊕3, near the marinas.

⊕ 3 • 07°02,15'S 034°51,35'W Near the marinas

This mooring area gives access to three sets of facilities:
• Marina Club Jacaré
• Marina Jacaré Village
• Iate Clube da Paraíba
• A little upstream it is possible to anchor opposite Praia de Jacaré.

MARINA CLUB JACARÉ

This is a small yacht club, mainly frequented by local motor boats.

MARINA JACARÉ VILLAGE

This marina was set up by Frenchman Philippe Feissard, and it is the preferred location for visiting boats.

Facilities – Services ***

The floating facilities are made up of two pontoons that can hold around forty boats.

Water and 220 volt electricity.

Fuel.

Comprehensive washing facilities with toilets, showers and washing machine.

Wi-Fi internet connection.

There is a slipway for lifting out boats up to 12 tonnes. It is also possible to ground boats against the jetty for work between two tides.

There are also leisure facilities, with swimming pools, restaurants, barbecue and *pétanque*.

☏ (83) 3248 3638
Contact@marina-Jacare-village.com
www.jacare-yacht-village.com

IATE CLUBE DA PARAIBA

There is a pontoon and an area of mooring buoys. Additional imorovementsb are planned according to teh president, Bernardo.

CABEDELO NÁUTICA

This boatyard near the Iate Clube is run by an Englishman, Brian I. Stevens, and can be used for all types of maintenance and repair work, engineering, electrics, polyester work, painting, etc.

Jacaré

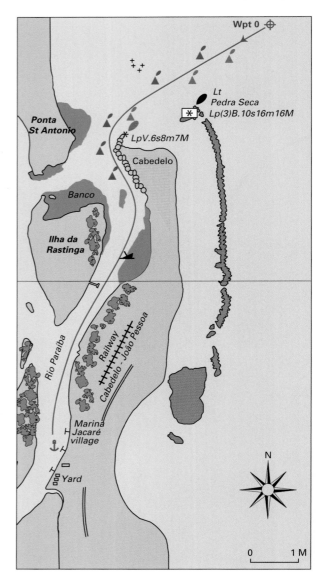

CABEDELO

There are a few mooring buoys in front of the boatyard, and a slipway for lifting out boats up to approximately 10 tonnes.

Cabedelo Náutica, Praia de Jacaré, 99 – Cabedelo
☏ (83) 3248 1478
Email brian@cabedelonautic.com.br

JACARÉ ANCHORAGE

Quality of moorings ***

In the whole marina area, holding is good in 3.5m of water on sand and mud, but it is also possible to use the club's mooring buoys. The mooring area is calm but there is quite a strong current.

Facilities – Services **

Some repairs can be carried out on site, or contact the Cabedelo Náutica boatyard, about 100m upstream.

Supplies **

There is a small supermarket 15 minutes' walk away.

Jacaré. A calm anchorage but the current in Rio Paraíba may run fast

In João Pessoa, which is around 10km away, there is a large Carrefour supermarket on the João Pessoa – Cabedelo road.

Buses stop at the service station around 2km from the Iate Clube.

Cabedelo. A lively holiday resort

Location and surroundings ★★★

The surroundings are pleasant; next to the Iate Clube, Praia de Jacaré is very lively, with several riverside bars and restaurants.

Useful telephone numbers

Area code ☎ (083).

Capitania dos Portos da Paraíba (Paraíba Port Captain's Office), Rua Barão do Triunfo, 372, Cabedelo ☎ 221 1293

Hospital Pronto Socorro (Emergency Medicine), Av. Júlia Freire, 1038, João Pessoa ☎ 224 1520

Tourism

João Pessoa and Cabedelo are modern towns of no particular interest, apart from the beautiful church of São Francisco (1589) in the centre of João Pessoa.

There are however some lovely beaches from north to south that form numerous natural pools at low tide.

Ponta de Seixas offers an excellent scuba diving site in very clear water.

STATE OF RIO GRANDE DO NORTE

Natal

Very shortly after the discovery of Brazil, the region of Natal was occupied in turn by the French in 1535, the Portuguese in 1598 and the Dutch in 1633, and then taken back for good by the Portuguese.

The Fortaleza Dos Reis Magos, an imposing 5-point star shaped building, was built at the mouth of the Rio Potengi, and remains a symbol of the bloody battles that took place here for possession of these lands.

Like neighbouring Paraíba, the State of Rio Grande do Norte is one of the smallest in Brazil. It too offers beautiful sandy beaches with natural pools inside a barrier of reefs. The orientation of the coast changes here to southeast-northwest, and the strong onshore breeze contributes to the formation of a line of dunes running the length of these vast beaches.

Natal, the State capital, is a modern town with a population of 700,000 stretching to the south of the Rio Potengi; today, it is a large seaside resort that is constantly expanding, with roads and luxury hotels being built along the seafront.

Yachts heading for the north of Brazil can be found here, as well as a few boats arriving from Europe or Africa.

Navigation

Brazilian Chart DHN No. 802.

Approach

Conspicuous landmarks

By day From the south:

- Natal lighthouse, a white tapered tower that is located above the town, approximately 2.5 miles south of the mouth of the Rio Potengi.
- The imposing viaduct that straddles the river near its mouth.

- Fortaleza Dos Reis Magos, built on the reef and extended by the southern breakwater, which has a green tower at the end.
- The northern breakwater with its red tower.

By night
Natal lighthouse, Lp(5)B.25s87m39M and a fixed red light at a height of 150m (TV antenna).
The lights of the channel half a mile offshore.
The lights Lp.V.5s13m17M on the southern breakwater and Lp.E.6s8m7M on the northern breakwater.

Tide and currents

Mean tide level is 1.1m above the chart datum.

The flood and ebb currents are on average in the region of 1.5 knots, but they can reach 3–4 knots on the ebb in spring tides or after a period of heavy rainfall.

Hazards

From the north, watch out for the reefs of Baixa Grande and Cabeça Negra, to the north of the mouth of the river.
Make landfall at

⊕ 0 • 05°44,84'S 035°11,54'W Natal landfall

You then enter the marked channel and once past the viaduct, after buoy No. 6, the facilities of Iate Clube do Natal can be seen one mile away to port (the name is written on the roof of the Iate Clube).

Anchor nearby.

IATE CLUBE DO NATAL

This very old club (est. 1955) willingly accepts visiting boats and makes its facilities available to their crews.

Quality of moorings ***

The club has a few mooring buoys and a floating pontoon on which the limited number of berths is reserved for members.

It is possible to anchor nearby in 3–4 metres of water with good holding on sand. The mooring area is often disturbed by the comings and goings of boats from the commercial port. There is a significant current.

A *jangada* returning from a fishing trip

Entrance to Natal. The green tower at the end of the southern breakwater

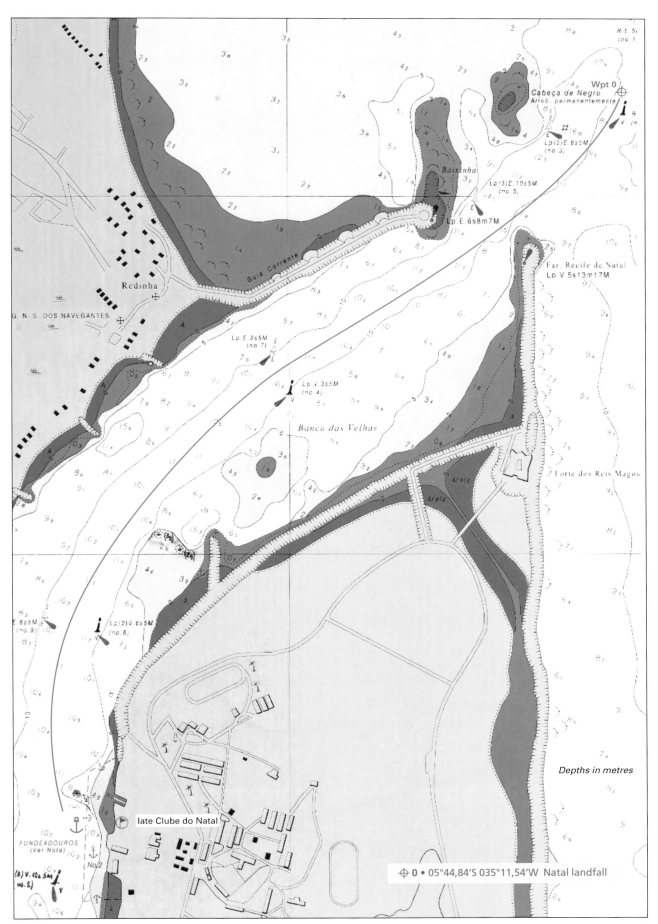

Depths in metres

⊕ 0 • 05°44,84'S 035°11,54'W Natal landfall

NATAL - RIO POTENGI

Iate Clube do Natal, at the mouth of the Rio Potengi

Facilities – Services ***

The club has good facilities (bar, restaurant, toilets and showers, swimming pool, etc.) and all of the comforts of the Brazilian clubs.

There is a boatyard to the rear for all sorts of boat maintenance including engineering, electrics, refrigeration, polyester repairs, etc.

There is a slipway for lifting out smaller boats up to 35' or around 10 tonnes.

Water and service station on the reception pontoon.

Supplies ***

Supplies are readily available in town at several supermarkets:
Natal Shopping Centre, Praia Shopping,
Hiperbompreço, Carrefour, etc.

Mooring fees ****

As a guide, the price for access to the club is R$8 per day, with three days free of charge for visiting boats.

Location and surroundings **

The club is a little far from the town centre and shopping malls, but there is a bus stop nearby.

24-hour security.
Iate Clube do Natal, Rua Coronel Flaminio s/n, Santo Reis, Natal
☏ 3202 4402
Email iateclubedonatal@matrix.com.br
www.iateclubedonatal.com.br

Useful telephone numbers

Area code ☏ (84).
Polícia Federal (Immigration), Av. Mario Câmara 300, Nazaré, Natal ☏ 320 2255.
Capitania dos Portos do Natal (Natal Port Captain's Office), Rua Chile, 230, Ribeira, Natal ☏ 3201 9630.
Alfândega dos Portos (Customs), Rua Silva Jardim 83, Ribeira, Natal ☏ 3220 2238.
Hospital Mr Walfredo Gurgel, Av. Senador Salgado Filho ☏ 3221 4241.
Department of Tourism, Rua Mossoro, 352 ☏ 232 2486.

Tourism

- Fortaleza dos Reis Magos and several interesting museums.
- On either side of the town, long white sandy beaches backed by magnificent sand dunes that overlook the sea and provide excellent dune buggy rides (buggies can be rented with or without a driver from Genipabu), with some particularly impressive stretches.
- There is a barrier of reefs along the coast, providing excellent scuba diving sites in very clear water (off Praia de Genipabu, two miles out to sea).
- At the beginning of December, Carnatal, four days of madness all over town.

Natal is nicknamed Cidade do Sol (Sun City), and rightly so, as the weather is hot and dry all year round.

Entrance to Natal. The northern breakwater

STATE OF CEARÁ

Fortaleza

The northeastern State of Ceará has an extensive coastline, and its capital, Fortaleza, has a population of over two million.

It is a busy commercial port and fishing is also big business in this region. The seaside resorts mainly make their money out of tourism, and the hotel network is such that Fortaleza is the largest resort in the area.

The arid environment of the hinterland, or *sertão*, only allows for limited agriculture and animal husbandry. This lack of resources results in young people leaving for the coast, which unfortunately leads to high levels of delinquency in the seaside resorts.

The normal safety precautions should therefore be taken all along this stretch of coast.

For yachts heading for the north of Brazil with good sailing conditions and beam winds, Fortaleza is an interesting port of call and a good rest stop before the long leg to the mouth of the Amazon.

Jangada on the beach. The fishing harbour and commercial port are in the background

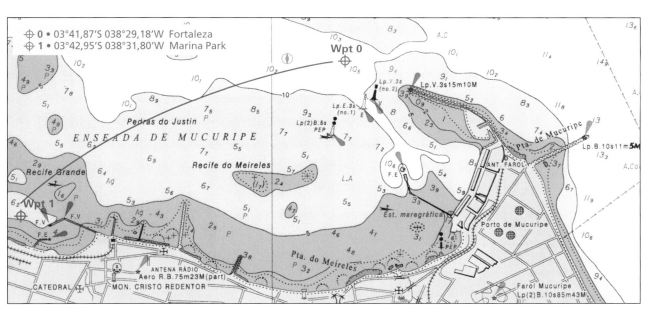

FORTALEZA

By day and especially by night, a close watch should be kept for fishing boats, which are particularly numerous in these waters. Similarly, *jangadas*, the small traditional sailing craft used for fishing, are hard to see against a white-capped sea and always pose a risk of collision, particularly at night.

Navigation

Brazilian Charts DHN No. 700, 710 and 800.

Navigation along a line of depths of 50m avoids the hazards of the coast and allows for trouble-free coverage of the 250 miles between Natal and Fortaleza.

Offshore hazards

Between Cabo de São Roque and Cabo Calcanhar, the coast is littered with shoals and it is preferable to sail offshore towards the Risca do Zumbi cardinal buoy R(3)B.10s8M, located 12 miles to the east of the cape.

Similarly, 35 miles to the west of Cabo Calcanhar is a shoal area on which the sea breaks; the drying reefs of Coroa das Lavadeiras and Urca do Minhoto, 12 miles from the coast, are marked by a lighthouse Mo(U)B.5s39m15M.

Further northwest, the reefs of João da Cunha are located 15 miles offshore.

Approach

Conspicuous landmarks

By day

- The Mucuripe lighthouse, a black and white striped cylindrical tower.
- A group of four wind turbines stands out clearly on the breakwater.

By night

- Mucuripe lighthouse, Lp(2)B.10s85m43M, can be seen from a long way offshore.
- From the southeast, to port, Praia do Futuro lighthouse, LpB.10s11m15M.
- There is a light on the end of the northern breakwater of the commercial port, Lp.V.3s15m10M.

Tide and current

Mean tide level is 1.55m above the chart datum.

The offshore current is two knots and flows west-northwest; it is generally weaker from July to December.

Winds

Generally, light northeasterly winds blow from November to June. From July to October they blow from the east at speeds of Force 4 to 5.

Landfall

From the southeast, make landfall near the commercial port breakwater at:

⊕ 0 • 03°41,87'S 038°29,18'W Fortaleza

There are two possible destinations:
- the mooring area at Iate Clube de Fortaleza, near the commercial port,
- Marina Park, located to the west of the town.

The Iate Clube has beautiful facilities but Marina Park is more convenient and the best option in terms of security. Head towards:

⊕ 1 • 03°42,95'S 038°31,80'W Marina Park

This waypoint is opposite the entrance to the marina and the riprap breakwaters. Watch out for the carcass of a grounded ship; stay well clear of it, as only part of the wreck is visible.

MARINA PARK

The marina is located in front of a luxury hotel, a long white 4-storey building that is easy to spot. The entrance is protected by two riprap breakwaters.

Quality of moorings ***

The marina can hold around one hundred boats split between the single pontoon and the protective breakwater; mooring is on buoys, bows or stern to the pontoon.

Water depth is 3–4m and the mooring area is well-protected.

Before entering the marina, it can be a good idea to anchor at the entrance, near the Indústria Naval do Ceará boatyard, and visit the reception office; however, watch out as the depth decreases rapidly.

Facilities – Services ***

It is possible to use all of the hotel's facilities (bar, restaurant, internet access, etc.) including the beautiful pool.

Water Taps on the pontoon.

Electricity 220V power outlets on the pontoon; the floating pontoon could however do with a serious overhaul and renovation of the wiring.

The marina entrance; the wreck of the grounded ship can be seen to the north of the breakwater

Luxurious leisure facilities

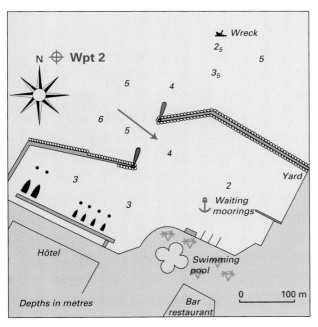

The Marina Park and the hotel. In the background is the cathedral

MARINA PARK

For maintenance work, contractors can work on site, but there are no facilities for lifting boats out of the water.

Supplies ***

Supplies are readily available; Fortaleza has several Pão de Açúcar supermarkets, which will also deliver.

Mooring fees **

As a guide, the price on the pontoon is US$0.50 to 0.60 per foot per day; note that the monthly price is discounted by 20%.

Location and surroundings **

The marina is not far from the town centre and there is a bus stop nearby. There are also always taxis on the hotel forecourt.

The surroundings are attractive with lovely gardens around the hotel and pool, but in contrast the Indústria Naval do Ceará boatyard, near the marina, detracts from the pleasant setting.

Marina Park Hotel, Av. Président Castelo Branco, 400, Fortaleza
☎ 4006 9595
Email marina@marinapark.com.br
www.marinapark.com.br

IATE CLUBE DE FORTALEZA

The Iate Clube is located near the commercial port and the fishing harbour and has excellent facilities that can be seen near some tall buildings on the left of Enseada do Mucuripe.

However, anchoring off the Iate Clube is unadvisable for safety reasons; there have apparently been several thefts and even physical attacks on yachts.

The club does not therefore recommend that you stop in this area, and when we visited there were hardly any boats moored here.

In spite of this, the Iate Clube does accept visitors and makes all of its facilities available to them.

The terrace restaurant is delightful and the shady gardens are particularly pleasant given the oppressive heat in the northern part of Brazil.

Iate Clube de Fortaleza, Av. Abolição, 4813, Enseada do Mucuripe, Fortaleza
℡ 263 1744
Email iateclubfort@uol.com.br

Useful telephone numbers

Area code ℡ (85).
Polícia Federal (Immigration), Av. dos Jangadeiros s/n, Cais do Porto ℡ 3263 6470.
Alfândega dos Portos (Customs), Av. dos Jangadeiros, Cais do Porto ℡ 3263 2115.
Vigilância Sanitária (Health Surveillance), Cais do Porto
Capitania dos Portos (Port Captain's Office), Cais do Porto ℡ 3219 7555 (comes on board).
Hospital Santa Casa de Misericorda, Rua Barão do Rio Branco, 20, Centro ℡ 3231 1752.
Centro do Turismo (Tourist Centre), Rua Senador Pompeu 350 ℡ 3231 3566.

Tourism

- Lots of local crafts, pottery, statues, embroidery, etc. at the Mercado Central (central market) not far from the marina.
- A tour round an *engenho* (distillery where sugar cane is converted into *cachaça*).
- There are great festivities during the *jangada* regatta at the end of July.

Iate Clube de Fortaleza, seen from the mooring area

FORTALEZA TO THE RIO PARÁ

Navigation

Brazilian Charts DHN No. 310, 400 and 410.

It is a 600-mile journey between Fortaleza and the mouth of the Rio Pará, with generally good sailing conditions along this coast, beam winds and a favourable current. It is of course preferable to sail offshore to avoid coastal hazards, shoals, reefs and fishing areas obstructed with large nets.

From Fortaleza to Baía de São Marcos, the coast is low, uniform and devoid of marked geographical features, with the hills of Ilha Maranhão in the background.

For most of the year, easterly and southeasterly winds blow at a speed of Force 3 to 4, but they are stronger and southeasterly at the end of the year.

Some northeasterly Force 3s blow at the beginning of the year.

There are a few fishing harbours along this stretch of coast, the ease of access of which varies depending on the weather conditions.

The fishing harbour of Luís Correia, approximately 240 miles from Fortaleza, makes a good shelter from northeasterly to southerly winds and if necessary emergency repair services can be found here. It is located between Ponta de Itaqui, LpB.6s39m17M to the southeast, and Ponta Pedra do Sal, LpB.6s15m10M to the northwest. It is made up of a long breakwater ending in two moles; the end of the northern mole has a white tower with a light LpV.3s10m5M. It is possible to anchor inside the two moles in 3.5m of water, or at high tide the village can be reached up the Rio Igaruçu, which runs alongside the breakwater.

The ebb current is particularly strong in this channel and, running against strong northeasterly winds, it forms a bar at the approach to the port that can sometimes be difficult to cross. Entry on the end of the rising tide is therefore strongly recommended.

To the northeast of Luís Correia, Baía de Tutóia is well-sheltered from the winds in general, but access to the port of Tutóia requires good local knowledge in view of the entrance obstructed by constantly shifting sandbanks.

Further northwest Baía de São Marcos opens out, with the town of São Luís on Ilha de Maranhão and the port of Itaqui. This bay is home to the largest tides in Brazil, with an amplitude of over 6.5m; low tide uncovers large numbers of sand banks. The tidal currents are also very strong, in the region of six knots.

For further information about the tidal currents in Baía de São Marcos, consult the DHN documents entitled *Cartas de Correntes de Maré – Baía de São Marcos* and *Portos de São Luís-Itaqui*.

From Baía de São Marcos to the Rio Pará, the coast is low, sandy, hard to see from offshore and peppered with islands and rivers.

Generally, the offshore currents flow north-northwest all year round; they can reach two knots in January and February but are weaker (less than one knot) from July to December.

Travelling via the ports of Luís Correia and São Luís-Itaqui requires a 140-mile detour compared with the direct route to the Rio Pará. Most yachts, particularly sailing boats, which generally enjoy good wind conditions in this area, do not stop on this leg and choose the direct offshore route.

LUÍS CORREIA

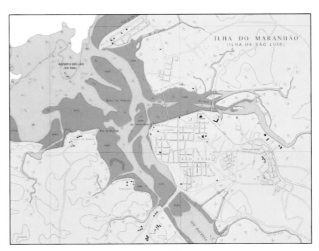

BAÍA DE SÃO MARCOS – SÃO LUÍS

STATE OF PARÁ

Belém – Ilha de Marajó

Belém

The port of Belém is located in the Amazon delta on the Rio Pará, 80 miles from the ocean.

This part of the Amazon region was previously occupied by the Tupi Indians, before colonisation by the Portuguese, who settled here in 1616. They built a fortress to protect themselves from invasions by the French and Dutch, who also coveted this territory and organised expeditions inland, travelling up the rivers.

A few years later, the King of Portugal appointed Francisco Caldeira Castelo Branco to found the city of Santa Maria de Belém.

Today the State of Pará, located in the eastern Amazon, covers an area of one and a half million square kilometres and its capital Belém is a large town with a population of around 1,500,000.

The town expanded significantly in the 19th century as a result of the rubber trade, and it is now the largest port in the Amazon delta. Most journeys inland are made by boat; large commercial ships can be seen and numerous craft ply the river carrying a whole range of goods, such as wood, building materials, food, craft products, etc. There are also numerous fishing, trip and passenger boats on the river.

As is the case in most of the Amazon, the humid equatorial climate brings a rainy season from December to June and a drier season from July to December.

The name is well justified here; the close heat is humid, with daily rains that struggle to lighten the oppressive atmosphere.

Rio Pará. The best means of transport on the river

For yachtsmen, Belém is a mythical port of call, full of charm and interest. Despite its expansion, the bustling town retains a good many traditions.

It is also the gateway to the Rio Amazonas, which can be reached from the Rio Pará along secondary channels (*igarapés*). This enables you to go deeper into the continent by boat up part of this enormous river, which is navigable for almost 3,000km.

Navigation

Nautical documents:

Brazilian Charts DHN No. 310, 314, 315, 316 and 320.

Notices to Mariners: a free booklet published fortnightly by the CHN, available on request at Capitanias dos Portos (Port Captain's Offices; this booklet is important for navigation on the Amazonian rivers).

General

At 6,400km, the Amazon is the longest river in the world. Its enormous flow rate of 120,000m^3 per second doubles in spate periods, resulting in a significant rise in its level (over 8m at Manaus). This is a period of intense geomorphologic activity for the river and its tributaries; banks are destroyed with trees and plants ripped out, sediment is moved, causing erosion and the creation or changing of position of sandbanks, etc.

The land areas shown in dark green on the charts are subject to constant change, and it is a good idea to steer well clear of them.

The conditions on the Rio Pará are different from the Rio Amazonas, with a much smaller rise in level (around 1m in spate periods); however, in the rainy season, these changes can also be found, although to a lesser extent.

The charts require regular updates and must always be interpreted with caution, particularly in the secondary channels.

For boats planning to sail on the Rio Pará and the Rio Amazonas, it is therefore advisable to use the very latest version of the Brazilian Navy charts and check the *Notices to Mariners* periodically.

Valuable information can also be obtained by contacting the Capitania dos Portos (Port Captain's Office) or the Comando do 4e Distrito Naval (4th Naval District Command) in Belém (*see Useful telephone numbers*).

Tide and current

Throughout the Amazon delta, the tides are semi-diurnal.

Pay close attention to the tide table and the information relating to currents (charts DHN No. 310 to 316). Depending on the period, high tide in Belém is three to four hours behind the mouth of the Rio Pará, and up to five hours behind the tide times in Salinópolis.

In Belém, the mean tide level is 1.8m, with a maximum amplitude of approximately 3.8m in spring tides.

The tidal currents are particularly strong and depend on the flow rate of the river, the influence of which is felt up to 10 miles offshore.

Approaching the Rio Pará, the flood current flows west and the ebb current flows east. The currents are still noticeable over an hour after the tide has turned.

In the Canal de Espadarte at the mouth of the river, the tidal current can reach 3.5 knots in spring tides.

Further upstream, in the Canal de Mosqueiro, the flood current is particularly strong from the 4th hour of tide, and can reach five knots in spring tides.

However, in spate periods these figures can change, as the level of the river can increase significantly depending on how much rain has fallen.

Winds

During the rainy season, from December to June, gusty northeasterly winds generally follow the calm periods. They then turn gradually southwest, through north, and are accompanied by heavy rain and violent storms.

In the drier season, from July to November, east-northeasterly and east-southeasterly winds prevail; they are moderate in July and August, but fresher at the end of the year, sometimes with strong gusts known as *marajós*.

Navigation on the Rio Pará

Navigation on the approaches to the Amazon delta requires great vigilance, and the same applies to the Rio Pará.

Make landfall at the mouth of the river, in the Canal do Espadarte, preferably at the end of the night or at daybreak. It is possible to enter at low tide in order to take advantage of the flood current, which is quite strong in the channel.

Sailing at night is always dangerous on the river due to the invisible floating obstacles, and a close watch must be kept for vessels of all sorts that ply the river and often travel with unreliable, or even no, navigation lights.

A powerful long-range light is very useful for spotting drifting plants, branches and even uprooted trees, carried by the current and often half-submerged.

If it is necessary to stop and anchor at night on the river while waiting for the tide to turn or for visibility to improve, etc., if possible it is best to anchor outside the ebb current and keep a close watch when anchored.

With regard to safety for yachts, the Capitania dos Portos advises against anchoring in isolated locations at night on the Rio Pará.

Conspicuous landmarks
Once past the mouth of the Rio Pará, the following can be seen to port heading towards Belém:

• Ponta de Taipu lighthouse, Lp(3)B.15s39m16M.
• Ponta Maria Teresa lighthouse, a white tower, Lp.B.6s42m15M.
• Ilha Quati lighthouse Lp(2)B.6s14m10M.
• The Chapéu Virado light, on the western point of Ilha de Mosqueira, Iso.V.2s11m13M.
• The white metal tower on Ilha Tatuoca, R(2)B.6s9M.
• The white tower of Forte da Barra, R.B.13m9M (visible sector 220°), located on a rocky islet on the right bank of the Belém approach channel.

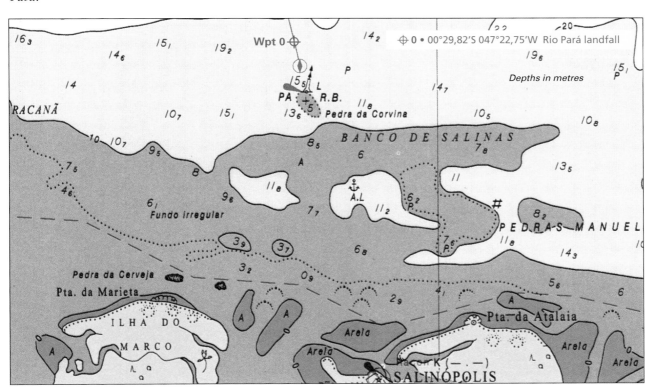

BELÉM 1, RIO PARÁ APPROACH

Precautions

- The Coroa das Gaviotas shoal, which is uncovered at the start of the falling tide.
- The Andorinhas reefs, one mile to the north of the Chapéu Virado light.
- A bank of rocks one mile northeast of the light on Ilha Tatuoca.
- The Pedras da Barra, Pedras do Forte and Pedras Val-de-Cães reefs.
- Banco da Cidade at the entrance to Belém, and the shoal on the bend in the river, heading towards the Rio Guamá.

Approach

Make landfall eight miles to the north of the lighthouse at Salinópolis, Lp.B.6s61m46M, on the north cardinal buoy marking the Pedra da Corvina shoal.

⊕ 0 • 00°29,82'S 047°22,75'W Rio Pará landfall

Then steer a direct course of 280° towards ⊕1, approximately 27 miles away.

The mouth of the Rio Pará is very wide, around 30 miles, and there are no conspicuous landmarks as the low, featureless coast cannot be seen. When the river is in spate, cautious navigation is required as the depth and the position of the sandbanks (mostly invisible) near the normal navigation channels can change. It is possible to identify some of them by the presence of small breaking waves. If you are sailing at night, watch out for the large number of fishing boats and nets at the mouth of the Rio Pará.

It is important to position yourself correctly at the entrance to the Canal do Espadarte, and to accurately identify green buoy No. 2, Lp(3)V.12s, which is left to port.

This buoy marks Baixo do Espadarte, a large sandbank on which the sea breaks and which uncovers at the start of the falling tide.

It marks the northern entrance to the Rio Pará entrance channel.

⊕ 1 • 00°23,89'S 47°50,02'W Buoy No. 2, Canal de Espadarte
⊕ 2 • 00°25,18'S 48°55,13'W Buoy No. 6
⊕ 3 • 00°27,63'S 47°57,75'W Buoy No. 8, No. 3
⊕ 4 • 01°07,32'S 48°29,56'W abeam Ponta do Chapéu Virado

Then head towards:

⊕ 5 • 01°11,87'S 48°29,24'W Ilha Tatuóca lighthouse abeam to starboard
⊕ 6 • 01°18,50'S 48°30,00'W near starboard buoy off Icoaraci

Go towards the next starboard beacon:

⊕ 7 • 01°20,37'S 048°29,48'W Starboard beacon
⊕ 8 • 01°22,23'S 048°29,58'W Pedras da Barra

Leave to port Pedras da Barra (green beacon and isolated danger mark) and head towards:

⊕ 9 • 01°23,64'S 048°29,98'W Pedras Val de Cães

Avoid the Pedras Val-de-Cães reefs to port (port beacon and south cardinal buoy), to reach ⊕10.

Then travel alongside the port facilities at the entrance to Belém, the naval base and various terminals and quays (watch out for any large commercial ships manoeuvring).

⊕ 10 • 01°24,45'S 048°29,84'W Beacon No. 1, Belém channel

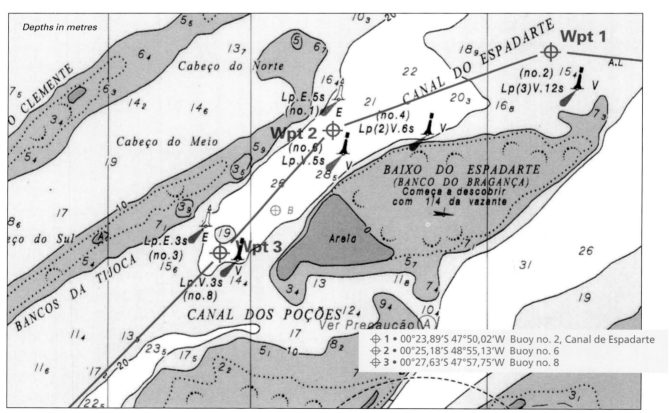

BELÉM 2

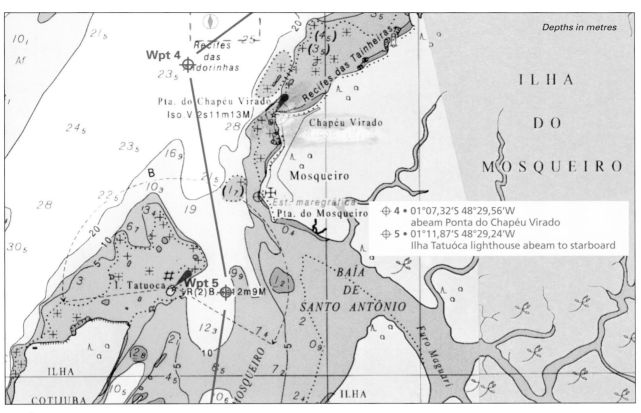

Depths in metres

⊕ 4 • 01°07,32'S 48°29,56'W
abeam Ponta do Chapéu Virado
⊕ 5 • 01°11,87'S 48°29,24'W
Ilha Tatuóca lighthouse abeam to starboard

BELÉM 3

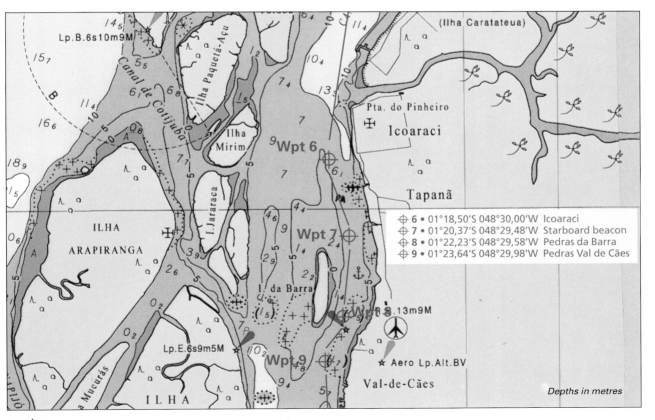

⊕ 6 • 01°18,50'S 048°30,00'W Icoaraci
⊕ 7 • 01°20,37'S 048°29,48'W Starboard beacon
⊕ 8 • 01°22,23'S 048°29,58'W Pedras da Barra
⊕ 9 • 01°23,64'S 048°29,98'W Pedras Val de Cães

Depths in metres

BELÉM 4

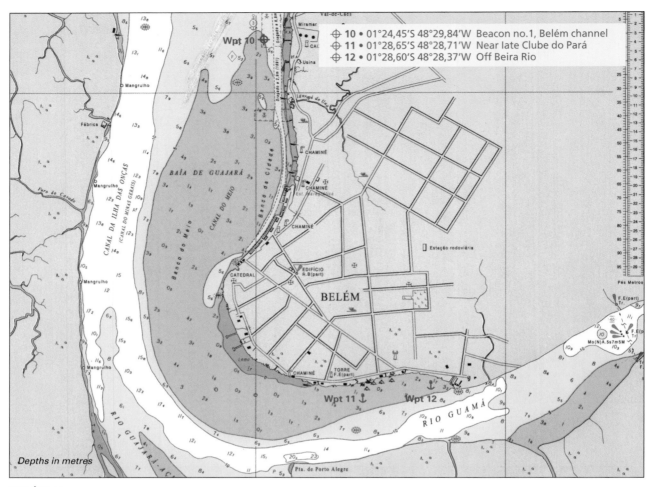

⊕ 10 • 01°24,45'S 48°29,84'W	Beacon no.1, Belém channel
⊕ 11 • 01°28,65'S 48°28,71'W	Near Iate Clube do Pará
⊕ 12 • 01°28,60'S 48°28,37'W	Off Beira Rio

BELÉM 5

Approaching Belém

The marked channel leads to the port docks and further upstream the old restored docks can be seen, identifiable by a series of yellow cranes lined up on the quays.

Travel alongside the quays for approximately 50m until you are level with Forte do Castelo, which can be seen to starboard with the cathedral in the background.

The river then enters a long bend to the east, and in order to avoid the large sandbank extending into it, move away from the quays towards the middle of the river, staying well clear of the bend on a line of depths of 4–5m.

You then enter the Rio Guamá, and around two miles further on to port, a small group of mooring buoys marks the former facilities of Iate Clube do Pará.

⊕ 11 • 01°28,65'S 48°28,71'W Near Iate Clube do Pará

The old Iate Clube do Pará

IATE CLUBE DO PARÁ

A few years ago, I stopped off at this Iate Clube and found it to be a friendly, very lively place. It was very hot and the pool was crowded; the lovely riverside terrace was also full of people.

This time (September 2005) I found a deserted, desolate, lifeless place in an advanced state of dilapidation.

Iate Clube do Pará is closing down!

The manager, Neto, is on site and former employees still maintain a few boats stored in the sheds; they can still be relied on for a minimum level of service, but for how long is anyone's guess.

Due to a comprehensive restructuring of the entire quarter, the facilities at Iate Clube do Pará are soon to be demolished. The project includes provision for the construction of a new municipal marina, managed by Belém town council.

⚓ HOTEL BEIRA RIO ANCHORAGE

This anchorage is currently preferable to the Iate Clube.

Around one mile upstream, beyond the Iate Clube, the single-storey building of the Hotel Beira Rio (painted yellow) can be seen, with a terrace and a pontoon on the river. Anchor in front of the hotel or nearby.

Tenders can be left in complete safety on the pontoon.

⊕ 12 • 01°28,60'S 48°28,37'W Near Beira Rio

Quality of moorings **

At both the Iate Clube and Beira Rio anchorages, it is possible to anchor in 3–4 metres of water with good holding on sand and mud; the mooring area is calm with a 1.5–2 knot current on the ebb.

Facilities – Services *

A little way upstream of the Iate Clube there is a small boatyard where some maintenance, mechanical repairs and electrical work can be carried out.

Just next door, boats can be grounded against the quay for work under the waterline.

Supplies **

Supplies are readily available and there are several supermarkets in town:
Shopping Center Iguatemi, with a 24-hour bank, is the closest;
Shopping Center Castanheira (quite far away).

For fruit, vegetables, fish and many other items, go to the Ver-o-Peso market. You will find a phenomenal range of Amazonian products at very reasonable prices.

For fish, choose the covered market in preference to the market on the quay (where the fish may go off in the sun).

Location and surroundings *

The surroundings can seem a little desolate, but this is all part of the scenery on this part of the river, near the Cidade Velha: a collection of dilapidated buildings with corrugated iron roofs and old jetties built on piles that always seem on the point of collapse.

It's a veritable patchwork of rusty roofs, gaudy tarpaulins, faded paint and pot-bellied boats grounded on muddy banks, waiting to be refloated in coffee-coloured water.

On land, this district, Bairro de Jurúna, doesn't enjoy the best reputation...

Belém. A display of fish at the fishing harbour

Belém. The boat bus terminal with the market in the background

Ilha de Marajó. The landing stage at Soure

Belém. Amazonian crafts at the Ver-o-Peso market

For safety's sake, it is categorically unadvisable to go through this district on foot, even during the day – always take a bus or a taxi.

With regard to the Iate Clube anchorage, although security here used to be provided by watchmen, this is no longer the case. Leaving the boat unattended under these circumstances could be rather risky. Caution is therefore the order of the day at this anchorage!

The Hotel Beira Rio anchorage currently seems better, more convenient and safer.

For going into town, there are taxis on the hotel forecourt and a bus stop in the street opposite.

Useful telephone numbers

Area code ☎ (91).

Polícia Federal (Immigration), Av. Castilho França ☎ 3223 4331.

Receita Federal, Av. Castilho França ☎ 3223 4331.

Vigilância Sanitária dos Portos (Health Surveillance), Av. Pt Vargas, 41 ☎ 3222 0790.

Pronto Socorro (Emergency Medicine) ☎ 192.

Capitania dos Portos da Amazôna Oriental (Eastern Amazon Port Captain's Office), Rua Gaspar Viana, 575, Vila Nova, Belém ☎ 3242 7188.

Comando do 4° Distrito Naval (4th Naval District Command) ☎ 216 4031.

Hospital Adventista, Av. Al. Barroso, 1758, CENTUR, Centro de Convenções.

BELEMTUR Tourist Office, Av. Nazaré, Belém ☎ 246 8686.

British Honorary Consulate in Belém ☎ +55 (11) 3094 2700 Email hc.belem@fco.gov.uk

Tourism

- Forte do Presépio (1916), a symbol of the founding of Belém; the first fortress built by the Portuguese, which still has its original canon.

- Catédral da Sé, built in 1755 and currently undergoing renovation.

- Museo Emilio Goeldi, which details the fauna, flora and indigenous culture of the people of Amazonia.

- The Mangal das Garças ecological park, in the historic centre.

- The Círio de Nazaré, celebrated on the second Sunday in October with the Romaria Fluvial boat procession on the Saturday; this is the biggest religious festival in Brazil, bringing together over two million people who accompany the Virgin, Nossa Senhora de Nazaré, on a procession through the streets.

- Estação das Docas, a giant food tasting and restaurant complex in the converted warehouses on the quays of the port.

The whole area has been renovated, repainted and decorated in a resolutely modern style.

The backdrop is a modernised scene of bridge cranes, storage sheds with complex metal frames and port cranes painted bright yellow, looking like huge wading birds standing motionless by the river.

There is a whole range of good restaurants and a great atmosphere.

Ilha de Marajó. Soure lighthouse at the mouth of the Rio Paracauri

- And of course, the Ver-o-Peso market next to the fishing harbour is a must.

  The atmosphere of this market is indescribable, with its displays of fruit and vegetables, medicinal plants with miraculous powers, magic potions, mysterious sacred amulets, a multitude of religious items, pottery, Indian sculptures, smells, tastes…

  The area around Belém is also worth a visit, with Icoaraci near Ponta do Pinheiro and Mosqueiro and its 15km of freshwater beaches, both very busy and lively at the weekends.

- A few hours' sail to the northwest is Ilha de Marajó.

Ilha de Marajó

The Marajó archipelago is located 25 miles northwest of Belém and covers an area of 49,000km².

The capital, Soure, has a population of 18,000. It is on the east of the island, on the Rio Paracauri, which flows into Baía de Marajó.

The island is encircled by the Rio Amazonas and the Rio Pará, linked by numerous secondary channels.

During spate periods, the volume of water in the Amazonian rivers and in the secondary channels increases considerably, and two thirds of the surface area of the archipelago is flooded.

Navigation

Brazilian Charts DHN No. 310 and No. 316.

Conspicuous landmarks

Lighted beacon No. 8, Lp(2)V.5s to the south of Banco de Muriçoca, which is uncovered at low tide.

Lighted beacons Nos. 10, 5 and 12, to the south of the Coroa Seca bank.

Joanes lighthouse, LpB.10s23m14M.

Salvaterra lighthouse on Ilha dos Amores, LpB.3s14m5M.

Soure lighthouse, a red and white striped square tower, Lp(2)B.10s35m16M.

Approach

On leaving Belém, go as far as ⊕4, then head towards ⊕13, located 10 miles north-northeast:

⊕ 13 • 00°57,00'S 048°26,13'W Green beacon No. 12

Landing on Ilha de Marajó

A course of 345° leads towards Ilha de Marajó, passing to the south of the Coroa Seca shoal (buoys Nos. 12, 5 and 10), to:

⊕ **14** • 00°50,72'S 048°28,65'W Green beacon No. 8

Then steer a course north and make landfall at

⊕ **15** • 00°45,00'S 048°29,30'W Soure landfall

This waypoint is opposite the mouth of the Rio Paracauri, approximately two miles from Soure.

As the current in the Rio Paracauri can reach four knots in spring tides, entry on the rising tide is highly recommended.

⚓ SOURE ANCHORAGE

Enter the river sailing in the right-hand half, and anchor approximately two miles further on to starboard, after the landing stage for the ferry between Soure and Salvaterra, the village on the opposite bank.

Anchor holding is good in 4m of water on sand and mud.

The guará. The red ibis, a very common species in the Amazon basin

The mooring area is calm, although there is a significant tidal current, especially on the ebb.

Soure is a small town and pretty much all types of supplies are available.

Tourism

The island is a haven of calm that will be much appreciated after a stay in the hectic town of Belém.

The natural surroundings are fertile and varied, with a large number of birds, particularly red ibis (*guará*).

The buffalo are also equally at home in town or in the fields; it's not unusual to go round a corner and find yourself face to face with one of these imposing beasts. They're big, but apparently harmless!

In the streets of Soure there are almost as many buffalo as bicycles which, along with horses, are one of the traditional means of transport on the island.

Ilha de Marajó offers a wealth of crafts, and in particular ceramics, pottery, sculptures and paintings.

There are numerous beautiful beaches, most of which are deserted or rarely frequented, such as Praia Aruaruna, Praia do Presqueiro, etc.

If you like music and dancing, let yourself be carried away by the rhythm of the local dance, the *Carimbo*.

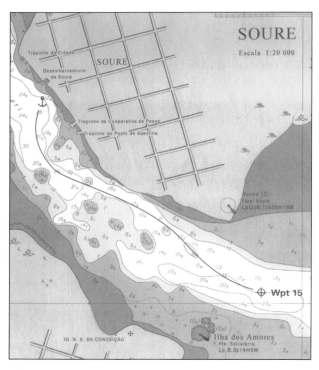

SOURE LANDFALL

Ilha de Marajó. The landing stage at Soure

Buffalo on Ilha de Marajó

Appendix

Brazilian Portuguese – English glossary

A

Area / area, zone
areia / sand
âncora / anchor
acima / above, up
abordagem / approach
abrigar se / to shelter
acesso / access
acatar / to respect, observe
afundar / to sink
assalto / assault, attack
água / water
água potável / drinking water
aguardar / to wait
aguardente / brandy
ajuda / help
alfândega / customs
anticiclone / anti-cyclone
aqui / here
ali / there, over there
amanhã, de manhã / tomorrow,
    tomorrow morning
amarelo / yellow
amarrar / to moor
angra / cove
antes / before
arco iris / rainbow
arquipélago / archipelago
arrebentações / breakers
atrás / behind
autorização / authorisation
azul / blue

B

Baía / bay
baixa / bank, shoal
baixa mar / low water
baleia / whale
banco / bank (sandbank)
bandeira / flag
barra / bar, mouth
Bombordo / port
Boreste / starboard

C

Cabo / cape
cachaça / sugar cane spirit
caipirinha / cachaça-based drink
cadeia / chain
camarão / shrimp, prawn
Candomblé / cult of African origin
    practiced in the Bahia region
canoa / dug-out canoe
chuva / rain
concha / shell
coroa / bank (of coral, rocks)
costa / coast

corrente / current
comunicação / communication
chamada / call

D

Declaração / declaration
depressão / low pressure
deriva / drift
desabrigado / unprotected, exposed
descobrimento / discovery
desembarque / disembarkation, landing
desmontar / dismantle, remove
dia / day
diesel, diésel / diesel
documento / form of identification,
    papers
dragado / dredged

E

Encarnada / red*
enseada / cove, small bay
escuna / traditional sailing boat of the
    Bahia region
entrada / entrance

F

Farol / lighthouse
farolete / tower
ferragem / ironmongery
fundear / drop an anchor
fondeio / anchorage
frente / front
frente quente / warm front
frente fria / cold froid

G

Gaivota / seagull
galon / gallon (3.6 litres)
gasolina comum / petrol (outboard
    motors)
gelo / ice
gelo filtrado / ice made from filtered
    water
gelo escama / ice chips (non-drinking
    water, for fishing)
guiar / to guide
guincho / winch

H

Hélice / propeller
hora / hour, time

I

Iate / yacht
Ibama, Institute Brasileiro de Meio
    Ambiente / Brazilian Institute of
    Environment and Renewable Natural
    Resources

Iemanja / Candomblé goddess of the sea
igreja / church
ilha / island
informação / information
itinerário / itinerary

L

Lagoa / lake
laje / rock, reef
lama / mud
lampejo / light (on a buoy)
lancha / motor boat
Lanchonete / small snack bar
litoral / coast, seashore
lixo / rubbish, garbage; dustbin, trash
    can
latitude / latitude
longitude / longitude
lugar / place, berth (in port)
lula / squid
luz / light

M

Maré / tide
maré de echente / rising tide
maré de vazante / falling tide
marinha / navy
marinheiro / mariner, sailor
mercado / market
mercadinho / small grocery shop
mergulhar / to dive (scuba diving)
milha náutica / nautical mile
molhe / mole, breakwater
morro / hill

N

Náutico / nautical, maritime
Nivel / level
nivel de baixa-mar média / mean low
    water level
norte / north
nome / name
nublado / cloudy

O

Oceano / ocean
onda / wave
orixá / Afro-Brazilian Candomblé deity
ostra / oyster
oficina / garage (for repairs)

P

Peixe / fish
ponta / point, tip
ponte / bridge
ponto / point, dot
poluição / pollution

posição / position
praia / beach
preço / price
pressão atmosférica / atmospheric
    pressure
previsão do tempo / weather forecast
profundidade / depth
pronto-socorro / emergency medical
    services
protecção / protection

R

Rampa / slipway
rajadas / gusts
rebocar / to tow
rebocadore / tug boat
recife / reef
ribeira / stream, brook
rio / river
rocha / rock
rodoviária / bus station
rum / rum
rumar / to steer for, head for

S

Saco / inlet, cul-de-sac
saveiro / traditional sailing boat of the
    Bahia region
sair / to exit, to leave
saida / exit, departure
salvamento / rescue
SALVAMAR / Brazilian Maritime Search
    and Rescue Service
sinal / signal
socorro / assistance, help
sul / south
subir o barco / to take the boat out of the
    water

T

Tempestade / storm
tempo / weather; time
temporada / season
tinta / paint
travessia / crossing, voyage
tráfego / maritime traffic
tubarão / shark

V

Veleiro / sailing boat, yacht
vento / wind
vermelho / red*
viagem / voyage, journey
visibilidade / visibility
voltar / to return, come back

X

Xérox / photocopy

List of Brazilian Navy Charts

No.	Name of chart	Scale
310	De Salinópolis a Belém	1:200,000
315	Da Boca da Vigia a Mosqueiro	1:50,000
316	Do Mosqueiro a Belém	1:50,000
320	Porto de Belém	1:50,000
400	Do Cabo Gurupi a Ilha de Santana	1:300,000
411	Baía de São Marcos	1:50,000
412	Proximidades de Baía de São Marcos	1:135,000
504	Proximidades do Porto de Tutóia	1:42,000
515	Porto de Luís Correiá	1:15,000
710	Proximidades do terminal de Pecém e do Porto de Mucuripe	1:50,000
802	Porto de Natal	1:8,500
830	Porto de Cabeledo	1:15,000
52	Arquipelago de Fernando de Noronha	1:30,000
901	Porto de Maceió	1:17,500
902	Porto de Recife	1:50,000
906	Porto de Suape	1:15,000
930	Proximidades do Porto de Recife	1:100,000
1000	De Maceió ao Rio Itariri	1:300,000
1110	Baía de Todos os Santos	1:65,000
1104	Baía de Todos os Santos parte nordeste	1:30,000
1105	Porto de Madre de Deus	1:80,000
1107	Baía de Todos os Santos parte oeste	1:30,000
1100A	Fundeadouros do Morro de São Paulo	1:50,000
1100	Do Rio Itariri a Ilhéus	1:300,000
1131	Porto de Camamu	1:30,000
1200	Do Porto de Ilhéus à Ponta Cumuruxatiba	1:300,000
1201	Porto de Ilhéus	1:12,500
1250	Baías Cabrália e Porto Seguro	1:30,000
1210	Proximidades do Porto de Ilhéus	1:50,000
1300	Da Ponta Cumuruxatiba ao Rio Doce	1:300,000
1301	Barra de Nova Viçosa	1:30,000
1310	Canal de Abrolhos	1:100,000
1311	Fundeadouros de Abrolhos	1:10,000
1312	Porto de Caravelas	1:30,000
1401	Portos de Vitória e Tubarão	1:15,000
1402	Porto de Ubu	1:15,000
1403	Da Barra Itapemerim ao Cabo São Tomé	1:134,000
1404	Enseadas de Perocão e Guarapari	1:5,000
1420	Terminal da Barra do Riacho	1:15,000
1501	Baía de Guanabara	1:50,000
1508	Do Cabo Frio a Ponta Negra	1:75,000
1511	Barra de Rio de Janeiro	1:20,000
1620	Da Barra do Rio de Janeiro a Ilha Grande	1:120,000
1621	Baía da Ilha Grande – Parte Ieste	1:40,000
1631	Baía da Ilha Grande – Parte central	1:40,000
1632	Baía da Ilha Grande – Parte centro norte	1:40,000
1633	Baía da Ilha Grande – Parte oeste	1:40,000
1634	Da Ponta de Juatinga a Ilha das Couves	1:40,000
1635	Da Ilha das Couves a Ilha do Mar Virado	1:40,000
1635	Enseada de Ubatuba	1:40,000
1636	Porto de Angra dos Reis e proximidades	1:20,000
1637	Baía de Ribeira	1:25,000

No.	Name of chart	Scale
1641	Da enseada do Mar Virado ao Porto de São Sebastião	1:40,000
1645	Canal de São Sebastião	1:50,000
1700	Da Ilha São Sebastião a Ilha do Bom Abrigo	1:300,000
1701	Porto de Santos	1:25,000
1711	Proximidades do Porto de Santos	1:80,000
1721	Baía de Guaratuba	1:25,000
1804	Porto de São Fransisco do Sul	1:27,000
1810	Enseada do Porto Belo	1:27,000
1822	Portos de Paranaguá e Antonina	1:25,000
1901	Porto de Laguna	1:10,000
1902	Proximidades da Ilha Santa Catarina	1:100,000
1903	Canal norte de Santa Catarina	1:50,000
1904	Canal sul de Santa Catarina	1:50,000
1908	Porto de Imbituba	1:75,000
2110	Porto de Rio Grande	1:50,000

Distance Tables (in Nautical Miles)

Rio Pará and Rio Amazonas, Belém to Almeirim

Belém
16	Mosqueiro
28	12	Farolete Cotejuba
43	27	15	Farolete Arrozal
51	35	23	8	Vial do Conde
54	46	26	10	11	Farolete Capim
68	52	40	26	27	19	Farol Mandii
75	59	47	33	34	26	8	Foz do rio Tocantins
92	76	64	50	51	43	32	24	Cocal
111	95	83	69	70	62	51	43	19	Curralinho
143	123	111	97	98	90	79	71	47	28	Boca de Estreito de Boiuçu (Fte. S. Helena)
162	142	130	116	117	109	98	90	66	47	19	Boca da Passagem do Vira-Saia
229	209	197	183	184	176	165	157	133	114	86	67	Entrada no Rio Amazonas (Pta. do Vieira)
262	242	230	216	217	209	198	190	166	147	119	100	33	Gurupá
277	257	245	231	232	224	213	205	181	162	134	115	48	15	Foz do Rio Xingu
323	303	291	277	278	270	259	251	227	208	180	161	94	61	46	Almeirim
889	869	857	843	844	836	825	817	793	774	746	727	660	627	612	566	Manaus

Costas Norte, Belém to Cabo Calcanhar

Belém
110	Fundeadouro de Salinòpolis
414	304	Terminal da Ponta da Madeira
415	305	1	Itaqui
421	311	7	6	Terminal da Alumar
477	367	173	174	180	Tutòia
512	402	211	212	218	58	Luís Correia
558	448	259	260	266	108	65	Camocim
725	615	432	433	439	294	245	186	Fortaleza
852	742	555	556	562	414	375	308	137	Terùinal de Areia Branca
860	750	559	560	566	420	380	321	140	13	Areia Branca
870	760	579	580	586	430	390	330	162	38	51	Macau
941	831	648	649	655	501	461	402	216	112	125	100	Cabo Calcanhar

Cabo Calcanhar to Cabo Frio and the Oceanic Islands

```
Penedos de Sao Pedro e Sao Paulo
394  Atol das Rocas
340   93  Ilha de Fernando de Noronha
505  114  192  Farol Calcanhar
534  144  200   52  Natal
          237  137   89  Cabedelo
630  260  295  207  159   84  Recife
               321  275  198  126  Maceió
               429  381  306  234  122  Aracaju
1010 648  670  595  547  472  400  284  183  Salvador
1028 658  680  605  557  482  410  294  193   10  Aratu
1031 661  683  608  560  485  413  297  196   15       Madre de Deus
               634  586  511  439  315  220   65   75   78  Camamu
               678  630  555  483  364  265  117 1277  130   62  Ilhéus
1262 892  942  845  791  716  644  530  433  303  313  315  259  197  Farol Abrolhos
1398 1068 1118 1015 967  892  820  706  609  479  489  492  431  375  176  Tubarão
                         820            710  720  723                      617  Ilha de Trindade
1401 1071 1121 1018 970  895  823  709  612  482  492  445  434  376  179    6  620  Vitória
1531 1163 1208 1110 1062 987  915  799  704  592  582  585  528  466  269  112       115  Farol São Tomé
          1174 1126 1051 979  865  768  638  648  651  594  532  335  164       167   48  Macaé
1625 1259 1305 1206 1158 1083 1011 897  800  670  680  683  624  574  367  204  715  207   96   45  Farol Cabo Frio
```

Cabo Frio to Arroio Chuí

```
Cabo Frio
 75  Rio de Janeiro
125   72  Ilha Guaíba
143   90   18  Sepetiba
160  107   20   38  Angra dos Reis
199  146   98  116   86  São Sebastião
273  220  173  191  163   70  Santos
403  350  304  322  295  211  168  Paranaguá
433  380  325  350  322  235  192   60  São Fransisco do Sul
442  389  348  366  345  268  226  104   63  Itajaí
457  414  376  394  373  289  254  142  105   54  Florianòpolis
511  458  415  433  412  331  286  181  143   93   82  Imbituba
530  477  433  451  425  349  302  200  162  112  100   25  Laguna
622  569  534  558  531  456  420  313  275  225  213  135  118  Tramandaí
808  755  720  738  717  642  606  499  461  411  399  322  304  190  Rio Grande
833  780  747  765  744  669  633  526  488  438  426  349  331  217   27  Pelotas
969  916  884  902  881  806  770  663  625  575  563  486  468  354  164  153  Porto Alegre
904  851  816  834  813  738  702  595  557  507  495  420  400  286  134  161  298  Arroio Chuí
```

Index